NO AVERAGE DAY

NO AVERAGE DAY

THE 24 HOURS OF OCTOBER 24, 1944

RONA SIMMONS

University of Missouri Press, Columbia, Missouri 65211
Printed and bound in the United States of America
 First printing, 2024.

ISBN: 9780826223173

Library of Congress Control Number: 2024940723

∞™ This paper meets the requirements of the
American National Standard for Permanence of Paper
for Printed Library Materials, Z39.48, 1984.

Typeface: Adobe Caslon Pro and Aktiv Grotesk

All maps created by Rona Simmons.

THE AMERICAN MILITARY EXPERIENCE SERIES

JOHN C. MCMANUS, SERIES EDITOR

The books in this series portray and analyze the experience of Americans in military service during war and peacetime from the onset of the twentieth century to the present. The series emphasizes the profound impact wars have had on nearly every aspect of recent American history and considers the significant effects of modern conflict on combatants and noncombatants alike. Titles in the series include accounts of battles, campaigns, and wars; unit histories; biographical and autobiographical narratives; investigations of technology and warfare; studies of the social and economic consequences of war; and in general, the best recent scholarship on Americans in the modern armed forces. The books in the series are written and designed for a diverse audience that encompasses nonspecialists as well as expert readers.

Selected titles from this series:

No Sacrifice Too Great: The 1st Infantry Division in World War II
Gregory Fontenot

Patton's War: An American General's Combat Leadership, Volume 2: August–December 1944
Kevin M. Hymel

Patton's War: An American General's Combat Leadership, Volume 1: November 1942–July 1944
Kevin M. Hymel

Patton: Battling with History
J. Furman Daniel

Lessons Unlearned: The U.S. Army's Role in Creating the Forever Wars in Afghanistan and Iraq
Pat Proctor

Loss and Redemption at St. Vith: The 7th Armored Division in the Battle of the Bulge
Gregory Fontenot

Military Realism: The Logic and Limits of Force and Innovation in the US Army
Peter Campbell

Omar Nelson Bradley: America's GI General, 1893–1981
Steven L. Ossad

The First Infantry Division and the US Army Transformed: Road to Victory in Desert Storm, 1970–1991
Gregory Fontenot

Dick Cole's War: Doolittle Raider, Hump Pilot, Air Commando
Dennis R. Okerstrom

To all those who perished on October 24, 1944,
whether private or seaman, colonel or commander.

CONTENTS

MAPS

PREFACE

October 24, 1944, was the 1,052nd day of America's participation in World War II. It was a Tuesday. The first American soldier to die that day did so at a Japanese prisoner-of-war (POW) and slave-labor camp in Hanawa, Japan. The prisoner, Paul Miller, a US Army private first class, knew he was near death. His breath was shallow and slow. Every joint and muscle in his emaciated body ached. His fingers were stiff and unresponsive. He knew he would not return home or ever see his family again. But hours before dawn broke, he harbored one bright thought: he would not be forced to labor in the mine when the guards came for him at daybreak.

The last to die perished minutes before midnight aboard a landing ship returning from the Philippines to its base in New Guinea. Far below deck, Seaman Wanza Matthews was settling in for the night. His thoughts turned as they often did to home and his mother and father, and he pondered what he would write in his next letter home. In an instant everything changed. An Imperial Japanese Navy submarine that had been tracking the landing ship attacked. The volley of torpedoes failed to sink the ship, but it sent twenty-two men, including Wanza, to their deaths.

The day may have dawned like any other grimy day of World War II. But on this particular Tuesday, twenty-six hundred Americans, including Paul Miller and Wanza Matthews, would perish. The toll exceeds the twenty-five hundred Americans killed during the

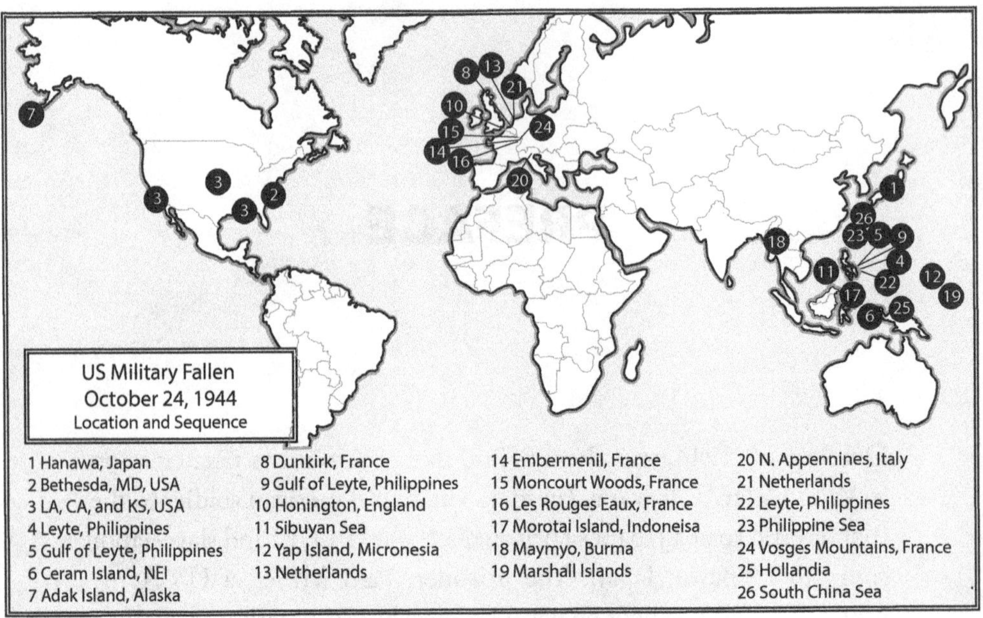

1. US Military Fallen, October 24, 1944: Location and Sequence

Normandy invasion; the twenty-four hundred killed in the attack on Pearl Harbor; the one thousand who fell in the incident dubbed "Little Pearl Harbor" at Bari, Italy; and the nine hundred who perished in shark-infested waters after the USS *Indianapolis* sank. It is also more than the number of US forces killed in any one day during the iconic battles of the war, including Midway, Guadalcanal, Anzio, and the Battle of the Bulge.

Compared with the losses of the war's other major participants, the twenty-six hundred American lives lost on that one Tuesday may seem insignificant. They were, for example, a fraction of what historians estimate were lost during any one day of arguably the greatest battle of the war: the six-month Battle of Stalingrad. While estimates vary by source and are fraught with error, losses in Stalingrad averaged more than five thousand per day and left over a million Russian soldiers dead. The same might be said of the losses incurred over the course of the war. While America lost four hundred thousand members of its military (less than a third of a percent of the country's population), the Soviet Union suffered a staggering ten million military deaths, or about 5 percent of its population.[1]

Regardless, the American losses were nine times the average of three hundred American fatalities per day from the attack on Pearl Harbor in 1941 to the surrender of Japan in 1945. They far exceeded what the political and military leaders and the families on the home front had come, albeit reluctantly, to think of as normal. Statistically, then, that Tuesday was far from just another day.

The day's events went largely unreported. After the attack on Pearl Harbor, headlines on the country's newspapers had shouted, "Japan Declares War," and after D-day, "Heavy Fighting Rages on French Beachhead." On those occasions, the newspapers canceled advertisements to allow space for war news and rushed extra editions to the streets.[2] But on October 24, they were silent. In part, this oversight is due to the fact that no Allied forces witnessed the sinking of the *Arisan Maru*, a Japanese hellship, in which two-thirds of the day's losses occurred. The remainder, some eight hundred Americans, fell in locations scattered across the globe in large and small battles. They died while engaged with the enemy in hand-to-hand combat; by small-arms, machine-gun, sniper, and artillery fire; by missiles, rockets, strafing, torpedoing, and dive-bombing. They died from stepping on land mines, drowning, freezing, burning, being crushed in the wreckage of their aircraft, or hurtling to the ground when their parachutes failed to open or were shot full of holes. They died suddenly as a result of a heart attack or traffic accident or finally relented to death after a prolonged struggle with disease or malnutrition. They died from beatings, stabbings, and beheadings and by taking their own lives. Some were casualties of friendly fire.

To tell the stories of each of the twenty-six hundred fallen Americans would be a daunting, if not impossible, task. And so, on the pages that follow are the stories of some three dozen fallen, including Paul Miller and Wanza Matthews. This handful of souls bears the heavy burden of representing and honoring the memory of their fallen comrades. But it is a job they do well.

They were for the most part seaman, corporals, and privates, "small" men and women by many standards, often the unsung and overlooked soldier or sailor. Among them are members of the military who served in the Army, Army Air Corps, Navy, and Marines and in all major theaters of war across the globe and in the continental United States, and thus they represent a good cross-section of the US military.

They came to the military from small towns across the country, like Waycross, Georgia; Mason City, Iowa; and Gunnison, Utah. Most grew up as members of lower- and middle-income families, in households with four, five, and six siblings, and many had only a grammar school education. But they were not of a kind—in their midst were white and black soldiers, as well as Hispanic, Native, and Japanese Americans.

For the most part, they died not in one of the major air, ground, or sea battles, but in lesser-known incidents. They died on obscure photo-reconnaissance patrols, training exercises, and seemingly safe and mundane and supply-ship convoys. Here, the sailors and soldiers at the center of the narrative cross scrabble-strewn hillsides, huddle among dense forests rocked by artillery, and take advantage of time away from the battle to visit a historic site or swim in placid waters.

Some are frightened to their core, while others forge ahead into the teeth of enemy fire, oblivious to or in spite of the obvious peril. Regardless of heritage, place of birth, gender, or age, they are Americans. And whether draftee or volunteer, each one served for what they held dear—their family, their friends, their faith, their country, and their freedom.

Perhaps most important, the stories show us the soldiers as flesh and blood, individuals with mothers and fathers, sisters and brothers, and wives or husbands or sweethearts at home. We see them journey in a few short months from civilians contemplating their future to battle-hardened warriors on the ground, in the air, or on the seas. We slip our feet into their shoes. We hold our breath as their final moments click by and feel their hearts beat a last time in their chests.

Portraying the last moments of these individuals is like stepping through a field laced with land mines. Uncovering what occurred to one individual and at what hour in any battle of any war is an exercise fraught with error. For the stories taking place at sea, war diaries, action reports, and ships' logbooks proved invaluable. These sources provide as accurate an account as can be rendered amid the chaos of war. They note, for example, when a ship's crew sighted the enemy, at what day, hour, and minute they took evasive or offensive action, and they chronicle the results of those actions.

Accounts of those who died in skirmishes on the side of an unnamed hill while hunkered in foxholes and slit trenches far from their command post, however, naturally lack any pretense of precision. The last moments of these soldiers may have transpired without witnesses, and hours or even days might have passed before anyone located, counted, and identified the fallen.

Further, unlike prominent World War II military and political leaders who left behind correspondence, diaries, and memoirs, or who have had their lives recorded in countless biographies, most of the soldiers mentioned here left little or no record behind. A son or daughter, a grandson or granddaughter, might have saved a faded and fragile letter on vellum or a hazy sepia-toned photograph. A Silver Star Medal commendation or the digitized copy of a soldier's draft registration might sit in an archive. Finding these details involved months of scouring US military archives, books, magazines, and articles; watching videotaped interviews; and, here and there, perusing memoirs, letters, journals, and photographs the soldiers' descendants graciously contributed.

Where known, the precise time of day and source of a soldier's death are cited. Where the details are sketchy or absent, the circumstances are described as accurately as possible along with the rationale for assigning a specific or approximate time to the soldier's or sailor's death. All the stories unfold in local times and dates, despite the difference in time zones and the international date line. For example, if a sailor is killed at 6:00 a.m. in the South Pacific on October 24, 1944, and an infantryman dies in France at 6:00 a.m. on that same date, the two stories are presented as occurring simultaneously.

Finding the bits and pieces that remain of these "small" lives has been for me like discovering flecks of gold in a rock-strewn stream. In gathering the color and binding the bits together, I hope to have made their stories whole. And I hope you will realize as I did that their deaths were not small deaths, after all, that they were not average people, and that Tuesday, October 24, 1944, was no average day.

ACKNOWLEDGMENTS

Accurate counts of America's fallen during World War II are elusive. Even today, nearly eighty years after the war ended, the total number remains a debatable figure and varies by source. Further, breakdowns by theater of operation, branch, rank, sex, and race are even more fraught with errors. And so, an accounting of deaths on a particular date and at a particular time of day is doubly problematic. Where known, the times of death of the individuals portrayed in this work are cited; in other cases, they are estimates based on available research or acknowledged as being unknown. While the resources mentioned herein have been invaluable in this effort, I bear all responsibility for any errors.

I am indebted, as any writer on the topic of World War II is, to the extensive accounts of the war from those who oversaw the conflict or had a front-row seat, whether documented by the Center of Military History, the Office of Air Force History, or the Naval History and Heritage Command. I am also grateful to the following: the National Archives for preserving and now digitizing many of the war diaries, action reports, and Missing Air Craft Reports; the Library of Congress and other organizations' Veterans History Projects, which include collections of firsthand interviews of World War II veterans on video or in interview transcripts; the Defense POW/MIA Accounting Agency that continues to this day to unearth records of the fallen across the theaters of war, in cases aided by individuals such as Peter Ranfranz with the "Missing Air Crew: The Search for the Coleman B-24 Crew Project"; and the Regimental Histories often written by members of a company, battalion, regiment, or division and now maintained and updated by the sons and daughters of those who served. With regard to the accounts of the Japanese prisoner-of-war camps, the hellships, and the *Arisan Maru* in particular, the POW Research Network Japan's website (powresearch.jp/en/), the Center for Research (mansell.com), and the list of *Arisan Maru* prisoners at West-Point.org were invaluable.

It is impossible to mention all the websites that have collected and now house records of a particular military unit, whether historical lineage, roster, interview transcripts, or lists of resources. A few of the sites that proved fundamental to the research of this work, and without which it could not have been done, include FindaGrave.com, HonorStates.org, Fold3.com, TogetherWeServed.com, American Battle Monuments Commission (abmc.com), and genealogical sites such as Ancestry.com. Among the websites maintained by individuals dedicated to preserving the history, records, and personal stories of World War II veterans, I found the following particularly helpful: MtMestas.com (Eighty-Eighth Infantry Division), BataanProject.com (192nd Tank Battalion), benkaplow.com (26th Infantry of the Yankee Division), and 351inf.com (the 351st Infantry Regiment).

I also want to thank the handful of descendants of people across the country mentioned in the book for responding to an email or online message from a complete stranger, as well as those who took my call or answered my letter and graciously shared their memories and artifacts. Thanks goes as well to the many individuals who have created and maintained social media pages dedicated to individual military units and lists of the fallen from World War II.

Finally, as always, I am eternally grateful for the support and encouragement of early readers of sections of the manuscript who concurred with my belief in its merits, including author and historian Jonathan W. Jordan; professor, author, and military historian John C. McManus; and editor in chief Andrew J. Davidson of the University of Missouri Press. And always and most of all, thanks goes to my very understanding husband, who never complained of the incessant tapping of my keyboard long into the night and who graciously read every word in my manuscript on the military topics with which he is most knowledgeable from his years as a US Navy pilot.

NO AVERAGE DAY

PART ONE

MORNING

For the first few days there were 1,800 of us together in one hold. . . . We were just kind of stuck together.
—Private Anton E. Cichy

00:01 a.m., Pacific Theater, the *Arisan Maru*, Bashi Channel in the South China Sea

Today, nearly eighty years after World War II ended, if there is one event that resonates in the minds of Americans, it is the attack on Pearl Harbor on December 7, 1941. President Franklin D. Roosevelt famously declared it a "date which will live in infamy." On that same day, although excluded from Roosevelt's "Day of Infamy" speech, the Imperial Japanese Navy also attacked other military assets in the Pacific. They made air raids and amphibious assaults on British, Indian, and Canadian installations in Malaya (part of present-day Malaysia), in Hong Kong, and in Singapore. And they bombed and strafed American garrisons on US-controlled Guam, Wake Island, and the Philippines. The United States had no choice but to respond to the threat to its far-flung Pacific outposts.

US military and political leaders had known from the start of the twentieth century that defending those outposts would be problematic. In the late 1930s, during his second administration, President Roosevelt recognized the situation was more than problematic; it was urgent. He would soon be forced to bring the country into the

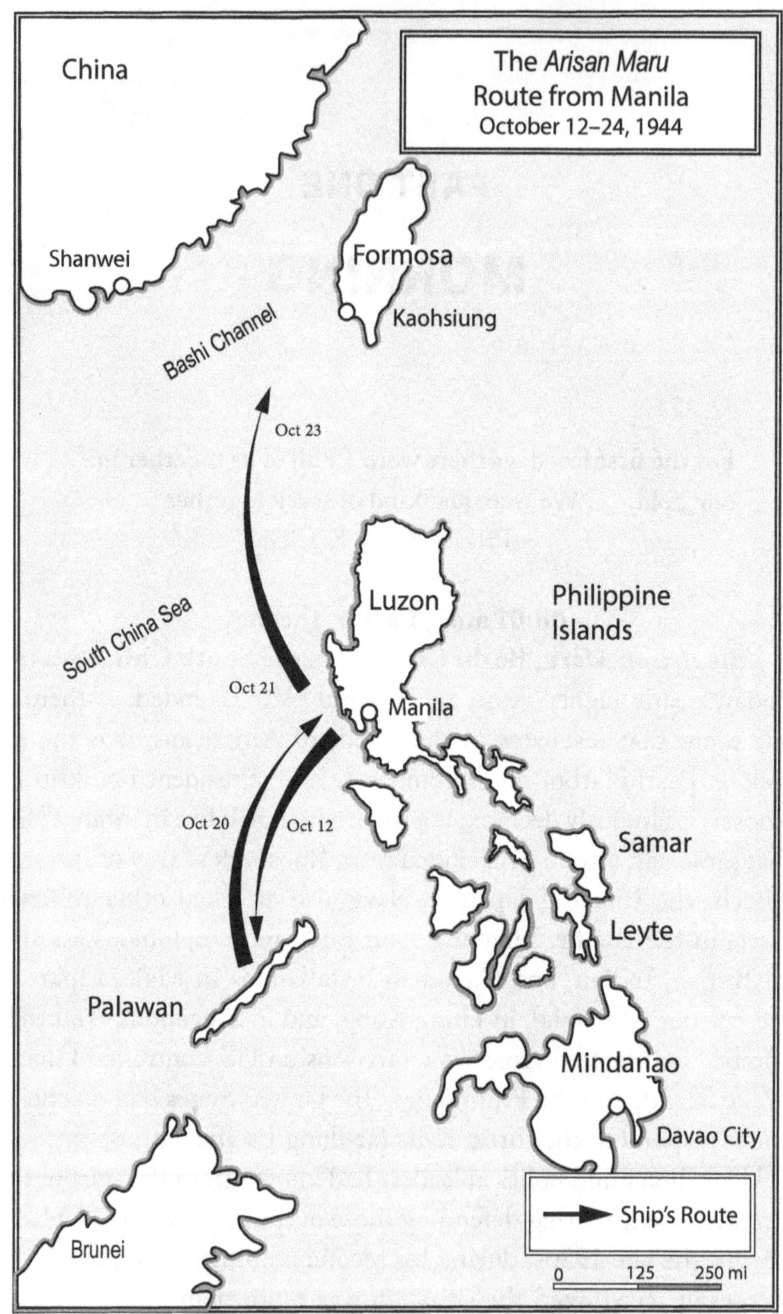

2. The *Arisan Maru* Route from Manila, October 12–24, 1944

conflict in Europe and was already determined to avoid the peril of fighting on two fronts. Roosevelt's military advisers retrieved and dusted off "War Plan Orange" from the shelf where it had languished for decades. Initially formulated in the 1800s but modified several times afterward, the plan outlined actions the United States should take if Japan invaded US territories. After much discussion, the administration modified War Plan Orange again. This time the color-coded plan included more specifics regarding the strategically sited Philippine Islands. It called for the US Army Forces in the Far East to delay the enemy's advance as long as possible, then withdraw to Luzon's Bataan Peninsula, across the bay from Manila. Should the circumstances become dire, the USAFFE was to cede Luzon and make a last stand on Corregidor Island in Manila Bay. In a worst-case situation, the USAFFE forces were to abandon the Philippines altogether.[1] The man Roosevelt chose to execute the plan—also a topic of much discussion—was Gen. Douglas A. MacArthur, whom Roosevelt had recalled from retirement to active duty to take command of the USAFFE.[2]

Two weeks after Pearl Harbor, Japanese forces landed in the Philippines. A sprawling archipelago, the Philippines comprise seven thousand separate islands. Yet only a handful of these islands, Luzon to the north, Samar and Negros at the center, and Mindanao to the South, account for the bulk of the Philippine landmass. Any plan for invasion had to incorporate the nation's daunting geographic challenges. Taking a multipronged approach, the Japanese landed first at Batan Island, off Luzon's northern coast, and then at Gamiguin Island, only miles from the Luzon mainland, before making their major push on Luzon's west coast through the Lingayen Gulf and its southeastern shores through Lamon Bay, where combined American and Filipino forces fought a desperate but doomed battle to try to repel the Japanese. Overwhelmed by the widely dispersed and nimble Japanese forces, despite their superior numbers, the combined Allied forces withdrew to the Bataan Peninsula in concert with War Plan Orange. Then, after failing to hold Bataan, the American-led forces, again reverting to the plan, transferred personnel and matériel to Corregidor.[3]

Under orders to leave the Philippines for his safety, in late February 1942, Gen. Douglas MacArthur transferred his command of the combined defending forces to (then) Lt. Gen. Jonathan M. Wainwright and, shortly thereafter, departed Corregidor with his family. Unfortunately, in the haste and chaos of the poorly planned and disorganized operation, more than sixty-five thousand Filipinos and ten thousand US troops under the command of Maj. Gen. Edward P. King were stranded on Luzon. All but a few hardy and defiant souls soon surrendered. Just two months later, in April, the Japanese drove the prisoners of war on foot from the tip of the Bataan Peninsula to Camp O'Donnell, a prison camp sixty-five miles north of Manila. During the arduous weeklong journey, later dubbed the "Bataan Death March," those prisoners not executed by the Japanese endured beatings, thirst, and starvation at the hands of their captors.[4]

Troops who had avoided capture or refused to surrender fell back and tried to reach Corregidor to make a stand with Lieutenant General Wainwright. But that resistance effort failed too, and on May 6, 1942, with dwindling supplies of both food and ammunition, Wainwright surrendered. He and the eleven thousand troops under his command were housed temporarily at the Bilibid Prison in Manila. From there, the Japanese sent the prisoners either to prison camps in Luzon such as Camp O'Donnell, where they joined the survivors of the Bataan Death March, or to POW camps in other Japanese territories.[5]

The death rate at Camp O'Donnell quickly became unacceptably high (fifteen hundred Americans alone died in the camp's first two months of operation). As a result, the Japanese transferred most of the prisoners forty-two miles east to a larger facility, Camp Cabanatuan. There, for two more years, the men lived and worked in appalling conditions, suffering physical abuses, unsanitary conditions, and malnutrition. Then, in 1943, the Japanese began emptying the prisons and shipping able-bodied prisoners to the Japanese home islands or other Japanese-controlled territories. The country's shipyards; wharves; coal, copper, and nickel mines; steelworks; and road-building and wood-cutting operations were suffering a severe shortage of manpower and needed workers to feed the nation's war effort. The Japanese trove of prisoners of war offered the perfect solution.[6]

From camps across the Philippines, guards called for the prisoners to prepare to move at a moment's notice—not that they had anything to pack or needed much time to prepare. The prisoners had little or no idea what lay ahead, and so they braced themselves, suspecting their circumstances would soon worsen. When the time came, the Japanese herded the prisoners into groups of one hundred and sent them to Manila. There, the prisoners sat for hours in the tropical sun without food or water. Finally, the guards rousted the men and pushed and prodded them into a waiting ship's hold until there was no room to sit or stand. Who first coined the name for the prisoners' ship is unknown, but soon the tens of thousands of men transported in them recognized and knew the horrors the term *hellship* represented. Lost, with countless Japanese records destroyed at the end of the war, is the precise number of ships, voyages, prisoners transported, and prisoners who died during transit. By some estimates, however, well over fifty ships and perhaps as many as one hundred crisscrossed the South Pacific with as many as sixty-eight thousand prisoners in their cargo holds. Some twenty-two thousand men are believed to have perished during these voyages. Some died from the miserable conditions on board, while others perished as submarines and bombers attacked and sank what they believed were nothing more than enemy cargo transports. In one case a typhoon raged and caused a ship carrying prisoners to sink. Of the total fatalities, about thirty-eight hundred were Americans.[7]

The Japanese freighter *Arisan Maru* was one of those hellships. On October 10, 1944, the ship stood at anchor in the Manila port, preparing to take aboard eighteen hundred American prisoners, most of whom came from Camp Cabanatuan. Of those the Japanese forced aboard, more than half had served in the US Army's Coast Artillery and Infantry Regiments and the Army Air Corps. The other half were Marines; hospital and medical staff; men from US Navy ships, including the *Canopus*, *Tanager*, *Pigeon*, *Finch*, and the *Napa*; and one hundred civilians. The bulk of the civilians were Americans who had been working in the Philippines prior to the start of hostilities.[8]

The prisoners were a mix of officers and enlisted men. Among the officers were three hundred holding the rank of commander or lieutenant colonel to second lieutenant and warrant officer. The fifteen hundred enlisted men included those with ratings from senior and chief petty officers to sergeants, seamen, and privates. At first, the Japanese separated higher-ranking American officers, like Generals Wainwright and King, from the rest of the troops and held them in relatively humane quarters. When their value as sources of intelligence and propaganda failed, however, they too were sent to the labor camps and later transported aboard hellships.[9]

Regardless of rank or position, branch of service, or given name, all suffered tremendous hardships. As the prisoners entered the hold designed to accommodate four or five hundred people, they clambered into makeshift bunks or were left standing with no room to sit or lie down. They stood or sat slumped against each other. Weakened and emaciated from dysentery and with little or no access to a handful of five-gallon oil cans that served as latrines, their excrement soon covered the floors. Once all were on board, the crew closed and locked the hatches. Darkness blanketed the hold. The lack of light was uncomfortable and the stench was all but unbearable, but when temperatures soared to more than one hundred degrees, the situation turned deadly. As General Wainwright later recalled during his experience transiting on the *Noto Maru* and then on a steamer to Formosa, "There was so little air in the place, many of us feared death by suffocation."[10]

The *Arisan Maru* departed Manila on October 12. Based on the snippets of information gleaned from their guards or overheard in conversations, the prisoners guessed they were destined for labor camps in Japan or China. But because the Japanese believed the Allied invasion of the Philippines was imminent and bombing raids and naval patrols in the surrounding sea lanes likely, the *Arisan Maru* turned south, away from Japan and China. It sailed four hundred miles south-southwest and anchored in a cove on the coast of Palawan Island.[11]

The already wretched conditions in the hold grew even more intolerable. Some men developed heat blisters and collapsed from heat exhaustion. Others moaned and screamed in agony from the lack of food and water, and some went mad. On October 15, while anchored off Palawan, the first death occurred. According to one account, Maj. Robert B. Lothrop, an Army engineer, wriggled his way through a porthole and dropped into the sea. A slightly different version claimed that he talked his way onto the deck and then dove over the side. Whichever story is the more accurate, the Japanese spotted the former West Point athlete swimming away from the ship. When an alarm sounded, a patrol in a rowboat spotted the splash from Lothrop's long strokes through the water. He took aim and fired. Then he fired again and again, hitting Robert four times. The Japanese retrieved Lothrop's body, only to bury him at sea shortly afterward. Lothrop's death was the first, but not the last.[12] Five other men died in the first forty-eight hours off Palawan. Then they began dying in larger numbers, thirty to thirty-five a day, according to a postwar interview with a former prisoner, Anton E. Cichy, an Army private. Their bodies remained in the hold, crumpled or stretched alongside the living until dark, when the crew allowed the prisoners to carry the corpses to the deck and drop them over the side.[13]

US Army Air Corps radio operator James T. Murphy, a prisoner aboard the *Noto Maru* that had sailed to Japan in August 1944, recalled the conditions he faced.[14] "We were sick, starved, and suffocating," he said. "There were only buckets provided for bathroom facilities. We were given one cup of water and two small rice rations daily. As we got underway, the hatch covers were partially opened, and this gave some air to the POWs lucky enough to be near the center of the hold."[15] For those on the *Arisan Maru*, blowers in the hold had been cut off, but a modicum of relief came when, with a combination of Yankee ingenuity and determination, the prisoners restored power to the blowers. Anton Cichy recalled, "Some of the prisoners were able to wire the ship's blowers into the power lines . . . [but] the blowers were disconnected, two days later, when the Japanese discovered what had been done."[16]

With the death toll showing no sign of abating, the Japanese transferred six hundred men to a second hold. The conditions in that hold were hardly an improvement, as the latter carried a cargo of coal that filled one-third of the space. The transfer was made not for humanitarian reasons, but because the ship's authorities had orders to deliver viable labor to Japanese industrial sites.[17] In December 1942, the Japanese War Ministry had issued explicit instructions: "Prisoners should arrive at their intended destinations in suitable condition to immediately perform their assigned duties." Like many hellship crews, that of the *Arisan Maru* largely ignored the instructions.[18]

If asked, most of the eighteen hundred aboard the hellship would have said they were just average young men, that they were nothing special. But the roster included more than a few remarkable people. There was one man with the given name of George Washington (Pearcy), one Andrew Jackson (Napier), three men with the name Benjamin Franklin (Coon, Harrison, and Van Sant), a Woodrow Wilson (Kazart), and one John Pershing (Patton). Unfortunately, no evidence remains to say these men harbored any greater sense of patriotism or duty than any of the others aboard. There were also four members of the Cabanatuan Cats orchestra aboard the hellship. They were John H. Kratz, who had organized the prison-camp musicians; Martin D. Salas and Edwin T. Booth, pianists; and Chester R. McClure, a guitarist who had played with the "Ace, Deuce, and

Spades" band and once on a Phoenix radio station. During the last weeks on Corregidor, the four privates first class and a few other soldiers from the Fifty-Ninth Coast Artillery Regiment buoyed spirits by playing swing music for the stranded men. According to a War Department report, "Men in the fortress claim the musicians are one of the best 'pickup' bands west of the international dateline and east of the China Sea." While the men were stripped of most of their belongings on the Bataan Death March, the Japanese, purportedly fond of music, allowed those who had small musical instruments to keep them. They even sanctioned transporting a piano from the former home of one captive from Manila. "For a few brief moments the horror of reality vanished," as Cabanatuan prisoner Col. Eugene C. Jacobs recalled in his memoir.[19]

Those relatively good times were now a thing of the past. Prior to boarding transports from Cabanatuan, the prison guards strip-searched the men and confiscated most of their personal items, including their musical instruments. It was unlikely even a harmonica could have been smuggled aboard the transport ship. Still, in the cramped hold, nothing could prevent John Kratz and the other musically inclined from leading the men in song or humming a few bars of "Sentimental Journey," "Stardust," or even "God Bless America" to alleviate their misery.[20]

Also in the hold, nearby, Lt. Cdr. Herbert C. Brokenshire offered solace of another kind to the prisoners. Brokenshire had worked as a medical missionary in the Philippines in the early 1900s. He took that calling into the military, serving in World War I and now again in World War II. In the dark, the man of faith reached out to grasp a hand or touch a shoulder of the fearful. He bowed his head and heard their prayers.

For ten days, the *Arisan Maru* remained in its hideaway at Palawan. While there, as the Japanese had predicted, Allied forces intent on retaking the Philippines bombed Manila and its surroundings. In their flights to and from Manila, the bombers missed the *Arisan Maru* in its hideaway. But later, when the bombing routes expanded, Allied aircraft returning from a raid on Palawan's airfield spotted and strafed the hellship. Whether this action caused additional loss of life is unknown.[21]

Finally, on October 20, when the air strikes on Manila abated, the *Arisan Maru* returned to Luzon. The stay in Manila was brief, and on October 21 the ship departed at 11:40 p.m. in a convoy bound for Takao, Formosa (present-day Kaohsiung, Taiwan).[22] Nine days had elapsed since the ship's first departure. During that time, except for the men charged with preparing the captives' meals, the prisoners remained in the dark, heat, and stench of the holds. Belowdecks, the ninth and tenth days of confinement passed, one day and night blurring into the next. On October 23, the eleventh day, although unbeknownst to the prisoners below, radios crackled across the convoy. In their path through the Bashi Channel, two hundred miles west of Luzon, convoy defenses had detected a wolfpack of eight Allied submarines lying in wait.[23]

At 5:24 p.m., the wolfpack's leader, the USS *Sawfish* (SS-276), attacked. The ship's logs recorded the sinking of a large cargo or transport—later identified by Japanese records as the *Kimikawa Maru*, a seaplane tender. Fearing more attacks, the convoy scattered, each ship proceeding toward Formosa at its own pace. The fears were justified, as the submarines attacked again at midnight, with the USS *Snook* (SS-279) striking another large cargo ship or oiler and sinking what postwar records revealed as the *Shinsei Maru*. Throughout the night, a classic sea battle raged. Convoy escorts chased the pack and deployed a series of depth charges, only to have the submarines escape, speed away, and then return to make another attack. The encounter was a devastating loss for the Japanese, leaving a total of eight ships lying at the bottom of the sea.[24]

Making only seven to eight miles per hour, the *Arisan Maru* trailed the former convoy through the Bashi Channel. For the moment, it had escaped detection. By day's end and 150 miles to the north, the ship would reach its final destination, its service as a freighter and cargo carrier of any ilk ended.

CHAPTER 1

A Pencil for a Pick

It stays with you forever.
—Staff Sergeant Lester I. Tenney

3:00 a.m., Pacific Theater, Sendai POW Camp No. 6-B, Hanawa, Japan

In the suffocating confines of the *Arisan Maru*'s hold, prisoners like Anton Cichy, James Murphy, John Kratz, and Herbert Brokenshire could only imagine what trials awaited them. Consumed by the grim specter of that future, they contemplated their odds of surviving and speculated about their impending deaths. One person, however, knew exactly what lay ahead. His name was Paul Henry Miller, a private first class in the US Army.

Paul Miller was born in 1920 in Virginia to Samuel and Crissa Miller, both staunch members of the Church of the Brethren, a Christian denomination that encouraged living simply and peaceably. By the time he graduated from high school and began attending Bridgewater College, rumblings of war reverberated across the horizon. Simplicity and peacefulness were at great risk. The Millers did everything they could to shield their son from the brewing tempest—that is, until he began dating a young woman outside the church. With America still squarely on the sidelines of the multinational conflict, Crissa Miller decided a stint in the peacetime military might be just the thing to end the budding romance.[1]

On October 14, 1940, after weeks of some not so gentle persuasion, Paul Miller made his way to the local recruitment center and inked his commitment to the military. A few months later, he arrived at Fort William McKinley in the Philippines. His assignment as a clerk in the US Army Forces in the Far East finance department was a "plum" assignment, perhaps the plumpest plum. Fort William McKinley sat on an idyllic neck of land south of Manila and away from the capital city's hustle and bustle. Verdant stretches of farmland sloped down and away from the post to Laguna de Bay on its eastern flank, and along the post's tree-lined avenues stately homes stood like islands in a sea of manicured grass. Across the city, during the social season, the local society's upper class and the military's high-ranking officers in white jackets with gold epaulets supped by candlelight. True, as an enlisted man, Miller was excluded from these affairs. But when not on duty, he could enjoy a round of golf at the post golf course, go to the theater, or shop for sundries at the exchange. And while his barracks sat more than a stone's throw from the stately homes and the semiluxurious officers' quarters, his accommodations were better than the bare essentials most other soldiers found in the military.[2]

The young man took to his surroundings and his assignment. Just two months into his tenure, he received a promotion to chief clerk. The setting, the plum job, and his rise in fortune notwithstanding, Miller sensed the building tension in his tiny corner of the South Pacific. Rumors of war circulated on and off the post. When the attack on Clark Field came, however, it caught everyone off guard. Life in the Philippines changed in an instant—the candles snuffed, the last round of golf scored, and the theater curtains drawn. Within two weeks, the Japanese were knocking on Manila's door, prompting the Americans to withdraw to the Bataan Peninsula and then, according to War Plan Orange, from Luzon to Corregidor.[3]

The holdouts sheltered inside the Malinta Tunnel, a large bombproof storage and personnel bunker the Americans had constructed on Corregidor. There, realizing their stand would soon be over, Col.

John Vance, a USAFFE finance officer, and his assistants destroyed small arms, burned documents, and spent several hours cutting up large stacks of Philippine pesos. It is possible that Paul played a role in the destruction as his last official act with the Army.[4]

After Lieutenant General Wainwright surrendered his troops in May and the last holdout of Americans followed in June, Paul Miller became a mere statistic. He was just one more of the tens of thousands of American, British, Australian, and Filipino prisoners in Japanese hands. Records do not show how he endured the subsequent months of captivity, but it is likely he participated in the forced march to Camp O'Donnell and was imprisoned at Camp Cabanatuan. In February 1943, Samuel and Crissa Miller received a telegram stating their son was "well" but that it was "impossible to get mail to him at present." The family rejoiced with the news—the first in more than a year. Other families with husbands or brothers or sons imprisoned in the Pacific theater had long since given up hope. But drawing on their faith, the Millers told a reporter from their local newspaper, the *Staunton (VA) Evening-Leader*, "We are sure he is all right."[5]

By this point, the Japanese had begun dispersing prisoners from the Philippines to other Japanese-controlled areas and the Japanese home islands. Paul Miller was among them, possibly transported aboard the *Noto Maru* that sailed from Manila on August 27, 1944, with more than a thousand survivors of the Bataan Death March. Shortly after departing, the *Noto Maru* became the target of an unidentified American submarine, the crew of which had no idea as to the nature of the ship's cargo. The *Noto Maru* zigzagged desperately through the water to escape the submarine's torpedoes. Two streaked beneath the ship's hull but left the *Noto Maru* unscathed. The ship sailed on and, after twelve days at sea, arrived in Moji, Japan, on September 4, 1944. There, it unloaded its human cargo for transport to their assigned prison camps.[6]

Paul Miller found himself in the newly established Tokyo No. 8 Branch Camp at Osarisawa-cho, Kazuno Gun, Akita Prefecture (later renamed and placed under the Sendai jurisdiction as Sendai No. 6-B Branch Camp). The camp was one of more than 150 in the Japanese home islands designated for prisoners of war, a third of which sat in close proximity to the capital city. Thirty other camps in the vicinity held civilian captives. Outside contact was virtually nonexistent. The International Red Cross made occasional visits to the prisoner-of-war camps to encourage humane treatment practices. The supervised visits, however, were largely superficial gestures, as the authorities barred the Red Cross representatives from direct contact with the prisoners. Families sent packages to their loved ones in good faith, but the guards pilfered the contents and discarded or set aside the packages. And while the prisoners wrote letters home, only a meager number of them reached their families. Those that did were censored heavily and long delayed.[7]

Sendai No. 6-B housed more than five hundred American, British, and Australian prisoners in crude barracks connected by covered passageways. The prisoners slept on straw mat–covered platforms flanking each side of the barracks. At mealtime, a team of prisoners manned buckets from which they doled out the rations to their fellow prisoners, who sat or squatted on packed-dirt floors in the center of each barracks. The meals were scant. In the morning, they consisted of a cup of rice or barley and a cup of thin soup. On occasion, for the dinner meal, the prison cooks added a scrap of fish or meat.[8]

Camp prisoners labored at the Mitsubishi Mining Company's Hanawa, Osarisawa, copper mine. Overseers assigned the men to work details based on their claimed competencies, whether electricians, mechanics, machinists, or other skilled trades. They dispatched those like Paul, who could not lay claim to a specific useful expertise, to the lower, most unpleasant depths of the mine, where they helped bring up the copper. Sgt. James T. Murphy, a survivor, remembered on his arrival the commander gave the prisoners notice "that we would stay in this camp until the Japanese won the war, that we had to bow to all guards and obey their instructions, that we had to obey all camp rules and that we would be severely punished for any infractions to these rules, and that we would be working at the Mitsubishi copper mine and must work very, very hard." Very hard indeed, Murphy recalled. Just getting to the work site from the barracks entailed a taxing hour-and-a-half climb two miles up a mountainside to the mine's entrance. Once inside the mine's tunnels, the men walked until they could no longer proceed upright, and then they crawled on their hands and knees to their workstation. For eight hours, they blasted and dug out the ore, hand loaded it into wheeled carts, pushed the carts out of the mine, dumped the ore into large holding bins, and then returned to dig for more. The work was "dirty, dangerous and difficult," sometimes conducted in standing water, under poor lighting, and in areas susceptible to cave-ins.[9]

Each day, the men faced the very real prospect of death. Besides the inherent dangers in mining, they endured backbreaking work in both extreme heat and bitter cold temperatures, all while suffering under a near-starvation diet. Equally deadly were the constant beatings they endured from overseers, mining officials, and prison guards.[10]

For five months, the Millers heard nothing about their son from the International Red Cross Committee who throughout the war supplied the military with information on prisoners of war and in some cases communicated directly with the families. After the War Department and staff verified information received from the Red Cross, details went by Western Union under the name of Maj. Gen. James A. Ulio, the US Army's adjutant general, with a confirmation letter to follow. To his credit, despite the overwhelming number of telegrams and letters, numbering six thousand a day at the peak, Ulio insisted the letters not be form letters. And though the office had committed to keeping families updated with new details, often there was little or nothing the department could add.

Finally, in January 1945, an official card arrived in the Millers' mailbox. The card stated the Japanese had transferred Paul Miller from the Philippines to the Japanese home islands. The scant information held little practical value. There was no mention of where or how they might contact him. Calling the War Department to ask for more details would have been unproductive, with more than twelve hundred calls per day coming into the department from families desperate to know more.[11]

And so the Millers waited. Two months later, on March 18, 1945, the Red Cross sent the Millers an updated report. It noted their son had died five months earlier, on October 24, 1944. Japanese prison records released after the war list the cause of his death as beriberi, a sign of malnutrition. Miraculously, only nine men died before the camp closed. Paul Miller had been the first.[12]

While the exact time of Paul Miller's death is unknown, this account places his demise in the first hours after midnight, imagining death was merciful and spared him another day of hard labor.

On receiving notice of Paul Miller's death, the military located his younger brother, Robert, who was serving in Italy and sent him home to his family. It had been much to Crissa's chagrin that on finishing his college studies, Robert had followed Paul into the military. Robert's enlistment, however, had been of his own volition. According to Robert Miller's son, in 1948, the Red Cross recovered Paul's dog tags and ashes and delivered them to the Miller family, who buried the remains in Bridgewater, Virginia. Being able to bury their son's remains, however, was little comfort, particularly for Crissa, who, until the day she died, regretted having been instrumental in sending her son to war.[13]

In the decades following the war, Japan made several statements regarding the mistreatment of their prisoners of war, although the former prisoners and their families often characterized the comments as "too little, too late."

In a public event in July 2015, Mitsubishi Corporation executive Hikaru Kimura apologized to a group of US World War II veterans once forced to labor in Japan's prisoner-of-war camps. One of those in the group was former US Army sergeant and radio operator James Murphy. He was then ninety-four years old and was the only survivor of the Mitsubishi mining company camp able to make the ceremony at the Los Angeles Museum of Tolerance. Perhaps realizing this was as close to atonement as he would ever receive, Murphy said, "It's my high honor to accept the apology from the Japanese delegation."[14] Not all were so forgiving. Lester I. Tenney, who survived the Bataan Death March, a voyage on the hellship *Toro Maru*, and imprisonment at a prisoner-of-war camp in Omuta, Japan, once said of his experience, "It stays with you forever."[15]

Later, the Mitsubishi Corporation placed a plaque at the entrance to the former Hanawa mine where Miller and Murphy and hundreds of others toiled. The plaque reads, "Working conditions for the POWs were exceedingly harsh and left deep mental and physical wounds that the lapse of time would not heal. . . . With the deepest sense of remorse, Mitsubishi Materials offers its heartfelt apologies to all former POWs who were forced to work under appalling conditions."[16]

In August 2015, on the seventieth anniversary of Japan's surrender, Prime Minister Shinzo Abe, using carefully chosen words, "reiterated his support for past apologies for the country's imperial expansionism." He added that Japan "did inflict immeasurable damage and suffering" on "innocent people."[17] Critics maintain a full apology is lacking, but given the delicacy of the situation and the great length of time that has passed, they are unlikely to ever hear anything more direct.

CHAPTER 2

A Petty Officer of Pigeons

It's up to the women.
—Eleanor Roosevelt's 1933 call to action

3:45 a.m., Zone of the Interior, USA

Forty-five minutes later and halfway across the globe, Petty Officer Margaret Nancy Neubauer of the US Navy drew her last breath. Doctors pronounced her dead at Bethesda Naval Hospital in Washington, DC, and then informed her parents. Two days earlier, after returning from leave, Margaret had walked through the entrance gate of the Navy Proving Grounds at Dahlgren, Virginia, heading for her quarters. The driver of a Navy truck did not see Margaret and struck her, sending her to the ground with severe injuries.[1]

Margaret, the youngest child and second daughter of Dr. Ferdinand John Thomas and Margaret Duryea Neubauer, was born in 1923 in Chile, where her father worked as head of the Valparaiso observatory staff. Her mother was a graduate of Stanford University—an exemplary accomplishment as fewer than 4 percent of women could claim to hold a college degree at the time. The Neubauers returned to the United States in 1929 and settled in San Jose so that Margaret's father could continue his work in astronomy, this time for the Lick Observatory. Both daughters, no doubt influenced by their parents' educational and professional achievements, finished high school and then enrolled in college. Phoebe followed in her mother's footsteps and attended Stanford, while Margaret chose to attend the University of California at Berkeley. There she graduated with honors in mathematics in 1944. A few months before her graduation, with the war in full swing, Margaret enlisted in the military to use her education and talent in the service of her country. She joined the US Navy's Women's Reserve, better known as the WAVES, or the Women Accepted for Volunteer Emergency Service.

Although women had served as nurses in both the Army and the Navy since the early 1900s, they were not eligible for the draft and not allowed to enlist in the military. Changes were afoot, however. Eleanor Roosevelt had supported the idea of women in service—although not specifically military service—as early as 1940. Finally in 1942, Congresswoman Edith Rogers's bill to allow mobilization of women passed, and President Roosevelt signed it.[2]

Now there were promises that by answering the military's call, women would help bring the war to a close sooner than otherwise and further that it was a woman's *duty* to serve. Recruiting centers displayed posters with the slogans "Join the WAC (Women's Army Corps) . . . it's my war too" and "Bring him home sooner, join the WAVES." But there was also the equally prominent admonishment to join this or that service and "free a man to fight." In theory, women who joined the Army, Navy, Air Force, Marines, or Coast Guard would be assigned to stateside positions or to administrative, training, and nursing roles overseas, releasing their male counterparts for combat.[3]

Margaret became one of the 300,000 women who served in the military by the end of the war, 100,000 of which served in the WAVES. Approximately 150,000 served with the Women's Army Corps (WAC), 23,000 in the US Marine Corps Women's Reserve, 10,000 in the US Coast Guard Women's Reserve (SPAR, for *Semper Paratus*—Always Ready), and 1,100 in the Women Airforce Service Pilots (WASP).[4] Some women came to have second thoughts about their service, not in the sense of serving their country, but in the realization that by accepting their assignment, they sent a man in harm's way. "Somewhere out there was a woman somewhere who hated me," said WAVES lieutenant Eleanor Millican Frye, referring to an unknown sweetheart or wife of a soldier or sailor.[5]

Assigned to a role that fitted her background, Margaret likely had no such thoughts. College-educated women with math, physics, chemistry, and engineering degrees were in high demand and in the Navy assigned directly as petty officers in "specialist" roles. The largest concentration of women in the Navy's reserve, 20,000, including Margaret, served in Washington, DC. And there she found her niche with other mathematicians and technicians with a specialist (X) rating at the Bureau of Ordnance. Many of the bureau's assignments had to do with proofing and testing the Navy's arsenal and computational devices, including such highly skilled tasks as calculating bomb trajectories, and many were classified. Records note Margaret completed her basic training with other female recruits at Hunter College. Her official rating at that time was one of the most obscure: pigeoneer. Pigeoneers had the responsibility to train and care for the flocks of birds used by the military to deliver messages between units and their stations.[6]

The birds were first used as message carriers by the United States in the late 1800s. From on board the USS *Constellation*, a handler would place a note inside a tiny capsule and tie it to the homing pigeon's leg and release the bird to fly back to its home—a loft onshore. By the turn of the century, a half-dozen Navy yards housed pigeons in lofts. Although the program was discontinued once radio communications became the standard, the pigeon service returned during World War I under the auspices of the quartermaster. The military continued use of the birds through World War II. Thousands were dropped into France during the Normandy invasion so that the resistance could send back messages about German troop movements. And the Navy carried the birds aboard Navy ships for communications where radio silence was required or in the event technical failures prevented normal means of communication. Interestingly, while the Navy had opened its doors to women to serve, one former pigeoneer, Pearl Nill Robbins, stated, "When homing pigeons came back to base, a male officer retrieved the encrypted messages, not the WAVES."[7]

The pigeon service was finally discontinued in 1961 and the pigeoneer rating discontinued. It was perhaps an odd assignment for Margaret (as it would have been for any Navy recruit), but it may have been only a temporary one. When she was killed, she was awaiting final officer training and possibly serving in an un- disclosed mathematics capacity at the Proving Grounds.[8]

Margaret Neubauer was awarded posthumously the American Campaign Medal and the World War II Victory Medal. She was buried at Arlington National Cemetery with full military honors.

Of the 350,000 women who served in World War II, approximately 300 lost their lives. Margaret Neubauer's death was the only known death to have occurred October 24, 1944. Two days earlier, Army nurse Lt. Sarah B. Vance of West Virginia was killed while serving at the Thirty-Third General Hospital in Italy. And two days later, on October 26, Gertrude V. Tomkins Silver, one of the 1,100 WASPs, disappeared after taking off from Los Angeles Municipal Airport to ferry a P-51 aircraft from California to Arizona. Neither she nor her aircraft has ever been located.[9]

CHAPTER 3

A Dress Rehearsal

Our future supremacy in the air depends on the brains and efforts of our engineers.

—Gen. Henry "Hap" Arnold

4:00 a.m., Zone of the Interior, Barksdale Field, Bossier City, Louisiana

The first B-29 Superfortress prototype sparkled as it emerged from the hangar at Boeing Field in Seattle, Washington, into the morning sun. It was 1942, and the behemoth of a bomber was the US military's answer to the demands of the war in the Pacific. Dubbed a "very long range bomber," the aircraft could cover the Pacific's long overwater distances, capable of flying to its targets from bases in China and India and later from islands across the South Pacific. The B-29 brought with it the capacity to fly at higher altitudes, at faster speeds, and to carry heftier payloads than the workhorse B-17 and B-24 bombers already in service in World War II. The drive to develop ever more advanced aircraft and thereby achieve supremacy in the skies was a key element of America's strategy for winning World War II. And that goal depended on, as Gen. Henry "Hap" Arnold said, the brains and efforts of our engineers. Engineers, working now in concert with the military, incorporated the latest in aviation technology into every aspect of the bomber's design, including a pressurized cabin, an electronic fire-control system, and remote-controlled machine-gun turrets.[1]

Boeing had secured the contract to supply the B-29 and launched the first model with a test flight on September 21, 1942. It should have been a triumphant moment for everyone involved. Instead, a series of engine failures cast a dark shadow on the aircraft's promise. The aircraft engineers returned to their drawing boards and made alterations, and, in short order, the company unveiled an improved second B-29 prototype. Ninety days later, on the second model's maiden flight, the aircraft's engines erupted in flames. Fortunately, the crew returned to the airfield and landed safely, avoiding what would have been a complete disaster. Boeing fitted the second prototype with engines salvaged from the first model and then fine-tuned and tested every nut and bolt and system on the bomber. Second, third, and fourth test flights followed, and all seemed to be going well. On February 18, 1943, Edmund "Eddie" Allen, Boeing's chief test pilot, took the controls for the B-29's ninth test flight. Eight minutes into the flight, the number-one engine caught fire. The crew onboard extinguished the fire, and everything seemed in order. Still, with an abundance of caution, Allen turned back toward the airfield. The fire in the number-one engine erupted for a second time, followed shortly by an explosion, although the plane continued flying, shedding parts as it went. The crew bailed out, but they were too low for their parachutes to open. Then the aircraft hit the ground, exploding in a cataclysm of fire and smoke. No one survived.[2]

Despite the mishaps, the military was determined to make the Superfortress a success and turned to the best man they had: Brig. Gen. Paul Tibbets. At the time, Tibbets was in Europe serving as the deputy group commander for the Eighth Air Force. He accepted the mission and returned to the United States to train B-29 crews. To his surprise, he found many pilots reluctant to fly the Superfortress, thinking it untested and too dangerous. Tibbets devised an ingenious plan to change the young pilots' minds. He asked two female pilots (Dora Dougherty Strother and Dorothea Johnson Moorman) to learn to fly the bomber. Neither woman had flown a four-engine aircraft before, but after three days they were ready and took the Superfortress on a series of stateside demonstrations. The plan was a resounding success, dispelling the concerns among the male pilots—or perhaps shaming them into flying the B-29 regardless of its reputation. By 1944, the Superfortress had become an indispensable element of the US Air Force.[3]

Among the many crews comfortably flying B-29s in late 1944 was Capt. Paul Dowling and his ten-man crew from the 484th Bomb Squadron, 505th Bomb Group. In the wee hours of October 24, 1944, they took off from Harvard Army Airfield, Nebraska, in a B-29 for a cross-country training mission. For them, the flight was a dress rehearsal of sorts. In days, they were to depart for duty in the Mariana Islands. The flight was likely to be their last before deploying.[4]

Dowling was accustomed to the early-morning flights; he might have even preferred flying at that time of day, with generally calmer air and less crowded skies. Their planned route would take them south and east to Barksdale Field in Louisiana, where they would refuel and then return home. As they cruised at a comfortable altitude, Dowling glanced outside at the still-inky black canopy of the sky. The clouds that had hung in the skies earlier were dissipating, and patches of stars shimmered overhead. The temperature was a balmy fifty-six degrees. A clear fall day lay ahead.[5]

The B-29's shaky start and later record of fatal accidents were facts the bomber's pilots knew. What Paul Dowling did not know was that over the past few days, two B-29s had crashed at US Army Air Force airfields in China. One incident occurred on October 20 at Pengshan Airfield. There on the bomber's final approach, the aircraft crashed, killing the eight-man crew. On October 23, the tragedy repeated itself at the Hsin-Ching Airfield, taking the lives of ten more airmen. From the latter incident, Dowling could have taken small comfort in knowing that poor weather had caused the crew to lose their way and exhaust their fuel supply. The plane had crashed just short of the airfield.[6] But like other pilots, had he known, Dowling would likely have shrugged off the statistics. It couldn't happen to him. Besides, he had much to do yet with his life. He had graduated from the University of Nebraska College of Law and had been admitted to the bar in 1941. And Jeanne Rustenbach, his wife of six months, was taking flying lessons on her own during his absence. He looked forward to sharing stories of flying and perhaps one day flying together. It couldn't happen to him.[7]

The flight down to Louisiana proved routine. Dowling and his crew landed safely, refueled, and prepared for their flight home. At 4:00 a.m., Barksdale ground control cleared the Superfortress to taxi for takeoff. Short of the runway, he ran up the four twenty-two-hundred-horsepower engines. Then, with clearance from the control tower for takeoff, he turned the B-29 onto the runway, released the brakes, and let the massive plane roll forward. On reaching takeoff speed, Dowling eased the control column back and watched as the ground dropped away. The Superfortress was airborne and headed home.

Barely a handful of heartbeats into the takeoff, the B-29 wavered. The hair on Dowling's arms stood erect. He shifted in his seat, turning toward his copilot just as the aircraft's wing clipped a treetop on the Fullilove Plantation at the south end of the runway. As light as the impact was, it sent the faltering aircraft into the ground, nose down. The impact ruptured the now full fuel tanks, engulfing the bomber in flames and incinerating the eleven men onboard, everything inside the aircraft, and a sizable swath of the Fullilove forest.[8]

Hours before news of Dowling's crash could be reported, Louisiana residents opened their morning newspapers to the front-page story of yet another crash. Six of its own had died the day before in a B-26 Marauder bomber crash in Canfield, Arkansas. That plane, too, had been on a routine training mission. Engine trouble was believed to have precipitated the crash.[9]

March Field, Riverside, California

By noon, both the Canfield and the Barksdale crashes had already settled into the realm of old news. There were new developments unfolding in the aviation drama. At 6:30 a.m., a B-17 Flying Fortress had engine trouble and crashed onto farmland in Worthington, Minnesota. Fortunately, in this case the ten crewmen had parachuted safely before the crash.[10] Then in Riverside County, California, that same day, although the exact time is not known, 1st Lt. Anthony "Vito" Galioto of the Army Air Forces' 420th Base Unit was completing a training exercise as the navigator in a B-24J Liberator. On approach to land at Riverside's March Field runway, his aircraft lost an engine. In an all too familiar story, the plane plummeted nose down toward the earth. Galioto and five others perished. They, too, were in their final stages of training for combat. Like Paul Dowling's crew, they soon would have deployed to the Pacific.[11] So common had local aircraft accidents become, the outcome of the Sunday football game between the Fourth Air Force of March Field and the Marine's El Toro Base teams was still headline news days later. The report of the deaths of the six young men had disappeared overnight.[12]

Russell, Kansas

Remarkably, another fatal accident occurred on October 24. In the skies above Russell, Kansas, Capt. Herbert "Bud" Keadin was at the controls of a B-17 when he experienced engine trouble. With a population of a mere forty-eight hundred and surrounded by miles of open land, the town was never in danger. Keadin was able to guide the failing bomber to an open wheat field. Eyewitnesses reported that for the first few seconds after the aircraft came to a stop, nothing happened. An eerie stillness hung over the scene. And then, without warning, the plane ignited. An explosion rocked the area, killing all aboard. In the aftermath, investigators examined the blackened and twisted metal and sifted through the ashes, but they failed to find the cause of the deadly incident. The crash was chalked up to yet another training accident, despite Captain

Keadin's considerable experience. He had served in the military since 1941 and completed tours of duty in Panama, Puerto Rico, and the South Pacific.[13]

Two other crashes on October 24 are also worth mentioning. Thankfully, they had happier endings, that is, without the loss of life.

On a training mission off the California coast, the crew of Patrol Bombing Squadron 106 from Camp Kearny, California, became lost in bad weather. Besides the eleven-man US Navy crew, two female Marines and the squadron's canine mascot were on board the PB4Y-2 Privateer (a long-range bomber derived from the B-24 Liberator). The crew searched for a suitable landing site, or any expanse of dry land for that matter, until the aircraft's fuel gauge registered empty. Out of options, they ditched the aircraft in the Gulf of Baja. All thirteen on board and the canine mascot exited the aircraft safely and swam to a six-man life raft retrieved before the plane sank. While the men took turns swimming alongside the raft to give the others room, they drifted with the current and made it to Angel de la Guardia, a deserted island on the east coast of Baja, California. There they subsisted by eating raw clams and fish for four days. With survival in doubt, five of the crew set out on the life raft in a desperate attempt to find help. Their efforts succeeded. The crew of a Mexican fishing boat spotted and rescued the group, who guided the Mexicans to the other survivors. Soon, a US Coast Guard team arrived in Bahia de Los Angeles to fly the crew home.[14]

The Robinson Crusoe–like story splashed across the country's newspapers. Everyone wanted to hear how the two women Marines and the eleven Navy crew members survived, in that order. Headlines read, "Women Marines, 11 Fliers Downed on Desert [*sic*] Island," "Girl Marines Marooned Four Days on Desert [*sic*] Isle with 11 Men," and "Girls Decide It's Hardly Paradise." In fact, while PFC Helen L. Breckel and PFC Edna H. Shaughnessy were named in article after article, only two or three of the eleven men were ever mentioned by name. And the mascot remained simply the squadron's "canine mascot."[15] Curiously given the crew's makeup, no one asked what the mission's purpose was, at least not publicly.

Finally, coming "full circle," a B-29 crashed in Harvard, Nebraska, Paul Dowling's home station. After experiencing engine failure, the 482nd Bomb Squadron pilot made a belly landing in a farm field south of Harvard Army Airfield. Once again, the aircraft erupted in flames, but in this instance, the crew managed to escape unharmed.[16]

The dizzying list of accidents during training exercises on October 24, 1944, that took the lives of twenty-eight pilots and crew did not escape the notice of other bomber crews, whether they flew in B-17s, B-24s, B-26s, or B-29s. Still, the fallen were but a small fraction of the twenty-six thousand men who lost their lives to aircraft accidents during the war. Of those, fifteen thousand perished without ever leaving the United States. Several factors contributed to the deadly statistic, including rushed design and production efforts, abbreviated aircraft testing, lax or less rigor in pilot selection, and expedited pilot training. The dangers were no secret to the pilots and their crews. They nicknamed the B-24 bomber the "flying coffin" and the B-26 the "widow maker" because of their design problems and flying difficulties. But the avid pilots with wings on their chests shrugged their shoulders and carried on. It couldn't happen to them.[17]

CHAPTER 4

The First "Kamikaze"

I have returned.
—Gen. Douglas A. MacArthur

8:40 a.m., Pacific Theater, San Juanico Strait, Philippine Islands

In 1942, after Gen. Douglas A. MacArthur arrived in Australia where he established his new headquarters, he vowed to the world, "I shall return." Now that moment was at hand. And he returned to the Philippines with a wider than ever influence. He had turned down an opportunity to run for president of the United States, settling as of March 1942 for the lofty title supreme commander of the Southwest Pacific area.[1] Under his purview, he had an extensive organization that was well prepared to do what he had come to do—retake the Philippine Islands. The troops under his command included the Sixth Army's Ninety-Sixth and Seventh Infantry Divisions and the First Cavalry and Twenty-Fourth Infantry Divisions, the Army Services of Supply in the Southwest Pacific, and the Seventh Fleet.[2]

On the morning of October 20, 1944, the general paced the deck of the cruiser USS *Nashville*, sitting two miles off the eastern coast of Leyte Island in the Philippines. All he needed was a signal that the beaches of Leyte were secure. The notice came at 1:00 p.m.

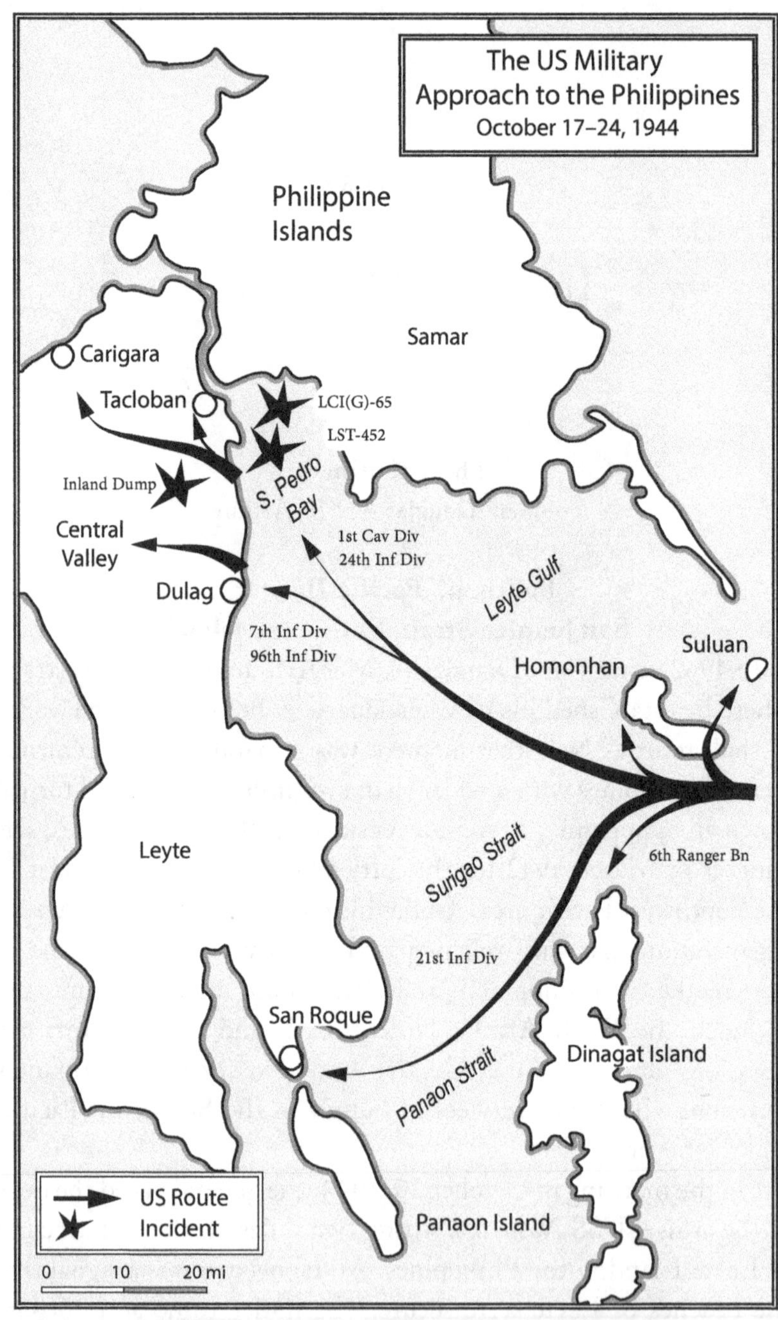

3. The US Military Approach to the Philippines, October 17–24, 1944

Accompanied by his staff and Army photographers, MacArthur disembarked the *Nashville*, boarded a landing craft, and headed for shore. Minutes later, with the landing craft unable to pull up onto dry land, the general stepped from the craft into knee-deep water and waded ashore. Within days, photos of the landing splashed across the front pages of America's newspapers. Front and center was MacArthur, a scowl on his face, a determined forward lean, and water-stained pants. The photograph became one of the iconic images of the war.

Once on the sand of "Red Beach," the general strode to a mobile radio set behind the beachhead. From there, MacArthur made his announcement: "I have returned. By the grace of Almighty God our forces stand again on Philippine soil—soil consecrated in the blood of our two peoples."[3] It was perhaps MacArthur's finest moment.

"A-day," as the landing on the Philippines was dubbed, had come about only after much deliberation. Throughout the summer of 1944, Navy admirals, the Joint Chiefs of Staff, and even President Roosevelt had strategized behind closed doors, each arguing for a favorite approach to retaking the Philippines. At play were when and where to land, whether on Luzon to the North, home to Manila, the Philippine capital; Leyte in the central Philippines; or Mindanao to the south.

Military reconnaissance in the South Pacific helped sway the decision. During his island-hopping campaign, Adm. Chester W. Nimitz, the commander in chief of the Southwest Pacific area, had encountered the Imperial Japanese Navy off the island of Mindanao and sensed their vulnerability. MacArthur concurred, believing early Japanese operations—much of which had been successful—had spread the Imperial forces thinly across the Pacific. Thus, on September 15, 1944, the Joint Chiefs arrived at their decision. They elected to begin the invasion on Leyte Island and accelerate the operation timeline, moving it up from December 20 to October 20.[4]

The Plan

The landing was a complex, multistage operation. In the first stage, a battalion of MacArthur's Sixth Army would land on Suluan, Homonhon, and Dinagat Islands, fifty miles east of Leyte. In the second stage, four of his Army's divisions would come ashore on Leyte Island's east coast, landing on a series of beaches dubbed White, Red, Blue, Orange, Violet, and Yellow. Simultaneously, one of the Sixth's regiments would invade the southern tip of Leyte.[5]

In stage three, after establishing a beachhead on Leyte, the Sixth Army's ground troops, at an estimated strength of more than 130,000, were to move inland.[6] Their goal was to capture four strategic points: the gulf's eastern gateway, access to the straits at both the northern and the southern tips of Leyte Island, and the island's central valley region.

If successful, the Americans would wrest control of the island and its numerous airfields from Japanese hands. Most important, they would have a defensible position from which to continue across the Philippine archipelago. And they would have a secure base of operations from which to launch an attack on the Japanese home islands.

Despite the noted vulnerability of the Japanese Navy, as A-day approached, American submarines made numerous sightings of Japanese warships as well as tankers and repair ships heading for the Philippines. What they did not know, but had to assume, was Japan was well aware of the strategic value of the area and determined to keep the Philippines from falling into the hands of the Allies.[7] In fact, the Japanese were amassing ground forces from across the Pacific to defend Leyte and reinforcing their air-raid shelters and coastal and garrison defenses.[8]

The Landing

At 6:00 in the morning on October 20, "A-day," US forces commenced a two-hour naval bombardment, rupturing the early-morning calm along a three-mile swath of the eastern coast of Leyte. Battleships, cruisers, and destroyers pounded the shoreline and then turned their guns inland and to the left and right flanks of the landing zone. Air strikes supplemented the ship-to-shore barrage. In theory, the bombing and strafing were to weaken or eliminate Japanese resistance before the Americans went ashore.[9]

The first troops of the Twenty-Fourth Infantry Division landed at precisely 10:00 a.m. on Red Beach. They encountered no significant resistance. The same could not be said for those arriving afterward. Besides the enemy rifle and machine-gun fire raining down on the troops, they had to battle the difficult terrain, clambering across trenches and through tunnels and wading through knee-, waist-, and, in places, armpit-deep swamp.[10]

The action was reminiscent of the Normandy landings. One of the first of the Twenty-Fourth's elements, the Thirty-Fourth Infantry Regiment, landed north of its assigned area on Red Beach and was immediately pinned down by heavy machine-gun and rifle fire. Col. Aubrey S. Newman, the unit's commanding officer, grasped the desperateness of the situation and shouted, "Get the hell off the beach. Get up and get moving. Follow me." His words resonated across the pockets of huddled men. They jumped into action and followed Newman inland to a more protected area.[11]

Despite the mild-to-moderate resistance encountered during the landings and the more intense opposition found as they moved inland, the Sixth Army claimed initial success. They had gained the sea route through the Panaon Strait and taken two key airfields, and troops were moving north through the Leyte Valley toward the coastal town of Carigara.[12] They had yet to face the enemy in force, but that day was coming.[13] The ground battle for control of Leyte, however, proved to be a longer, drawn-out affair, and much blood would be shed over the coming months.[14]

LCI(G)-65: At Sea in the San Juanico Strait

In support of the invasion, seven LCIs (landing craft, infantry) and their counterparts, the larger LCI(G)s, provided close-in troop support. LCIs were designed to transport troops—each capable of carrying a company of infantry or Marines—approximately one hundred men and twenty-five officers and crew. LCI(G)s were LCIs converted to gunboats that carried greater armaments and as many as seventy officers and crew. After the bombardment from battleships, destroyers, and cruisers ended, they began shelling the beaches in a flank formation.[15]

And although the landing craft did not stay longer than needed to beach and unload their cargo, they and the troops and crews aboard the craft were also subject to attack. Here and there, a Japanese attack aircraft succeeded in penetrating the naval and shore defenses and strafed, bombed, or crash-landed on targets of opportunity, including carriers and battleships, as well as the smaller landing craft.

For the moment, while the crash of a Japanese aircraft might have been a deliberate, last-ditch effort by a dying pilot to cause destruction and death, the military did not consider the attacks to be an organized suicide-bombing program. Instead, the military attributed these early Japanese air-raid successes to enemy fighters that successfully defeated the US Navy's air defenses by attacking at night, hiding in cloud cover, or flying in groups outside the range of radar and then overwhelming a US ship's ability to track individual fighters that broke away from a group of fighters. An attack on October 30, 1944, by three Japanese fighters, one of which crashed on the USS *Franklin*'s deck and a second on the USS *Belleau Wood*'s deck, is often cited as the first true "kamikaze" strikes.[16]

Regardless of how the military classified the attacks, C. J. Macaluso, a junior grade (j.g.) lieutenant in command of the LCI(G)-65, reported what he believed was a suicide attack on his vessel. After the initial landings, Macaluso's ship had taken a position offshore in the San Juanico Strait. There they kept watch for signs of enemy barges or torpedo boats. Although they found no threats, the ship remained at the mouth of the strait (anchored in San Pedro Bay off Jinamoc Island) from October 20 through October 23 without incident. Then, at 8:40 a.m. on October 24, twenty-five enemy twin-engine bombers came from the west. One left the formation and headed toward LCI(G)-65. Macaluso wrote,

"As he came in we opened fired with our 3" 50, 40 mm, 20 mm's and .50-calibers scoring several hits while the plane was still some distance away. However, he would not fall and as he came in low he made a strafing and torpedo attack. The torpedo passed under our stern. After numerous hits, the plane crashed into our fan-tail."[17]

The one casualty sustained was the death of one of the ship's cooks, Lester E. Aiston, who had been at his battle station near the ship's stern when the bomber hit. Lester, the eldest of the five children of Theodore and Mildred Aiston, had been looking forward to celebrating his twentieth birthday that December.[18]

LST-452: At Sea Off Leyte Island

LSTs (landing ship, tanks) were giants when compared with LCIs. They measured more than three hundred feet from stem to stern—the length of a football field, twice the size of the LCIs. An LST could carry up to nineteen hundred tons of cargo and 150 troops and their equipment in addition to the ship's 117 officers and crew members. Referred to fondly or derogatorily as the "large slow targets," the LSTs could make only twelve knots, making them more vulnerable to attack than most of the Navy's other vessels. The LSTs were indispensable for amphibious landing operations. They had a shallow draft, which allowed their crews to beach them during action, drop their clamshell-shaped bow doors, and unload troops, trucks, and tanks onto the sand.[19] American journalist and war correspondent Ernie Pyle watched the ubiquitous craft operate and later described them in one of his reports. "An LST isn't such a glorious ship to look at—it is neither sleek nor fast nor impressively big," he wrote, "and yet it is a good ship, and the crews aboard LSTs are proud of them."[20]

LST-452 had the distinction of being the first ship of LST Flotilla Seven to leave the US West Coast in March 1943 and the first to arrive in the South Pacific a month later in April 1943. The landing ship was but one of the nearly one hundred LSTs supporting the landing and subsequent actions during the invasion of Leyte. The

LSTs participated in combat actions throughout the area. Their lists of battles in the spring and summer of 1944 alone read like accounts of the US Navy's South Pacific island-hopping campaign. They saw and participated in actions at Hollandia (present-day Jayapura), Wakde and Biak Islands in New Guinea, Morotai Island in Indonesia, Rabaul and Cape Gloucester in New Britain, and the Admiralty Islands. During their months at sea, they had been the target of more than one aerial assault from torpedo dive-bombers.[21]

By the time they arrived for the Philippine invasion, the LST crews were combat tested and considered themselves experienced. Later, the battle-tested commander of LST-171 who knew better wrote, "Thus, on the eve of the Philippine operations, the men aboard 171, survivors of eight invasions, had acquired the cocky feeling of hardened veterans. Two months later they would realize that no one is ever a hardened veteran."[22]

Like the many soldiers and sailors Ernie Pyle met and interviewed, thirty-two-year-old Lt. James A. Dunn might have been proud of his ship, too. He certainly would have been proud to come home and tell his family of his exploits during the war and his two promotions while at sea aboard LST-452. And he would have been excited to return to his professional career. From the time he graduated from Waseca Central High School, in Minnesota, then Rochester Junior College, and finally the University of Oklahoma, he had had big plans for his future. His early interest in a variety of business ventures, including managing a branch of the Marigold Ice Cream Company, led him to a promising career in investment banking—that is, until the war broke out.[23]

James Dunn wrote home frequently, and, although saying little about his exact duties, he encouraged his family to read news about the war in the Pacific. He, of course, had a front-row seat. On October 21, LST-452 was approaching Red Beach to disembark its cargo of vehicles and troops when an enemy field of fire found its mark. The landing ship was hit in the wheelhouse, the wardroom, the chartroom, amidships on the port side, and on the ship's ramp.

"The ship grounded on a sand bar off the beach," according to the captain writing later in his action report, "but the screws dug hard in the sand and the momentum carried the ship over the bar. . . . The ship stopped on beach with three feet of water off bow and three fathoms of water off the stern." All the while, the LST came under intense rifle and submachine-gun fire. Nevertheless, as soon as they could, the ship's crew lowered the ramp. "Unloading was started at once."[24] Amid the chaos of the amphibious operation, James Dunn was wounded. Two days later, on October 24, he died of his wounds, although the exact time is not known. Regardless, he would send no more letters home.[25]

For its efforts during the landing on Leyte, LST-452 bore numerous shell holes in the hull and sustained damage to the ship's superstructure, guns, and equipment as testimony to recent enemy air attacks and heavy mortar and artillery fire. Despite the damage, LST-452 continued to serve in the invasion and the subsequent retaking of the Philippine Islands. "During this period," reads the *History of LST Flotilla Seven*, the flotilla "established a record for assault landings and transportation of troops and cargo that no other Flotilla could equal. During amphibious operations from Sydney to Yokohama, ships of this Flotilla were bombed, shelled, and torpedoed, but the holes were plugged, the fires extinguished, and not a ship was lost." The account continues, "Of all the ships of LST Flotilla Seven, perhaps the most recognition for services rendered should go to LST-452, the Flotilla's flagship. This LST was the first to arrive in the Southwest Pacific, and operated in the forward area for a longer period of time than any other LST in the Pacific."[26]

Quartermasters at Palo, Leyte Island

Close on the heels of the combat troops, the Navy began delivering rations, equipment, jeeps, trucks, tanks, and bulldozers to the shore. Once offloaded, the Army took over, sorting, arranging, and dispersing the supplies. The seemingly routine act of unloading cargo, however, was not without its perils. The operation was hampered by the terrain, with some cargo crates sinking into wet sand and vehicles having to navigate through several feet of water, the dearth of workers, and the haphazard mountains of crates blocking ingress and egress. Despite the difficulties, most supplies were available to the troops within a day or two of the landing.[27] Having delivered the supplies, however, the Quartermaster Corps had not finished their job. Supplies at the coastal dumps as well as dumps established as the troops moved inland had to be guarded from attack by the Japanese.

Cpl. Garret J. Glum, a soldier with the Twenty-Fourth Quartermaster Company, participated in the unloading, storage, and security of the supplies. A ruddy-complexioned young man with brown hair and hazel eyes, Glum hailed from Bismarck, North Dakota, where he had worked on his family's farm and at a local stable. With only a grade school education, he joined the Army on October 24, 1941, setting an example for the family. His enlistment inspired his three brothers: Joseph enlisted in the Navy and served aboard a battleship in the Pacific, George became a gunner in the Naval Air Corps in Miami, and William became a gunner in the Army Air Corps in Kingman, Arizona. One of Garret Glum's five sisters became a Navy nurse. He had looked forward to seeing his family before deploying, but that was not to be, as his parents reported later. In the spring of 1942, he deployed to the Pacific.[28]

With other members of the quartermaster company, Corporal Glum helped move the supplies inland, following the advancing combat troops. On October 24, four days after the landing on Leyte, he was standing watch at an inland supply dump. The day passed uneventfully, but that night, the Japanese, using the cover of darkness to attack, set fire to a group of trucks at the dump site. In the fierce battle that erupted, three years to the day after Glum had enlisted, he was fatally wounded. Later, his commanding officer commended the young man, mentioning that Glum's actions and the sacrifice of his life inspired the other troops to redouble their efforts to protect the supplies.[29]

In all, from 8:40 a.m. until the late-night attack at the supply dump on October 24, thirty-four soldiers were killed on the push inland. It was a relatively small toll, considering the size of the operation. Two days later, although Japan withdrew its ships from the area, the battle was not over. The "mop-up" with more loss of lives would continue until May 1945.[30]

In his after-action report on October 25, General MacArthur wrote, "Our ground forces have made extensive gains in all sectors. On the front of the XXIV Corps . . . the 7th Division penetrated the enemy's covering screen to seize San Pablo airdrome and fan out to the north toward Dagami. Elements of the 96th Division . . . have enveloped Catmon Hill and are approaching Tabontabon. In the northern sector, the X Corps has made substantial gains to the west of Palo and Tacloban and is pushing forward from the line of hills seized from the enemy which dominate the coast between Palo and Tacloban."[31] Everything was proceeding as or better than planned.

Back home, Americans rejoiced. Newspapers cheered with the headlines "Yanks Win Philippine Foothold." President Roosevelt sent his congratulations to MacArthur, noting that the "whole American nation exults at the news that the gallant men under your command have landed on Philippine soil." The events could not have come at a more fortuitous moment. The 1944 presidential race was winding down, with Election Day less than three weeks away. While the outcome was not unexpected, the good news emanating from the Pacific contributed to Roosevelt winning an unprecedented fourth term in a landslide.[32]

Two months later, Christmas Day 1944, MacArthur delivered his gift to the Allies—declaring Leyte secure, with the United States having control over the supply and communication routes.[33] Then, on January 9, 1945, MacArthur again waded ashore to announce his return, this time at Luzon, whence he had been forced to leave three years earlier. He strode ashore with the same forward lean and wet pants legs, but bearing a triumphant expression on his face.

Douglas MacArthur received dozens of medals over his career, among them the Medal of Honor for defense of the Philippines and a Congressional Gold Medal. He was a controversial figure, alternately loved and reviled, honored, blamed, and exonerated, the blessing and bane of Presidents Roosevelt and Truman. Nevertheless, he kept the image of the consummate military professional until his death in 1964.

Aubrey Newman served in the US Army for thirty-four years. He commanded airborne troops, served as deputy commanding general of the Army Infantry Center, as chief of staff of the Iceland Defense Force, and as chief of staff of the Army Continental Command. He attained the rank of major general. His words "Follow me," shouted to the troops on Red Beach in 1944, became the rallying cry for the Twenty-Fourth Infantry Division. Newman was awarded several medals, including a Distinguished Service Cross, the second-highest award for valor in combat.[34]

Lester Aiston's body was returned to his family and interred in the Lulu Cemetery in Ida, Michigan, his hometown.

When he entered the military, James Dunn was married and the proud father of a seven-year-old girl and four-year-old boy, his namesake. On his death, he was buried at sea with full military honors. Demonstrating the responsibility that commanders of ships shoulder and the relationships they have with their crew on smaller ships like the LST, when he returned home to the United States, Cmdr. and Lt. G. W. Morris visited Dunn's parents, James and Julia Dunn. Morris had officiated at Dunn's burial at sea and offered more details about James's death and the burial ceremony for which the family was grateful, having not even known the exact day he died. Dunn is memorialized at the Manila American Cemetery and Memorial in the Philippines.[35]

Garrett Glum is also memorialized in the Philippines. His siblings all survived the war.

CHAPTER 5

And Then Another

The ship gave a heavy lurch to the port side and a wave of flame passed over the entire midship section.

—Lt. Walter R. Wurzler

8:45 a.m., Pacific Theater, Dio Island, San Pedro Bay, Leyte Gulf, Philippine Islands

As a tug of the Task Group 78.2.9, the USS *Sonoma* (AT-12) was a workhorse of the fleet with responsibility for rescue of other ships, including salvage, towing, and firefighting. It had launched in 1912 and served in the Atlantic during World War I. In the early months of World War II, the *Sonoma* was back on duty in the Pacific, busily towing ships to repair facilities. The ship saw its first combat of the new war in 1943 when it helped down a Japanese aircraft during an attack off New Guinea. By 1944, it was a veteran of the war with a long history of service. Newer, larger, and more capable tugs, however, had joined the fleet. Now, with the *Sonoma* officially considered an "old" tug, the Navy redesignated it to ATO-12, the *O* for "old." Old, perhaps, but it was still a valuable asset. With a draft of less than fifteen feet, the *Sonoma* and other old tugs were capable of performing close inshore work, which some of the newer and larger ships could not.[1]

On October 20, ATO-12 took part in the landings at San Ricardo, Leyte, as well as in the invasion on White and Red Beaches. During

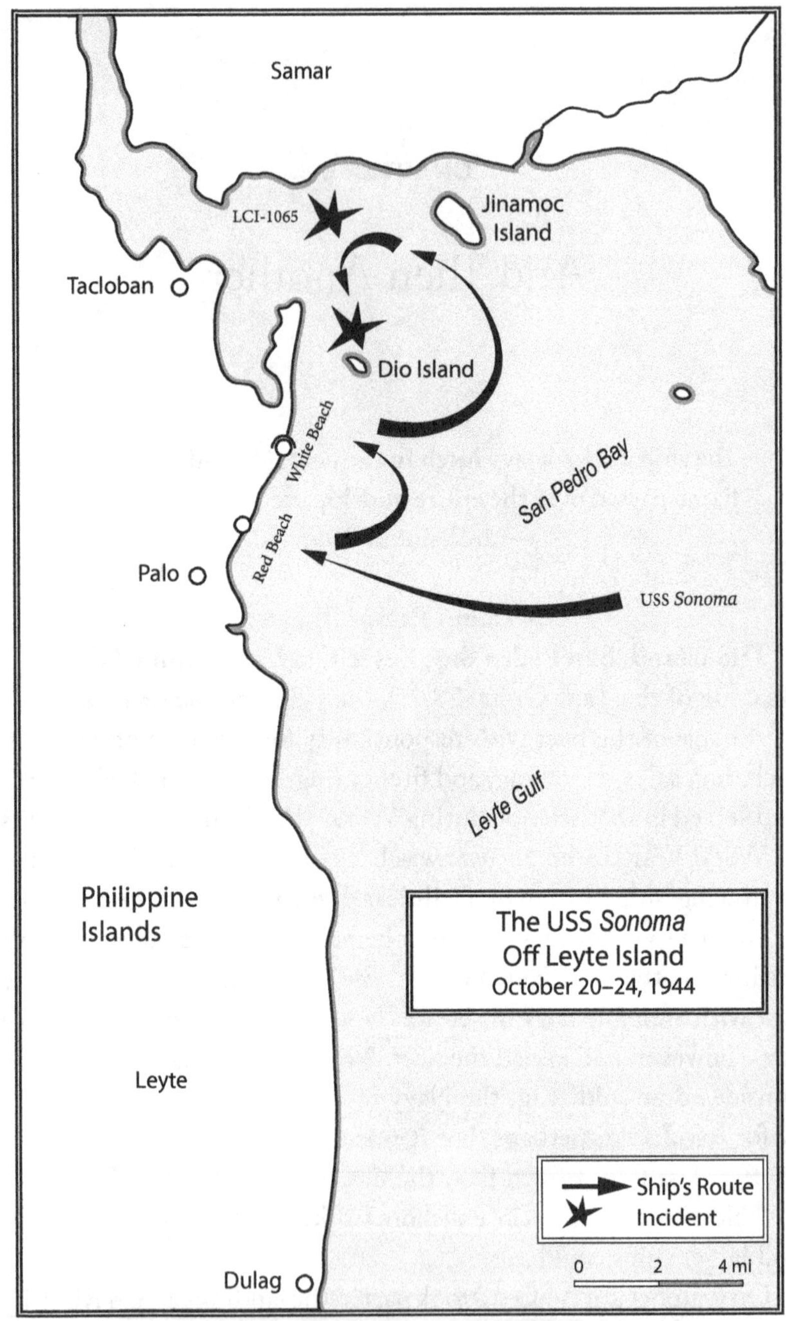

4. The USS *Sonoma* Off Leyte Island, October 20–24, 1944

the battle, it pulled several grounded LSMs (landing ships, medium) from White Beach and then another fleet tug, the *Quapaw* (ATF-110), off Red Beach. Four days later, on October 24, ATO-12 stood anchored in San Pedro Bay off Leyte when it received reports of possible danger in the area from below, above, and on the surface in the form of drifting sea mines, Japanese "Betty" bombers, and water spouts. The American military had bestowed many of Japan's bombers with female nicknames—among them "Sally" for Japan's Mitsubishi Ki-21, "Nell" for the Mitsubishi G3M, and "Betty" for the later-model G4M, a mainstay of the Imperial Japanese Navy during World War II. The bombers were ubiquitous, but so far the US fighters and antiaircraft artillery had easily dispatched them. Still, the Japanese attack planes like the Yokosuka D4Y dive-bomber, nicknamed "Judy," were about to become much more dangerous and deadly as organized suicide bombers.[2]

Sonoma's crew was on high alert, but even though Japanese aircraft continued raiding the area, no Allied ships were hit and no enemy planes were shot down.[3] At 8:00 a.m. after the action subsided, the *Sonoma* came alongside the Liberty ship SS *Augustus Thomas* to take on freshwater. Besides water, the hold of the supply ship carried three thousand tons of ammunition and a thousand barrels of high-octane gasoline, military equipment, and 548 men. The *Sonoma*'s timing could not have been worse. After the two ships were moored together, the Japanese returned. Crews on both ships watched as a number of enemy planes were hit and then fell in flames on White Beach. The *Sonoma* went to general quarters, and the order was given to cast off lines. But before the two ships could separate, without warning, a Betty bomber appeared overhead. Gunfire from ships in the harbor had found their mark on the Betty; both of its engines were engulfed in flames. Leaving a trail of smoke and flames behind, the pilot took aim at the *Sonoma* and the *Augustus Thomas*, still side by side. The bomber's wing hit the *Sonoma*'s stack and crashed into the tug amidships at the main deck level. A member of the Navy's armed guard aboard the Liberty ship was an eyewitness. He recalled, "We were at anchor on the morning of October 24, 1944, when we were hit by a twin engine Japanese Betty Bomber. . . . We were loaded with aviation gas and ammo, and a deck cargo of landing mats for the air field. They got us good, the plane hit us at midships."[4]

Lt. Walter R. Wurzler, commanding officer of the *Sonoma*, posted a note in his war diary at day's end, stating that the ship "gave a heavy lurch to the port side and a wave of flame passed over the entire midship section and bridge and around the forward and after bulkheads of the main deckhouse. There were two distinct explosions followed by a deluge of water from the port side." The plane had struck with such force that it penetrated the deckhouse, wiping out the forward engine-room bulkhead, sections of both starboard and port outboard bulkheads, and two intermediate longitudinal bulkheads. Burning fuel spewed into the engine room and throughout the midships section, setting the radio shack afire. Two other bombs, released before or as the plane struck, fell between the *Sonoma* and the Liberty ship and exploded beneath the *Sonoma*'s hull. In the first few seconds, as the rush of water from the explosion beat back the flames, many of the crew escaped.[5]

To prevent a further catastrophe from developing, a second Liberty ship, the SS *Benjamin Ide Wheeler*, came alongside the *Augustus Thomas* and helped offload the ammunition from the cargo hold. Miraculously, although several men on board the *Augustus Thomas* and the *Wheeler* were wounded, no one was killed.

The *Sonoma* was soon dead in the water, burning at midships. Still, Wurzler held out hope for his ship's survival. "It has not yet been determined whether the salvage of the *Sonoma* is possible or economically worthwhile," he wrote in his diary. An infantry landing craft, LCI-72, and the fleet tug *Chickasaw* came alongside the *Sonoma* to fight the fires on board and offload casualties. Other ships helped rescue men from the *Sonoma* who had jumped or been propelled into the water. With a severe list and rising water, it became apparent the *Sonoma* was lost. All salvageable supplies, guns, sights, and instruments; important documents; and anything else of value were transferred to the *Chickasaw*. In a last-ditch effort, the *Chickasaw* tried to tow the *Sonoma* to safety. When salvaging the ship was deemed impossible, it was beached off Dio Island. At 4:30 in the afternoon, the *Sonoma* was abandoned. The ship proceeded to sink in eighteen feet of water.[6]

Petty Officer Roy L. McMillan, a Texan and an old hand aboard the *Sonoma*, was killed in the fire in the aftermath of the bomber attack. He was twenty-three years old and had been serving as a machinist mate, thus likely well below deck when the bombs hit. While all the deaths of those killed in the attack on the *Sonoma* dealt their families a severe blow, Roy's death (declared after failure to retrieve his remains) was particularly grievous. His parents, Walter and Media McMillan, had already lost three children before they had reached the age of ten. Now the household had only five of their nine children left from whom to take comfort.[7]

Cox. Donnas H. Boyd was severely injured on October 24. He had enlisted in June 1943 and had been aboard the *Sonoma* since December 1943 as a seaman second class. He was manning the port midships boat deck's .50-caliber gun directly above where the Betty had crashed. Burning gasoline covered the area and sprayed Boyd's clothing. Although badly burned, and with his clothes still in flames, he remained in the area and forced open the jammed door of the radio room, releasing two men trapped inside. The two were uninjured, but Boyd's life was in peril. With his clothes smoldering, he jumped over the gunwale and into the water. Boyd was rescued from drowning in the water but succumbed to his wounds three days later.[8]

Lieutenant Wurzler had the respect of his men and a sense of honor. He was young—scarcely a year or two older than many of the crew he oversaw—and gifted, with a thin face free of the creases and crow's-feet of a more seasoned captain. At the helm of a relatively small ship, Wurzler had the luxury of being able to become more familiar with the men under his command and was well liked by his crew. As one sailor said of life aboard the *Sonoma*, the smaller size of their ship meant the crew was closer than the crew of a larger ship, and operations were carried out with less rigid routines.[9] Exhibiting the characteristics of a true leader, he wasted no time in recognizing the sacrifices made the day the *Sonoma* was hit. Soon afterward, he recommended Donnas Boyd for a Navy Cross. He also took time to assess the actions that led to his ship's demise, speculating that the bomber pilot had intended to inflict as much damage as he could before losing control of his aircraft. Wurzler noted that in the future he would be more aware of the damage bombers could do after they were hit, not just as they approached and released their bombs. Finally, with honor and humility, he openly shouldered part of the blame for the incident.[10]

LCI-1065: San Pedro Bay, Leyte Gulf

At approximately the same time the Betty bomber hit the *Sonoma*, a second bomber struck the LCI-1065. It was a "Nell" bomber that along with the Betty had first taken aim at two Liberty ships in the area, but after narrowly missing the mast of one ship, it crashed into LCI-1065, setting it afire just forward of amidships. Although nearby ships came to the rescue, by the time they were in place, the stricken landing craft was burning out of control and shortly sank. The *Fremont* (APA-44), a staff and command ship, received some of the casualties from both the *Sonoma* and LCI-1065. Reports stated the injuries were unusually severe and included second- and third-degree burns. Many of the wounded, working under the tropical sun or in hot quarters, were stripped to the waist at the time they were injured, accounting in part for their extensive burns.[11]

When a count of the survivors and casualties was made, two of LCI-1065's crew were declared missing: Ens. Sigurd J. Bjertness and the ship's radioman, Petty Officer Gordon A. Judson.[12]

Neither the attack on the *Sonoma* nor the attack on LCI-1065 was officially declared the result of a suicide bomber, or kamikaze, attack. The first such attacks are often considered to have occurred on October 30, 1944.[13]

Roy McMillan was memorialized at the Lometa Cemetery in his hometown in Texas.

Donnas Boyd was awarded the Navy Cross, posthumously, for his actions in saving two of his fellow crewmen. The award cited his extraordinary heroism and devotion to duty while serving on board the *Sonoma*. He remained "within a gasoline fire to release two men trapped inside a burning compartment. . . . Though covered with burning gasoline, and with complete disregard for his own safety, Coxswain Donnas Hank Boyd courageously delayed in escape and exerted great presence of mind in remaining amidst the fires engulfing the midships section of the *Sonoma* to free two radiomen trapped inside the burning radio room, the door of which had been jammed by the several explosions that eventually caused the loss of the ship."[14]

The remains of Sigurd Bjertness and Gordon Judson were not recovered. News that the Navy had abandoned hope for recovering Bjertness arrived at his family home in May 1945. Within the week they also learned that a second son, Sgt. Martin Luther Bjertness, a technician fifth grade, was killed at Okinawa on May 2, 1945. C. S. Bjertness, a pastor and father of both Sigurd and Martin Luther, would conduct a double memorial service for his sons in Minneapolis. Judson was officially declared dead in December 1945.[15]

Both men are memorialized at the Manila American Cemetery and Memorial in the Philippines. Dates of death are often misstated on memorials. Bjertness, for example, is listed as having died on October 25 and, on a marker in his home state of Minnesota, Judson on October 17.

Walter Wurzler carried a sense of guilt from the loss of his ship and two of its crew with him. But the Navy recognized his abilities as a leader and in April 1945 gave him command of another tug. This time, it was not an "old" tug, but the *Chimariko* (ATF-154), a newer and larger fleet tug. He remained in the Pacific through the end of the war and lived to the age of sixty.[16]

CHAPTER 6

The "Photo Joes"

Unescorted, unarmed, and unafraid, Joe wings his gutsy way.

—Tom McGuire, from the poem "To Photo Recon Joe"

9:00 a.m., Pacific Theater, Ceram Island, Maluku Province, Netherlands East Indies

With the first rays of sun clearing the hilltops behind them, on October 24, 1944, two F-5s taxied to the end of the runway and paused. Their elongated shadows stretched before them like a pair of arachnids eyeing their prey. The pilots, engrossed in their meticulous preflight rituals, failed to notice. Satisfied that everything was in order, twenty-two-year-old Clair J. Bardsley of the USAFFE, Twenty-Sixth Photographic Reconnaissance Squadron (Sixth Photo Reconnaissance Group), glanced over his shoulder toward Madison Gillaspey in the second aircraft. Bardsley signaled his partner with a thumbs-up and pushed the throttles forward. Engines roaring, his F-5 rolled a few yards and then accelerated down the runway. As aircraft #42-6874 lifted from the earth, Bardsley eased the wheel back. Gillaspey followed, joining Bardsley in the skies above their home base at the Mokmer Airdrome in Papua Province, Indonesia. After a quick check of their gauges, they set a course for the mission's target, Ceram Island in Maluku Province, Netherlands East Indies.[1]

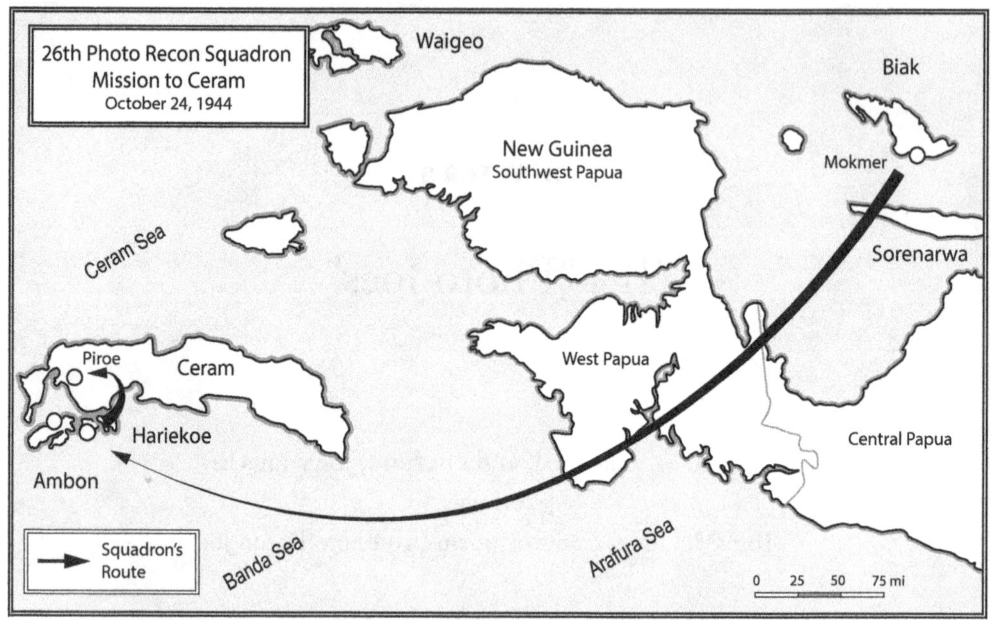

5. 26th Photo Recon Squadron Mission to Ceram, October 24, 1944

As they cleared the coast, the sun, still low on the horizon, slipped behind a solitary cloud. Clair Bardsley stole a moment from the war to admire the landscape below, crystal-clear expanses of turquoise waters studded with hundreds of rocky and jungle-clad islets. Then the radio sputtered alive, jolting Bardsley from the scenery. It was Gillaspey's voice grumbling about the weather and the gathering clouds. Cloudy skies could mean their efforts would be for naught.

They had had their share of aborted missions, some for equipment malfunctions, like losing an aircraft canopy on takeoff, or an engine blowing out at altitude, or navigation equipment failing as they flew over open water. But the weather proved as big a foe as all the mechanical glitches combined. The South Pacific, with its unpredictable and often poor weather, wreaked havoc on the unit's high-altitude reconnaissance efforts. This was particularly true during the rainy season that ran from November into March in what often seemed like one endless torrent. An unidentified member of the Eighth Photographic Reconnaissance Squadron said of a day in February 1943, "I sometimes wonder why we are over here, and today is one of those times. We were so completely socked in that not an engine turned over."[2]

Bardsley, Gillaspey, and the other reconnaissance pilots, dubbed "Photo Joes," flew F-5 aircraft, which were P-38s reconfigured for aerial photography missions. The modification stripped the 20-millimeter cannon and .50-caliber guns from a standard P-38 fighter aircraft and replaced the armaments with a payload of cameras. The trade-off left the F-5 pilots unarmed, except for the relatively useless pistol each pilot carried in the cockpit, but with a newfound nimbleness and a speed advantage over the enemy. Yet that advantage was fickle. While making a photographic pass, the pilot, absorbed in computing speed, altitude, and angle combinations, or flying to maintain their aircraft at a level and precise altitude, might not catch sight of approaching enemy fighters. Further, the Photo Joes flew without fighter accompaniment. They were cautioned to do everything necessary to avoid combat.[3]

Even on the ground, the reconnaissance pilots were at risk. The base at Mokmer itself was a target of the Japanese, intent on destroying the unit's planes and killing its personnel. As the first wail of the airfield's sirens punctuated the air, pilots resting in their barracks and ground crews working under the sweltering sun took cover. Some sought shelter in one of the station's buildings or dove into slit trenches, cursing as they dusted themselves off and resumed whatever they were doing once the threat had passed.[4]

How Bardsley and his cohorts summoned the courage to become Photo Joes is due in part to the indomitable spirit of youth and in part to confidence gained from thorough training and hours of flight experience. The first reconnaissance pilots in the South Pacific were understaffed and underequipped, but their belief in what they were doing and confidence in their abilities—well placed or not—inspired them to keep flying and gain the requisite experience. Much of the credit for the success of photo reconnaissance in the Southwest Pacific goes to Karl L. "Pop" Polifka. According to Walter Boyne, a writer for the *Air & Space Forces Magazine*, beginning with a single F-4 at Port Moresby in April 1942, Polifka, then a captain, "almost single-handedly mapped large portions of New Guinea and New Britain." As important, if not more so, was his charismatic leadership. "He created a squadron of pilots with his own daring, initiative, and skill. He would do the same thing in North Africa and the Mediterranean, each time overcoming faulty equipment and a lack of supplies."[5]

Another exemplary leader was Alexander Guerry Jr., a lieutenant who started as a pilot with Polifka's Eighth Photo Reconnaissance Squadron, became the Eighth's commander, and later led the Twenty-Sixth Squadron. Guerry earned a Distinguished Flying Cross for a flight made in May 1943, the first ever over the Panapai Airdrome, at Kavieng, New Ireland. A newspaper article, published in his hometown of Chattanooga, Tennessee, explained that flying to New Ireland itself was dangerous, as the island sat at the maximum range for Guerry's aircraft. Undaunted, the lieutenant completed his photographic mission and then, despite worsening weather, flew another 150 miles to photograph enemy activity at Rabaul.[6] Other pilots took far more unnecessary risks in displays of pure bravado. Some of the young daredevils enjoyed the simple, albeit dangerous, pleasure of "buzzing" an enemy airfield at high speed and defying antiaircraft artillery volleys to hit their mark. Others, with their reconnaissance photographs captured, returned for a second pass or, like Lt. Vince E. Murphy of the Eighth Reconnaissance Group, performed acrobatic maneuvers over the enemy airfield.[7]

Clair Bardsley was born a middle child to a middle-class family in Gunnison, Utah, a town squarely in the middle of the state. He may or may not have known his hometown was named for John W. Gunnison, who was a reconnaissance Army officer of sorts in the mid-1800s. A noted explorer, Gunnison was hired by the government to survey the Rocky Mountains with the hope of finding a route west for the transcontinental railroad. Nearly a century earlier to the day Clair Bardsley took off to survey enemy activity in the South Pacific, Paiute Indians attacked the Rocky Mountain surveying expedition and killed Gunnison.[8]

Bardsley graduated from Gunnison Valley High School in the summer of 1940 and enrolled at the University of Utah that fall. But the war interrupted his plans. In November 1942, he was inducted into the Army, earning his wings less than a year later. At the time, he had no inkling he would become a reconnaissance pilot. Nor did he imagine where he would serve until he deployed for duty in the Pacific in April 1944.[9]

Despite the dangers, his assignment to New Guinea had its upsides, namely, the opportunity to travel across the South Pacific. In June, Bardsley wrote to his parents, mentioning a recent trip to Australia during which he had watched the curious game of Australian football. He wrote, too, that his squadron was organizing an orchestra and had purchased various instruments. He made no mention of whether he would be playing in the ensemble or which instrument, if any.[10]

Today, however, Bardsley and Madison had not dwelled on the weather, trips to Australia, or the budding New Guinea orchestra. They had nothing more on their minds than returning home in time for lunch. The day's mission was routine. The two had made reconnaissance runs in the area before and were familiar with the route and the terrain. They had been in the Southwest Pacific for a year flying long-range, unarmed aerial photography missions to capture enemy troop positions and activity at Japanese airfields, harbors, and beach defenses. At first, they had flown from Sydney and Brisbane, Australia. Then, moving forward with the Allied advances, they launched from Port Moresby and Nadzab. Most recently, they had flown from the forward airfields of Mokmer on Biak Island to Leyte, obtaining valuable information about the Japanese defenses on the island. Unbeknownst to the Photo Joes at the time, the information had helped the Allies plan the amphibious assault on Leyte.[11]

Bardsley and Gillaspey flew an uneventful hour and a half, skirting weather here and there along the route. Ceram and the smaller Ambon and Haroekoe Islands, home to several Japanese airfields, sat just minutes ahead.[12] Army intelligence wanted to know if the Japanese had repaired the airfields in the area after an Allied bombing raid two weeks earlier.[13] Unfortunately, as Gillaspey had predicted after takeoff, the weather was not cooperating. They would have to rely on the art and science of photographic reconnaissance to find clear images of the ground on their film. Cameras clicked in rapid succession as each pilot passed over the target. After he pulled up at the end of his run, Gillaspey radioed to say he would make a second pass over the area. Bardsley did not respond. And although Gillaspey tried to raise his partner several more times, the result each time was the same: silence. As he banked to turn back, he spotted Bardsley making a wide sweep and turning north into a bank of dense, gray clouds hugging the coastline. He guessed Bardsley was skipping the second pass over Haroekoe and heading toward Liang Airdrome on Ambon or perhaps Piroe, farther north on Ceram Island. With a bit of luck, he might find better visibility there. Bardsley's F-5 punched through the clouds and disappeared from sight. Gillaspey completed his second pass and thought he had captured at least a few seconds in the clear. He turned and set his course for Mokmer. In seconds, he was back in the soup. It would be instruments all the way home.[14]

At 12:15 p.m., Madison Gillaspey touched down. He eased his F-5 to its spot on the hardstand and made a quick scan of the airfield. At the end of the runway, he noticed two reconnaissance aircraft waiting on clearance for their mission. And at the spot on the hardstand where Clair Bardsley's plane should be parked, he saw an empty span of concrete. The sky, now as clear as it had been when the two had taken off at first light, was empty. Gillaspey deplaned and watched the intelligence crew remove the five heavy metal camera boxes from the nose of his aircraft. They stowed the cameras in their jeep and gestured toward an empty seat. Gillaspey hopped aboard for the ride to the intelligence tent, anxious as anyone to see what the film revealed about the airfields at Ceram and Haroekoe Islands.

Shortly after 1:00 in the afternoon, Gillaspey was called to the operations tent. There he gave his statement to the operations officer for a Missing Air Crew Report. The facts were noted, typed, and filed. The operations officer then notified fighter control that #42-6874 was an hour overdue. By 2:00 p.m., an air and sea rescue call was made. Despite several sorties, no sign of Clair Bardsley or his plane was ever found.[15]

In November 1944, the Sixth Reconnaissance Group moved to the Philippines, photographing parts of Luzon and Mindanao still in contention. The group continued to gather intelligence across the Pacific and over the Japanese home islands.[16]

Clair Bardsley was awarded an Air Medal and Purple Heart posthumously. Two years later, the military officially declared him dead and killed in action. In a letter home dated October 23, 1944, Bardsley had told his parents of his pending promotion to first lieutenant. He also shared that with 190 combat hours, he had passed the halfway point to 300 combat hours. Once he reached that mark, he would receive a furlough back to the States and be able to spend some time with his family.[17] He is memorialized on the Tablets of the Missing at the Manila American Cemetery and Memorial.

Madison Gillaspey, too, would perish and be declared missing in action after a reconnaissance mission in 1945.

As a lieutenant, Vince Murphy flew eighty-five missions and received a Distinguished Flying Cross with Oakleaf Cluster and an Air Medal. He rose to the rank of major and served in both World War II and Korea.

Karl Polifka survived World War II and returned to make reconnaissance missions for the Korean War as commander of the Sixty-Seventh Tactical Reconnaissance Wing. He was killed in action in 1951 while flying over North Korea.

After a sterling record from 1942 to 1943 with the Eighth Photographic Reconnaissance Squadron, Alexander Guerry was made commander of the Sixth Reconnaissance Group. He had well over 400 combat hours and, according to John Stanaway, one of the most prolific authors on the P-38 Lightning, "probably contributed more to the success of the squadron than any other man."[18] He became a lieutenant colonel before leaving the Army and then joined and later chaired the Chattem Drug & Chemical Company board of directors in Tennessee.[19]

CHAPTER 7

The Second Time Around

A typical day was gray: Rain, snow, or sleet, and wind at a velocity that very often knocked you off your feet.
—Petty Officer Earl W. Long

9:00 a.m., Pacific Theater, Adak Naval Operations Base 230, Adak Island

As July 12, 1943, dawned, George H. McElroy found himself in a familiar place, the doorway to the US military recruiting office in Mason City, Iowa, his hometown. This time, it was for another war. He might have thought he was done with the military, having served during the Great War, the "war to end all wars." Yet here he was again, twenty-five years later, fuller bodied, deeper creases to his smile, and a line or two etched on his forehead. At the ripe old age of forty-one, he stood in a sea of boyish faces, most of them belonging to men born after the echoes of the earlier world-shattering conflict had faded. Unlike the innocents in line, McElroy knew what war held for him, but he believed in what the military was doing and understood how he could help. Since that earlier war, he had stayed connected with the military. McElroy's was a familiar face at the American Legion Post in Mason City, where he held the office of vice commander. He needed to set the example, and so he enlisted again.[1]

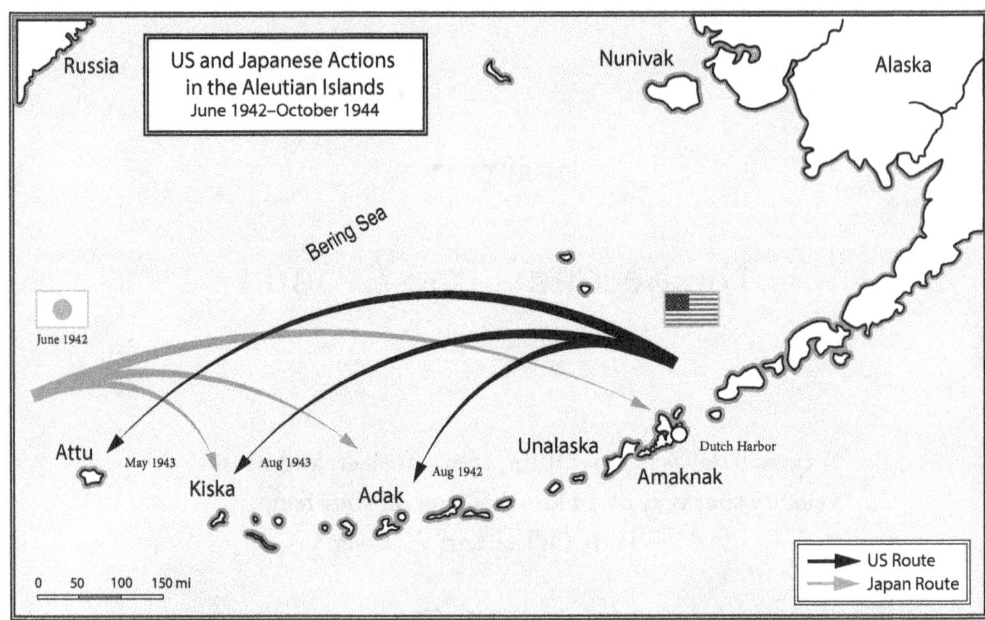

6. US and Japanese Actions in the Aleutian Islands, June 1942–October 1944

In December, the Navy called. George bid his wife, Olga, good-bye, promised to return soon, and reported for duty. After a short period of training, George McElroy, now a seaman first class, stepped aboard the *Fletcher*-class destroyer *Rowe* (DD-564) on March 13, 1944, the day of its commissioning in Seattle. With an impressive top speed of thirty-five knots and a range of sixty-five hundred nautical miles, the destroyer was ready to take on the challenge of the Pacific's expanse. Further, as a war machine, it boasted an arsenal that surpassed its predecessor: 20-millimeter to 5-inch guns, ten torpedo tubes, and six depth-charge projectors. The four-hundred-foot "tin can" had everything necessary to conduct antisubmarine and antiaircraft warfare and participate in surface action.[2]

McElroy and the other three-hundred-plus crew were at sea in no time. Following a brief shakedown period off the coast of California, they sailed for Pearl Harbor, arriving at the end of May. In those idyllic waters, they underwent a few more weeks of training, honing their skills for the battles ahead. The ship's first action came as part of a convoy escort run to Eniwetok in July. A month later, as the flagship of a destroyer squadron of the Ninth Fleet, it set a course for one of the most remote places on earth, Adak Island, an outpost at the terminus of the Aleutian Island chain.[3]

In the opening months of World War II, the Imperial Japanese Navy had focused its efforts on the Central and South Pacific. Rear Adm. Robert A. Theobald, who had assumed charge of Alaska's defense in 1942 from commander in chief, US Pacific Fleet, Adm. Chester W. Nimitz, believed Japan would soon pivot northward. Midway Island stood squarely in their path in the Central Pacific. And to the north sat the long arc of the Aleutian Island chain, stepping-stones eastward through Alaska and then to the US mainland.[4]

The military described Adak as a "weather-beaten, uninhabited island . . . 30 miles long and has a maximum width of twenty miles. Terrain is rugged and mountainous. . . . The treeless ground is covered with tundra." It added, "The island is subject to frequent storms of rain, snow, sleet and to high velocity wind. . . . Annual rainfall averages 40 inches, with 100 additional inches of snowfall."[5] Petty Officer Earl W. Long with the Navy's Eighty-Sixth Construction Battalion spent eleven months on Adak and attested to the military's characterization of Adak. In a postwar interview, he recalled, "The weather in the Aleutians can be dramatic, shifting suddenly and with severe consequences. . . . A typical day was gray: Rain, snow, or sleet, and wind at a velocity that very often knocked you off your feet." Earl also remembered having to remove the windshield wipers of his truck each night to prevent the wipers from blowing away.[6] Given the choice, it would not have taken much to convince men on the *Rowe* or on Adak to trade places with the photo reconnaissance pilots two thousand miles away in tropical Papua Province, Indonesia.

On June 2, 1942, the Japanese attacked the Aleutians. Behind the scenes, the United States had cracked the Japanese naval codes and knew of Japan's true intent. The enemy's planned attack on the Aleutians was a smokescreen. Midway was their primary objective.[7]

Although surprised by the American presence they encountered in the Aleutians, the Japanese inflicted significant damage on the US facilities at Dutch Harbor in Unalaska Bay, a point midway along the island chain. As swiftly as they had come, however, the Japanese ships withdrew to engage in the Battle of Midway, what many military historians later claimed to have been the turning point in the war in the Pacific. Japan lost four carriers and a cruiser during the battle. Stunned by their losses, they returned to the Aleutians and its softer targets. After taking Kiska on June 6 and Attu on June 7, the Japanese declared the results a great victory and again withdrew. Still suspecting Japan would try to use their tiny foothold in the Aleutian chain to invade the Alaskan mainland, the United States fortified its positions in the North Pacific. In August 1942, five thousand troops landed unopposed at Adak. They secured the island and within two weeks established an airfield there. The United States retook Attu in May 1943 and Kiska in August that year.[8]

By August 1944, the Navy had transformed an expanse on Adak from its earlier bleak and barren landscape to a bustling forward base. Operations included an air station, ship-repair facilities, fuel and ammunition storage, administration buildings, and officer and troop barracks to house several thousand men.[9] With the chain having become a significant military outpost, none other than President Franklin D. Roosevelt elected to tour the US Aleutian installations. At Adak, after the tour concluded, the president hosted a lunch for enlisted men. The grand gesture would long be a fond memory for the sailors and soldiers in attendance. Few missed an opportunity to point out their proximity to the head table in photographs of the luncheon. It was an event a "newspaperman" like McElroy rued missing when he heard the news and how close he had come to being in the right place at the right time.[10]

By the time the *Rowe* arrived at Adak in the late summer of 1944, however, all was back to "business as usual." The *Rowe*'s crew trained together as a destroyer group or as a composite destroyer and cruiser group with other US Navy ship crews in the area. On October 2, it received orders to depart for what the ship's muster rolls label "dangerous waters." In fact, the cruise would take it to the northwest Pacific Ocean for strikes in the Kurile Islands from November through February 1945.[11]

The day the *Rowe* cast off its moorings from Adak, the tenuous nature of Navy assignments favored George McElroy. He was transferred from duty aboard ship to shore duty at the Adak Naval Operations Base 230. The bleak outpost had its own daily newspaper, which proved to make life for all there a bit less bleak, particularly for the newspapermen, and McElroy soon joined the staff. The *Adakian* was the brainchild of Dashiell Hammett, the acclaimed hard-boiled detective author and fervent anti-Nazi and antifascism activist. A veteran of World War I and forty-eight years old, Hammett was determined to serve again. Assigned to the Signal Corps but relegated to the distant Aleutians, he "wrote training manuals and gave lectures and radio broadcasts on the progress of the war in all theaters," ensuring the troops knew what was happening at home and abroad and how their duties fitted into the war effort. By the time McElroy came ashore and joined the newspaper staff, though, Hammett was often absent from Adak on tours around Alaska. His larger-than-life persona persisted, however. The staff regarded him as a mentor and father figure. Like them, McElroy would have been in awe of Hammett and worked hard to please.[12]

It was a job where McElroy could leverage his prewar experience with both the *Mason City Globe Gazette* and the *Cedar Falls Record*. In a matter of a few days, the news made it home to Iowa. The October 19, 1944, issue of the *Globe Gazette* gave Mason City readers an update on their hometown hero. The article mentioned McElroy's current work was "newspapering" with the welfare department at the station, noting that George found his assignment pleasant. "Nice comfortable base here as far as advanced bases go," McElroy said. Despite living in a Quonset hut on the side of a mountain, he had access to a "good gym for showers and sun lamp . . . plenty of movies . . . chow is very good."[13] Although he had missed a chance to see the president, George McElroy's timing was otherwise serendipitous, not only for the chance to work with Hammett but also because September and October were the two best weather months in Adak.[14]

His good luck and timing did not last, however. Nine days later, the *Globe Gazette* ran a second article about McElroy. This one was his obituary. On October 24, while editing the station's newspaper, George McElroy suffered a heart attack and died.

George McElroy's body was returned to his family. He was buried at the Memorial Park Cemetery in Mason City, Iowa. Eight years later, in 1952, Olga McElroy met another World War II veteran. They married and spent thirty-five years together.

CHAPTER 8

A Most Unlikely Place to Land

The desire to fly is an idea handed down to us by our ancestors who . . . looked enviously on the birds soaring freely through space . . . on the infinite highway of the air.
—Wilbur Wright

9:30 a.m., European Theater, Dunkirk, France

Herman J. Adolfae began his military career in the Navy, enlisting in 1932—nearly a decade before America's entry into the global conflagration that was World War II. He committed to serve for four years, and during that period he rose rapidly through the ranks. From his modest first assignment as an apprentice seaman, he became a seaman second class, then a seaman first class, and then an aviation machinist's mate third class. In November 1936, having finished his four-year term, he received an honorable discharge. But his papers had a thin veneer of finality. After considering his prospects, he reenlisted, committing to another four years of service. Not knowing where or when his new assignment would take him, before deploying the young man with piercing blue eyes and brown hair made a trip home to see his family in Kansas City, Missouri.[1]

After his second tour of duty expired in 1940, he returned home, but the old world order had disappeared and in its place was an unrecognizable geopolitical landscape. The Treaty of Versailles that

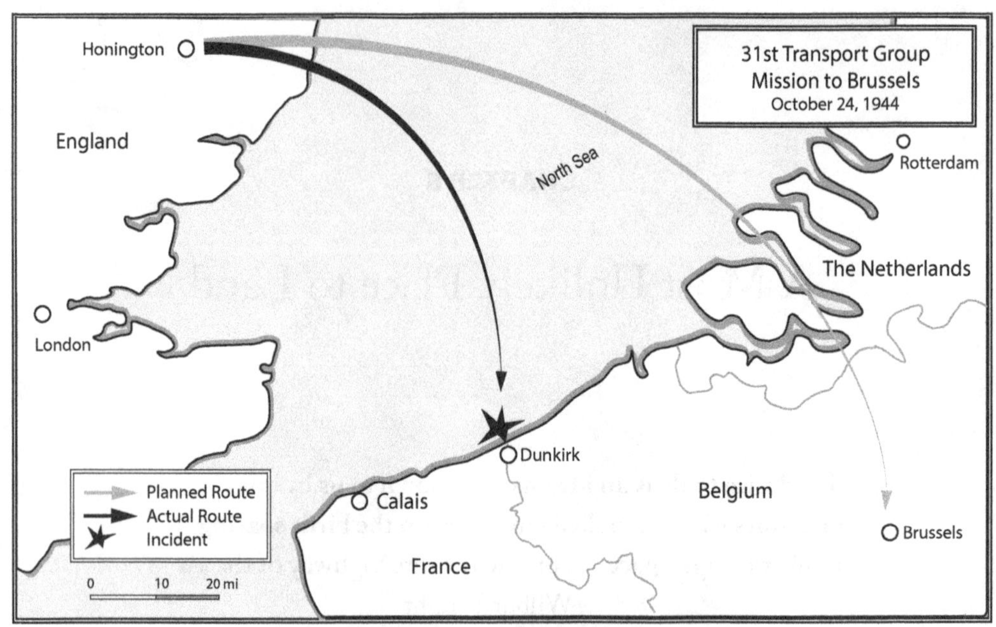

7. 31st Transport Group Mission to Brussels, October 24, 1944

had put an end to World War I lay in tatters. Germany had rearmed and invaded Poland, prompting Britain and France to declare war on Germany, followed shortly by Canada. Despite the upheaval, the United States remained a spectator on the war's periphery.

For now, Adolfae figured he would be sitting on the sidelines along with his country. But he was wrong. The Royal Canadian Air Force (RCAF), now fully engaged in the war, realized they needed far more pilots than they could muster from their own citizenry. Rumors began circulating. One young man told another and that young man told a third that the RCAF welcomed Americans and men of other nationalities to join the RCAF ranks. And so, by word of mouth, the RCAF hoped to augment its ranks while at the same time skirt US laws prohibiting foreign countries from actively recruiting Americans into their military. Canada had banked on the belief that patriotic, freedom-loving Americans who wanted to join the fight would cross the border, just as many of them had two decades earlier in the run-up to World War I.[2]

A trickle of volunteers appeared in Canadian recruitment centers. The trickle grew as word spread, and soon the centers strained under the influx of eager souls. The young men were a mosaic of motivations and backgrounds. The cadre included adventure seekers as well as principled champions of the fight for democracy. They were men who followed the beacon of opportunity to become a pilot when that door had been closed to them at home. It was, in other words, their chance of a lifetime. As author Spencer Dunmore observed, they were a "colourful" group and counted among the lot "professionals and playboys, convicted felons and husbands on the run, idealists and mercenaries, kids seeking adventure, youngsters seeking nothing but an opportunity to fly, middle-aged men looking for work." By the end of the war, almost nine thousand Americans answered the call from north of the border.[3]

Adolfae had gained experience in aviation during his last military deployment, and that experience had left him wanting more. He soon joined the border-crossing volunteers. Surrounded by a young, fresh-faced group of men, however, Adolfae worried his age would disqualify him. He was already thirty, and Canada restricted applicants to men under thirty. So, as he worked through the enlistment forms, he altered his birth date and prayed no one would ask to see his birth certificate. Then, with care, he listed dates for his elementary school years, his high school years, and his dates of previous employment and made sure all flowed seamlessly with his contrived timeline. At the bottom, he signed his name. His artful script brimmed with swirls and tendrils and a bit of bravado. His ruse worked. Adolfae reported to Windsor, Ontario, for training under the auspices of the British Commonwealth Air Training Plan (BCATP), established in 1939 to develop aircrews for the United Kingdom, Canada, Australia, and New Zealand. After completing ground instruction at the Elementary Flying Training School, he proceeded to individual flying and technical training and then bomber-crew training. The cadets trained in any aircraft the RCAF could spare—generally, aircraft that had been outclassed on the front line and relegated to the BCATP program. This included the Fleet Finch and the World War I–vintage Avro Anson. Only after months of training did the trainees transition from the outdated aircraft to state-of-the-art frontline aircraft.[4]

On receiving a commission as a flying officer for the RCAF on July 31, 1941, Adolfae had realized his dream. His prospects looked brighter than ever. So in December when the United States entered the war and half of the Americans who had gone to Canada transferred back to the United States to join the Army Air Corps, Adolfae remained with the RCAF.[5] He flew his first missions in Canada and then transferred to a Canadian air station in England. But then, a week after D-day and the Normandy invasion, Adolfae had a change of heart. He decided to join his countrymen and transferred from the RCAF to a temporary position as a first lieutenant with the US Army in England. His orders sent him to the United States Army Air Forces airfield at Honington (Station 375), originally a bomber base and then a fighter base and air depot, and then home to the 313th Transport Squadron, Thirty-First Transport Group. The group had flown the first air cargo mission to supply troops on Omaha Beach and was the first to return from the Continent bearing Allied wounded five days after the invasion. Following the move inland, the group played an instrumental role in transferring Army and Army Air Force units to the Continent, carrying supplies and establishing depots to conduct repair and resupply operations.[6]

Although he had left the RCAF, Adolfae still carried with him the RCAF's Pilot's Flying Log Book, embossed with his name and Canadian serial number (J-13062). And he continued to record his flights in the book, as a copilot on Douglas C-47D Skytrain missions between England and France in June 1944 and then, at last, as a full pilot in July.

The transport effort grew exponentially as the Allies moved inland from the beachheads. Some of its aircraft had been flying with more than the maximum payload specified for ferrying supplies—a prescription for disaster. By August, the US military recognized the need to augment its fleet. Washington gave the green light to move a hundred C-47s to Europe and at the same time reshuffled the transport hierarchy to address resupply inefficiencies. The Thirty-First (Adolfae's group) and the Twenty-Seventh Transport Groups were reassigned to the 302nd Air Wing operating directly under the auspices of the Air Service Command (ASC) for the US Strategic Air Forces. In its revamped and consolidated role, the 302nd now ferried aircraft for all Air Force units in the European theater of operations, transported mail and supplies between bases, and evacuated wounded men from the Continent back to England. Wherever they flew, the C-47 cargo bays bulged with medical supplies, whole blood, blankets, overshoes, and helmets. On board, bayonets, ammunition, flares, and rockets shared space with cigarettes, heaters, aircraft engines, gas pumps, tires and gasoline, and even telephone poles.[7] One of the few items they did not carry was troops. Troop transport remained the responsibility of the Troop Carrier Command. However, the 302nd did transport civilians, including war correspondents and entertainers, as well as German prisoners and freed Allied prisoners.[8]

On October 24, 1944, the now seasoned First Pilot Herman Adolfae, known to his crew as "Bud," sat at the controls of his C-47, nicknamed "Skip." Alongside him were his copilot, Lt. Glenn Goodwin, and two aerial engineers, Sgt. Leroy W. Holliday Jr. and Sgt. Floyd R. Myers. They were one of four teams in line for takeoff from Honington Airfield for a routine mission to transport materials to Brussels, Belgium, via what was designated Corridor 18. At 9:10 a.m. they were away, and a mere twenty minutes later the four aircraft reached the coast of the Continent.[9]

The first two crossed at a bearing of fourteen degrees off their intended course. Antiaircraft fire erupted. For a moment, the pilots believed the incoming fire to be from Allied emplacements along the Belgian coast—a case of "friendly fire." The lead airplanes pushed through without incident. But the last two aircraft, including

Adolfae's C-47, were not so fortunate. They had veered even farther off course, coming in over Dunkirk, a port city near the border between France and Belgium. The city still lay in German hands, and on spotting the errant transports, antiaircraft batteries came alive. One of the C-47s made it through and landed in Brussels. The other, piloted by Adolfae, did not.[10]

Later, Capt. Richard Launder and his copilot, 2nd Lt. John B. Hill Jr., one of the aircrews on the day's mission, reported having seen Adolfae's C-47 crash near the harbor of Dunkirk. The 302nd could not launch a rescue operation, however, as Dunkirk was at the center of an ongoing battle between Canadian and Czechoslovakian troops and relentless German army, navy, and air force troops. For now, all the personnel of the air wing could do was list Adolfae and his fellow crew as missing in action.[11]

After the war, the American Graves Registration Command of the Army's Quartermaster Corps investigated the incident, hoping to recover the C-47 crew's remains. In 1950, while in Dunkirk to interview local citizens and former German soldiers, AGRC members located an eyewitness to the incident. The man, a former German POW, recounted a harrowing tale: "Violent firing from the German artillery brought the four planes down. One fell on the land, the other three in the sea; among these one fell at about 50 yards from the Neuvelle Ecluse. Out of this plane, three bodies came out to the surface of the water. They had died from wounds received in the plane."[12]

The recollections were incomplete and faded with time and clearly contradicted the military's record of the date and number of aircraft involved.[13] But they revealed one important detail, the approximate resting place of the C-47 Skytrain #44-186277, a point in the water between the harbor's east and west jetties.[14] According to further testimony, this time from harbor authorities, after the crash, a part of the plane remained protruding from the water. The wreck was not only a hazard to shipping, but an impediment to

German submarine pen operations. In a frenzied endeavor, the Germans tried to remove the wreck from the harbor. After a series of futile attempts, they resorted to demolition charges to break up the wreckage. The AGRC hired a diver to search an area of the harbor. Amid the silt and shadows, he recovered a brass plate. The AGRC affirmed the plate was a remnant from the tail of a C-47 and concluded its investigation, declaring Adolfae's remains unrecoverable.[15]

In 1945, the contents of Adolfae's locker were returned to his wife, Helen. They included his clothing and toiletries, as well as a photograph, flask, softball, cribbage set, and a handful of chessmen. The US Army also forwarded a check for the amount of $12.44, representing funds due Adolfae as deferred pay from the RCAF after his discharge and reenlistment in the US Army. Herman Adolfae was posthumously awarded the Purple Heart. He is memorialized on the Tablets of the Missing at the Ardennes American Cemetery in Belgium, approximately 175 miles from where he lost his life, and the twisted metal of his aircraft, "Skip," remains beneath the sand.

While Adolfae's remains were never recovered, during their investigation, the AGRC located the graves of his crew in the dunes near Dunkirk Harbor. They exhumed the bodies, positively identified them, and sent them home for burial, Goodwin in Baltimore National Cemetery and Holliday in Highland Cemetery in Kentucky.[16]

CHAPTER 9

To the Rescue

Our steel ships, too, are served by iron men.
—Thomas B. Inglis, captain, USS *Birmingham*

9:39 a.m., Pacific Theater, Gulf of Leyte, Philippine Islands

Bruce Harwood was born in Claremont, California, in 1910 to Harrison and Belva Harwood. Harrison was a dentist, but on graduating from high school, his son Bruce did not see a future in dentistry or, for that matter, any form of medicine. In fact, he had not picked any particular path forward. Only eighteen, he believed he had a lot of time ahead to decide how to spend his adult years. He enrolled in Arizona State Teachers College and completed four years of study there in the early 1930s. After graduating, he tried his hand at a few occupations, but still nothing appealed to him. In Europe, however, the seeds of war were being sowed, and it was the war that would finally decide Harwood's future.[1]

In early 1935, Hitler announced the reestablishment of the German armed forces in violation of the Treaty of Versailles and created Germany's air force, the Luftwaffe, enlisting twenty thousand men for its two thousand aircraft. That summer, at President Franklin D. Roosevelt's urging, Congress passed the first Neutrality Law, a measure designed to keep the country from becoming embroiled in the war in Europe. Nevertheless, at the same time, the

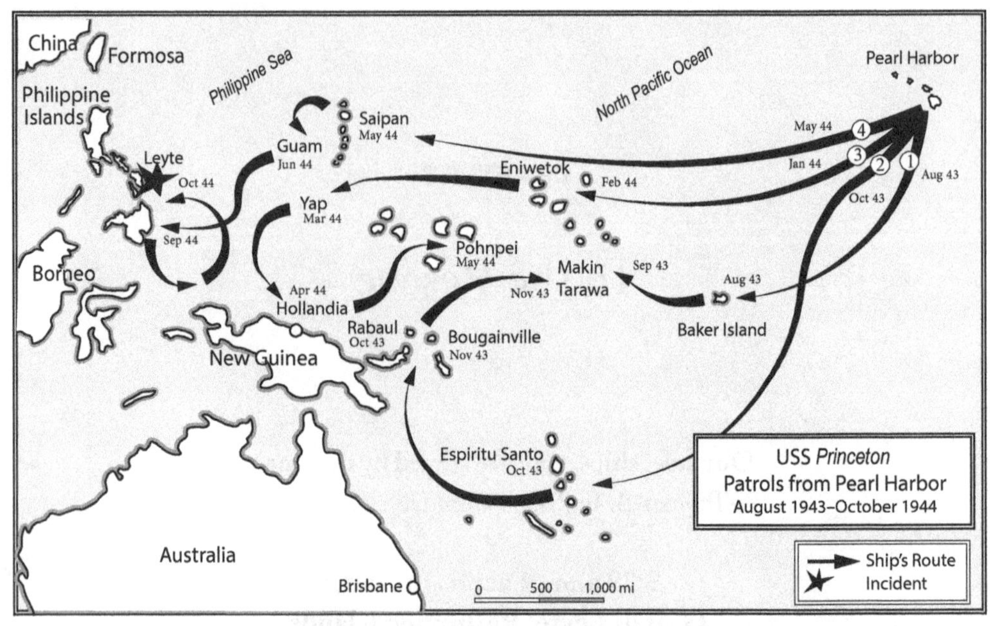

8. USS *Princeton* Patrols from Pearl Harbor, August 1943–October 1944

United States established a general headquarters for its air units, naming Henry "Hap" Arnold as the commander of the first wing of the US Army Air Corps based at March Field in California.[2]

Like so many people across the country, Bruce Harwood knew war was imminent. Whether inspired by the movement of pieces on the chessboard of the geopolitical environment or the siren call of flight, he enlisted in the Navy that same summer. Harwood expressed a desire to fly, and when accepted into the Navy he crossed the country to train at Naval Air Station Pensacola, Florida. Without the urgency of a nation at war, it would be four years before he finally received his wings and a commission as an ensign. His promotion to lieutenant (j.g.) followed in 1940. Impressed with his performance, the Navy sent him to the nearby Naval Air Station in Miami as an aviation instructor. There beneath the sunny Florida skies, in his dress whites and naval aviator's wings, Harwood cut a dashing figure and caught the eye of Sadie Frances Clark. The two fell in love, and in short order he asked for her hand. Whether she understood what marriage to a naval officer in wartime held in store for her—the long absences, the worrisome silences—she accepted. Bruce Harwood and Sadie Clark married in October 1940. They would have little more than a year to begin their lives together. In early 1942, the Navy sent the lieutenant halfway around the world, landing him about as far away from Sadie as he physically could be. He soon found himself in the middle of the Pacific aboard the carrier *Saratoga* (CV-3), off the deck of which he would fly torpedo bombers as part of Torpedo Squadron Eight.[3]

Twice during the battle in the Solomons, Harwood was selected to carry along with him a news correspondent while he conducted raids against the Japanese. On July 2, Associated Press correspondent Clark Lee climbed into the cockpit and took a seat behind Harwood. Lee later described the young lieutenant as a "big, easy going pilot who was itching for his first action of war." Lee also noted Harwood's calm, businesslike manner as he went about his assignment.[4] In August, Jack Singer, an International News Service correspondent, described the action from the back seat of Harwood's plane. Singer's admiration for the Navy flyer and his abilities was evident, writing that he was a handsome young man whose features are "chiseled, grim, hard lines and whose cool voice snaps orders to his squadron when they sight four Japanese ships." During the encounter, the squadron survived a hail of antiaircraft fire and successfully bombed their targets. For the newspaperman it was a memorable experience. He wrote, "The throb of screaming shells jars the plane and I hold my breath. There isn't time to pray."[5]

Adm. Chester W. Nimitz pinned a Navy Cross on Harwood a few months later in Pearl Harbor.[6] The award's citation read, in part: "Leading his squadron in an unsupported aerial torpedo raid against a Japanese task force, Lieutenant Harwood pressed home his attack through a bursting hail of fire from hostile anti-aircraft batteries. He contributed to the relentless fighting spirit and aggressive courage, which enabled his squadron to score one certain hit and two estimated hits on an enemy aircraft carrier. His superb airmanship and unyielding devotion to duty aided greatly in the defeat of a persistent foe and were in keeping with the highest traditions of the United States Naval Service."[7]

Two months later, in lieu of a second Navy Cross for "extraordinary heroism," while flying from the carrier *Hornet* (CV-8) in the Guadalcanal area, Bruce Harwood earned a Gold Star. The award citation noted that "he and his bombers again sought out the enemy and, flying on instruments through violent tropical storms to Rekata Bay, bombed the shore installations at that point, in spite of fierce opposition by Japanese fighter planes which rushed to the attack. Lieutenant Harwood's outstanding courage and intrepid leadership contributed to the high morale of his squadron and to the successful defense of our base on Guadalcanal."[8]

By early 1944, Harwood, now a hero in newspapers at home, took another step up the chain of command. He was appointed the air officer for the light carrier *Princeton* (CVL-23). Should a formal occasion aboard ship call for dress whites, besides his naval aviator's wings, Bruce Harwood had a chest full of medals, including the Navy Cross and Gold Star. He ranked among the most decorated men aboard. By day's end on October 24, 1944, he would earn a third Navy Cross (in the form of a second Gold Star), awarded posthumously for his actions on the deck of the carrier.[9]

The *Princeton*

The *Princeton* began life as the *Tallahassee*, a light cruiser, its keel having been laid in June 1941 in Camden, New Jersey, by the New York Shipbuilding Corporation. The ship was a "work in progress" when the Japanese attacked Pearl Harbor and drew the United States into the war. At Navy headquarters in Washington, it was evident they needed more aircraft carriers than they had originally figured. The *Tallahassee*'s blueprints were altered to reconfigure it as an aircraft carrier, though a lighter, faster version whose construction might proceed more quickly.[10]

The *Princeton*, in the form of an *Independence*-class light aircraft carrier, launched on October 18, 1942, and officially joined the US Navy when commissioned on February 25, 1943, with Capt. George R. Henderson in command. By late summer, it was ready for war service and headed to the Pacific. The ship's first of four sorties across the North Pacific began in late August 1943 when it sailed southwest from Pearl Harbor in tandem with the light cruiser *Belleau Wood* (CVL-24) to provide aircraft cover for landings on Howland and Baker Islands, atolls in the Central Pacific. Following successes at those locations, the *Princeton* joined the carrier *Lexington* (CV-6) and three cruisers to execute air strikes against Japanese installations on Tarawa and Makin in the Gilbert Islands. One of the three cruisers in the formation was the USS *Birmingham* (CL-62), with whom the *Princeton* would be inextricably linked in history. From there, the *Princeton*'s logbook reads like a history of the naval battles of World War II. It launched planes against Japanese fortifications on Rabaul on the island of New Britain in October and Buka and Bonis on Bougainville in November. In the opening days of 1944, it supported attacks on and then the occupation of the Marshall Islands and Eniwetok. In its first year in operation, the *Princeton* achieved an exemplary record, covering seventy thousand miles and launching forty-four air strikes that dropped 440,000 pounds of bombs and torpedoes on the enemy.[11]

After serving as an understudy aboard the *Princeton*, in February 1944 Capt. William H. Buracker assumed command from Henderson. Buracker's next few months were eventful, as the *Princeton* engaged in battles at Parry Island; the Palaus; Woleai, Ulithi, and Yap in the Carolines; and then Hollandia in New Guinea. In June, he oversaw strikes off the Marianas, Saipan, and Guam as well as during the Battle of the Philippine Sea, more popularly known as the Marianas Turkey Shoot, in which US forces downed more than 450 Japanese aircraft.[12]

By this time, two key figures had joined the *Princeton*: Bruce Harwood as the air officer in March and Capt. John M. Hoskins,

Buracker's understudy, as commander in September.[13] Besides the fact that he was eminently qualified for the positions, Hoskins's appointment was part of the Navy's standard protocol to rotate men in command of its ships. Moreover, he was a Naval Academy graduate, although he had a difficult time in school and finished nearly last in his class, earning him the dubious honor of "anchor man." Apparently, he made up for his lack of scholastic and athletic ability with his "good, rare human qualities: warmth of understanding, the ability to work with men, a buoyant sense of humor, and plain guts." Further, Hoskins had served aboard a series of battleships, as a pilot of catapult-launched observation aircraft, and as commander of the *Saratoga*'s air squadron. No doubt, too, another factor in favor of his appointment was the time he spent networking and building his résumé in Washington as chief of staff to commander, Fleet Air, Rhode Island.[14]

Due to the level of hostilities that fall, however, Buracker decided to remain in command. Hoskins instead served in a "make learn" period. Neither man could have known how short-lived that period would be. At 5:20 a.m., on October 24, 1944, with enemy submarines and aircraft reported in the vicinity, Buracker called for general quarters. Fighter aircraft left the decks to protect the carrier, while other aircraft took to the skies on scouting missions. More of the ship's forty-five aircraft sat on deck, ready to be called for attack missions. Crewmen led out fire hoses in the hangar and on the flight deck in preparation for what lay ahead.[15]

The *Birmingham*

Off the coast of Luzon, a short distance from the *Princeton*, Harry Popham and Vernon Trevethan were beginning their watch on board the *Birmingham*. The two young men had much in common. They had grown up in California—Popham in the bustling Los Angeles metropolitan area and Trevethan in Watsonville, a town of fewer than twelve thousand in the center of the state near redwood forests, mountains, and beaches. Both had played football during their high school years, Popham at James Garfield High School and Trevethan for the Cowboys at Salinas Union High School. Were it not for the war, they would have gone their separate ways and graduated in 1944. Instead, they set aside their studies and their athletic pursuits to join the Navy and serve their country. The two, both machinist mates, mustered aboard the *Birmingham* within days of each other in January 1943. They likely saw the same duty and might have stood the same watches. Regardless, they soon became best friends.[16]

The *Birmingham*'s keel had been laid in February 1941 at Newport News, Virginia, by the Newport News Shipbuilding and Dry Dock Company and had launched a year later. Capt. John Wilkes was at the helm of the *Cleveland*-class cruiser in January 1943 when the two young machinists came aboard. After weeks of full-power speed runs, fire and rescue drills, firing the gun batteries, and testing of everything from radios to taking battle stations under simulated general quarters, the *Birmingham* went to sea.[17]

The ship escorted troop carriers to the Mediterranean and then provided support for Operation Husky, the Allied landings in Sicily on July 9, 1943. It returned home from the Mediterranean, underwent repairs, and then headed for the Pacific, passing through the Panama Canal in August. During the crossing, the crew had little to do. By the end, they welcomed a break from the monotony and the confines of the ship. At Balboa on the canal's eastern terminus, while on liberty, a number of the men elected to visit the local tattoo parlors to ink the memory of the war, their ship, or their sweetheart on an arm or chest. Whether Popham or Trevethan was among them is not known.[18]

Once in the Pacific, the *Birmingham* supported the US Navy's task forces at Tarawa, Makin, and Wake Island and escorted troop transports headed for the Solomon Islands. On the evening of November 8, 1943, the ship came under attack. Although the ship shot down an attacking Japanese bomber, the plane released one of its bombs before crashing into the sea. That explosive skipped through the water and blasted a fifteen-foot hole in the *Birmingham*'s hull. A second aircraft dropped a torpedo that exploded near the *Birmingham*'s port bow, blowing another hole in its hull twice as large as the first. A third bomber, hit by the ship's guns, exploded over the deck, taking out a gun turret. No one on board, not even Popham and Trevethan in the engine room well below the deck, could have missed the thunder of the ship's guns, the crash of the exploding bomber, or the ripping of the *Birmingham*'s hull. They had been to battle and survived the horror.[19]

While the ship wore deep scars from the encounter and lost two of the crew, it refused to yield. The *Birmingham* stayed afloat and remained with the cruiser formation and its protective shield. On the following day, it underwent temporary repairs in the Solomons, then returned to the US mainland for a major overhaul. The stateside visit was relatively brief, considering the extent of the damage. By February 1944, the *Birmingham* was back at sea and supporting amphibious operations in the Central Pacific. In May, the warship escorted a convoy to the Marshall Islands and then headed west to conduct mine-sweeping and underwater-demolition activities for the Marianas invasion. There it came under fire from enemy shore batteries that showered the deck with shrapnel. This time, the ship suffered only light damage.[20]

One battle after another followed in quick succession. The crew now knew "what" to expect and "how" they would react in the face of battle. The "where" was the Philippines. Only the "when" was unknown.

The *Birmingham* joined the seventeen carriers, nine fleet carriers, and eight light carriers of Adm. William F. Halsey's Third Fleet. But it was soon once more sent to handle tasks far from the main fleet. The ship assisted with strikes against Okinawa and Formosa and, in mid-October, provided defensive cover for two damaged warships, the *Canberra* (CA-70) and the *Houston* (CL-81), as they were towed to repair facilities. Finally, on October 24, the *Birmingham* rejoined the Third Fleet zigzagging toward Luzon.[21]

According to reports from the *Lexington*, the weather and visibility were very good. "The sea was slight with low swells moving from the east. The sky was eight-tenths covered with cumulus, alto-stratus and cirrus clouds. A fresh breeze blew from the northeast."[22] On that pleasant, clear day, naval intelligence spotted the Japanese fleet approaching from the west. The American carriers took the offense and attacked. They damaged two enemy ships and sank a third. In response, in the heart of the Philippines, Clark and Nichols Airfields rumbled to life. Though earlier US naval bombardments and air strikes had damaged the Japanese-occupied airfields, they had not been neutralized. Dozens of land-based enemy fighter and bomber aircraft took off and headed to the brewing conflict.[23]

From his vantage point on board the *Birmingham* and what he learned after the incident, Harry Popham described the action vividly:

> To start the day, *Princeton* contributed 20 fighter planes to the air battle over Leyte Gulf. The first wave of 40 to 50 Japanese planes was intercepted and their attack broken up with many enemy losses. A second group of about 30 enemy aircraft quickly took to the air. Out of the two waves, *Princeton*'s planes alone shot down 34 enemy aircraft with a loss of only one. Pilots became aces in a matter of minutes. The planes returned to the carrier for refueling and re-arming in preparation for an airstrike against a Japanese force of 4 battleships, 8 cruisers and 13 destroyers southeast of the island of Mindoro.[24]

Action reports also recorded the fight in minute-by-minute accounts. At 7:55 a.m., the crew of the *Lexington* sighted a large bogey group. Ten minutes later, it launched eleven fighters and maneuvered to repel an enemy air attack. At 8:37 a.m., it came under a dive-bombing attack on the starboard beam and opened fire from all its batteries. The *Lexington* ceased firing at 8:39 a.m. In another ten minutes, low-flying planes approached, sending the

Lexington into another series of emergency turns. At 9:38 a.m., it opened fire to starboard on a lone dive-bomber making a run at the *Princeton*.[25]

The Attack

That lone enemy aircraft, a Yokosuka D4Y "Judy" dive-bomber, emerged from the clouds and hurtled toward the *Princeton*. It fought back with its 20-millimeter and 40-millimeter forward guns, and the captain took evasive measures and "put the helm over" to port. One of the Judy's two 550-pound bombs fell into the sea, but the other landed with a resounding thud amidships. The impact reverberated throughout the ship, a harbinger of the destruction to come.[26]

The flight deck bore the brunt, the bomb tearing a jagged fifteen-inch hole in its surface. Buracker said in a later interview, "I wasn't too much concerned. I thought it was a small bomb and we could patch up the damage quickly."[27]

Piercing the deck, the bomb continued downward. At 9:39 a.m., it crashed into the hangar deck where six Grumman TBM Avengers sat, having been prepared for their next strike, their gas tanks full and torpedoes mounted. After possibly striking one aircraft, the bomb penetrated to the galley below. There, it finally exploded, creating a massive fireball that triggered secondary explosions. A thick cloud of white smoke billowed from every hangar opening and covered the ship in a gray shroud, rendering it all but uninhabitable.[28]

Despite months of training and constant drills, chaos followed, stymieing the firefighters. An electrical short circuit singed the control switches for the sprinklers in the hangar. An emergency power source failed to engage. Then more explosions erupted, the new blasts throwing needed hands overboard. Still other crewmen, after hearing what they thought was a call for unnecessary personnel to abandon the ship, descended rungs on the aft of the ship or lines over the side.[29]

Bruce Harwood, who had remained at his station on the bridge's port side to help direct firefighting, left the safety of the bridge and entered the hangar deck to determine the extent of the damage. The area was engulfed in intense flames, the fire uncontained and spreading toward the torpedo- and bomb-stowage areas. Ignoring the immediate danger, Harwood continued with his efforts to assess the risk. He entered several endangered areas as he went, pulling men from compartments where they had been overcome by heat or exhaustion.[30] As Captain Buracker said later, "Bruce had been conspicuous all day long, going into places where he might have been killed at any time."[31]

Petty Officer Manuel L. Pino died out of sight of anyone. As a water tender and fireman second class when he came aboard in February 1943, he was responsible for tending to the fires and boilers in the *Princeton*'s engine room. Pino would have been in the thick of the firefighting.[32]

The Rescue Attempt

Four nearby ships, the light cruisers *Birmingham* (CL-62) and *Reno* (CL-96) and the destroyers *Irwin* (DD-794) and *Morrison* (DD-560) rallied to the *Princeton*'s aid. With ocean swells growing and the smoke and heat rising from the raging fires, as the *Birmingham* and *Irwin* pulled alongside the stricken *Princeton*, they had difficulty keeping their ships close. The *Princeton* was "dead in the water," and the assisting vessels had to use their engines to maneuver to keep even with the carrier. On several occasions, with the increasingly choppy seas, the *Princeton* and *Birmingham* collided, their hulls scraping and clashing, inflicting significant damage to both ships.[33]

Capt. Thomas B. Inglis of the *Birmingham* believed his ship was better able and better equipped to fight the carrier fire than was the *Irwin*. His ship had more hoses, a larger deck space on which to operate the hoses, and a superior pumping capacity. The *Irwin* yielded and moved away to allow the *Birmingham* to take a better position. Inglis ordered a line run to the *Princeton* to keep the two ships together.[34]

As crews on both ships battled the fires, those aboard the *Princeton* began salvage operations. The crew had performed exhaustive drills for both firefighting and salvage under simulated battle conditions, but live battle was altogether different. Inglis asked for volunteers to board the stricken *Princeton*. Forty men stepped to the head of the line, demonstrating, as Captain Inglis would later say, "Our steel ships, too, are served by iron men."[35] By 1:30 in the afternoon, the fires were mostly under control. But as luck would have it, a new threat emerged with reports of enemy air and submarine activity in the vicinity. The risk of keeping the *Birmingham* tethered alongside the *Princeton* was too high. All but a handful of the volunteer firefighters returned to the *Birmingham*. It and the other nearby ships pulled away. Although Japanese aircraft probed the formation's defenses, no material threat developed. Two hours later, the assisting ships ventured back. The *Birmingham* made ready to tow the *Princeton*, which had remained afloat without any noticeable list. Lacking proper towing gear, it set lines again to maintain a fifty-foot separation between them and act as a tug.[36]

Then, without warning, at 3:23 p.m., five hours after the initial strike, a tremendous explosion ripped through the *Princeton*. Many sailors aboard the *Birmingham* who normally would have been belowdecks had come topside to watch the firefighting effort. Hundreds were wounded or killed in an instant.[37] Captain Hoskins was severely injured, the explosion severing his right leg above the ankle. In a 1950 *Life* magazine article, Hoskins recalled the incident: "We were knocked flat. The whole stern of the ship was blasted off. Everyone started to run forward—but I couldn't get up. There was my bare right foot . . . hanging by a tendon almost completely severed. They carried me forward and the doctor, who was injured himself, went to work on me with a sheath knife." Humorist that he was, as members of the crew carried him on a stretcher from the *Princeton*, Hoskins smiled and asked Captain Buracker, "Permission to leave the ship, sir?" Without a moment's hesitation, Buracker gave his permission, and Hoskins was transferred and shortly flown out for further medical care. Despite the expedited transfer and treatment, Hoskins lost his foot.[38] Still belowdecks, carrying on with his damage assessment, Commander Harwood was among those killed. Paying tribute to his air officer later, Buracker said, "Like every man on the ship, he thought of saving it first and not of personal danger."[39]

The carnage was not limited to the *Princeton*. The force of the blast blew off the ship's stern and showered hot debris across the *Birmingham*'s crowded deck. For years afterward, the horrific scene stayed with many of the *Birmingham*'s survivors. They remembered being blown across the deck, limbs broken, bearing cuts, bruises, and burns. Body parts littered the deck. Blood ran across the ship in rivers and drained into the ocean. Hot shrapnel burned hundreds of tiny holes in the crew's clothing and singed bare skin. A relentless hail of debris bombarded the cruiser's deck—steel plates, gun barrels, uniforms, life jackets, gas masks, beams from the flight deck, pieces of machinery, tool chests, and an assortment of other items, all remnants of the disaster.[40]

Harry Popham witnessed the last minutes of life for his close friend Vernon Trevethan. While fighting for his own life, he saw Vernon, also blown back by the force of the blast, in a somersault backward. "I saw him land on his feet and run around the barbette of No. 3 turret." There he disappeared from Popham's sight. Sometime later, however, Harry learned Vernon had dropped dead on the other side of the turret.[41]

The ship's chaplain was in the wardroom at the time of the explosion. Minutes later, the wounded were brought in for aid. The chaplain wrote, "It was impossible to fully comprehend its magnitude." As more and more wounded arrived, he observed, "All of these casualties were not only suffering from shock but from major wounds of head, chest, stomach and severed of badly mutilated arms and/or legs. This was one occasion when it was not figuratively but literally a time when, 'the decks ran red with blood.'"[42]

Captain Inglis suffered a broken arm and other less serious injuries, but remained in command until he began to lose consciousness. Before he went below to tend to his injuries, he handed the conn to his gunnery officer and the ship's command to his executive officer, Cdr. Winston P. Folk.[43]

The Sinking of the *Princeton*

At 4:00 p.m., on the *Princeton*, Captain Buracker weighed the odds and decided the fight was over. He ordered the damage-control and salvage party to abandon ship and then went over the side himself to the *Gatling*. Adm. Frederick C. Sherman, on the *Essex*, issued orders to the *Irwin* to sink the *Princeton*. The carrier's end was as troubled as the day's events. The *Irwin* fired a torpedo at the burning but still floating hulk of the *Princeton*, but the torpedo ran foul, veering left and hitting the *Princeton*'s bow. A second torpedo missed astern. And continuing the almost tragicomic display, a third torpedo porpoised, turned on itself, and headed back toward the *Irwin*. With six hundred survivors crowding its decks and fearing being tossed into the water a second time, the *Irwin* took evasive maneuvers and succeeded in evading the torpedo's track by a slim thirty-foot margin. A fourth and then a fifth torpedo missed the mark as well, and then a sixth mirrored the path of the third, turning back on itself, missing the *Irwin* by an even narrower margin.[44] Finally realizing that the *Irwin*'s torpedo capabilities had been damaged while moored alongside the *Princeton*, the order to sink the carrier was transferred to the *Reno*. It responded, directing two torpedoes at the Princeton's main magazine, and, at 5:49 p.m., a massive explosion sent debris soaring two thousand feet into the air.[45] While a devastating loss, with the tide of the war turning, the *Princeton* was the last US carrier to be sunk in the Pacific.[46]

Neil W. Wirick, an aviation ordnanceman who had jumped from the *Princeton*, was bobbing up and down in the water with the passing swells. When he crested one swell, he saw a black cloud fill the sky. In a heartbeat, with the next swell, he looked again, but the cloud had lifted and the ship was gone.[47]

Later, Commander Folk commended the crew of the *Birmingham*, writing that men from across the ship heeded the call for manning hoses during the firefight. "I recognized engineers, storekeepers, radiomen, signalmen, gun strikers, gunner's mates, and all manner of men whose duties normally would not require them to man hoses, doing exactly that. Because of the number of hoses, it was essential that these extra men be brought into service. The point I wish to make is that they brought themselves into service before it was necessary to pass the word. They were eager to participate directly in the firefighting operations, nor were they in the least deterred by the numerous minor explosions that continually took place."[48]

Smaller tales of valor surfaced. One sailor in the water witnessed another swimming with a rope in his teeth. At each end, a wounded sailor or perhaps someone who could not swim clung to the rope for life. Other seamen drew upon their lifeguard training and swiftly grasped struggling swimmers, swung them around and under their arms, and dragged them toward a rescue craft.[49]

Three days after the incident, more than two hundred of the worst of the wounded sailors were transferred to a hospital ship, the USS *Samaritan*, which set sail on October 31 for the US mainland. Harry Popham was among them.

In total, 349 men were killed or missing and 546 wounded. Of those, the *Birmingham* reported 229 dead, 4 missing, and 420 wounded. Half of the wounded were seriously injured, and 8 of them would die within hours. The *Princeton* claimed 108 dead and 126 wounded. Miraculously, 1,361 of the *Princeton*'s crew and just over 1,000 of the *Birmingham*'s crew survived.[50] The dead came from across the service occupations aboard the ships, including seamen, electrician and machinist mates, metalsmiths, shipfitters, ordnance men, firemen, and water tenders, plus bakers, painters, radiomen, pharmacist's mates, and signalmen.

The *Morrison*, *Irwin*, and *Reno* were more fortunate. Although they suffered damage, they incurred no loss of life.[51]

William Buracker earned a Silver Star, the Navy Cross, and the Legion of Merit for his actions during the war in the Pacific. In 1945, he served as commander of naval training at the Massachusetts Institute of Technology, holding the position until he retired in 1947 as a rear admiral. He passed away in 1977.[52]

John Hoskins received a Purple Heart and the Navy Cross and recovered stateside, eventually taking command of the next (and fifth) ship to carry the name *Princeton*. Affectionately known as "Uncle John" to some and "Our Peg-Leg Admiral" to the nation, he was profiled in *Life* magazine's August 14, 1950, issue. He achieved the rank of vice admiral, retired in 1957, and passed away in 1964.[53]

Bruce Harwood received, posthumously, a second Gold Star in lieu of a third Navy Cross. In his honor, the USS *Harwood* (DD-861) was commissioned on September 28, 1945, and christened by Sadie Frances Clark Harwood.[54]

Thomas Inglis was awarded the Navy Cross for his actions in the Pacific. He remained in the Navy and retired as a vice admiral. He passed away in 1984 at the age of eighty-six.[55]

Harry Popham lost a leg but recovered from his wounds and wrote of his memories aboard the *Birmingham*. He passed away in 2000.[56]

Vernon Trevethan was buried at sea. He received a Purple Heart and was memorialized on the Tablets of the Missing at the Manila American Cemetery in the Philippines.[57]

Manuel Pino, the *Princeton* water tender who perished in the attack, was memorialized at the Manila American Cemetery and at Mount Olive Catholic Cemetery near his hometown in Colorado. His remains were unrecoverable.[58]

A boat from the destroyer USS *Gatling* rescued Neil Wirick, who no doubt at one point thought he might drown. He survived and returned to his home in Idaho, finished his education, became a science teacher, and pursued his many hobbies before passing in 2014 at eighty-seven years of age. In a videotaped interview seventy years after the incident, his tears flowed freely as he recalled that horrific Tuesday in October 1944.[59]

CHAPTER 10

Qualifying for the Scouts

The white nose Mustangs . . . frequently passed up opportunities to raise their victory scores while sticking to the prime mission—protecting the bombers.

—Bill Marshall, *Angels, Bulldogs & Dragons: The 355th Fighter Group in World War II*

10:00 a.m., European Theater, Honington Airfield, England

In 1943, B-17 Flying Fortress bomber pilots flying with the Eighth Air Force faced stark odds. The harsh reality gnawed deep in their gut as they knew they had only a one in four chance of finishing their tour of duty, at the time set at a grueling twenty-five missions. Capt. Charles F. Hess defied the odds. He completed his twenty-fifth mission on June 12, 1944, when he returned from a mission to Vitry-en-Artois, France.[1]

Those long odds were not the only ones Hess faced in his short life. Born and raised on a farm in New London Township, Pennsylvania, he was not dissuaded by challenge. In 1940, fresh out of high school, he strolled to the nearest Army Air Corps recruiting station and walked through the doors. Like hundreds before him, he asked to join and train to become a pilot. A routine physical examination, however, revealed his eyesight fell short of the military's stringent 20/20 vision requirement for pilots. Undaunted, he

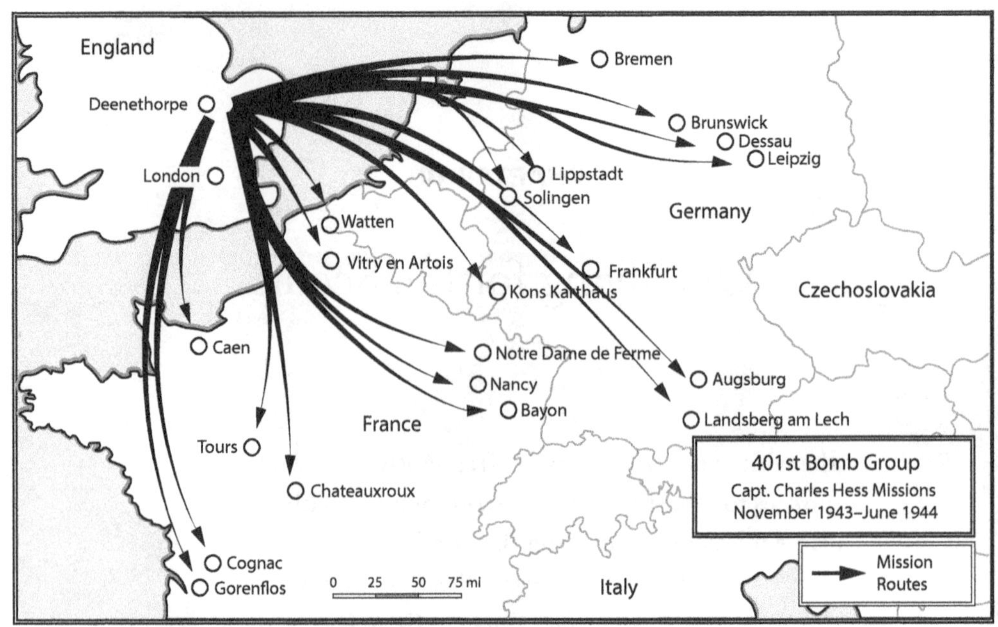

9. 401st Bomb Group: Capt. Charles Hess Missions, November 1943–June 1944

began feasting on large quantities of carrots, a regimen the recruiter suggested. He didn't stop there. He sought help from a higher power as well. Charles Hess was a regular attendee of New London's Presbyterian Church, and sitting among the other faithful, he said his prayers and asked for what he wanted most. Diet and faith aside, tenacity was the young man's cornerstone. Hugh Morgan, the principal at Hess's high school, remembered the student years later. In a letter to Hess's sister, Morgan wrote, "I watched with keen interest Charles' dogged determination to get ahead in the Army."[2]

While waiting for his homegrown remedy to take effect, Hess enrolled at Lincoln University in Oxford, Pennsylvania. Two years into his studies, in 1942, he attempted to qualify as a pilot a second time. This time, the military granted his wish. Perhaps his vision had improved, or maybe the military now realized how desperately they needed pilots. Or both. The Army Air Corps had raised the number of pilots inducted into training programs from an initial thirty thousand men to fifty thousand. And by the time Hess reappeared at the recruiting station, the bar had reached a staggering one hundred thousand.[3]

After a half year in training, Charles Hess received his commission as a second lieutenant and a coveted assignment as a B-17 pilot to the Eighth Air Force's 613th Bomb Squadron, 401st Bomb Group. He deployed with the group to Deenethorpe Airfield, Station 128, near Deenethorpe, Northamptonshire, England, sixty miles north of London. It was a land transformed. Where once an open patch of ground lay, now stood a purpose-built airfield for American heavy bombers, boasting two-thousand- and fourteen-hundred-yard runways. Three weeks after his arrival, Hess flew his first bombing mission. The target was the port of Bremen in Germany, but engine trouble aboard Hess's B-17 bomber, the "Betty J" (#42-31072), forced him to return to base. The aborted flight did not count toward his goal of twenty-five. Six days later, he was back in the skies in another B-17, this one the "Lopin Lobo" B-17 (#42-3940), on a mission to Solingen, Germany. This time, after bombing his target, engine trouble resurfaced. Ground and air artillery had hit their marks, putting out two of his four engines. As he limped toward home, flying perilously low across the Channel, Hess ordered his crew to bail out. But he, his copilot, navigator, and bombardier remained with the battered plane and brought it back to England, albeit to Manston, a coastal airfield 150 miles closer than Deenethorpe and home.[4]

From there, Hess and his crew flew deep into Germany as far east as Leipzig and south to Landsberg am Lech, to Cognac near the west coast of France, and east to Bayon in the mountains along the French and German border. Hess and his nine crewmen finished their quota of twenty-five missions on June 12, 1944. Hess earned a promotion to captain and returned to the United States to spend time with his family in Russellville, Pennsylvania. The skies above him were now free of bombers, contrails, and flak. Only an occasional thunderclap could interrupt the quiet of his summer afternoons. Yet the war was not finished with Hess, nor was Hess finished with the war. Word reached him that Maj. Allison C. Brooks, his former 401st Bomb Group operating officer, had transferred from the 401st to the First Scouting Force, 364th Fighter Group, at Honington Airfield in England. Flying still coursed through Hess's veins, and the opportunity to fly a fighter beckoned irresistibly.

The First Scouting Force was Col. Budd J. Peaslee's brainchild. The colonel had served as group commander of the 384th Bomb Group. In October 1943, he had led the Eighth Air Force's attack on Schweinfurt. The raid resulted in a tremendous loss of men and planes: sixty B-17s and six hundred men perished. The disastrous incident exposed the flawed practice of sending bombers on daylight missions without fighter escorts.[5] But beyond the additional safety an *escort* could provide, Peaslee believed in having fighter aircraft *precede* bomber formations on missions over Europe to report on weather along the planned route and near the target. If conditions were deemed unfavorable, the "scouts" would redirect the formation to secondary or tertiary targets. Peaslee's aircraft of choice for the scouting force were "fast fighters" with long-range flight capabilities, planes like the Lockheed P-38 Lightning or the North American P-51 Mustang. The pilots he sought were those with a unique combination of skills: knowledge of bomber operations and good navigational skills—particularly in the art of instrument flying. In essence, he wanted mostly tour-expired bomber pilots.[6]

Besides, having the right skills, Peaslee believed former bomber pilots would jump at the chance to try their hand in the cockpit of a fighter. He needed no other proof than to watch a throng of 401st bomber pilots swarm a P-51 Mustang on the tarmac at Deenethorpe. They stared at the sleek fighter, ran their hands along the curve of its wingtips, and jockeyed to ask the pilot questions. Upgraded with British Merlin engines, the "B" model P-51 was the state-of-the-art fighter, capable of flying higher and faster than earlier models.[7]

On July 16, 1944, Peaslee's scouts made their first flight, but testing and refinement continued at the Steeple Morden Airfield in England. All did not go as planned. On July 26, 1944, Lt. Richard T. Bennett was killed while making a gunnery pass behind a Tow Target B-26. The accident was attributed to engine failure. A month later, during another training exercise, Peaslee's deputy, Lt. Col. Gerald C. Price, "pulled the wings off of his P-51, 'Starduster,' while recovering from a high speed dive." He was killed on impact.[8]

Despite the losses, in August 1944, satisfied with Peaslee's plans, the Army Air Corps approved the concept and created three scouting forces within existing air divisions flying from Steeple Morden, Honington, and Wormingford Airfields.[9]

Charles Hess rushed to enroll and then made the long transit back to England to train with the still "experimental" First Scouting Force at Honington Airfield. Most of his bomber transition training occurred thirty miles away under the auspices of the 555th Fighter Training Squadron, 496th Fighter Training Group, at Goxhill, Lincolnshire. After completing twenty hours of flying time in a North American AT-6 (an advanced fighter trainer), he moved on to the P-51. With fifteen to twenty-five more hours in the fighter, the former bomber pilots were considered ready to fly the P-51 in combat.[10] Another Scout pilot, Bill Schofield, remembered, "Our checkout procedures in those days was [*sic*] not as time consuming as modern methods used today." Like Hess, he received a checkout in an AT-6 but then graduated to the P-51 the next morning.

On October 24, 1944, Charles Hess was on the cusp of completing his training with a checkout flight in the P-51. As he soared over the airfield aboard the fighter (#43-6768) nicknamed Black Lace, the engine sputtered, belched a plume of smoke, and lost power. Desperate attempts to regain control and return to the airfield proved futile. Hess bailed out, but it was too late. He had lost altitude while maneuvering the aircraft and was now too low, his parachute failing to open fully. Like Colonel Price, he was killed on impact.[11]

In the aftermath of the tragic mishap, Charles Hess's former bombardier Robert W. Rowe, a good friend and fellow second lieutenant, paid tribute to his fallen friend. He hailed Hess as "the best damn bomber pilot that ever sat in a cockpit." Rowe added that he "was good with his hands and spent a good deal of time making useful items out of junk cast off by the military." It was a trait he shared with many other young men who came from family farms and a testament to their ingenuity. "He made a bed out of old shipping crates," Rowe remembered, "ash trays out of old ammo casings, and lights out of chunks of wood and bits of metal." Unfortunately, those skills, while perhaps making him a superb pilot, failed him when the P-51's engine quit.

Charles Hess earned a Distinguished Flying Cross for the bomber mission to Solingen in December 1943 and an Oak Leaf Cluster for his second DFC for a bombing mission on a German airfield in France in June 1944. The citation for the latter noted Hess's great courage and skill "materially aided in the success of these missions and his actions are an inspiring example for fellow flyers."[12]

P-51 scouts played a significant role during the war, guiding bombers around treacherous weather and suggesting altitude changes to avoid icing or severe contrail problems. They also helped maintain bomb-wing formation integrity by spotting vulnerable gaps between bomb wings en route and helped bomber pilots avoid German fighters. Occasionally, with adrenaline pumping through their veins, the volunteer fighters had the opportunity to do what they had only dreamed of and tangled with the Luftwaffe's attack aircraft in aerial combat.[13] Nevertheless, they generally maintained a sense of honor among their comrades in the air. According to one historian, "The white nose Mustangs frequently passed up opportunities to raise their victory scores while sticking to the prime mission—protecting the bombers."[14]

Charles Hess was buried with full military honors at the Cambridge American Cemetery in England. Two of his siblings also served during the war, his brother William in the Army and his sister Gladys in the Navy's Reserve Women's branch, Women Accepted for Voluntary Emergency Services.[15]

Raymond Nield, one of the men who bailed out during the Hess bombing mission to Solingen in December 1943, became the 401st Bomb Group's first successful evader from capture by the Germans. He returned to England and his squadron in February 1944 before returning home to the United States.[16]

Allison Brooks, the man Charles Hess followed into the scouting force, remained in the military after the war, rising to the rank of major general. He also served during the Vietnam War as vice commander of the Second Air Division and then as commander of the Air Rescue and Recovery Service and finally retired from the Air Force in 1971.[17]

CHAPTER 11

Even the Best of the Best

I'd pick out my plane, then he'd [Rushing] make his. We'd make an attack, pull up, keep our altitude advantage, speed, and go down again. We repeated this over and over.

—Cmdr. David McCampbell

10:22 a.m., Pacific Theater, Leyte Gulf, Philippine Islands

The USS *Intrepid* (CV-11) was one of twenty-four formidable US Navy *Essex*-class aircraft carriers that formed the backbone of the US Fleet. On deck and in their hangar decks below, they carried an assemblage of eighty to ninety aircraft, primarily Grumman F6f Hellcat fighters, Curtiss SB2C Helldiver dive-bombers, and Grumman TBF Avenger torpedo bombers. The aircraft complement gave the ships a potent advantage in both offensive and defensive airpower.[1]

In April 1943, following its launch and the rigors of the shakedown cruise, the *Intrepid* sailed to the Pacific, arriving at the military's bustling naval station at Pearl Harbor in January 1944. There it joined forces with two other carriers, the USS *Cabot* (CVL-28) and the USS *Essex* (CV-9), for the final stages of the naval campaign in the Gilbert and Marshall Islands. After successfully wresting control of the islands from the Japanese and destroying

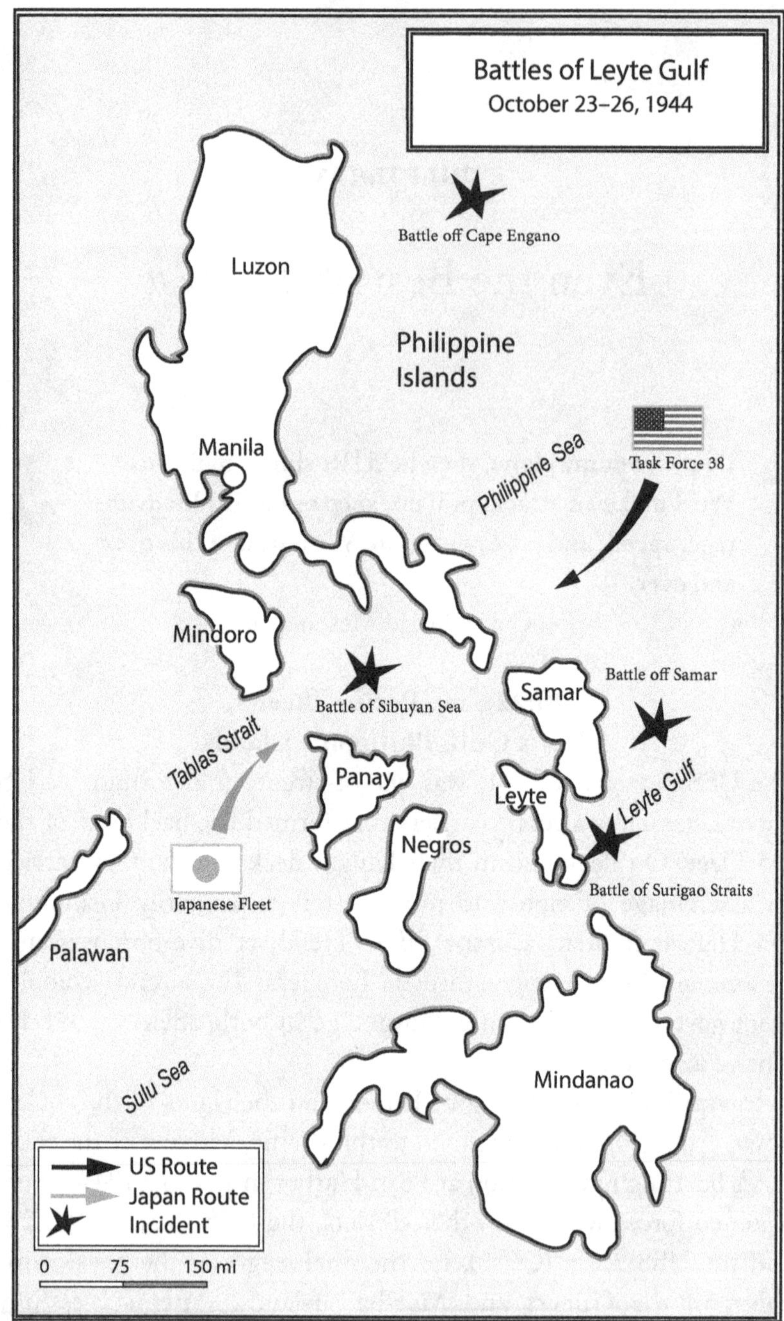

10. Battles of Leyte Gulf, October 23–26, 1944

more than eighty enemy aircraft in the process, the *Intrepid* joined Task Group (TG) 38.2.[2] The task groups, referred to as "fast carrier task groups," were the US Navy's primary attack unit in the Pacific. Each comprised three to four aircraft carriers and their supporting vessels. And in the Pacific Fleet hierarchy, each task group reported to a task force and each task force to one of the numbered fleets.

Task Group 38.2 headed southwest to Micronesia to attack Truk, an atoll with a natural harbor set within its protective reef. The harbor offered the Japanese fleet sanctuary in the South Pacific. Truk was, in essence, Japan's own Pearl Harbor. After mounting successful attacks throughout the day on February 17, the *Intrepid* was hit below the waterline by an aerial torpedo. The blast breeched the carrier's fortified hull and flooded several compartments. Despite the blow, it returned to Pearl Harbor under its own power and then sailed on to the continental United States for repairs. By late summer, the ship was ready to resume the fight and returned to the Pacific. In a series of zigs and zags across the area, it attacked enemy airfields and artillery emplacements at Peleliu, then at Mindanao in the Philippines, then at Peleliu again, and then back at the Philippines.[3]

At the start of October, the *Intrepid* again sailed with TG 38.2. Although the composition varied based on needs at any particular time, besides the *Intrepid*, this time the group's ships included the carriers *Bunker Hill*, *Independence*, *Cabot*, *Oakland*, and *San Diego* and the destroyers *Benham*, *Colahan*, *Halsey Powell*, *Stockham*, *Twining*, *Uhlmann*, *Wedderburn*, and *Yarnall*. That first week found TG 38.2's ships clashing not with the Imperial Japanese Navy but with "mother nature." A typhoon limited their movement and forced the ships to suspend flying activities. The delays required them to reprovision for battle before returning to their assignment.[4]

Once back at sea, the "Fighting I," as the *Intrepid* was known, took its place with sixteen other carriers in Task Force 38 and set a course back to the Philippines. While under way, the ships dispatched multiple air patrols to scan for signs of the enemy. The weather turned foul again, but despite the heavy rain squalls, the task group launched an attack on Okinawa and Formosa. The actions were part diversionary strikes and part strategic calculations. Should they succeed in neutralizing the Japanese airfields on the islands, the Pacific Fleet could avoid enemy aerial attacks during the impending invasion of the Philippines. With at least measurable damage inflicted on the enemy, the *Intrepid* quickly resumed its course toward the Philippines.[5]

As the task force edged closer to the Philippine Islands, however, the enemy threat increased. Joseph F. Bolger, the *Intrepid*'s captain, wrote that the bogeys (unidentified and potentially unfriendly aircraft) became "more than just annoying." Round-the-clock surveillance continued, with fighters taking to the skies day and night.[6]

Soon, intelligence operations confirmed what the fleet had suspected: the Imperial Japanese Navy was approaching the Philippines to stop or stall the invasion at Leyte and the fleet's westward progress. Although the task force had not yet sighted the enemy, they attacked the Philippines, striking at northern Luzon on October 18 and northern Negros Island on October 21.[7] The attacks left no doubt among the commanding officers in the Imperial Japanese Navy. The US Fleet's course was clear: their next objective was the Philippines. The Japanese also understood the engagement would be a decisive battle in the war in the Pacific.[8]

Briefings increased. With each one, anticipation for the coming surface action quickened, touching every shoulder on each ship's deck and in each corridor. Finally, just after midnight on October 23, while on patrol, the US submarines *Darter* and *Dace* detected the clandestine approach of the Japanese attack force off Palawan Island in the Philippines. They radioed the enemy position, heading, and makeup to the fleet. On a sortie at 8:20 a.m. the next day, *Intrepid* reconnaissance aircraft spotted the approaching enemy ships. And in the midst of the formation, they saw the unmistakable outline of the superbattleship *Yamato*.[9] It and its sister ship, the *Musashi*, were the pride of the Imperial Japanese Navy. The two were behemoths, with a 40 percent greater displacement (sixty-five thousand tons unloaded) than that of the largest US battleships at the time, the US *Iowa*-class battleships. They symbolized Japan's commitment to build quality—bigger and better ships—rather than quantity. They flaunted a devastating armament, including the largest guns ever mounted on a warship, nine eighteen-inch guns compared with an equivalent US ship's nine sixteen-inch guns. Further, their hull, decks, and gun tubs were sheathed with 20 percent more armor.[10]

The enemy ships were steaming through the Tablas Strait, still two hundred miles distant from the Allies' current position. If left unimpeded, the island-studded passageway between Mindoro and Panay Islands would bring the enemy from the Sulu Sea to the south and west of the Philippines, to the Sibuyan Sea to the east, and ultimately to the Philippine Sea. There they would find the Pacific Fleet operating off Leyte. In his war diary, Bolger noted, "This day is distinguished by the fact that at last the Japanese Navy has stirred itself into action in the area of our present operations—the support and protection of the Leyte landings."[11] The eagerly awaited word swept across the fleet.[12] At 10:22 a.m., two hours after the sighting, aircraft from the *Intrepid* and *Cabot* were aloft, shifting the encounter from anticipation to action.[13]

Among the attackers flying an SB2C-3 dive-bomber from the *Intrepid* was twenty-six-year-old Lt. Wilson C. McNeill. After flight training at the Pensacola Naval Air Training station, he had yearned for an assignment to a carrier. But because of his demonstrated prowess, the Navy held him back to serve as a flight instructor at Barin Field in Alabama. Now, much to his chagrin, three years into his service as a naval aviator, only the last eight months of that time had been at sea. He loved what he was doing and had every reason to be proud of his accomplishments and the prospects of a splendid career ahead. There is no doubt he wanted to make his days at sea count toward that end. Another twentysomething, Clarence F. English was flying as McNeill's radioman and gunner.

Both men had young wives at home, in Wilson's case a wife of less than a year and a baby daughter he had not seen.[14]

As the dive-bomber climbed away and headed toward the enemy, their wives and families were not a topic of conversation. The men in the cockpit were all business. The broad and easy smile that often graced McNeill's face was absent. Little did McNeill or English, or any of the other aviators that day, realize the curtain was rising on one of history's largest and the Navy's most costly air and sea battles. Postengagement debriefings gathered the vivid tales of the skirmish in the air and on the water. One mentioned the intense pink and purple antiaircraft artillery fire and some shells resembling "large ball-bearings, which burst forward with shrapnel effect." McNeill and English did not have the chance to add their thoughts to these observations. Hours later, when the strike forces returned to the *Intrepid*, it was without McNeill and English and their SB2C-3.[15]

The *Intrepid*'s pilots were not alone in facing the enemy or losing pilots. Carrier operations across the task group grew hectic, with launch schedules nearly impossible to meet. The *Cabot*, for example, launched eight VFs (fighter aircraft) and five VTs (torpedo bombers) at 8:55 a.m. and recovered them at 9:20 a.m. Fifteen minutes later, enemy fighters approached, interrupting the *Cabot*'s schedule. In a near miss, a bomb dropped from twelve thousand feet, hitting the water a mere one hundred yards off the carrier's port side. At 12:31 p.m., the *Cabot* was back on schedule. It launched eleven VFs and four VTs and, an hour later, eight VFs and three VTs. At 4:00 p.m., the 12:31 p.m. flight returned, and at 5:00 p.m. the 1:30 p.m. group did so, less one TBF Avenger in the latter group. The pilot, twenty-one-year-old Ens. Donald Lampson Jr., and his gunners, Albert A. Granger, an aviation machinist mate, and William H. Odom, an aviation radioman, both twenty years old, were missing. Their plane is believed to have crashed into the sea after being shot down.[16]

The USS *Franklin* joined in the attack at 1:30 p.m., launching "ten fighters armed with rockets, twelve bombers and ten torpedo planes with torpedoes." They located two groups of ships, one in disarray after an earlier attack and the other with an undamaged *Yamato* at the center, heading full speed to the west. As the planes closed within eight miles, they encountered a maelstrom of antiaircraft artillery. Curiously, the enemy ships did not launch their own fighters. So, despite the wall of fire, the Allied aircraft attacked, damaging the *Yamato* and the battleship *Nagato* and sinking a light cruiser. The cost to the *Franklin* included the SB2C-3 Helldiver with Lt. (j.g.) Marshall D. Barnett and his gunner, Leonard Pickens; the torpedo plane with Lt. (j.g.) Richard H. Clive and his gunners, Robert W. Bogert, an aviation machinist mate, and Eugene E. Black, an aviation radioman; and a second torpedo plane with Ens. Robert Freligh and his radioman and gunner, Samuel A. Plonsky. Clive's superiors described him as "an aggressive and intrepid airman, experienced in combat flying." His plane was shot down as he made a "daring run on his target in bold defiance of the intense withering barrages of anti-aircraft fire from all warships in the force and, pressing home his determined, relentless attack at perilously low altitude, scored a direct hit on an enemy battleship. By his superb flying ability, his indomitable fighting spirit and cool courage, maintained at great personal risk, Lt. (j.g.) Clive contributed immeasurably to the extensive and costly damage inflicted on the Japanese during this and numerous other brilliantly executed strikes against Japanese shipping and shore installations in the Pacific War Area."[17] Later that day, good news reached the *Franklin*. Freligh and Plonsky had survived and were in the hands of friendly Filipinos.[18]

Meanwhile, after launching from the deck of the *Lexington*, Cdr. Richard McGowan led a fighter squadron toward the Japanese fleet as it entered the San Bernardino Strait east of the Tablas Strait. McGowan's dive-bomber developed electrical problems, forcing him to give up the pursuit and return to the *Lexington*. Accompanied by Lt. Jack Scott, his wingman, McGowan "limped" back in foul weather. A Japanese fighter spotted the aircraft and approached, but fled when, despite McGowan's aircraft's difficulties, Scott and McGowan counterattacked. Unfortunately, as the two were on approach to the *Lexington,* the ship itself came under attack. McGowan and Scott had no choice but to circle out of range until the threat passed. When released to land, just before he reached the ship, McGowan's plane crashed into the sea. Scott circled the site, dropped a smoke flare, and then landed aboard the carrier. Although McGowan perished, the crew of the *Lexington* rescued his gunner, E. A. Brown, from the water.[19]

Heroics flourished in the skies above the task groups, but nowhere more than aboard the *Essex.* A Japanese force of sixty Luzon land-based aircraft took off and headed toward the *Essex* and its accompanying ships, the closest targets. In the scramble to launch a defensive strike, the commander of Air Group 15, David McCampbell, and six other Grumman F6f Hellcat pilots launched their sapphire-blue fighter aircraft hastily, some without a full load of fuel. They took the enemy head-on, the chaos of the fight once described by McCampbell: "I'd pick out my plane, then he'd [Rushing] make his. We'd make an attack, pull up, keep our altitude advantage, speed, and go down again. We repeated this over and over."[20] By the end of the encounter, McCampbell had dispatched nine of the enemy and his wingman five. According to later reports, McCampbell returned to the *Essex* nearly out of ammunition and fuel, but the *Essex* waved him off as other aircraft ready to launch filled the deck. He was diverted and landed on the USS *Langley,* having only six rounds of ammunition and an empty fuel tank.[21] For his display of gallantry, he earned the Medal of Honor, a tribute to his "great personal valor and indomitable spirit of aggression under extremely perilous combat conditions." It was not McCampbell's first act of valor. In June 1944, he and his squadron of fighters had faced eighty Japanese aircraft and routed the much larger force.[22]

Lt. (j.g.) Conrad W. Crellin and his radioman, Carl E. Shetler, also of the *Essex* and also launched in haste with McCampbell, were not so fortunate. After dodging heavy cloud cover, they went after the battleship *Musashi* with their one-thousand-pound bombs. "While still out of range, they were taken under fire by the ships below, and the fire never slackened." Their planes bounced around, but at about 2:30 p.m., Crellin dove toward his target and dropped his bomb. Antiaircraft fire found their mark, however, hitting Crellin's Helldiver as he pulled out of the dive. The dive-bomber burst into flames. Eyewitnesses later reported the plane "turned over on its back and crashed into the sea and left no evidence of survival."[23]

A second fighter also somersaulted into the sea. This time, however, the incident was of the pilot Ens. Ralph A. Mayhew's own making—a tale of triumph undone by a fleeting moment of elation. After shooting down two Japanese aircraft, the twenty-two-year-old pilot headed back to the USS *Savo Island* (CV-78). In a momentary lapse of judgment, Mayhew decided to celebrate his success with a "victory roll" in view of everyone on deck. As he started through the acrobatic maneuver, the fighter's engine faltered. The Wildcat rolled, crashed, and sank. No trace of Mayhew or his aircraft remained.[24]

The tally at day's end had both gains and losses. Carrier-based aircraft sank the battleship *Musashi* and damaged two other battleships, a cruiser, and the infamous *Yamato*.[25] The task groups, however, bore their own sacrifices, losing "3 torpedo and 3 bomber planes to flak," which, according to the returning pilots, was so thick that it was "capable of being walked upon."[26]

At 8:30 p.m., bloody and bruised, the Japanese fleet gave all appearances of a turn back to the west. Believing the Japanese central and southern surface forces bested, Task Group 38.2, in what would go down in the annals of naval history as a major miscalculation, set a new course. They headed for what Capt. S. J. Michael, commanding officer of the *Cabot*, described in his diary as "a Japanese carrier unit reported about 200 miles north of us," east of Luzon.[27] The Japanese forces heading north proved to be a siren's song. Their turn north was designed to lure the Third Fleet away from the San

Bernardino Strait. The ruse worked. Yet through the valiant efforts of the remaining forces east of Leyte, a potential disaster for the Pacific Fleet was avoided. The saga of the Battle of Leyte Gulf, the head-to-head encounter between the Imperial Japanese Navy and the Pacific Fleet, unfolded over several days and in different locales. These included the Battle of the Sibuyan Sea (October 24), the Battle of Surigao Strait (October 24–25), the Battle off Samar (October 24), and the Battle off Cape Engano (October 25–26). The result was a decisive victory for the United States. During the period, more than three thousand Americans lost their lives, three carriers were sunk, and over two hundred aircraft were lost. Japan lost nearly ten thousand men, four carriers, and almost five hundred aircraft.[28]

Wilson McNeill received a Distinguished Flying Cross (Knight). His remains were not recovered. He is memorialized at the Tablets of the Missing at the Manila American Cemetery. In what might have been an oversight, unlike other gunmen who perished, Clarence English received only a Purple Heart.[29]

Donald Lampson Jr. received a Distinguished Flying Cross. His gunner, Albert A. Granger, received an Air Medal and radioman William H. Odom a Purple Heart.[30]

Marshall Barnett and Richard Clive were each awarded posthumously a Navy Cross for their attacks on a Japanese cruiser despite intense and accurate antiaircraft fire and damage to their own aircraft. Barnett's gunner, Leonard Pickens, received a Distinguished Flying Cross, as did Clive's gunners, Eugene Black and Robert Bogert.[31]

Richard McGowan had earned a Silver Star for actions near the Nansei Shoto Islands on October 10, 1944, two weeks before his death. On that day, despite enemy air opposition and continuous antiaircraft fire, he scored a direct hit on an enemy warship.[32]

David McCampbell finished the war with thirty-four kills in the air (and twenty more on the ground), granting him the honor of being the third-highest US ace of all time and the leading Navy ace. President Roosevelt presented McCampbell the Medal of Honor at the White House on January 10, 1945. He also earned the Navy Cross and the Legion of Merit.[33]

Conrad Crellin earned a Navy Cross and Air Medal. His crewman Carl Shetler received a Distinguished Flying Cross.[34]

Ralph Mayhew, too, left behind a young wife whom he barely got to know, having deployed three months after they were married in April 1944. He received a Distinguished Flying Cross and an Air Medal for his actions.[35]

CHAPTER 12

A Distant and Unnecessary Death

It is questionable if the results were worth the cost.
—Stanley Falk

10:30 a.m., Pacific Theater, Yap Island

How Girvis Haltom Jr.'s nickname "Snooks" originated during his high school years in Stephens, Arkansas, has been lost to history, but the moniker stuck and followed him to Magnolia A&M College. By 1941, as he was nearing graduation, news of the attack on Pearl Harbor reverberated through A&M's halls and reshaped his trajectory as well as that of most of the other young men of his class. After the first reports of the attack, "a radio was hurriedly set up in the A&M armory so stunned students could gather to hear news reports. . . . Listening to the radio in the armory made distant events at Pearl Harbor seem immediate and close. In mid-January 1942, news came that brought the attack even closer to A&M. . . . Marine Private Carl E. Webb Jr. had died aboard the USS *Arizona*, a battleship that Japanese attackers had sunk. Webb had been an A&M student in 1939–40." Haltom persevered through the remainder of the school year, but the war was omnipresent. In September 1942, he transitioned from academia to military service, joining the Marine Corps with dreams of becoming a pilot. He got his wish. On gaining his commission and wings, he attended the Marine Fighter Training wing at El Centro, California. In due

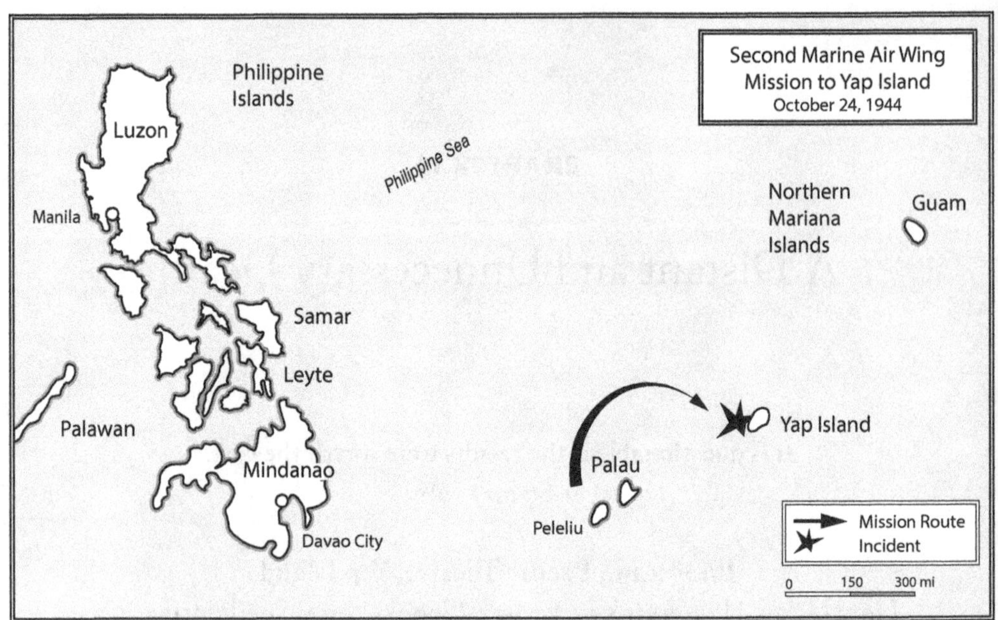

11. Second Marine Air Wing Mission to Yap Island, October 24, 1944

course, but what might have seemed an eternity to Haltom, orders arrived. He was to report for duty in the Pacific as a member of the Marine Fighting Squadron (VMF) 122, Marine Aircraft Group 11, Second Marine Aircraft Wing.[1]

Peleliu

Embarking from the West Coast aboard the escort carrier USS *Hollandia*, Lt. Haltom arrived on the shores of Peleliu in the Palau Islands on September 24, 1944. The battle for the six-by-two-mile spit of land five hundred miles east of the Philippines had just begun. "The U.S. invasion of the Palau Islands . . . was considered a necessary element in Gen. Douglas MacArthur's recapture of the Philippine Islands en route to the Japanese homeland." Enemy aircraft operating from Peleliu presented a formidable threat to Allied actions in the area.[2] As Stanley Falk, author and former chief historian of the US Air Force, described the operation to eliminate the threat, the United States "plastered the Japanese positions with bombs and napalm and strafed them freely, but rarely managed to inflict too much damage. They tried steep-angled glide-bombing and low-level treetop attacks. They dropped 500- and 1,000-pound bombs. They fired rockets and machine guns. And above all, they tried to burn out the Japanese with thousands of gallons of napalm."[3]

At Peleliu, Snooks became a member of the "Werewolf" squadron and acquired another nickname, "Tommy," presumably a derivative of his surname. He could not have been more excited and immediately took to the skies in the distinctive gull-winged Vought F4U Corsair. With its huge thirteen-foot spanning propeller and Pratt and Whitney twenty-eight-hundred-horsepower engine, the Corsair was the "largest and one of the most powerful engine-propeller combinations ever flown on a fighter aircraft." What's more, pilots flying the Corsair could walk with a bit of swagger in their step. America's aviation hero Charles Lindbergh was flying the same fighter for Marine Air Group 31 in the Pacific. While Lindbergh flew routine bombing missions with his group, he also made flights to demonstrate the aircraft's hauling capabilities, carrying bombs with payloads of three and four thousand pounds.[4]

Haltom's missions were more routine. His first assignments were to provide close air support for the invading Marines in the Palau Islands. "This was one of the few times in the Pacific war when Marine aircraft were able to support a Marine assault landing (usually carrier planes handled the job) a source of satisfaction to both the flyers and the troops."[5]

Routine or not, the fighting was ferocious and casualties extraordinarily heavy. An early skirmish for Umurbrogol Mountain, a cave-pocked elevation on Peleliu the Marines had dubbed "Bloody Nose Ridge," was waged in plain sight of the troops stationed on the island. In Haltom's words, captured in a letter to college classmate and friend Harold G. Alford, he said, "All hell is breaking loose about 300 yards over the hill. Snipers are still active as hell here and they have cornered one in the brush. Seems funny—we just ignore a war going on at our own doorstep practically. Guess we get tired being excited, for this was a rough spot for a few weeks and still is pretty hot at times. Have you heard or read of Bloody Nose Ridge? Our camp is 200 yards from it."[6]

He was correct. The fighters had to operate in an unusually limited space when defending their station at Peleliu. "Marine aviators could go on a strike mission against the Umurbrogol and return to the field without retracting their landing gear. They could be over the caves and tunnels, about 1,000 yards from the strip, in 15 seconds."[7]

As Falk noted, above, the battle at Peleliu also involved the Allies' use of napalm, a new weapon. According to Col. Kunio Nakagawa, commander of the Japanese forces at Peleliu, the plan "seems to be to burn down the central hills post to ashes by dropping gasoline from airplanes." Japanese troops responded, keeping "their heads down when the Corsairs attacked." And when October arrived, so did the tropical rains that held the flames in check. Both factors made the Allied effort more arduous.[8]

Yap Island

Haltom found time again to talk of his experience. This time, a Marine Corps combat correspondent submitted Haltom's comments for publication. He had boasted, "Over enemy positions on Babelthuap I haven't run into any Jap anti-aircraft fire, but one afternoon, a Jap sniper took a pot shot at me while I was standing in the chow line here. That is the closest call I've had here."[9] The Marine fighter and bomber squadrons also made sorties, deemed "milk runs," to neutralize the opposition on other nearby islands. Haltom's squadron was among them. He made flights to Yap Island and soon found his earlier jest about no close call was misplaced. In fact, twenty-eight Marine planes were shot down on the so-called milk runs to that remote island, some three hundred miles from Peleliu over open ocean.[10]

The war was devastating to the people of tiny Yap Island, an arrowhead-shaped strip of land measuring less than fifteen miles from tip to tip. Having fallen under Japanese control in 1914, it now served as a Japanese naval base. The Allies hoped that by neutralizing the opposition and capturing the island, they could gain another strategic outpost of their own, as well as access to a recently constructed airfield for refueling and repair operations. And so Allied bombing began in the summer of 1944 and, with the combined efforts of the Navy, Marines, and Army Air Forces, continued in a relentless aerial assault until the end of the war. On October 17, Corsairs from the Second Marine Air Wing (MAW) attacked, hitting the Japanese airfield and setting two enemy planes on the ground afire. That same day, a single Navy Ventura search plane bombed gun positions south of Yap Town. And then on the following day, the Seventh Army Air Force took its turn, unleashing a flight of B-24 Liberators on Yap Town and nearby bridges. The attacks paused for a few days, but they resumed on October 21. For the rest of the month, Second MAW pilots executed bomb runs and strafed enemy positions in the Northern Palau Islands, while Liberators repeatedly attacked Yap Island's airstrip. Throughout the onslaught, the enemy offered only light to moderate opposition by antiaircraft fire.[11]

On the morning of October 24, at 10:30 a.m., seven Second MAW aircraft, with Major Pierce in the lead, took off from Peleliu to assess the damage inflicted on the airfield at Yap Island. If necessary, they were to bomb the area again to ensure the field remained inoperable. Among the sortie were 1st Lt. Girvis Haltom Jr. and his wingman, Edwin R. Zolnier.

It was a good day for flying, with scattered clouds and good visibility. When they arrived over Yap Island, the pilots had a clear sight of their target. Both of its airstrips bore the scars of earlier conflict, and several wheelless aircraft with patches on their fuselages stood propped up around the airfield. Yap Island's airfield presented nothing in the way of a target, nor did it seem much of a threat to Allied activity. Nonetheless, the squadron bombed and strafed the airfield and enemy gun positions. Then, as Haltom passed over the field at six hundred feet, antiaircraft fire erupted and he was hit. He made a slow roll to the right before his plane crashed and exploded at the northwest end of the airstrip.[12]

On returning to the Second MAW base, Major Pierce filed a Missing Air Crew Report for Girvis Haltom and his plane. Members of the squadron sent a letter to Haltom's parents, sharing their memories of their fallen friend. They wrote, "Girvis was building up one of the finest records among us. He had sunk several barges and had strafed and set afire innumerable fuel and ammunition dumps and Japanese trucks; moreover he was officially credited with destroying one and a half Jap float planes on the water. It is more than any of us have done thus far in winning the war."[13] This closed the story on "Tommy." Or so it seemed for three long years. In 1947, an article appeared in newspapers across the country with the title "Unknown Flier Buried on Yap Island." The article described the solitary American grave on the island as one of the loneliest in the Pacific. It lay in the shade of a grove of palm trees. While it may have been lonely because of the location, the article said, "It is not forgotten. Each day, the natives place fresh flowers at the base of a crude cross and push back the encroaching jungle growth."[14]

Another individual who might have placed flowers in a favorite place in honor of Haltom's memory was a young woman known only as "Fuzzy." In that same letter of October 17, Haltom had shared joyful news with his friend. He wrote Harold Alford, "Fuzzy and I are going to be married as soon as I get back. I decided that as soon as I came over here."

In mid-October, the island was declared secure, although fighting continued until the end of November.[15] Despite MacArthur's belief in the need to neutralize Japanese forces at Peleliu, military historians later claimed the actions on Peleliu and the surrounding island airstrips had likely been unnecessary. Falk was among them, saying, "It is questionable if the results were worth the cost."[16]

Sadly, that conclusion came too late for Girvis Haltom and the eighteen hundred Marines killed or missing in action in one of the bloodiest battles of the war.[17]

Girvis Haltom had a brother who survived the war and two cousins who were killed during it. His brother, Lt. John F. Haltom, with the Army Air Force in England, survived the war and later served in both Korea and Vietnam. One of the cousins, Capt. Winfield S. Haltom with the US Army, was a prisoner of war in the Philippines, later transported aboard the hellship *Oryoku Maru* from Manila to a prisoner-of-war camp in Formosa or on the Japanese home island. He was killed in an attack on the ship on December 15, 1944, and his remains buried in a mass grave initially on Formosa. His remains were later exhumed and transferred to the Manila American Cemetery in the Philippines.[18] The other cousin, a second cousin, was Lt. Gambrell W. Haltom II, killed in action on April 22, 1943, in North Africa while serving with the Army's 687th Signal Air Warning Company.[19]

In 2005, Peter Ranfranz, whose uncle Sgt. John R. McCullough was killed in the crash of a B-24 on the southeastern tip of Yap Island in June 1944, visited the island and spoke to the local citizens about the war and the battles at Yap Island. He was hoping to learn more about his uncle's service and to find his grave site under the auspices of the project "Missing Air Crew: The Search for the Coleman B-24 Crew." While Ranfranz did not find McCullough's grave site, the islanders led him to where Girvis Haltom had initially been buried. In 2010, Ranfranz helped erect a memorial to Haltom on Yap Island. He also helped create a partnership between the project and the Yap Visitors Bureau to document and share the history of Yap during World War II.[20]

Girvis Haltom's remains were eventually returned by the military to his home for burial in Stephens, Arkansas.[21]

CHAPTER 13

Boots on the Ground and in the Air

Next time I'll take a parachute.
—Maj. Gen. William C. Lee

11:00 a.m., European Theater

For an eternity, the land of the Onondaga Nation (the People of the Hills) lay south of what is now Lake Ontario in Onondaga County, New York. With five other nations, the Mohawk, Oneida, Cayugan, Seneca, and Tuscarora, the Onondaga made up the Haudenosaunee (People of the Longhouse) and stood together to preserve their traditions against the onslaught of immigration and forfeiture of their land. Today, only seven thousand acres, or 5 percent of the original Onondaga territory, remain intact.[1]

When World War I broke out, Native Americans had yet to be acknowledged by the federal government as US citizens and thus fell outside the purview of conscription. Yet this slight did not extinguish the sense of duty to their nation for the twelve thousand Native Americans who enlisted in the US armed forces to serve. A few years later, after the dust of the Great War settled, the Native American military veterans were granted citizenship. Not long thereafter, in 1924, all Native Americans received full US citizenship.[2] As testimony to their continued loyalty to the United States, during World War II Native American males volunteered in numbers far surpassing those of the general population, percentage-wise.

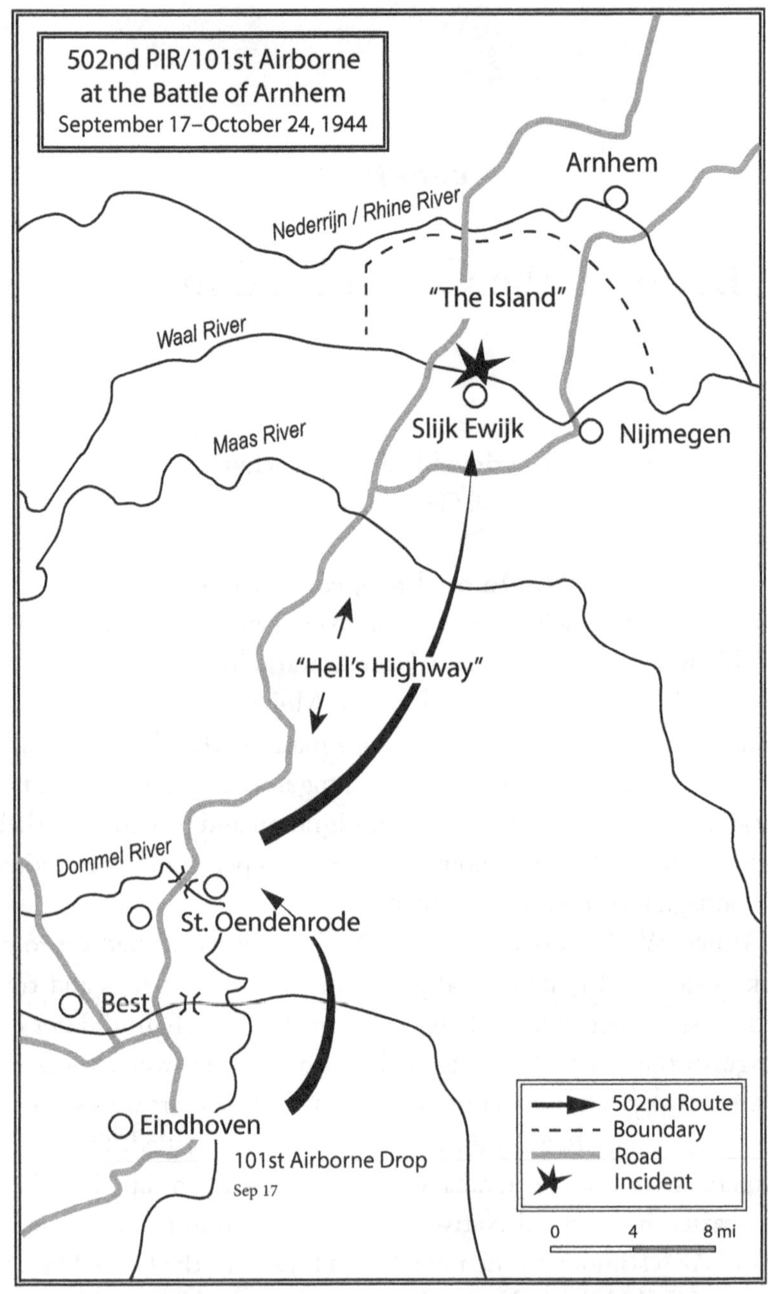

12. 502nd PIR/101st Airborne at the Battle of Arnhem, September 17–October 24, 1944

Close to 99 percent of those eligible registered for the draft, and one-third of all able-bodied Native American men, approximately forty-four thousand, served. They were a people or descendants of those who had fought for their land before and understood the need to defend their land once more.[3]

One of those men was Sylvester J. Thompson. He was born and raised in the territory in the early 1920s, the son of an Onondaga father, Chief Joseph Thompson, and a Mohawk mother, Hazel Mae Jones. In 1940, when he reached the age of eighteen, Thompson, like his cohorts among the Onondaga, became eligible for the draft. Without hesitation, he joined the Army, and, when he came of age, his younger brother Miles enlisted in the Navy. Four years later, Sylvester Thompson became a private with I Company, Third Battalion, 502nd Parachute Infantry Regiment (the "Five-Oh-Deuce"), 101st Airborne Division.[4]

Paratroopers were not run-of-the-mill soldiers. Lightly armed and without the backing of artillery or tanks, they arrived at the front lines before anyone else to face what might be overwhelming odds. On some occasions, they dropped behind enemy lines while a battle was in progress and then, with the element of surprise, attacked from the rear. Expected to play multiple roles—parachuting, fighting, and gathering and reporting intelligence—their training went beyond standard infantry training to include multifaceted combat exercises and physical conditioning specific to jumping. They mastered the techniques of landing after a parachute jump, practiced jumping at increasing heights and from both stationary and moving objects, and learned how to identify and handle parachute malfunctions and to manipulate their parachutes before landing. In an interview decades after the war, Staff Sgt. Earl E. McClung, a Native American with E Company, of the 506th's Parachute Infantry Regiment, described the training in one succinct statement, "It's pretty rugged."[5]

Once they arrived in England, the 101st and Eighty-Second Airborne Divisions were called together to participate in the

Normandy invasion on June 6, 1944. As they waited for the signal to assemble, one 506th paratrooper, Native American Sgt. James "Jake" McNiece, part Choctaw from Oklahoma, shaved his head in the fierce Mohawk tradition and applied "war" paint to his face. McNiece sought both to honor his heritage and to inspire his men. He succeeded. Eleven of McNiece's men, also Native Americans, embraced his example without hesitation. Shortly, twelve men wore a Mohawk under their helmets. Left to the imagination is what might have occurred had a German soldier encountered one of the dozen sans helmet. The paratroopers might have gained the upper hand without firing a shot.[6]

First to touch down on the Continent were volunteers from each of the units, aptly named "pathfinders." Their mission was to set beacons and transponders to mark designated drop zones for those to follow. Many of the pathfinders, however, missed their spots by considerable margins and wasted precious time scrambling across the labyrinth of marshes and hedgerows to find their comrades in the dark and reassemble for their mission. Less than an hour after the pathfinders landed, the Five-Oh-Deuce dropped into Normandy, plunging toward the ground at a heart-pounding sixteen feet per second. As they scanned the terrain, the ground raced toward them. They prayed to land in their drop zone, or at least in a clearing and not in a nest of Germans. Long after the war, the image still resonated with Earl McClung, who had jumped earlier. He recalled, "It was horrific. It looked like everything was coming right between your eyes. There were Germans all around. Machine-gun rounds, small arms, tracers." Still, the parachutists' efforts were highly successful. Maj. Gen. William C. Lee, considered the father of the US Airborne, had such regard for the troops, he once quipped, "Next time I'll take a parachute," when considering the choice of a glider or parachute.[7]

The 502nd's goal was to take a position west of Utah Beach and seize the causeway bridges, clearing the way inland before ground troops arrived. Fortunately, the winds were kinder to them. They landed in reasonable proximity to their target. After regrouping, without cover and "facing steady fire as they moved forward," the battalion worked its way down the causeway. The airborne troops then took up arms as infantrymen, suffering a considerable loss of men and matériel.[8]

Eventually, the paratroopers were relieved. They returned to England to rest, replace equipment, and train new soldiers for their next mission: the two-pronged Market-Garden offensive in the Netherlands. As historian Antony Beevor wrote, "It was quite simply a very bad plan right from the start and right from the top," and "almost everything went wrong, usually due to incompetence compounded by bad luck."[9] The plan, under British command, called for the 101st and Eighty-Second to join with the First British Airborne (the Market forces) to parachute into the Netherlands near the village of Eindhoven. Once on the ground, they were to seize nearby roads and bridges and secure a corridor for the British troops to advance from Eindhoven to Arnhem, forty miles north and east. If all went well, the route would place British ground troops (the Garden forces) ten miles from the banks of the Rhine and the German border. Should the parachute infantry regiment's mission fail, the British would be forced to struggle their own way across dikes, drainage ditches, rivers, and canals at every turn and likely forfeit their goal.[10]

The September 17 daylight drop succeeded. Almost seven thousand men made the jump, their parachutes dotting the skies like flocks of blackbirds. Postwar documents revealed the initial thrust was so expansive that no commander "could begin to estimate the scope and strength of the Allied operation. Reports and rumors of landings at almost every conceivable spot in the Netherlands spread through every headquarters."[11]

As with the other airborne units, the 502nd landed and quickly extricated themselves from their parachute harnesses. They picked up their arms and set off to secure their objectives. One battalion took the town of St. Oedenrode and the bridge over the Dommel

River, ten miles north of Eindhoven, and a second battalion seized the town of Best.[12] After recovering from the surprise drop of Allied troops, the Germans correctly surmised the Allied plan's goal was Arnhem. With this knowledge, they called for reinforcements. Fresh German troops surged into place, presenting a stronger than expected opposition to the Allies and precluding their farther advance. To compound the situation, the weather turned foul, hampering the fight and resupply efforts. The Allies had little choice but to withdraw and regroup for a subsequent push to Arnhem along a stretch of road the soldiers quickly dubbed "Hell's Highway" for the unrelenting and murderous enemy fire along the road.[13]

The 101st troops believed they were about to be relieved from the fighting when they learned the harsh reality. They were to advance. They moved to Slijk Ewijk, southwest of Arnhem, situated in an area of the Netherlands known as "the island," a spot of land bounded by earthen dikes between the Waal and Lower Rhine Rivers. First, they erected tents in an orchard, but when frequent German artillery volleys made the area untenable, they took refuge within the walls of nearby houses. There they remained in place through October, protecting the rear while British troops advanced. After a period of relative calm, the Germans, who had taken a strategically advantageous position on the hills north of the island and across the Rhine, resumed their attacks. They showered the area with artillery fire. The men had little defense, either while on foot patrols to prevent enemy infiltration or as they sheltered behind walls or in their foxholes. These foxholes, shallow and hastily dug to prevent groundwater from the Waal and Lower Rhine seeping through, provided little cover. There was no escape, and the 101st sustained heavy casualties. "That island was the worst period of my life," one officer later said.[14] While for the most part the Germans withdrew in mid-October, shelling continued, adding to the ever-growing list of Allied casualties. One of the wounded was Sylvester Thompson. Hit by enemy mortar fire while on patrol on October 23, he succumbed to his wounds the next day, October 24, 1944.[15]

The battle to take Arnhem stood as one of the fiercest battles the 101st encountered that fall.[16] They withdrew in defeat from the nightmare during the last week of November. Then, finally granted respite from the war, they traveled to Rheims, France, where they did nothing more strenuous than engage in gymnastics exercises and attend Red Cross entertainment events.[17]

Stephen Ambrose's best-selling 1992 book, *Band of Brothers*, and the widely acclaimed 2001 television miniseries of the same name highlighted the 506th's "Easy Company" and their remarkable achievements from 1942 through the end of the war. Despite the praise showered on them, Earl McClung also said in a postwar interview, "The praise . . . could have just as easily been based off of any number of the airborne companies. They all went through the same things we did."[18] Sylvester Thompson is testimony to McClung's sentiment. He and more than two thousand other men lost their lives during Operation Market-Garden.[19]

A poem credited to Raymond D. Cready and Robert N. Bryant of the 502nd, titled "Purple Heart Lane," pays tribute to the battle's participants. The poem concludes with:

> The long battle over, we trudged up the hill
> There we paused to look back at our comrades so still.
> We think of the boys, who died not in vain,
> Our pals, yes, the heroes of Purple Heart Lane.[20]

Sylvester Thompson was buried in the Netherlands. He was one of twenty New York Native Americans killed in the war.[21]

James McNiece earned four Bronze Stars among other medals. He survived the war and recounted his story to Richard E. Killblane, with whom he coauthored *The Filthy Thirteen*. After seventy-two days of fighting in Holland, only three of the Filthy Thirteen paratroopers survived. In 1967, the story was reimagined in the film of ex-convicts who became *The Dirty Dozen*.[22]

Earl McClung survived the war, returned home, and worked in a variety of jobs, from log loader in the West Coast sawmills and mechanic to mail carrier. In his later years, he was a frequent speaker to children's groups, sharing stories of his World War II experience and about war in general.[23]

Native Americans earned numerous awards during the war, including Purple Hearts, Air Medals, Distinguished Flying Crosses, Bronze Stars, Silver Stars, and Distinguished Service Crosses. In all, seven Native Americans earned the Congressional Medal of Honor for their actions in the war.[24]

PART TWO

NOON

Pacific Theater, the *Arisan Maru*, Bashi Channel in the South China Sea

As the number of prisoners dying aboard the *Arisan Maru* soared, the crew allowed their charges to take shifts on deck and to have water and a cup of rice a day. Still, the conditions were deplorable and such that no one who was not there or on another of the hellships can adequately describe them.

By noon, the temperatures in the region reached ninety-five degrees despite a partial cloud cover.[1] Inside the holds, the temperature climbed well above that mark. The men stripped themselves of shirts and pants, wore only skivvies or loincloths, or went naked. The sides of the hull became hot to the touch, nearly searing the skin of any man inadvertently pressed against the metal. Sweat, such as the men could produce, having consumed little more than a few sips of water daily, poured from their foreheads, chests, and backs. Most stood pressed against each other, back to belly. One man's sweat was indistinguishable from another's. One man's urine and feces, like another's, pooled on the floor. Perhaps the semidarkness was a godsend.

Amid their misery, the prisoners welcomed the comfort of men like Herbert C. Brokenshire, a South Pacific missionary, and chaplains Thomas J. Scecina, Frank L. Tiffany, and James W. O'Brien, as well as the healing treatment of doctors. At least six doctors are known to have been on board: Cdr. George R. Hogshire Jr., Maj. Philip Bress, Maj. William R. Davis, Capt. Walter F. Bartz, Capt. Charles E. Osborne, and Lt. George T. Ferguson. Even the most basic skills of the more than one hundred imprisoned pharmacist mates, hospital apprentices, and medics would have been put to good use.[2]

Perhaps those who were most comforted were those who managed to have survived the fighting, the forced march, the beatings and other abuses, and the deprivations of the prisoner-of-war camp beside a brother. On the other hand, back at home, families with more than one member on a hellship or in a prison camp suffered doubly or triply. In the infamous case of the Sullivan family of Waterloo, Iowa, the family's grief was fivefold. Brothers Joseph, Francis, Albert, Madison, and George Sullivan, at their request, served together aboard the USS *Juneau* (CL-52). During the Naval Battle of Guadalcanal, in November 1942, the Japanese torpedoed and sank the *Juneau*, and all five were killed in the action. Despite the popular misconception that Congress later passed a law to prevent such an occurrence happening again, in fact, although the military discourages the practice in times of war, even today family members may serve together.[3]

The *Arisan Maru* carried more than one set of siblings on its final voyage. Sgt. Oscar W. Tubbleville Jr. and Sgt. H. M. Tubbleville, for example, were one such pair of brothers on board. They hailed from the quiet country town of Alba, Texas. Although the small eleven-square-mile town could boast work opportunities at seven coal mines, a career in mining did not appeal to the Tubbleville brothers. And when Alba fell on hard times during the Great Depression, they decided to look for work elsewhere. Oscar and H. M. took jobs in the motion-picture industry—about as far from coal mining as they could get. But then, in the late 1930s, they changed their minds and decided to join the Army. They enlisted on the same day (September 8, 1939), when Oscar was twenty and H. M. twenty-two, with a plan to see duty in the Panama Canal

Department. They stayed together during their service, both assigned as the Army would have it not to Panama but to the Fifty-Ninth Coast Artillery Regiment, responsible for harbor defenses in the Philippines.[4]

Staff Sgt. Henry M. Luther and his twin brother, also a staff sergeant, John P. Luther, remained together as well. Both were twenty-four years old and had been working as roofers in Rock County, Wisconsin, before the war. In an undated family photo, the two young men sit, left leg crossed over the right, left hand over the right, identical pocket squares and argyle socks, and the same slight smile. In the split-second shot, the other family members look directly at the camera, but one of the twins appears distracted and alone, looking off at something to his right.

The Luther twins joined the Thirty-Second Tank Company of the Wisconsin National Guard in 1939 and spent a year at Fort Knox, Kentucky. In federal service, the company was renamed Company A with the US Army's 192nd Tank Battalion. The Luthers participated in the Louisiana maneuvers in the fall of 1941 and learned shortly thereafter that the group was not being released from duty but instead slated to serve overseas. By Thanksgiving, the twins were in the Philippines and, though they could not know it, only weeks away from the Japanese attack at Clark Field. Later, as the enemy pressed its attack on the ground, Company A took up a defensive position and laid down fire. During the attack, as could be expected, there was a great deal of confusion. In the midst of the chaos, a Japanese soldier penetrated the company's lines and planted a bomb on a tank. After the bomb exploded, Henry Luther climbed aboard, maneuvering around the wounded men, and moved the tank to a safe location. The action earned him a Silver Star.

After the surrender in 1942, the Bataan Death March, imprisonment at Camp Cabanatuan, and working as mechanics in camps outside Manila, Henry and John Luther were transferring with a group from one work detail to another. As they passed through the port of Manila, where the *Arisan Maru* sat at anchor, the Japanese dragged the twins and their group aboard the hellship to take the place of a group of prisoners who had not yet arrived.[5]

In 1945, the Luther family received official notice of their sons' deaths in a letter from Maj. Gen. J. A. Ulio. The letter is testimony to his ongoing effort to personalize and soften the blow of the harsh news. In it he affirmed the comfort the twins shared, saying, "I know how inadequate my words are in alleviating your sorrow, but I cannot refrain from expressing the hope that, in time, you may find solace in the knowledge of your sons' heroic service to their country. I hope, too, that the fact that John and Henry were together during their service in the Army will be of comfort to you as I feel it must have been to them."[6]

Fay and Ray Baldon were another set of Wisconsin twins who had entered the war together and served together. They, like the Luthers, were also members of the 192nd Tank Battalion. Born in 1919, the Baldon twins were twenty-one years old when inducted into the Army from their service with the Wisconsin National Guard. Unfortunately, after his capture and imprisonment in the Philippines, Ray became ill while on a work detail repairing vehicles the Japanese had retrieved from Bataan. He was returned to Camp Cabanatuan and died there without his brother. Perhaps Fay had met and befriended the Luther twins somewhere along the way and remained close to them.[7]

Pvt. Pascual Garde from Vaughn, New Mexico, was in a similar situation to the Baldon twins. He and one of his younger brothers, Arturo or Arthur, had served with the 200th Coast Artillery and then were assigned to the 515th Regiment. After its capture, the 515th was sent on the forced march to Camp O'Donnell, during which Arturo died of dysentery. Pascual was more alone than he realized. Another of his younger brothers, Sebastian, had been killed at Betio during the Battle of Tarawa in November 1943, a fact he was unlikely to have known. On the other hand, another of the ten children in the Garde family, perhaps motivated by what he may have known of his older brothers' predicaments, did his part as well. Mariano Garde joined the Army in March 1942, becoming a member of the Sixth US Army Ranger Battalion. In 1945, he took part in the infamous and highly successful effort to liberate the prisoner-of-war camp at Cabanatuan. Under cover of darkness, the Rangers and two hundred Philippine guerrillas crossed thirty miles behind the Japanese lines to reach the camp, surprise the guards, and rescue the 511 prisoners. Fortunately, with three Gold Star emblems hanging in the window of the Garde family, they were spared a fourth. Mariano survived the war and lived until January 2000.[8]

A third set of twins was incarcerated at Camp O'Donnell, John W. and Don Franklin Parker, both US Army privates. Although still in high school when he enlisted, John had plans to become an architect when he graduated and boldly listed that occupation on his enlistment papers in 1942 at the age of nineteen. Like the Luther brothers, Don Parker claimed to be working in the theater when he enlisted in February 1941. The registration office assigned both Parker boys to the Sixtieth Regiment of the Coast Artillery, but they served in different antiaircraft batteries. After the fall of the Philippines, the two were captured but became separated. In early 1942, Don was transferred to the Japanese homeland, where he was incarcerated in the Shinjuku prisoner-of-war camp in Tokyo. John remained in a camp in the Philippines until 1944 when the Japanese placed his name on the boarding list for the *Arisan Maru.* Fortunately, Don was liberated and repatriated in October 1945. He survived until the age of sixty-two and was laid to rest in his home state of Tennessee.[9]

Brothers Gene and Dwayne Davis of Carlsbad, New Mexico, did much together. They were not twins but worked for their father's photography business before the war, later joined the National Guard together, and served in the Army in the Philippines. Gene was four years older than his brother and became a sergeant in the 515th Coast Artillery, while Dwayne rose to the rank of lieutenant and served in the 200th. Both young men managed to send a letter home while in captivity in the Philippines. And like many of the other letters home from that grim situation, although handwritten, they bore eerily similar statements. Gene Davis's letter of August 1943 mentioned that his health was excellent and that he and his brother hoped to be home soon. Nevertheless, the twins' father, Ray, was overjoyed: "All of the spelling of these names is correct, making me sure that my boys are all right." Ray Davis took out a full-page advertisement in the Carlsbad newspaper for a tribute to his sons, whether in fact their health was "excellent." For at least a brief moment, his refrain, "Yes, we heard from the boys today," was a tonic for everyone in town. Apparently, while in different regiments, the two brothers had found each other among the hundreds of prisoners and boarded the hellship together.[10]

PFC William M. Wight and his brother Donald C. Wight, also a private first class, of Bartley, Nebraska, served with the coast artillery in defense of the Philippines. Both were captured in 1942 after the fall of Corregidor. The two spent some time together in a prison camp from which they were able to send messages home. Not surprisingly, prison guards limited and heavily censored the letters. Nevertheless, in August 1944, the Wights back home in Nebraska received a note from William that read, "I am interned at Philippine Military Prison Camp No. 1. My health is excellent. Received your letter. Glad to hear all well. Am feeling fine. Thinking of you. Love to all." Donald's note, also reaching the family at home in August, read, "I am interned in the Philippine Military Prison Camp No. 4. My health is good. Dear Mother, Dad, and Davey, hope this finds you all in good health. Bill received your letter of June 1942 which I read. I have not received anything myself. Bill and I were together for some time, but were recently separated. He is O.K. Don't worry. Love to all."

As Donald mentioned, the brothers' time together did not last. William went aboard the *Arisan Maru*, while Donald was assigned to the hellship *Hokusen Maru* and sent to Japan to be interned at the Shinjuku prisoner-of-war camp. These are facts William would not have known. Donald survived the war, was liberated in 1945, returned home, married, and named his son William.[11]

A last account here of *Arisan Maru* prisoners with brothers in the service is that of PFC Frederick Thomas, who enlisted in 1940 and joined the US Marine Corps, First Battalion, D Company. With dogged determination, his unit had defended Corregidor until April 1942 and General Wainwright's decision to surrender and spare further loss of life. At home in Chicago, his family did not hear of his capture and imprisonment until July 1943. In the interim, they clung to any scrap of news of his brothers. Thomas I. Thomas, a bombardier in the Army Air Corps, was a prisoner of the Germans. As far as they knew, Richard Thomas, also in the Army Air Corps, and William Thomas, an infantryman in the Army in Italy, were safe. With the four brothers serving in separate locations, the family believed it unlikely the war would take them all.[12]

The lack of communication between the prisoners and their families at home was the same whether the prisoner was a mere private or a general. In her daily newspaper column to readers on the home front, Eleanor Roosevelt spoke of her friend Mrs. Jonathan Wainwright's concern for her husband, Lieutenant General Wainwright. For two and a half years since he was taken prisoner, he was able to send only seven very terse twenty-five-word letters home. And in that time, no communication from home reached him. Eleanor considered Mrs. Wainwright to be an inspiration to all. She put aside concern for her husband to speak publicly about the travails of the families of the prisoners. Most believed they would not hear from their loved ones until the prisoners were liberated and could only imagine the conditions in which they passed their time. Hearing anything before the end of hostilities was more likely to be notice of their death.[13]

Twin, brother, friend, or distant relative, all huddled together and struggled to survive. Occasionally, the sound of aircraft engines overhead penetrated the hull, and many of the prisoners prayed for an Allied plane to bomb the ship and end their misery. But the rumble faded, and the hellship sailed on. At noon, the *Arisan Maru* was fifty miles and five hours from its destiny.

CHAPTER 14

Rumors of a Rest

It's just like Tennessee maneuvers—only with live ammo.
—Unidentified GI

Noon, European Theater, Emberménil, France

Nestled in the heart of New York State, the town of Lassellsville boasts its most prominent feature: the sprawling twenty-five-hundred-acre Lassellsville State Forest. The forest, a tapestry of creeks and wetlands, undulating hills, and sandy plains, is a popular area for adventurous hikers and nature enthusiasts, as much today as it was a century ago. It was a place where Elwood Dempster likely hunted and hiked in his youth. He had been born and grown up in the state and, in the early 1940s, lived in the vicinity with his wife, Marietta Quackenbush Dempster.[1]

But with the war in Europe raging, Elwood set aside hunting and hiking. On November 6, 1943, at the tender age of twenty-three, he took his solemn oath and joined the ranks of the US Army's 315th Infantry Regiment, Seventy-Ninth Infantry Division. While he and his fellow recruits might have been fit enough for day-to-day life in peacetime, the war demanded a higher level of hardening and endurance. The Army immersed the men in weeks of arduous maneuvers across the rugged terrain of Tennessee and then, without pausing, a three-month exercise in the desert near Yuma, Arizona. Over the winter, they endured more training in equally

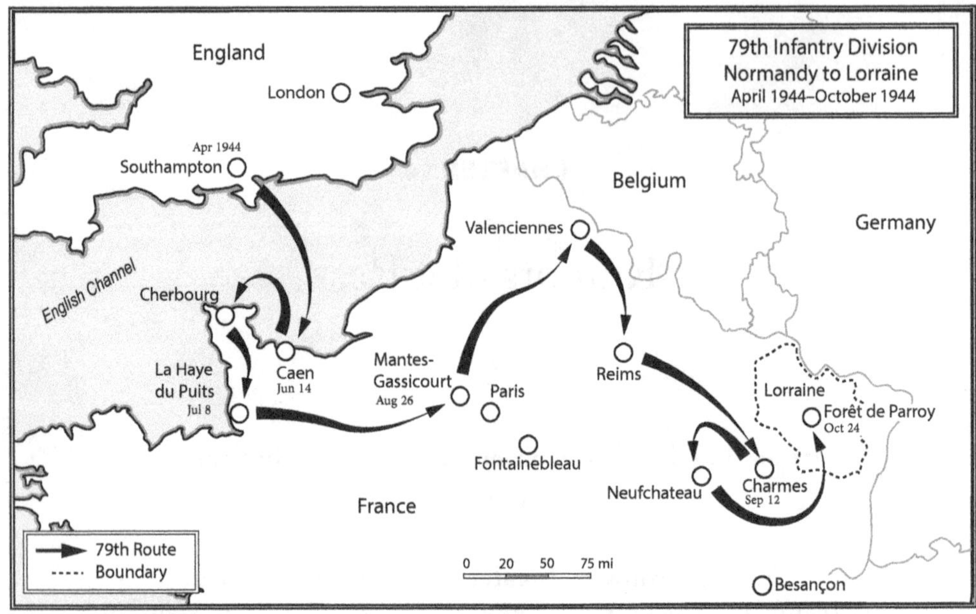

13. 79th Infantry Division, Normandy to Lorraine, April 1944–October 1944

harsh conditions at snowy, windswept Camp Phillips in Kansas. At last, when those exercises were concluded, the men were deemed as ready mentally and physically as they would ever be for the battlefields of Europe. In mid-April 1944, they transferred to the East Coast, boarded a troop transport, and sailed for England.[2]

With each passing day, the number of US soldiers in southern England swelled—all awaiting the call to board landing craft and take the war to the Continent and the waiting German Wehrmacht. In the interim, the Army kept the men engaged and their skills and resolve sharp through more training, including hiking, marching, and night-operation exercises. May passed and then the first week of June. Elwood watched and waited as troops to his left and right were called to board waiting landing craft for the cross-Channel invasion of Normandy, but neither he nor anyone from his unit was called. Whether disappointed or relieved, the Seventy-Ninth's regiments doubled down in their preparatory exercises. Finally, on June 14, a week after D-day, Elwood and his comrades were called to join the next wave of invading troops. After an uneventful crossing of the Channel, they disembarked and stepped onto the bustling shores of Utah Beach, no longer under immediate threat. The soldiers were swiftly dispatched west and north, where the fighting proved the war had not forgotten them. Three divisions charted the course up the Cotentin Peninsula amid flat land and hedgerows in the face of a fierce enemy who would not give up easily. The Seventy-Ninth took the lead to spearhead the capture of the vital port of Cherbourg at the tip of the peninsula. After accomplishing this task, they turned south and east, scrambling across northern France, engaging in both periods of heavy fighting and others with relatively light resistance.[3]

Elwood wrote home frequently, chronicling the events and the sights he had witnessed. He told of arriving on the shores of Normandy one week after the maelstrom of D-day and then advancing with the Army to Cherbourg and then, without a moment's rest, moving inland to a spot just north of Paris. In passing, he mentioned having received two Bronze Stars for his actions in as many battles. Those accolades propelled him through the military's ranks, bypassing promotion to corporal and going directly from private to sergeant in the heady confusion of war and the dearth of battle-tested leaders. Somewhere along the way, he wrote that he had been wounded, although he reassured his wife his wounds were not serious enough to keep him from the action. What's more, he said, he expected to receive a Purple Heart.[4]

Once they reached a position near Lorraine, the sight of the emblem the men wore on their uniforms, the *Croix de Lorraine*, might have struck Elwood as particularly ironic. World War I–era Seventy-Ninth Division troops had adopted the distinctive white cross embroidered on a blue background as their symbol—one that represented the area in which they spent most of their days in combat. Although the cross was the universal symbol for triumph, victory eluded the men of the earlier conflict. Now, two decades later, long after the echoes of the doughboys had faded, Elwood and his comrades of the Cross of Lorraine Division were back in France, seeking a new and, ideally, final victory on the same soil.[5] The Seventy-Ninth Division was not alone in pursuing and pushing the Germans back across France to their homeland. Troops from both the Twenty-Sixth Division and the Third Division joined the Seventy-Ninth in its push. Each approached the goal from different directions, forging three different histories. All left soldiers behind on October 24, 1944.[6]

Much like Lassellsville State Forest, the Forêt de Parroy, where the Seventy-Ninth was soon to be engaged, is a densely treed expanse ranging over a series of undulating hills separated by intermittent streams. Throughout the terrain, amid the nooks and crannies of the ridges and a cover of thick underbrush, opportunities for concealment were plentiful. And the Germans had exploited those opportunities. Long before the battle, they positioned their forces at strategically advantageous positions atop the mountain ridges and then surrounded them with defensive fortifications. A few Americans, like Elwood, however, felt if not at home at least comfortable in the familiar surroundings of tall hardwoods and pines, wandering rivers, and cool late-fall temperatures.[7] The forest in New York, however, did not have trees that burst apart, sending lethal barbs in every direction, or withering fire emanating from behind rocky outcrops. It was not teeming with figures bearing rifles made ghostly in the persistent heavy rain and dense fog that brought visibility down to inches. Nonetheless, the men of the Seventy-Ninth, having spent three months in combat in the theater, already considered themselves seasoned veterans. They looked up at the looming forest, drew a long breath, and prepared for what lay ahead.

Clearing the forest took two weeks, an endeavor made more daunting by deteriorating weather conditions. The Allies lost precious time waiting for the weather to clear so that their bombers could strike and soften enemy positions in advance of the infantrymen. That was their theory and their hope, but the weather significantly reduced the number of bombers that could take to the skies and the accuracy of the strikes of those that did. In short, the bombing proved futile. On reaching the edge of the forest, the troops came under heavy artillery and machine-gun fire.[8] Accounts likened the effort to jungle fighting. "The battle in the forest required small unit cohesion, tight control and, most of all, initiative on the part of small unit leaders." Nothing, however, seemed to deter the enemy. Reportedly, as in other similar situations in the area, Hitler ordered his army units to hold the forest at all costs. With no viable alternatives, the Seventy-Ninth committed all its regiments on October 1.[9]

After days of intense fighting, the Seventy-Ninth forced the Germans to release their hold on the town of Parroy. In mid-October, the Seventy-Ninth emerged from the forest's eastern edge to open terrain. While the fighting was far from over, once in the clear they enjoyed the luxury of time to regroup, patrol, weed the remnants of the enemy from their hiding places, and establish a new defensive position. As they waited for further orders and steeled themselves for what lay ahead, the men of the Seventy-Ninth could reflect on what had brought them to this point. They could congratulate themselves on their training and discipline while acknowledging the advantage of fighting with an experienced unit, one that had been together since they arrived in France. Such reflections were swiftly interrupted—intelligence reports revealed the enemy had taken the town of Emberménil, north and east of their position. With Elwood's unit taking the lead, the US troops attacked the town on October 13, wresting control from the Germans by the next afternoon. But the Germans withdrew only to take a stand on a high point to the east. As the Seventy-Ninth Infantry Division historian wrote, "It was only a matter of covering some two miles of ground, but what a price the doughboys would pay!"[10]

Drenching rain returned, transforming the unpaved roads and trails into mud-clouded rivers. The troops waited out the weather in place for a grueling five days. They had hoped clearing the Parroy would be the last bit of fighting for a while. But on October 20, orders came to straighten their lines, which they did under the fire of sporadic attacks. They complied as best they could and then took their place again, lingering and in limbo, pinned down by German artillery fire while they continued to wait for orders. With nothing to take their mind off their predicament, rumors of imminent relief spread quickly from man to man. The nearness of the opportunity to step back from the fight, eat a hot meal, take a shower, change clothes, and get much-needed sleep made every minute at the front line increasingly disquieting.[11]

Relief finally came on October 23. But as the Forty-Fourth Infantry Division stepped into place and the Seventy-Ninth exited, the enemy redoubled its efforts. Just after 6:00 in the morning, the Germans launched a strong artillery barrage and brought their tanks and infantry forward. US artillery returned fire, stalling the enemy for two hours, when a second assault began. By 8:45 a.m., two companies of the 315th Regiment, Elwood's unit, were driven from their positions. With their own tank-driven forces, they soon returned, counterattacked, and reclaimed their ground. In the next lull, the relief process resumed, and the last of the Seventy-Ninth left the area. The weary troops had been in constant combat for 128 days, from the day they arrived on the Continent. The reins of control for the area passed to Maj. Gen. Robert L. Spragins of the Forty-Fourth Infantry Division.[12]

Pvt. Melvin W. Johnson, with the 314th Regiment, wrote home on October 26, sharing how much he enjoyed the relief and particularly the food. "We've earned a rest. Don't know how long we'll be here. But it's wonderful to eat regular hot-cooked meals again and to sleep warm and dry at night. One day at dinner I ate 5 large hamburger steaks, besides potatoes, gravy, bread, etc. That morning had 5 pancakes for breakfast, plus other things! Can't seem to get enough to eat!"[13]

Unfortunately, the relief had arrived too late for Elwood Dempster. While the bulk of the troops rested and recuperated in the nearby town of Lunéville, sleeping in beds with sheets and pillows, Elwood lay in a field-hospital bed. This marked the second time in October that he had been injured and admitted to the hospital. This time, however, he did not return to the lines or join his comrades in the Seventy-Ninth. Instead, he died of injuries sustained from an exploding artillery shell in the waning days of the battle for Embermênil. On November 8, 1944, exactly one year after he had enlisted, the devastating news of his disappearance and presumed death arrived at Marietta Dempster's doorstep. The letter she received noted that he had died in the forests of eastern France on October 24, 1944, possibly during the early-morning German counterattack that day.[14]

Elwood Dempster might have earned his Bronze Stars in the hedgerows around Cherbourg that June or later at La Haye du Puits in house-to-house fighting in July. His efforts might have been rewarded as they crossed the Seine in August under heavy German counterattacks, or while taking Charmes in eastern France, or in clearing the Forêt de Parroy in October. Regardless, his was one of twenty-six deaths the Seventy-Ninth incurred on October 24.

For Alexander Patch, the Seventh Army commander, the relief that came too late for Elwood Dempster came too late for him as well. A barrage of German mortar fire on October 22 took the life of his son, Capt. Alexander M. Patch III, commander of Company C of the 315th Infantry.[15]

A and F Companies of the 315th received Presidential Citations for their efforts at Embermênil. The second citation underscored their heroism and contribution to the outcome of the engagement. It reads, in part, "Company F, 315th Infantry Regiment is cited for outstanding performance of duty in action against the enemy during the period 21 October 1944 to 24 October 1944 with the mission of closing a gap in friendly lines and seizing the high ground northeast of Embermênil, France. . . . By its heroic action in storming, seizing, and holding a strategic high point against overwhelmingly enemy superiority, Company F, 315th Infantry Regiment contributed substantially to the success of the regiment in this action."[16]

Elwood Dempster was buried in the Epinal American Cemetery in France.

CHAPTER 15

Yankees in France

We got them licked. Don't stop now.
—Lt. Col. Dwight T. Colley

Noon, European Theater, Moncourt Woods, France

In January 1941, the US Army mobilized the 104th Regiment, a Massachusetts National Guard unit, for war service. That fall, the regiment received its assignment to the Army's 26th Infantry Division—the Yankee Division, so named for the six New England states from which its World War I soldiers had hailed. As the division built to wartime strength, the men trained relentlessly. Two years later, during the harsh winter of 1943, they were still training, this time in the cold, rain-soaked terrain of middle Tennessee. Still not considered ready for deployment, in March 1944 they participated in one of the Army's forty-eight specialty-purpose maneuvers, an intense nine-week simulated combat exercise. The Tennessee Maneuvers were as authentic a representation of war as the Army could make them. The soldiers marched across rugged terrain, ate rations, and slept on the damp, muddy ground—everything combat promised except for live ammunition. In fact, the Army had chosen middle Tennessee because its river valleys and rolling hills resembled the areas in western Europe in which they expected the trainees to fight, particularly in the likes of eastern France, Belgium, and the Rhine. As fate or luck would have it, most of the units that

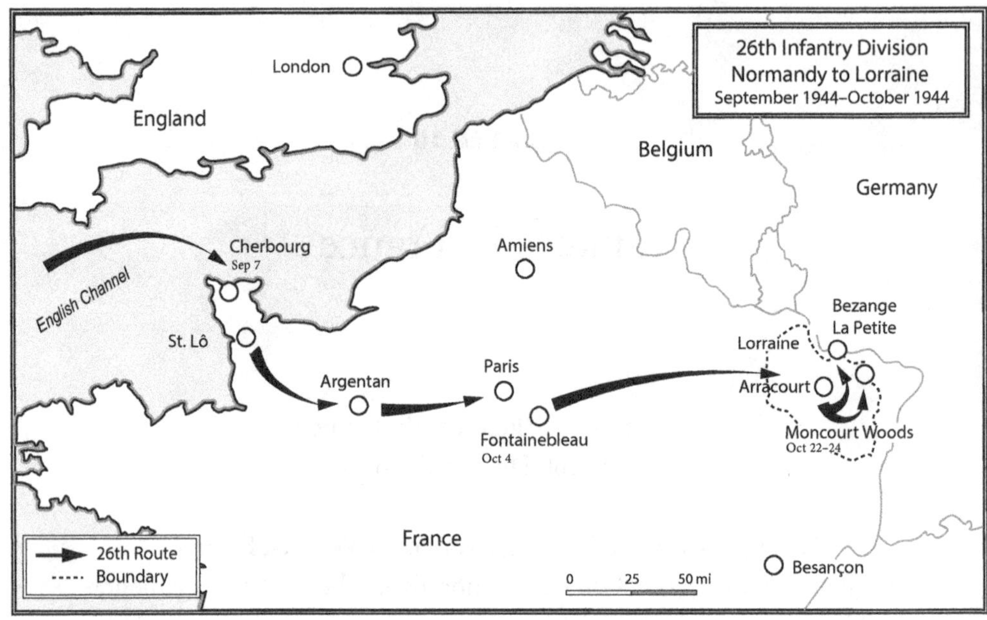

14. 26th Infantry Division, Normandy to Lorraine, September 1944–October 1944

trained in Tennessee did see action in those areas of the European theater of operations, and thus the battlefield conditions perhaps struck them as familiar ground.[1]

Following the exhaustive maneuvers, the division relocated through a series of camps while engaging in yet more training. One memorable exercise was a competition for the Expert Infantry Badge—the first of which went to Lt. Col. Dwight Colley. A natural leader, with the award Colley earned the admiration of everyone present, as he would later earn their respect and allegiance in combat.[2]

Still, to a man, the training seemed interminable. At one point, in the dog days of August 1944, an older man in the unit said, "This outfit will never go overseas." It was a thought PFC Robert B. Kuhl might have shared. Kuhl was a product of West Virginia's coal country, not a New Englander like many of his comrades. Like the other able young men, however, he was comfortable in the outdoors, including in mountainous terrain and harsh climates. At the age of twenty-two, he stood tall and lean. But on his young shoulders he carried the weight of responsibility to his country and his family at home, where his eight siblings and young wife waited, anxious for his safe return.[3]

For most of the summer, Kuhl remained stateside, enduring the demands of military training. Even when called up for deployment, after arriving at Camp Shanks, New York, he found himself in training. This time, the exercises covered new ground, amphibious landing drills. Then, abruptly, on August 27, 1944, the training concluded. The Army issued the 104th a twelve-hour pass, a brief respite with the opportunity to take in the sights of New York City or stay in the camp to rest and post quickly penned letters home. The twelve hours disappeared in what seemed like minutes. It was time to go to war. The men shouldered their heavy bags and made their way aboard the SS *Argentina*. As the ship cast off, fog rolled in, obscuring the New York skyline. A gentle drizzle fell.[4]

After a week at sea, the *Argentina* reached Europe a full three months after the D-day landings on the Normandy beaches. The troops disembarked at Cherbourg, now in friendly hands. The regiment might have earned the distinction of being the first troops to arrive directly in France from the United States, but their opportunity to engage in actual combat remained a month away. In the interim, they trudged through rain and mud to their staging area to await orders. The doubtful among them harked back to the rumor they would never go overseas and now wondered if the war might end before they had a chance to see action.[5]

As they idled away their time in camp, a few men of the 104th were commandeered to join the ranks of the Red Ball Express, the massive truck-based transportation group set up to expedite delivery of food, fuel, ammunition, and other mission-essential supplies to the Army as it pushed inland. Those assigned from the 104th spent two weeks loading, driving, and unloading cargo, while those who remained behind had liberty to explore the coastal towns on the peninsula. It was far from a sightseeing expedition. A half-dozen unwitting troops stepped on mines left behind by the fleeing Germans, offering the green infantrymen their first stark glimpse of the reality of war.[6] With a newfound respect, the volunteers helped remove a staggering seven thousand deadly devices from the area.[7]

At long last, after three and a half years of biding their time, the 104th received their orders to move to the front lines. Filled with a mix of excitement and trepidation, the men boarded trucks and rode through rain and cold across the northern expanse of France. In another day and time, the route would have been a tourist's itinerary of verdant fields and quaint villages. Instead, their path led them through the rubble of St. Lô and Argentan, into villages with houses and businesses open to the elements, and past orchards and forests reduced to little more than toothpicks. On and on they went, to Versailles, Fontainebleau, and Nancy. As they moved east, the Army held regular briefings intended to apprise the men of what to expect. But the lectures from improvised podiums did little to convey the reality of what they faced. Ahead lay a challenging tramp over rough ground on tired feet, no option but to shelter in rain-soaked foxholes, and, for some, the deadly whistle of a sniper's bullet as it passed a hair's breadth away.[8]

In the first week of October, they arrived at their camp near the village of Arracourt, in the Meurthe-et-Moselle area of Lorraine, where they found Patton's Fourth Armored Division bivouacked. The bruised but victorious tank unit was in a holding position during what would be called the "pause." The fuel, food, and ammunition necessary for the Third Army to advance east of the Moselle River and continue its race to the German border had been diverted. Gen. Dwight D. Eisenhower, supreme Allied commander in Europe, had requisitioned all the resources he could muster and sent them north to the Belgian coast, where he hoped to gain a deepwater port at Antwerp.[9]

Not knowing how long they might have to wait, the 104th took advantage of the lull and dug in just south of Moncourt Woods, one of a group of forests covering rolling hills with low ridges in eastern France. During the first few nights, the men remained on edge. They strained to hear the sound of Germans on patrol under the cloak of darkness, a footstep padding slowly over soft ground or a brier rustling as it caught the sleeve of a uniform. At the slightest hint of danger, they fired into the night, sometimes firing on their own men who were setting defensive wires around the encampment.[10]

Then the sleep-deprived men received a directive from headquarters to straighten their lines, removing vulnerabilities along the front. To comply, the 104th needed to dislodge the Germans from their vantage points on the forested hillsides and in the town of Bezange-la-Petite. And, to do that, they needed to remove two enemy outposts and establish their own on another hillside with a commanding height. As they embarked on their first foray, heavy fire from a German outpost rained down on them from north of Bezange-la-Petite, a point the troops thought the Germans had abandoned. In the torrent of artillery shells, the regiment suffered its first losses. The fight, later described as a "minor engagement on a nameless hill somewhere in France," was anything but minor and nameless to the former green troops. They proved the earlier predictions false. They had gone overseas, and they had seen combat. They had witnessed it in all its sound and fury, in the terror of close-quarter battle, and in standing face-to-face with the specter of death.[11]

Over the next few days, while continuing to hold their ground, the 104th fortified their positions. During this period, troops of the Second Cavalry arrived to safeguard the 104th's right flank. The added forces brought a measure of relief to the still jumpy men. It was time to launch their offensive and drive the enemy from the area. To soften the opposition, on the afternoon of October 21, a squadron of fighter aircraft roared over Bezange-la-Petite and Moncourt, strafing and bombing suspected enemy strongholds. The earth shook from the impact of five-hundred-pound bombs, and the concussions reverberated in the soldiers' chests. One witness said the concussions were "so severe men could feel themselves lifted within their foxholes although they were some five hundred yards away."[12]

The next morning, one battalion moved on Bezange-la-Petite, and another attacked along the western and southern edges of the woods. As they pushed forward, a well-entrenched German Army contingent returned heavy fire. Apparently, the Wehrmacht had taken advantage of the lull as well. During the preceding weeks, the Germans had fortified their positions and now had the protection of "massively thick earthen pillboxes, dense undergrowth and barbed wire." They had also deployed mines and added tank traps to the area. Hitler's intent was unambiguous and unquestionable, ordering the troops to hold Moncourt Woods under penalty of death. It was a matter of pride for the führer. He had experienced his first combat action in Moncourt Woods during World War I. Hitler had been successful then and was determined that his troops in this war would be as well.[13]

As if the thunder of heavy mortar rounds and crack of machine-gun fire were not enough to keep the 104th pinned down, fog and smoke rolled in, ensnaring the men in a disorienting haze. The battle-tested company commander knew what he had to do. Col. Dwight Colley emerged from the ranks, moving between and ahead of his men as they crouched low or advanced at a cautious pace. In a display of complete control, he tapped one soldier on the backside and placed an encouraging hand on another's shoulder, all the while issuing words of encouragement. "Let's go, son," he would say. "We got them licked. Don't stop now."[14] Nevertheless, by nightfall on October 24, the 104th had made only incremental progress into the forest's edge, now a tangle of broken trees and twisted branches. Sporadic but still deadly enemy fire, impassible trails, and the cover of night hampered close support and resupply efforts. Some units found themselves cut off completely. But the tenacious 104th persevered. The next day, with the support of their artillery units, they succeeded in pushing the Germans back. And, as a fitting end to the fight and the somber scene of destruction and fallen comrades, the rain returned.[15]

Losses in Moncourt Woods were considerable, and when the fighting ended Robert Kuhl was among the dead. He had sustained a grievous chest injury from an artillery blast on October 24 and succumbed during the fight, the exact hour unknown.[16]

Robert Kuhl was buried in the Lorraine American Cemetery in France, situated thirty miles from the woods that had claimed his life.[17]

Dwight Colley's leadership and bravery did not go unnoticed. On November 8, 1944, he received a Distinguished Service Cross for his actions in the ongoing battle for eastern France, a recognition he had also earned for his service in World War I. He lived to the age of eighty-six, passing in 1982.[18]

CHAPTER 16

Clinging to the Scrabble

Oh, gather 'round me, comrades; and listen while I speak
Of a war, a war, a war where hell is six feet deep.
—Audie Murphy

Noon, European/Middle East Africa Theater, Vosges Mountains, France

The Fifteenth Infantry Regiment, Third Infantry Division, embarked from Norfolk, Virginia, on October 24, 1942, with Walter J. Harris, a technical sergeant, among the thousands of men on board the troop transport. In passing time by playing cards or dice, Harris and his comrades might have made light of what lay ahead. All knew, once their boots touched North African soil as part of Operation Torch, their life could be taken at any moment. Little did they know just how great that likelihood was in their particular case. By war's end, the Third Division earned the distinction of seeing action in more campaigns and suffering more casualties than any other division. In fact, in a cruel twist of fate, two years to the day from his departure, Walter Harris's life met an untimely end. Until that moment arrived, he would face long periods of intense fighting, writing home to his father at one point that he had spent a staggering two hundred days in combat. He had also spent

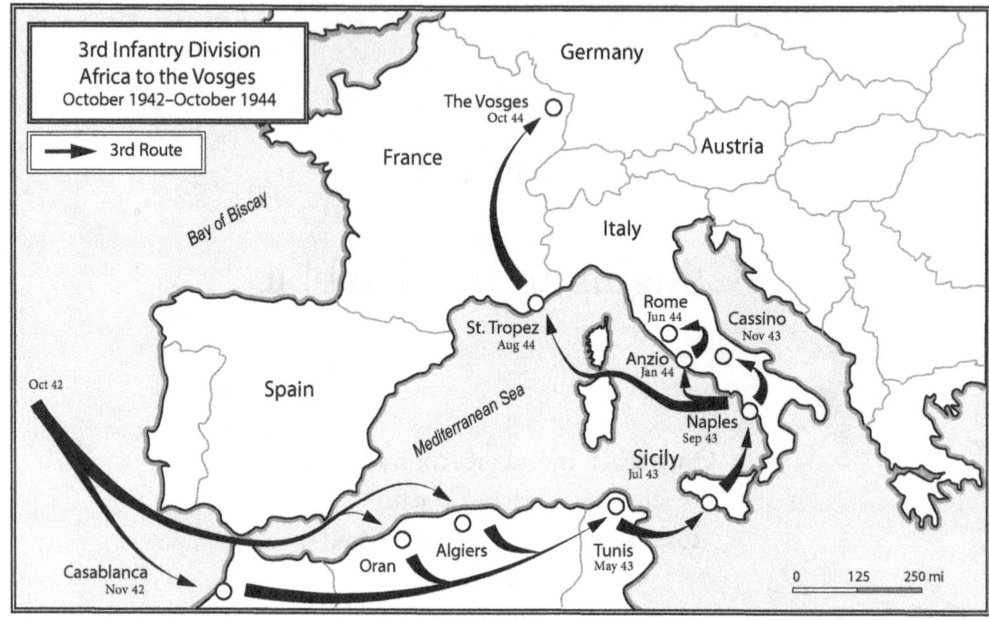

15. 3rd Infantry Division, Africa to the Vosges, October 1942–October 1944

protracted periods preparing for battle or simply marking time, something he did not bother to mention.[1]

Operation Torch was the code name for the amphibious landings in North Africa by the first US Army troops to arrive in the Mediterranean. Their goal was to wrest North Africa from the Axis and reinstate crucial shipping lanes for the delivery of Allied troops and equipment. The Third executed three simultaneous landings: at Casablanca on North Africa's northwest coast, Oran in the center, and Algiers on the east. Harris's unit, the Fifteenth Infantry Regiment, was assigned to Fedala, in French Morocco, just east of Casablanca. Regardless of their landing point, the Third Division troops exuded confidence in the outcome. They had trained for such a maneuver repeatedly before their deployment.[2]

Little did the troops know that, back home, Hollywood rushed the release of the Humphrey Bogart and Ingrid Bergman film *Casablanca* into production to capitalize on the Allied invasion of North Africa. The film captivated American audiences, despite the fact they barely knew where Casablanca was and were not aware of the landings of Allied troops on the continent until well after the invasion. The film went on to win the Academy Award for Best Picture in 1943. Of course, there was no casbah or Rick's Café Américain for men like Walter Harris. While they did not face stiff resistance on landing, he and his comrades were well aware of the dangers.[3]

The first domino, Casablanca, fell three days after the landings. Oran and Algiers followed in short order. And once the surrounding areas were secured, all eyes turned east, tracing the jagged contours of Africa's northern coast to Tunisia. Reaching Tunisia, however, consumed six months of arduous fighting. On May 20, 1943, the Allies held a victory parade in Tunis, the country's capital city, with General Eisenhower and other Allied military leaders in attendance. Remarkably, the Third still found itself in Tunis some forty days later, celebrating anew on the Fourth of July. Nevertheless, with Operation Torch behind them, Italy and what would be called the Italian Campaign loomed. To reach the Italian mainland, however, the men first needed to invade and take Sicily, an island they could practically see from their vantage point in Tunis.[4]

On July 10, Operation Husky launched, marking the Third's second amphibious landing. They came ashore on Sicily's southern coast at Licata, almost due east of Tunis. Then, in quick succession, the Third seized Palermo on the north coast and Messina to the east. Now the troops were staring at the toe of Italy's boot, a mere five miles across the Strait of Messina. Instead of surging forward, however, the Third once again paused to regroup. To some it appeared yet another seemingly unending hiatus.[5]

Welcome news arrived on September 3, 1943: Italy's government had surrendered. But taking control of Italy and liberating the country would still be far from easy. The German army, well entrenched across the boot of Italy, had no intention of capitulating.[6] Days later, together with the US Army's Thirty-Sixth and Forty-Fifth Divisions and British forces, the Third Division stepped out of their landing crafts and onto a miles-long stretch of beach on the Italian coast at Salerno. Fierce opposition greeted the Allies, but they pressed onward, carving a path inland and north in an unrelenting series of land battles that continued month after month. As they advanced, the terrain changed, and with it, so did the nature of the fighting. The toll in lives staggered comprehension. The Third alone lost one thousand souls at Anzio in the spring of 1944 and another five hundred in the battle for Rome in June.[7]

When orders called for the Fifth Army to take over the pursuit of the Germans along the Apennine Mountains, the Third Division enjoyed another "brief" reprieve. Rather than rejoining the troops pushing northward, they turned west, crossed by sea to the French Riviera, and joined Gen. Alexander Patch's Seventh Army to drive the Germans from France under Operation Dragoon.[8] The Third made an amphibious landing near St. Tropez in August, after which they pushed inland and lost another two hundred soldiers. Still, there would be no letup. The miles accumulated, and another series of towns and battles was but one long blur, from Orgon to Orange and then Marseille, Montelimar, and Lyon. The first week of September found them one hundred miles north, facing an obstinate foe at Besançon. In mid-September, it was Vesoul. Although the Allies pushed the Germans back again and again, each withdrawal left behind a hazardous maze of "mines, boobytraps, or log roadblocks," and the Wehrmacht simply dug in anew in a stand of heavily reinforced positions.[9]

The next confrontation took place east of the Moselle River. Another followed in the low, densely forested mountains of the southern Vosges. By now, the summer had given way to autumn, the days of the Mediterranean's sea breezes long forgotten. In their place were brisk winds, earlier than usual rain, and heavy fighting. The encounter with the enemy was close and ferocious. The terror the soldiers faced in the dark persisted long after the battle. For hours, the clatter and clang of the battle rang in their ears and the smell of spent gunpowder stung their nostrils. Surviving left them exhausted.[10]

At the end of the month, one of the war's most brutal battles occurred along the Cleurie River in the Vosges. The cliff-like walls rising on either side of the river valley harbored a labyrinth of stone quarries. Concealed within those quarries were miles of narrow, twisting passageways and hidden tunnels, providing natural defensive positions for the Germans. The Third's Fifteenth Regiment stalled outside L'Omet Quarry, where a barrage of artillery had failed to dislodge the entrenched Germans. Even the elements seemed to conspire against the Allies, as a driving rain, fog, and mist rendered air support impossible. Walter Harris and his cohorts could do little more than conduct a few offensive forays with negligible results. So, they sat, shoulders hunched against the cold and damp air, perched as best they could on the loose scrabble, while runners ferried supplies up the slippery slopes and returned bearing litters of wounded.

It is doubtful that while perched on the scrabble the men had time to reflect on life back home. Perhaps they did, though, to alleviate the stress. And for men from the country's heartland, like Walter, maybe they imagined the World Series—a battle of a different type, but this year, just a few weeks earlier, two Missouri teams faced off for the championship. No one doubted the outcome, with the St. Louis Cardinals, the odds-on favorite, trouncing the St. Louis Browns. Word might have reached Walter. The military had broadcast the Series on its mobile radio station, and tank operators received the signal on their radios. Perhaps he had been a Birds fan and was still reliving the details, imagining the hits and runs and the fans who reportedly consumed "three tons of peanuts, more than 100,000 hot dogs, almost 5,000 cases of beer, and 8,000 cases of soft drinks." At least the revelers and readers of the newspapers the next day had the opportunity to remember the men fighting in far-off lands. Just below the article about the World Series was a solicitation: "Our boys in the armed forces are giving all of their time for us. Give a day's wages to the war chest for them."[11]

"It was jungle warfare," one soldier remarked, "with thick nests of enemy snipers and infiltrating German patrols." Only when the division's tanks dismantled the enemy's stone roadblocks and carved a path into the quarry did the enemy's resistance falter. After a grueling six-day battle, the fighting ended and silence reclaimed the quarry's depths.[12]

Walter Harris's hometown newspaper, the *Moberly Monitor-Index*, in Huntsville, Missouri, reported his account of the battle in the quarries and his role in the effort. The paper proudly announced that Walter was with the "Yanks" who routed the Germans in a surprise nine-hour battle in a quarry in France. Using the cover of the forest, they reported, the "doughboys" climbed the slopes and bypassed the main German force.

But when a patrol party stumbled upon a small group of Germans, alerting them to the American presence, chaos ensued. Bullets flew, and in the firefight a German commander fell and his troops scurried for cover. The American platoons advanced, destroying German machine-gun nests and taking fifty-two prisoners. Then, the men of I Company dug in to wait for relief. The account, printed on November 1, must have made the Harris family proud. Unfortunately, the report lacked the full story.[13]

The saga continued, with the troops making their way north and east along the Cleurie River to the town of Le Tholy, which they captured on October 11. At that point, the Third Division's Seventh, Fifteenth, and Thirtieth Regiments had clawed their way deep into the Vosges Mountains. French troops relieved the men on October 17, but the relief was short-lived.[14] Three days later, the Third assisted with an assault on an enemy communication center in the nearby town of St. Die. The Seventh and Fifteenth Regiments attacked abreast near the town of Brouvelieures, seizing a bridge over the Mortagne River before the Germans could demolish it, and then proceeded northward along easier-going paved roads. On October 24, just short of the village of Les Rouges Eaux, the Fifteenth left the highway pavement and set out through rugged, forested terrain. They encountered light but persistent resistance in a skirmish that lasted through October 25. At that point, the Germans withdrew from the area, leaving scores of fallen Americans strewn across the landscape.[15]

On November 11, the *Moberly Monitor-Index* updated its account of Walter Harris, noting he had sustained serious wounds on October 24 while in France. They added that, although Walter had been wounded twice previously in Europe, neither of those injuries had been serious. Then, three days later, the paper ran a final update, this one reporting Harris had succumbed to the injuries he sustained on October 24.[16]

Walter Harris was awarded the Silver Star Medal for his brave acts in combat on August 14, 1944, during the invasion of southern France. While lacking details, the citation mentions Harris's "gallantry in action while serving with Company I, Third Battalion, Fifteenth Infantry Regiment, Third Infantry Division, in action against the enemy on 15 August 1944. His gallant actions and dedicated devotion to duty, without regard for his own life, were in keeping with the highest traditions of military service and reflect great credit upon himself and the United States Army."[17] Walter Harris was buried in the Epinal American Cemetery in France.

For actions in that same amphibious invasion of France, another soldier of the Fifteenth Infantry Division, second lieutenant and later poet, songwriter, and actor Audie Murphy received a Distinguished Service Cross. For his actions in the fighting along the Cleurie River, on October 2, 1944, he received his first Silver Star and at Tholy on October 5, 1944, his second. Murphy would become the most decorated soldier of World War II and earn the Medal of Honor. He survived the war, served with the Texas National Guard, and became a prominent figure in Hollywood. Audie was killed in a plane crash in 1971 and is buried in Arlington National Cemetery—his grave being one of the most visited of the cemetery's four hundred thousand.[18]

CHAPTER 17

Into Thin Air

Somebody sure could get hurt in one of these damned things.
—James Stewart, pilot

12:16 p.m., Pacific Theater, Pitu Airfield, Morotai Island, Indonesia

The men who took to the skies in the Boeing B-17 Flying Fortress during World War II did not see eye to eye with their counterparts flying the Consolidated B-24 Liberator. Nor did their crewmen. As suds sloshed in heavy glass mugs in pubs and bodegas across the globe, the men engaged in spirited debates about the merits and faults of the two aircraft. No matter which bomber they actually flew, flew in, or maintained, they were fiercely proud of *their* aircraft and believed it to be the superior bomber.

As proof of their convictions, B-17 pilots offered stories of the resilience of their aircraft. They mentioned limping back from a bombing mission in a plane shot full of holes, metal peeled away here and there as if a giant had wielded a can opener on the fuselage, with sections missing on the vertical stabilizer, and a single engine operating. But even missing a piece here or there, they had made it home. Not to be outdone, across the table a B-24 pilot would lean forward, smile, and mention his bomber's superior capabilities, citing the one-thousand-mile range advantage it had over the B-17.

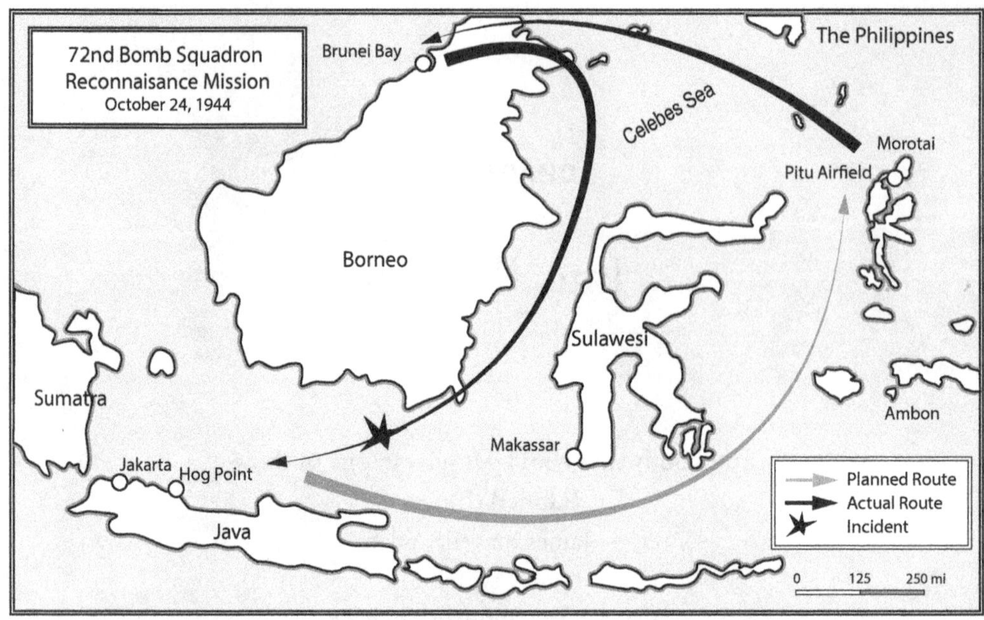

16. 72nd Bomb Squadron Reconnaissance Mission, October 24, 1944

Thus, in his plane he could deliver his payload not only six or seven hundred miles from airfields in East Anglia, England, to Berlin or Munich, as could the B-17, but on missions exceeding twenty-four hundred miles in China, India, and the Southwest Pacific. He could also tout the eight thousand pounds of cargo his B-24 could carry, if needed, a payload twice that of the B-17. So the argument went and on and on, long into the night, while the clinking of glasses and huzzahs played in the background.[1] Decades after the war, the aircrews' sons and daughters repeated the remembered scraps of conversations from their fathers' tales. They inherited their biases and guarded the memories like family heirlooms, firm in their belief in the superiority of the B-17 or the B-24, depending on which aircraft their father had flown.

No matter which side won the argument, if either ever did, the brutal truth remained: many men died in both bombers. As Hollywood film star James Stewart said, making light of what he knew from his experience as a B-24 pilot, "Somebody sure could get hurt in one of these damned things."

Nevertheless, 2nd Lt. William A. Albert Jr., a fervent advocate for the B-24, would have stood his ground, arguing vehemently for his particular Liberator, nicknamed "Red Butt." And those around the table would have yielded to his fact-based arguments. At the time he registered for the draft, William Albert had been working at the Boeing plant in Seattle. So, during the friendly back-and-forth, his firsthand knowledge of the strengths and weaknesses of the bombers lent a level of credibility few could match. Nonetheless, despite his unwavering confidence in his aircraft, the Red Butt perished in the South Pacific along with its crew, at least so the Missing Air Crew Report (MACR) #10018 attested in late 1944.[2]

Born in Canada, William Albert Sr. and his family, including his young son William Albert Jr., had immigrated to the United States and become US citizens in 1936. They settled in Seattle, where William would later attend the University of Washington. In June 1942, he enlisted in the Army Air Corps, and then, almost like clockwork, in July 1943 he received his commission, and in July 1944 he deployed to the Pacific with the Seventy-Second Bomb Squadron, Fifth Bombardment Group.[3]

The group had been in the Pacific since September 1942 when orders came to the Hawaiian Department: "Move one heavy bombardment squadron of B-17s to the South Pacific at once. The squadron dispatched should be the best trained and fitted for immediate combat of all those under your command." Initially, the Seventy-Second Squadron deployed to the Fiji Islands with the Eleventh Bombardment Group.[4] But by the time Albert and his crew arrived, the squadron was flying from Pitu Airfield on the island of Morotai, North Maluku Province, in Indonesia. The US military had built the airfield as a medium- and heavy-bomber base for use by the US Army Forces of the Far East to extend its access to Japanese shipping lanes, where it could hunt and bomb the Imperial

Japanese Navy ships. By the fall of 1944, Morotai was also seen as a strategic base from which the United States could support the retaking of the Philippines.[5]

On Tuesday, October 24, 1944, the squadron's mission was to search for signs of enemy shipping along the coast of Borneo. In the mission report, the route is described as running from "Cape Sempang, Mangayan, along the northeast coast of Borneo to Brunei Bay, then back to Cape Sempang, and then down the northeast coast of Borneo to a spit of land known as Hog Point and then back to Morotai." As such, the route was at least partially over enemy-controlled territory—nothing out of the ordinary for the team aboard the Red Butt or the other aircraft taking off.[6]

At 12:16 p.m., Albert's voice crackled over the radio, signaling the tower of his departure. The brief, routine transmission was the last communication received from the Red Butt. During the late-afternoon debrief, long after the Red Butt failed to return, an eyewitness claimed to have seen William Albert's crew bail out near the coordinates of latitude 0° North and 122° East. Later, that report proved to be in error, based on a garbled message from another crew. With the uncertainty, there remained at least a glimmer of hope for the Red Butt's recovery.[7]

Morotai operation staff dispatched two aircraft to search for the missing crew. As they scoured every inch of their assigned grid, one rescue pilot spotted the wreckage of what turned out to be a B-24. Hopes rose as he circled the area, only to be dashed moments later when they determined the wreckage must have been that of an earlier incident. As daylight dwindled, the search crews returned empty-handed to Morotai. Red Butt and its crew had vanished without a trace.

With the continued absence of concrete evidence, Pitu aircrews speculated about the fate of Red Butt's crew. Had they encountered adverse weather, experienced a mechanical failure, or faced enemy action? Some clung to the notion that if the aircraft had avoided a catastrophic failure, the pilot might have executed a water landing or the men might have bailed out prior to a crash—surviving one or the other incident. Others argued the crew might have been captured or hidden by sympathetic locals in one of Borneo's hidden coves or islets that stud the island's coast. Despite the speculation and the fact that such outcomes had occurred in the past, following protocol, the Army Air Forces listed the Red Butt crew as missing in action. A year later, in March 1946, with still no trace, the eleven men were declared dead and killed in action.[8]

The descendants of William Albert and his crew never gave up hope of finding an answer to the B-24's fate. In 2004, they held their breath when the POW Research Network Japan released a list of names of their prisoners of war by location. The lists were by no means complete, but the names of the Red Butt crew were absent, leaving the sons and daughters as perplexed and frustrated as ever.[9] Then a nephew of the Red Butt's engineer, Tech. Sgt. Josie W. Ivey, learned through unofficial channels that some of the crew might have survived. According to Josie's nephew, the US military launched an investigation after learning of a message scrawled on the wall of a Japanese prisoner-of-war camp cell in Makassar on South Celebes Island (Sulawesi today). While the Japanese had tried to obliterate such messages during and immediately after the war, in this case, the markings were legible and contained the names of several of the Red Butt crew: Lt. Robert M. Schow, navigator; Tech. Sgt. Donald Palmer, radio operator; Pvt. George H. Faust, aerial photographer; and 1st Lt. William A. Albert (written as Sergeant Major Albert).[10] Unfortunately, uncovering the message failed to put an end to the mystery.

Besides the scrawled message, two other artifacts remain for those who might continue the search: the Missing Air Crew Report and a photograph. The MACR includes minute details, such as the serial numbers of the aircraft's four engines (BP-443890, P-443436, BP-44463, and BP-44631) and those of the weapons mounted on the bomber.[11] The photograph of the crew posing in front of their bomber with the serial number 44-40947 provides another clue but also hints at an equally tantalizing and puzzling story. Painted on the aircraft's fuselage is the cartoon figure of a young woman bent at the waist to talk to a hound perched attentively on his hind quarters. The woman wears only a short polka-dot skirt, and in large print to the right of the woman's derriere are the words "Red Butt." Who conceived the image and named the aircraft and what they meant by the nose art are lost to history.

When the plane went missing, neither the image of the charming young woman in the polka-dot skirt nor the meticulously recorded serial numbers of the engines and armaments had the power to unveil the fate of the aircraft and its crew. Perhaps one day in the distant future, a weathered scrap of sheet metal with a piece of a polka-dot skirt will emerge and solve the Red Butt's mystery.

While the odds are slim, they are not nil. The search for the eighty thousand missing US soldiers of World War II continues under the auspices of government agencies and by dedicated groups and individuals. According to the Defense POW/MIA Accounting Agency, officially tasked with providing the fullest possible accounting for the missing, one thousand World War II soldiers initially listed as Missing in Action have been located and their remains retrieved since the 1970s.[12]

CHAPTER 18

Burma Bridge Busters

That's it! That's what we've been looking for. Bring on those bridges!

—Robert A. Erdin

1:42 p.m., China Burma India Theater, Maymyo, Burma

Washington could not afford to devote too many men or too much matériel or attention to distant Burma. Like the Philippines in the Pacific theater of operations, US military brass considered Burma in the China Burma India (CBI) theater a secondary front. But war on the far side of the globe was not a "forgotten war," as it is sometimes portrayed in postwar literature. With its expansionist ambitions, Japan recognized the strategic significance of Burma's 1,275-mile corridor separating China from India. By capturing and controlling the corridor, Japan would gain unfettered access to India. The United States, on the other hand, recognized the logistical value of keeping Burma open. The Allies funneled supplies through the corridor, a lifeline that ran north from the port at Rangoon on the Bay of Bengal and east from India's border with Burma to China. Bolstered by American resources, China could confront the Japanese forces at its back door while the United States, Britain, and Australia faced them in the South Pacific.[1]

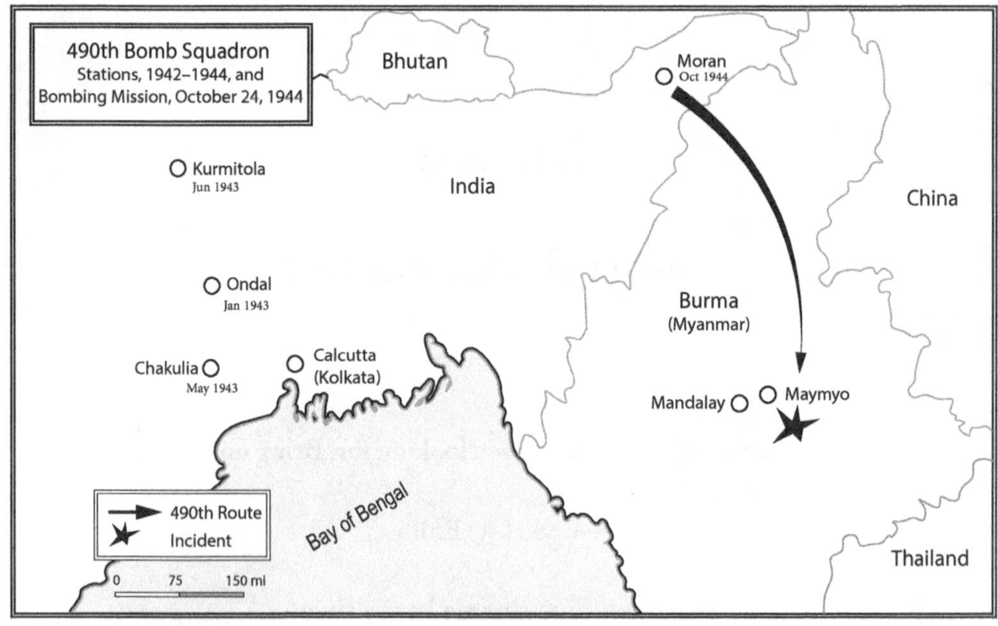

17. 490th Bomb Squadron, Stations, 1942–1944, and Bombing Mission, October 24, 1944

When established in 1942, the vast expanse of the CBI theater stretched from the western port of Karachi (then part of India) three thousand miles to the east coast of China. Southward it encompassed Southeast Asia.[2] The geographical sprawl posed a formidable challenge for the United States in organizing and staffing its forces for war. And while the United States considered its options, contemplated the potential outcomes of one action or another, and then formed and solidified its plans, the Japanese drove across the border and severed the Burma Road. By closing the primary overland supply route, Japan effectively blockaded China. Their troops poured into Burma, reaching a force of one hundred thousand soldiers and airmen, nearly twice the number of Allied troops in the theater. With the changed CBI landscape, the Allies had to pivot. They abandoned their land-based routes to resupply China and turned to the riskier alternative of flying cargo-laden transports between the towering peaks of the Himalayas.[3]

The job of managing air operations in the CBI theater fell to military leader Gen. Lewis H. Brereton, fresh from his command post with the Far East Air Force in the Philippines. Brereton's first challenge was to outfit the newly activated Tenth Air Force to handle the unique demands of the region. India and Burma were plagued with bad weather that rendered high-altitude precision bombing by heavy bombers difficult, if not impossible, particularly during the lengthy rainy season. Brereton's solution was to request a complement of aircraft, not only heavy bombers but also medium bombers like the North American B-25D "Mitchell." The latter were better suited for lower-altitude flying and capable of flying at higher speeds to avoid interception by Japanese fighter aircraft. Brereton also requested fighter and transport aircraft, ground-operation facilities, and personnel to support the Tenth.[4]

The buildup took several months. First, there was a dearth of available aircraft and supporting equipment. Troops in the CBI theater thought of themselves as stepchildren and supplied only when the higher-priority theaters, like Europe, had what they needed. Then came the logistics inherent in the supply line itself—a twelve-thousand-mile umbilical cord stretching from the US heartland to India. The odyssey for men and equipment traversing the route could take up to two months to reach the CBI theater. And once they arrived, a rugged journey lay ahead—a sixteen-hundred-mile trudge via truck, ferry, and rail from Karachi to airfields in northern and eastern India. This leg of the journey alone could easily consume another two months. But Brereton and his staff persevered. The first aircrews arrived in Karachi in early 1942.[5]

In the ever-shifting world of war, as luck would have it, Brereton was recalled to oversee actions in the Middle East. Before departing, he split his still meager forces, sending some aircraft and attendant crewmen to Gen. Claire Chenault and the China Air Task Force to help defend the supply route in southern China. This diversion further delayed the rebuilding of forces in India. Brig. Gen. Clayton Bissell took command and activated the India Air

Task Force, bringing it to full strength by early 1943. The initial defensive mission in northern India metamorphosed. Soon, the Tenth's 341st Bombardment Group was engaging in offensive sorties to disrupt Japanese operations. Their missions included attacking Japanese airfields and antiaircraft defenses and destroying the transportation infrastructure across Burma. Trucks, cars, ships, roads, bridges, and the sprawling two thousand miles of railroad tracks, railroad yards, and locomotives fell within their crosshairs. Among the group's most prized targets were the more than one hundred bridges along the routes between Rangoon and central and northern Burma. Taking one high-traffic bridge out could disrupt enemy military resupply efforts for weeks or months.[6]

Frank Finney was one of the 341st Group's bomber pilots. He had taught high school in Tennessee, but put his chalk and blackboard erasers aside to serve, enlisting in the Army Air Corps. In no time, he earned his wings, received his commission, kissed his pregnant wife good-bye, and was on his way to India. Assigned to the 490th Bombardment Squadron, he arrived in India with his crew in late 1942.[7]

The squadron soon knew as much about the area as anyone. For five months, the 490th claimed Ondal, India, as home, and then Chakulia for a week, then Kurmitola for three months, and then Dergaon for a year. Wherever they went, they lived like many of the local citizenry, often in primitive conditions. While in Kurmitola, for example, the men bivouacked in bamboo huts. They passed the time by complaining of the food, particularly in the early days when "the mess hall menu consisted of eggplant, beef, tea, and bread for all three meals." And then there was the weather. Perched in the middle of the Bengal jungle, Kurmitola suffered both blistering heat and torrential rain, followed by unexplainable cold. Monsoon season ran half the year, from May to October, drenching the mountains and valleys with periods of near-constant rain.[8]

As they acclimatized and trained for their coming missions, Finney and his cohorts adjusted to the routine of combat operations.

In the remote bases, there was a period of "intense activity followed by a period with no missions while aeroplanes underwent maintenance, waited for parts and gasoline, or sat out the weather." Luckily for the 490th, flying in the dryer central region, they were less likely than other units to have to abort their missions due to bad weather.[9]

In February 1943, Frank and his crew embarked on their first combat sortie.[10] Among their targets for the day were road and rail bridges in central Burma. But, as they would soon discover, destroying a bridge was not as easy as one might assume. According to one reporter for the *CBI Roundup* newsletter, "The crews had always dreaded bridge targets most of all, because they were hardest to hit. Whether the planes of the 490th bombed in formation from 5,000 feet or attacked singly at tree-top level, they seldom could hit a bridge." And unless the crews completely demolished a bridge or at least inflicted serious damage, the Japanese could rebuild the structure in short order.[11]

Often, the 490th Squadron's bombs either "ricocheted off their course, skipped clear over the bridge or slid under it to explode on the other side." So, after failing to take out one key bridge, the squadron stepped back to assess their tactics. They tried dive-bombing, but that did not suit the B-25's maneuverability. They tried attacking at treetop level, which was too low for their bombs to deploy effectively. They tried adding air brakes, then spikes, and even parachutes to the bombs. None of the changes made an appreciable difference in their performance. Then, on January 1, 1944, Maj. Robert A. Erdin, the day's squadron leader, stumbled on the flaw in the 490th's bridge-bombing tactics. Usually, the B-25s approached their target on a diagonal or at a right angle to drop their bombs. But on this day, Erdin aligned his bomber with the path of the Mu River bridge before releasing his bombs. As he came in for his pass, a large tree loomed in his path, forcing him to make a last-second maneuver, gunning his aircraft up, and then returning to his bomb run. He was now in a much shallower approach. After releasing his bombs, he looked back and instead of the expected splash of his bombs hitting the water, he saw that the bridge's two spans had collapsed into the river. The shallower dive had allowed the bombs to hit the bridge at a more favorable angle and detonate rather than bounce or skip over the target. "That's it! That's what we've been looking for," Major Erdin is said to have exclaimed. "Bring on those bridges!"[12]

The squadron refined the newfound and newly nicknamed "glip" bombing technique, which became the unit's standard operating procedure. Now, far more successful, the 490th earned a new moniker, the Burma Bridge Busters.[13]

Historians find no major battle or single incident to mark the turning point in the battle for Burma—not even the fortuitous change in bridge-bombing tactics. They point, instead, to the unrelenting attacks from fighters and bombers that gradually eroded the ability and will of the superior number of Japanese forces. With the first signs of progress, the British and US forces adopted a more offensive posture, initiating a ground campaign to regain control of Burma. The 490th supported that effort, too, delivering supplies and providing low-level air support for Allied troops on the ground and strafing and bombing enemy troops and installations. By October 1944, the Allied victory was on the horizon.[14]

Frank Finney moved once again, this time to a base in Moran, Assam, India. On October 24, 1944, with his copilot, navigator, and three gunners aboard, he headed out from Moran on a mission toward Maymyo, known before the war as the "pleasant summer capital of Burma, when administered by the British." If the counterparts of Finney and his crew in the group of B-25s flying along with them had their way, the day would be anything but pleasant in Maymyo. Their goal was to bomb a railroad line about fifteen miles northeast of the city, strafe other military targets, and gather vital reconnaissance. As usual, the pilots expected to encounter antiaircraft defensive fire on the approach to the target, but on that Tuesday afternoon, the flak greeting them was considerable.[15]

During one run at the railroad line, Lt. Ralph Everett and Lt. George Hyde, the pilot and navigator, respectively, of another B-25, saw what they believed was Finney's aircraft proceeding without difficulty. Then on another run over the area at about three hundred feet, Everett and Hyde saw the B-25 a thousand feet above them. This time, a stream of white smoke trailed from Finney's left engine. Everett changed course to follow the stricken bomber, but lost sight of it for a few minutes and then spotted it again, four hundred feet lower in altitude. As he kept pace behind Finney's B-25, its right engine began trailing smoke. From his higher vantage point, George Hyde caught a glimpse of two or three white specks emerge from the aircraft, but if they were parachutes, they did not open. A minute later, at 1:42 p.m., Finney's plane made a gliding turn and crashed into a mountainside. Ralph Everett turned back and flew over the wreckage. The fuselage appeared to be intact, but the tail section had broken away. For the next fifteen minutes, the accompanying pilots circled the densely foliaged and hilly terrain but failed to catch sight of the downed craft or any opened parachutes. On October 26, while carrying out another bombing mission, a dozen B-25s surveilled the area where Frank Finney's aircraft had last been seen, but they too could find no trace of the wreckage. Frank Finney and his crew were eventually declared lost in the line of duty.[16]

The 341st Bomb Group received a Distinguished Unit Citation:

> Waging an extremely successful and highly dangerous bridge-busting campaign along the land corridor then held by the Japanese . . . the Group developed and employed its own style of attack, "Glip Bombing." . . . The cost was not light to the Group, but the interdiction of this overland route was imperative. With extraordinary heroism, gallantry, determination and esprit de corps, the Group not only met the dangerous challenge but established a new record in economy of operations

> in doing so. These achievements . . . are worthy of the gallant traditions of the American military service.[17]

Robert Erdin received the Legion of Merit, Air Medal, and Distinguished Flying Cross in 1944 and retired from the military as a colonel in 1968. He later worked at Lockheed Aircraft Company in Georgia and died in 1996 in Atlanta.[18]

In 1949, the remains of Frank Finney and his crew were recovered and returned from Barrackpore, India, to the United States. They were placed in a common grave in the Zachary Taylor National Cemetery in Kentucky.[19]

CHAPTER 19

A Day at the Beach

War is not just the shower of bullets and bombs from both sides, it is also the shower of blood and bones on both sides.
—Amit Kalantri, *Wealth of Words*

2:00 p.m., Pacific Theater, Marshall Islands

Lloyd W. L. Poovey Jr. had everything going for him. He stood a commanding six feet tall with a slender but sturdy build, a head of wavy light brown hair adding a touch of charm. He was an attractive young man. And he was ambitious, with a business career in mind, in stark contrast to many of his peers—young men who had not yet chosen their life's calling. Lloyd had embarked on his career's journey at Kings Business College and then transferred to North Carolina State College and then to the University of North Carolina–Charlotte, anticipating a more rigorous and thorough curriculum there. Yet, deep into his formal education, he decided the best way forward was to gain more practical experience. He set aside his textbooks and took a job with the State Department in Raleigh, North Carolina. But fate intervened. When the United States entered the war, Lloyd Poovey changed course again. In May 1942, he enlisted in the Navy to serve his country, figuring his career could wait a year or two or however long it might take to defeat Germany and Japan. A year of intensive training as an aviation radioman followed, first at the naval hub of Jacksonville,

Florida, and then at Norfolk, Virginia, a second Navy stronghold. Two years later, Poovey was still in training and the war was no closer to ending. Then, finally, in March 1944, the Navy dispatched Poovey to the Marshall Islands, where he was promoted to aviation radio technician second class for Torpedo Squadron 305 with the US Pacific Fleet Air Force. In this role, he shouldered the responsibility for maintaining radio communications systems for torpedo-bomber aircraft at sea and on shore.[1]

Despite the demands of his war service, Lloyd Poovey found time to enjoy his assignment and his surroundings. He wrote home, regaling his family with stories of seeing Pearl Harbor rebuilding and recovering from the Japanese attack and later of distant Australia. One such letter arrived on his parents' doorstep in North Carolina on October 24.

Lloyd and Nancy Poovey were still savoring his news when, days later, a telegram arrived that shattered their world. It read, in part, "The Navy department deeply regrets to inform you of the death of your son, Lloyd William Poovey, as a result of drowning in the service of his country. No information is available at present regarding recovery of the remains, but because of existing conditions, the remains, if recovered, will probably be buried at sea or in the locality of death. If further details are received, they will be forwarded to you." The missive prompted more questions than answers. What did "drowning in the service of his country" mean? Was he at sea, and, if so, had he fallen overboard? Had he been aboard an aircraft and shot down over water? What was being done to recover his remains? What did the ambiguous "if recovered will probably" be buried at sea mean?[2]

In fact, like countless other soldiers stationed near the sea in temperate zones, whenever Poovey had a few hours of spare time, he joined his friends at the beach. On the afternoon of October 24, they drove to one of the many idyllic spots among the thousands of square miles of beaches on the Marshall Island atolls. There, the three swam, basked in the sun, and snapped photos of each other to send home. Shortly, Poovey took another dip in the ocean. The temperate waters turned deadly as a powerful current swept the young man out to sea and beyond the reach of help.

Lt. August V. Vorndam, Torpedo Squadron 99's commanding officer, included a note about Poovey's untimely loss in his "War Diary" for the month of October 1944. He recounted how Poovey had drowned while swimming near the reef on the ocean side of the island. "Efforts by three men with him that day, a life-boat crew, and a crash boat were unsuccessful in finding him after he was swept over the reef into deeper water."[3]

Accidental deaths, like Poovey's, that happened in moments of misfortune were not uncommon occurrences. Another accident on the same day, this one in San Diego, California, took the life of twenty-year-old PFC Donald M. Padgett. On furlough from the Marine Corps for the first time since he had enlisted, he was making a trip home to see his family. Tragically, at 10:00 p.m. at an intersection just east of downtown San Diego, a collision or ill-fated loss of control of his motorcycle took his life.[4] Half a world away, in Italy, a second, equally tragic, traffic mishap claimed the life of PFC Germain F. Miller. The young man was serving with the Army's Signal Corps, 560th Air Warning Battalion, and had survived operations in North Africa and battles at Corsica, Sardinia, and Italy. As a devout Catholic, when his unit neared the liberated city of Rome, he jumped at the chance to visit St. Peter's Cathedral and the Vatican. He was returning from the visit in a convoy of trucks when the mishap occurred. On a treacherous curve in the road near Montalto, Italy, where the pavement gave way to a gravel stretch of road, the driver lost control of the truck in which Miller was riding. The truck overturned, seriously injuring the young man. Capt. Foster Sweet, Miller's superior officer, sent a letter to his parents informing them of the incident. He mentioned he had summoned a priest to administer last rites. He also noted that while at the Vatican, Germain Miller had had an audience with the pope, and the supreme pontiff had blessed the rosary found in Miller's pocket. "The rosary," Sweet added, "is among his personal effects which are being sent to you."[5]

The Army as a whole, including the Army Air Corps, reported more than twenty-nine thousand accidental deaths during the war.[6] Another twenty-seven thousand soldiers succumbed to illnesses, victims of ailments as innocuous as the flu or pneumonia or to infections or lesions unrelated to battle wounds. According to the US Census Bureau, "World War II was the first war in which there were more American battle casualties, 74 percent of the total, than deaths from other causes, such as accidents, disease, and infections." In the Civil War, 61 percent of those who died did so from nonbattle situations; in World War I, the figure dropped to 54 percent.[7]

One such tragedy struck Capt. Bror H. Anderson. A second-generation Swedish American, Anderson graduated from Cornell University in 1938 with a degree in horticulture. He had a promising future and immediately put his education to use, becoming the head of the Floraculture Department at Alfred University in New York. Like Lloyd Poovey, he too had set aside his personal aspirations to serve his country. In June 1942, when the school term ended, he enlisted in the Army. Assigned to the 500th Armored Field Artillery Battalion of the Fourteenth Armored Division, he trained at Fort Knox and Camp Campbell in Kentucky and then at Fort Sill in Oklahoma. Still holding the image of his future in academia and one day having a family, he married before leaving for the war in Europe. Unfortunately, while in North Africa in the summer of 1944, he contracted meningitis and was admitted to an Army hospital. As his unit departed for Marseille, France, Bror Anderson was left behind. He died in the hospital on October 24, the victim of an unseen but equally deadly foe.[8]

Then there was Pvt. Clarence E. McGirk, a young man who had grown up in the tradition of the military—a member of the Sons of Veterans of the Civil War. In 1943, he enlisted in the Army and joined the 609th Engineers Light Equipage. After training at Camp Gordon in Georgia and Camp Forrest in Tennessee, and prior to deploying to Europe in the fall of 1943, he was granted leave to visit his family. The time passed all too quickly, and soon he was with his Army unit in Europe. He participated in the invasion of Normandy and the subsequent battles across northern France. Although exactly where and when he injured his foot in France is unknown, he sought treatment for the injury at a hospital in Paris. McGirk was discharged from the hospital, although his release might have been premature. Shortly thereafter, he suffered an embolism and was readmitted to the hospital, where he died on October 24.[9]

Most families would have preferred a nobler fate for their husbands, sons, or brothers. The soldiers themselves undoubtedly would have chosen a death that contributed to winning the war, rather than drowning at a tranquil beach, falling victim to a traffic mishap, or after languishing in a hospital bed. Still, they had heeded the call of duty whether they had enlisted or were drafted. Then they embraced their assigned jobs and pursued their objectives with unwavering dedication until they met their untimely end.

Lloyd Poovey's body was recovered on October 25 and shortly interred in a cemetery on Japtan Island in the Eniwetok Atoll, Marshall Islands. His family also placed a memorial at Oakwood Cemetery in Hickory, North Carolina, where other Poovey family members are buried.[10]

Donald Padgett was buried at Rose Hill Cemetery in his hometown of Mason, Warren County, Ohio.[11]

Germain Miller was buried in the Florence American Cemetery in Italy.[12]

Bror Anderson did not live to see his son born on December 8, 1944. After the war, his remains were returned home, and he was buried in Fort Hill Cemetery, Cayuga County, New York.[13]

Initially, Clarence McGirk was buried in a local cemetery in Solons, France. His remains, too, were returned home four years later, on October 24, 1948. He was reinterred in the Hopewell United Methodist Church, Downington, Chester County, Pennsylvania.[14]

CHAPTER 20

A Not So Quiet War

You grew up a poor man's son . . . you became a solider in time of peace. A Christian soldier . . . the war, the terrible war came here and ended all your earthly bliss.

—Olga Huebscher

2:00 p.m., European Theater, Vedriano, North Apennines, Italy

Formed in 1942, the Eighty-Eighth Infantry Division was the first of the US Army's "draftee divisions," units peopled largely by draftees as opposed to volunteers. The inductees were young and inexperienced men, initially from Ohio, Illinois, Missouri, West Virginia, and a smattering of other states. It was an experiment of sorts, a test to see if a group of conscripted civilians could be "quickly and efficiently converted into combat-ready units." The experiment was risky and had to overcome obstacles, mostly related to attitudes. The draftees did not necessarily want to be in the Army or to fight and risk their lives. They saw little they liked in the training camps. On the other hand, they knew a war was on and believed defending their country was the right thing to do. Having signed on the dotted line, they would have to do what the papers said they had committed to do. As Tech. Sgt. Delphia "Del" E. Garris with the Eighty-Eighth's 350th Infantry

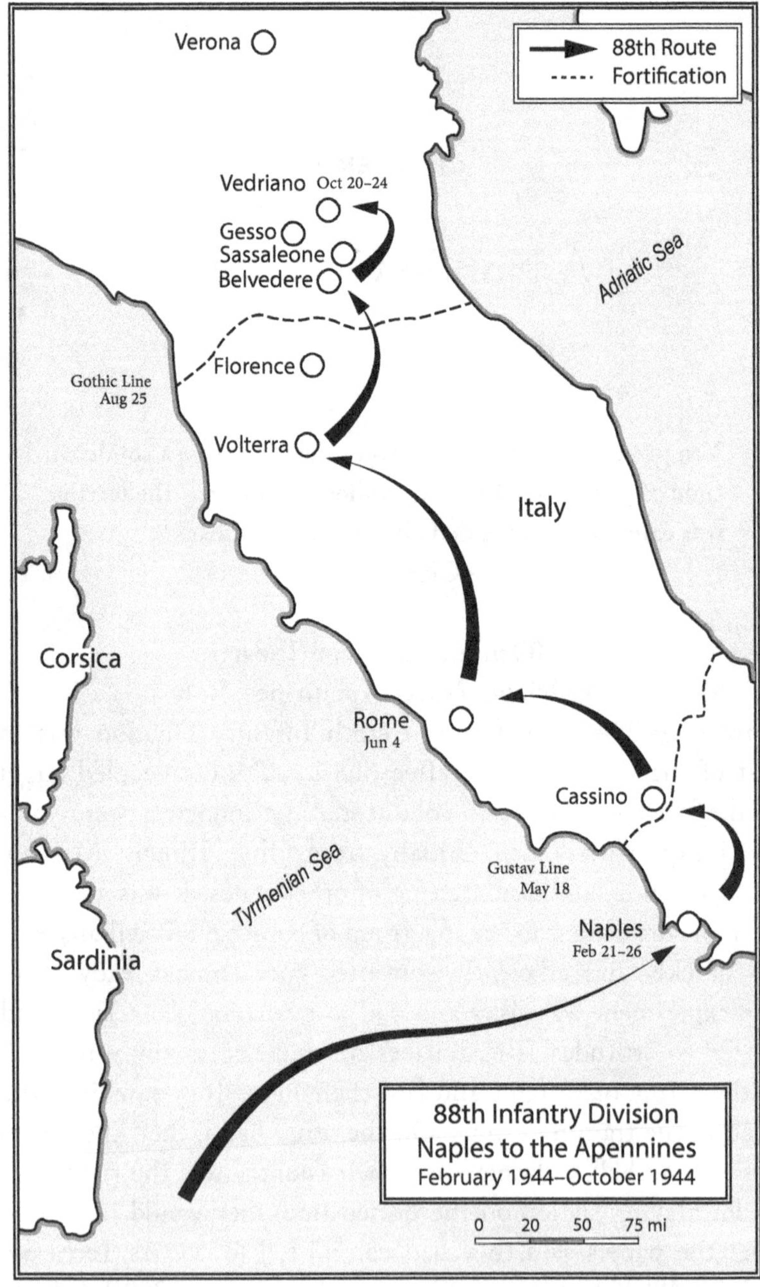

18. 88th Infantry Division, Naples to the Apennines, February 1944–October 1944

Regiment succinctly said, "It's just something that has got to be done. We have got to lick those bastards in order to get out of the Army."[1]

Over the course of the next sixteen months, the former farmers, factory workers, brick makers, and truck drivers underwent a dramatic transformation that defied their roots. They became fit and learned to march and load and unload, fire, and clean their weapons. Most of all, they learned to obey orders and work as a team. At the end of the period, in their case a relatively short one from activation to embarkation, the citizen soldiers of the Eighty-Eighth deployed to North Africa. They arrived there in late 1943, after the tumult of battle had subsided and the Allies operated from fortified bases strung across the coast of the continent—from French Morocco to Tunisia. Now, from those bases, the Allies were moving into the "underbelly of Europe," advancing from North Africa to Sicily and on to Italy. The Eighty-Eighth arrived with the purpose of relieving weary soldiers of earlier deployments—men who had been in action for months.[2]

The Eighty-Eighth was the first reserve division designated to serve as replacements, but the men had yet to prove their capability, not only to their superiors but also to themselves. So, after disembarking in Casablanca, to make doubly sure of their readiness, the Army put the troops through a more intensive curriculum of training than they had yet experienced. Then, in February 1944, the Army deemed them ready to face the enemy. Fourteen thousand men of the division made their second sea voyage, this one a considerably shorter trip—a mere nine hundred miles from North Africa to Naples, Italy. William Savich, then a lieutenant with the Eighty-Eighth's 349th Infantry Regiment, remembered every minute and mile of the crossing. Light rain had fallen throughout the day, and the seas became choppy. The ship swayed from side to side, rising and falling with each oncoming swell. The temperature dropped, chilling all aboard to the bone. Savich and many of his compatriots became seasick.[3]

On landing in Italy, the Eighty-Eighth relieved beleaguered British troops coming back from recent attempts to push north up the Italian peninsula. Now it was the new soldiers' turn to attempt to break through the one-hundred-mile defense labeled the Gustav Line and then make a turn toward Rome. The Gustav Line was the first of several formidable defenses the Germans had established across the peninsula. The second, the Gothic Line, lay another two hundred miles to the north. Both fortified lines ran from sea to sea, and the Allies would have to reach as well as cross them if they were to push the Germans out of Italy.[4]

Before they could reach, let alone challenge, the Gustav Line, the men of the Eighty-Eighth had to cross a hardscrabble of rocks and boulders, steep inclines and descents, and a swift river, easier said than done even without having to carry seventy to eighty pounds of gear, including a rifle, bayonet, ammunition, food, canteen, entrenching tool, first-aid kit, socks, underwear, gloves, and a raincoat or poncho. The landscape tested the men's physical fitness as much as the impending confrontation with the enemy haunted their thoughts. For two months, the Eighty-Eighth made steady progress toward the Gustav Line, establishing and then fortifying their positions across the area as they went. In May, they advanced to and, after several stages of bloody and costly battles on both sides, crossed the line. Their performance had exceeded everyone's expectations. At first, the Army kept the identity of the units responsible for the successful breaking of the line under wraps and far from the press. But eventually, none other than Gen. George C. Marshall allowed its release. Newspapers across the United States had something to cheer about, heralding the draftees as heroes. "All-Draft Divisions Chase Nazis 30 Miles," the *Washington Post* shouted from its front page.[5]

The excitement subsided quickly, and a brief quiet period followed. In June, however, the Eighty-Eighth was once again on the offensive, this time with Rome and the Gothic Line in their sights. For the upcoming assault, the Eighty-Eighth joined forces with the troops of other divisions fresh from a fight at Anzio. Together they liberated Rome on June 4. While the populace swarmed into the streets and cheered the Allies, the Eighty-Eighth had no time to bask in the glory of their success. Soon they were pursuing the Germans across yet another slice of the Italian landscape, this one in Tuscany's rolling hills. There too, the draftees found success. They routed the Germans from the Etruscan hilltop fortress of Volterra and then won a fierce battle at Laiatico, the latter resulting in a Distinguished Unit Citation for the Eighty-Eighth's 351st Regiment.[6]

As the Eighty-Eighth prepared for their next objective—to reach and break through the Gothic Line and then advance to the Po River—the Army was simultaneously preparing for the invasion of southern France. To bolster the invasion force, the Army pulled in as many as nine other divisions, including a few that had fought so well with the Eighty-Eighth in the liberation of Rome. Now a far weaker force, the Eighty-Eighth still had to reach and break through the Gothic Line. Before the assault could continue, the troops, who had been in almost constant combat conditions, rested and reorganized. And in the interim, the military leaders scraped and scrambled for reinforcements, eventually engaging the Thirty-Fourth, Eighty-Fifth, and Ninety-First Divisions as well as British, Canadian, and South African troops.[7] The Allies would need the additional forces. The Germans defending the Gothic Line fully grasped the imperative of holding the Allies, or at a minimum slowing their advance, and brought nine divisions to the front.[8]

The troops were in place, the Gothic Line in sight the last week of August. The battle erupted on August 25 and gathered in intensity through the opening weeks of September.[9] Once again, the attacking Allied troops faced steep ascents, this time up three-thousand-foot ridges defended by a very determined enemy. As the fighting began, so did the rain, turning creeks into rivers, rivers into torrents. The downpour washed out bridges and made quagmires of roads, which hindered critical supply lines. The men were wet, hungry, and tired, their guns clogged with mud. But as soon as the rains abated, they cleaned their weapons, rose, and advanced on the Gothic Line. The enemy waited, concealed in well-located nooks and crannies of the North Apennine's peaks. Conditions here mirrored or eclipsed the trials the Eighty-Eighth had endured in May at the Gustav Line. Long-range shelling, machine-gun fire, treacherous minefields, and yards of barbed wire all but stymied the troops. In places, the fighting came down to face-to-face encounters with bayonets fixed.[10] Finally, at the end of September, the Allies broke through. They stood a mere ten miles from the Po. Spurred on by their proximity to the German homeland, they moved forward, albeit at a snail's pace as they confronted heavy resistance from German armored units. In one eight-day period, they advanced fewer than eight miles—a mere mile per day.[11]

In the ensuing weeks, the Army reviewed and revised its plans to take advantage of more open terrain and to press on, hoping to make significant headway before winter snows blocked the passes. Having driven the Germans from the small towns of Belvedere, Sassoleone, and Gesso, the Allied forces arrived at Monte Delle Tombe. From there they set their eyes on a German stronghold on Monte Grande, still miles ahead. Unsettled by the steady Allied advance, the Germans stepped up their attacks, unleashing a phalanx of snipers and a barrage of shelling on the advancing columns. Allied casualties mounted under the fierce opposition, exhausting the Americans' resources and forcing them to take a defensive posture. When the German offensive quieted, the Allies attacked, fearing that the Germans were shoring up their fortifications. In the black of night, and in the throat of a driving rainstorm, the men of the Eighty-Eighth stepped from their bunkers and foxholes to ascend the steep slope of Monte Grande. Finally, at 11:00 a.m. on October 20, the Allies stood atop the peak with a clear view of the town of Bologna and the Po Valley, where they hoped to establish a base of operations.[12]

The saga of the Eighty-Eighth's march did not, however, end there. The 349th Regiment took Frasinetto and the 350th Farnetto on October 22. As the towns fell, the Germans stirred, reinforcing their divisions, and then commenced counterattacking anew. Two days later, on the morning of October 24, the 351st Regiment's G Company took the town of Vedriano and with it forty German prisoners. Two other companies were ordered to join and assist G Company, which despite their initial success had become surrounded. Intense fire on the Vedriano's perimeter, however, prevented the reinforcements from reaching G Company for the moment.

G Company held their ground and waited for reinforcements, expecting the Germans would try to retake the town. An intercepted enemy radio message—"Attack VEDRIANO. VEDRIANO is decisive!"—confirmed their suspicions. What the Americans did not know, however, was that the German forces mounting the attack had received one of Hitler's "stand and die" orders. They were to keep the town of Vedriano at all costs.[13]

As the 351st contemplated the coming battle, the Germans dispatched a message to the stymied troops of G Company. In exchange for the forty German prisoners, they offered the Americans the opportunity to leave Vedriano unharmed.[14] The offer was a tempting quid pro quo, but at 2:00 p.m., under orders from his command post, Capt. John F. Lanzendorfer, G Company's Second Battalion executive officer, declined the offer. Instead of walking away with his men, he led a new charge forward. More fierce fighting ensued, but by late in the afternoon, the sounds of the battle faded. Now another radio message was intercepted. This time, the Eighty-Eighth's headquarters was caught off guard. In the message, the Germans claimed to have retaken Vedriano, freeing their forty former captives and taking eighty prisoners of their own. Lanzendorfer had apparently surrendered. After nightfall, the Eighty-Eighth sent an attack force toward Vedriano to rescue G Company. When met by intense fire, their worst thoughts were verified. The Germans had indeed retaken Vedriano and reinforced their positions. Then, to the Allies' surprise, as night fell, the Germans slipped away into the fog and the dark with their prisoners.[15]

The fighting that took place as troops crossed first the Gustav Line and then approached the Gothic Line was called the "quiet war," one fought without fanfare and headlines. But not without bullets. By day's end, sixteen men of the 351st perished. As the Eighty-Eighth Headquarters Company later wrote, "It was a quiet sector, but men died there. And others became heroes."[16]

Today, we might call many of the men of the Eighty-Eighth heroes, although they themselves would likely have argued otherwise. To borrow Delphia Garris's words, they were just doing what had to be done. Among them was 1st Lt. William Savich, one of the former seasick members of the 349th Regiment. In June, at Volterra, he had described how an artillery shell exploded, blowing him into the air and killing the men beside him. Then, in early October, when he rose from behind cover to find the source of German gunfire, bullets raked across his calves. Twice wounded and twice evacuated, but undaunted in spirit, he returned to his men at the front both times.[17]

Also of the 349th, 2nd Lt. Alfred H. Vasholz was another man with an indomitable spirit. He had graduated from Technical High School in Crofton, Nebraska, but instead of pursuing a simple life in America's heartland, he elected to fight for his country. He was killed on October 24, leaving behind a wife and a daughter as well as an aunt who later penned a poem to remember his sacrifice.[18]

After a long-needed rest, the Eighty-Eighth Division rejoined the fight, relieving other battle-weary and exhausted troops. In April 1945, they finally crossed both the Gothic Line and the Po River and sent the Germans scrambling back toward the Alps.

In addition to Alfred Vasholz, 25 men from the Eighty-Eighth's regiments lost their lives on October 24, 5 from the 349th, 4 from the 350th, and 16 from the 351st. And, in all, during the nearly two-year deployment, the Eighty-Eighth lost 2,298 killed in action, 9,225 wounded, 941 missing in action, and 647 taken prisoner.[19]

Delphia Garris "licked the bastards," although at times his fate lay in doubt. He was hospitalized in July 1944 for cellulitis, in August for an abscess, in October for enterocolitis, and in November for bronchitis. Despite these misfortunes, he completed his service, was awarded a Bronze Star Medal, returned home, married, and spent more than fifty years with his wife. He passed in 2001 at the age of eighty-two.[20]

William Savich earned a Silver Star for rescuing one of his wounded men from a no-man's-land strewn with mines in the fighting in March 1945. He survived the war as well, married, had two children, and became an insurance agent, dying in 2017 at the age of ninety-eight. Engraved on his tombstone in the Georgia National Cemetery is the inscription "The Battle Is Over, Rest in Peace."[21]

CHAPTER 21

Of Wolfpacks and Windmills

A fighter pilot must possess an inner urge for combat.
—Col. Hubert "Hub" Zemke

4:15 p.m., European Theater, the Netherlands

A year prior to the war's start, the Fifty-Sixth Fighter Group came into being in the coastal city of Savannah, Georgia. The fledgling group was a skeletal entity, comprising merely 3 officers and 150 enlisted men. Their aircraft were equally bare-bones. Even after relocating to Charlotte, North Carolina, in the summer of 1941, where they hoped to augment their aircraft, they claimed a meager assembly of ten well-worn Curtiss P-36s and three Bell YP-39 Airacobras. Fortunately, the war was still six months away. Finally, in October, the nascent "pursuit group" received ten fresh-off-the-production-line Bell P-39s, affording them more effective air-defense exercises.[1]

When the Japanese attacked Pearl Harbor, their training ended abruptly. The group of anxious pilots and crew were entrusted with the job of guarding America's Atlantic Coast, or at least a long stretch of it. Their territory ran from the southern tip of South Carolina at Savannah to the Outer Banks at the northern reaches of North Carolina. The men split the territory between them in thirds, making their homes in the beachside towns of Charleston and Myrtle Beach, South Carolina, and Wilmington, North Carolina.

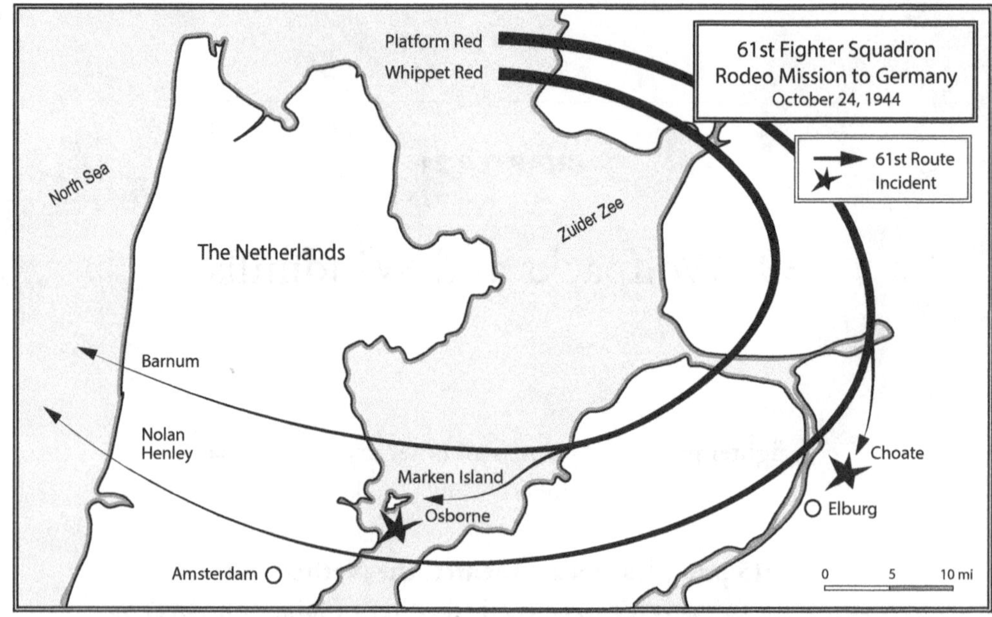

19. 61st Fighter Squadron Rodeo Mission to Germany, October 24, 1944

While now officially in the war, the Fifty-Sixth still flew what an engineering officer described as "an assortment of junk." Their fleet included everything from well-worn Seversky P-35s, Curtiss P-36s, and Republic P-43s to new P-39s and P-40s.[2]

One month into their coastal patrols, the group moved to defend the skies off the coast of New York. The now adept and flexible pilots began a transition to P-38s. But as their assistant material officer, Lt. Hubert Zemke, soon realized, factories could not churn out the new fighter fast enough. And so the group switched to the new and more abundant Republic P-47 Thunderbolt—the aircraft that would earn the Fifty-Sixth a place in history.[3]

Like the perennial debates about whether the B-17 bomber or B-24 bomber was the superior aircraft, pilots of the P-47 and P-51 had their arguments as well. The P-51, with its sleek, aerodynamic profile, had the edge in design, whereas the P-47 was the embodiment of power. With its two-thousand-horsepower engine, the P-47 stood toe-to-toe with any single-engine fighter in the world.

"With its superchargers, the plane climbed fast and performed admirably at high altitude. Its stubby appearance bespoke a ruggedness exceeding that of any other AAF fighter, and no plane of the war proved itself more versatile."[4] So endeared to its pilots for its ruggedness under fire and its ability to bring the pilots home from combat, the P-47 earned the nickname the "juggernaut" or, more affectionately, the "jug."

In January 1943, still languishing in the United States, like other units, the Fifty-Sixth feared they might never see combat. They would, however, soon get their chance. The order to deploy to Europe came that very month. After a six-day voyage on the *Queen Elizabeth* ocean liner turned troop carrier, they arrived at Kings Cliffe Airfield, their new home, albeit for only three months. Moving was nothing new to the group. From Kings Cliffe, they transferred to Horsham (Holton) Airfield in April and then to Halesworth Horton Airfield in July. With each move, while it seemed they frittered away precious time, they inched ever closer to the English coast. Halesworth was a mere eight miles from the North Sea. While noted for their speed and agility, fighter aircraft had a relatively limited range. By departing from England's coastal airfields, like Halesworth, the fighters were better positioned to escort bombers to the Continent and still have enough fuel to conduct strafing and dive-bombing missions of their own.[5]

For the next several months, the Fifty-Sixth did what they had trained to do. They flew "ramrod" and "rodeo" missions, borrowing code names from the British Royal Air Force. Ramrod missions designated standard bomber-escort missions, whereas rodeos were fighter sweeps in which the P-47s bombed and strafed ground installations to lure enemy fighters into combat and away from bombers approaching the area. As their successes mounted, the Fifty-Sixth gained a bit of notoriety.

Much of the group's renown and success was laid at the feet of Colonel Zemke, the former assistant material officer and lieutenant. He had downed five enemy aircraft, making him an "ace," and had been awarded a Distinguished Flying Cross by both the American and the British militaries. As a leader, he was inspirational but demanding. He had once said, "A fighter pilot must possess an inner urge for combat." He expected that urgency in his men and would accept nothing less. Further, as a flyer, he had a thorough grasp of combat tactics and had refined the way his pilots dove to attack and then climbed back to safety and had also established a formation they were to use on approach to targets. The formation, which became known as the "Zemke Fan," specified three echelons of fighters, a lead low squadron covered by a second squadron at a higher altitude with the second covered by a third even higher up and in reserve.[6]

The group's last move, in April 1944, took them to Boxted Airfield, about fifteen miles to the coast but fifty miles farther south and nearer to the Continent. A month later, and with many more missions completed, they earned a Distinguished Unit Citation for their aggressiveness in seeking and destroying enemy aircraft and attacking enemy airfields.[7] The Fifty-Sixth had become the most successful of the Eighth Air Force groups in air-to-air combat and was widely promoted by their moniker, the Wolfpack. Later, Flight Lt. Witold Lanowski, a Polish pilot who had joined the group, said, "When I arrived at Boxted, I quickly became aware that Zemke's Wolfpack was something special. There was an atmosphere about the place; you quickly became aware you were part of an elite organization."[8]

The Fifty-Sixth's next chapter was not as bright. On a mission over the Netherlands on September 18, the group lost sixteen pilots. Of the returning aircraft, fifteen suffered battle damage. Still, they received a second Distinguished Unit Citation for strikes against antiaircraft positions while supporting the airborne attack in the Netherlands.[9]

October was a relatively quiet period for the Fifty-Sixth. At least it was quiet for most members of the group. On the twenty-fourth, they launched a mission back to the Netherlands. Two flights were scheduled for the day. Whippet Red was the code name for the flight with Capt. Eugene E. Barnum Jr. in the lead and Platform Red for the one with Lt. Francis Nolan in the lead. The "red" designation came from the color of the band painted around the cowl of each of the P-47s. It was a visual aid for identifying friend from foe in the midst of aerial combat. In line behind each of the flight leaders were the rest of the members of Whippet Red and Platform Red, including two second lieutenants: William J. Osborne, a former teacher from Lackawanna, New York, in a P-47 christened "Pockey Doc," and George R. Choate, a former General Motors sheet-metal worker and Native American from Indianola, Oklahoma.[10] Osborne was flying with the Whippet Red flight, while Choate flew with Platform Red. Like his comrades, Choate was proud of what he was doing for his country and excited to be a member of the Fifty-Sixth. In a letter home earlier that month, he wrote of being busy at his air base, flying night missions, but also enjoying good food at his station, which included the all-American staple, roasted turkey. While on leave, he had even sojourned to London to take in the sights—an experience almost unfathomable to his Choctaw parents.[11]

On this autumn day in southeast England, low-hanging clouds made for a mere five-hundred-foot ceiling and reduced visibility to less than two miles. Captain Barnum hoped the weather would improve by the time his flight reached the Continent. Yet the overcast persisted over the Channel and grew heavier as they broke the coastline of the Netherlands. Barnum made the call to abandon the mission and return home. As he led the way, he descended below the overcast and followed a course of 270 degrees, taking him and his flight just east of the Zuider Zee, once an inlet from the North Sea. When they passed over the island of Marken, enemy guns opened fire. Their aim was, according to the report Barnum filed later, "very accurate as to range and lead."[12]

At 4:15 p.m., William Osborne's plane was hit by antiaircraft fire, setting his fuel tank ablaze. Barnum radioed Osborne, directing him to head for an open area to land. Osborne acknowledged the instructions and pulled up to about three hundred feet, crossing over Eugene Barnum's aircraft on his way. But then, as Barnum recalled in the debriefing on his return, Osborne "winged over and dove into the water. The plane's left wing struck the water and threw the plane on to its back." Still engulfed in flames, Barnum said, the plane "appeared to explode as it hit the water," just north of the island of Marken.[13]

Fifteen minutes later, Francis Nolan also decided to abandon the mission and return home. Determined to make the most of the situation, he dropped below the stubborn overcast to find a target of opportunity. Failing that, he would search for a safe place for his flight pilots to jettison their bombs, lightening their load before re-crossing the Channel and landing at their home base. Near Elburg, a small town east of the Zuider Zee, Nolan spotted a horse-drawn truck. The low visibility hampered his efforts to line up for a strafing run on the truck, so he pulled up and scanned the skies for George Choate, his number-two man who had been on Nolan's tail in the string of aircraft moments earlier. As he prepared to make radio contact, light flak rose around the Thunderbolts. A second later, he watched in horror as one of his flight made a steep dive from which the pilot did not or could not pull out. The aircraft hit the ground and burst into flames. Francis Nolan circled back over the area. He confirmed the wreckage was that of a P-47, but because of the fire and billows of black smoke rising from the wreck he could not make out the aircraft markings or determine if the pilot had survived.[14]

Also a member of Platform Red, 2nd Lt. Donald Henley reported much the same as he followed Francis Nolan's flight path. Henley had dropped his bombs, although they missed the truck, and so he too pulled up and away. As he left the area, he spotted a burning P-47, completely demolished except for a portion of its right wing. He glanced around for a landmark and noted the location as being near a windmill on a canal bank east of the Zuider Zee.[15]

On returning to Boxted, Francis Nolan and Donald Henley recounted the events of the ill-fated rodeo mission in their debrief, both suggesting the aircraft wreckage they spotted had been

George Choate's P-47. Knowing with certainty only that George Choate had so far failed to return, the station listed him as Missing in Action.[16] Unbeknownst to the Americans at the time, Choate had been killed. Sympathetic local citizens recovered his body and buried him in the village of Harlingen on the Netherlands coast.

After the war, as a symbol of their gratitude, thousands of Netherlands citizens adopted and cared for grave sites of fallen American soldiers. Some continued to visit and tend to their adopted grave site even after the remains were exhumed and reinterred in American cemeteries. Mia Hardy, who lived near George Choate's grave site in the Netherlands American Cemetery at Margraten, was one of those volunteers. She not only tended his grave, but also contacted George's mother and maintained a correspondence with her. Later, she enlisted her husband, Hans Roorda van Eijsinga, in the effort. Mia's dedication intrigued Hans, and he took it on himself to investigate the incident surrounding George Choate's demise. He located a farmer who witnessed the crash as a young boy and had collected remnants of the plane. Members of the van Eijsinga and Choate families eventually met, with the van Eijsingas presenting the keepsakes to George Choate's youngest sister.[17]

As good a pilot as he was, the weather was one element Col. Hubert A. Zemke could not outwit. On October 30, 1944, a thunderstorm took down his P-51 as he was flying over Germany. He survived but was captured and became a prisoner of war. When the war ended, he was liberated from Stalag Luft 1 at Barth, Germany, but remained in Europe, helping to locate and return former prisoners of war. He remained in the military until 1966, once serving at the Air Force's War College. He died in 1994.[18]

CHAPTER 22

Rough Roads and Seas

I furnished the soldier who was shooting the gun, the ammunition. I load the gun, and he shot it. . . . But if my duty was to do what they said, and they put me—if I'd have been put up there, I would have, but they put me here; so, I loaded the gun for the other man to shoot it.

—Lawrence Young Sr., Quartermaster Port Company

5:00 p.m., Pacific Theater, Leyte, Philippine Islands

One of the oldest US Army units is the Quartermaster Corps (QMC). Its roots reach back to the United States' origins in the American Revolutionary War. Often, however, the QMC has carried out its responsibilities quietly, in the shadows of the attention-getting infantrymen storming beaches, the bomber campaigns, and the clashes of battleships and destroyers. Hardly a word survives in World War II literature about those who served in the QMC, yet they were the backbone on which nearly every other unit relied during wartime. At first glance, the mission ascribed to the QMC appears deceptively simple—overseeing the distribution of supplies to Army depots and barracks. However, beneath this seemingly straightforward task is a far more complex undertaking. On the shoulders of the QMC's soldiers lay the responsibility for estimating matériel requirements for more than seventy thousand items, procuring the supplies, handling their storage, and distributing the supplies across the globe. In a historical account of the QMC, albeit one with a biased point of view, the corps is described as having "remained throughout World War II one of the most important of the supply, or technical services."[1]

Despite operating inconspicuously, the supply services have received their due from the highest level of command in the field. In a statement attributed to Napoleon Bonaparte, "an Army crawls on its belly," the French emperor complimented the companies that kept his army supplied with the essentials, in this case food. And in World War II, Gen. George S. Patton quipped that "the two-and-a-half truck is our most valuable weapon," acknowledging the importance of the Red Ball Express in rushing critical supplies from Normandy to the front lines and his rapidly advancing troops.[2]

At the outset of World War II, the supply demands of the war in the Pacific presented a particularly daunting challenge. Military leaders understood that moving supplies to and across the vast expanse of the Pacific theater's island-strewn seascape would be unlike anything encountered in the more familiar land-based maneuvers of the European theater. To worsen matters, the QMC had scant information about the proposed operation. They knew for certain that the United States planned to take Japanese-held territory and had an estimate of the size of the forces to be deployed. Thus, the QMC crafted plans based on their assumption that the United States would make an amphibious landing on a medium-size island. In their planning for the distances they would need to cover, the types of beaches where they would land, and the terrain they would need to traverse after landing to reach storage sites, the QMC used distant Yap Island in the western Caroline Islands as a stand-in. By April 1944, detailed logistical plans covered procuring everything from fuel to food and water to uniforms, loading and carrying the supplies from ship to shore, and establishing and filling island-based storage dumps. One month before the actual invasion of the Philippines, Washington informed the QMC the target would be not Yap Island but Luzon in the Philippines. Everyone returned to the drawing board to recalibrate their supply needs. Now they realized that "more rations, insect repellents, salt tablets, and atabrine were needed, not to mention such items as PX supplies and laundry soap for individual washing."[3]

As soon as US troops landed at Leyte in October 1944, supply and distribution services came to the forefront. Gen. Douglas MacArthur found himself in command of his version of Patton's Red Ball Express fraught with its own set of problems. The chaos of the landing and its aftermath wreaked havoc on the logistical plans so meticulously crafted with pen and paper in distant air-conditioned offices. As in all such matters, the realities of the war had the final say.

The QMC brought the supplies ashore, and then truck companies from the QMC or the Transportation Corps, the QMC's sister-service detachment, sorted and carried the supplies to their designated supply depots. And once the supplies were deposited in the depots, QMC troops were called back into play to guard the installations. In that capacity, they were considered combatants and issued "rifles, machine guns, grenade launchers, and in-trenching tools." This additional aspect of a QMC private's or sergeant's duties brought with it a greater awareness of the war and underscored the gravity of their role.[4]

Those who landed in the early stages and pushed inland faced a slew of issues the grand plan had overlooked. The quartermasters had the added grim task of clearing the beach of enemy dead and organizing captured war matériel. As if that were not enough, where QMC troops advanced ahead of or alongside the combat troops, they, too, had to contend with artillery barrages and deadly bombing raids and strafing attacks from hostile aircraft. The rationale for why the Army had issued them rifles, machine guns, and grenade launchers was made suddenly clear. Still, despite the peril, overall, the QMC troops suffered far fewer casualties than their comrades at the front lines.[5]

The quartermaster troops responsible for getting the supplies to the beach were a unit made up largely of African American men. In fact, an overwhelming majority of black troops were consigned to the service forces. Of the nine hundred thousand blacks in the Army during the war, 78 percent served in construction battalions. They wielded picks and shovels, served as bakers and launderers, tirelessly loaded and unloaded cargo, and executed other similar services. The same was true in the Navy, where blacks were for the most part relegated to positions as mess attendants and cooks. Eventually, when the Army ran short of more skilled manpower needed to transport men and matériel to the front lines, they began assigning blacks to the QMC transportation units. The black soldiers quickly proved themselves "indispensable to keeping the American war machine running."[6]

One such African American soldier, Charles B. Hall, was working in Washington, DC, in 1942 when he decided to enlist in the Army. He was assigned as a private to the Transportation Corps, where he worked his way through the ranks. By 1944, now a sergeant, he found himself assigned to the 164th Port Company in the Philippines, halfway around the world from his hometown in North Carolina. Port companies had already made their mark on D-day in Europe. There the men, again mostly black soldiers, set records for tonnage deposited onto the Normandy beaches in round-the-clock efforts. And while the "stevedores" were often transferring ordinary supplies, according to one account, "enthusiasm goes up when the cargo being taken off smacks loudly of the battlefront. Virtually all of the men prefer unloading military equipment with high priority."[7]

The men laboring alongside Charles Hall were seasoned and highly skilled. They were masters of operating winches and cranes while bobbing with the ocean swells and adept at unloading cargo on coral beaches that bore no resemblance to any port they had ever seen. And while the work itself was dangerous—with untold numbers of broken fingers and smashed arms or legs from shifting loads or snapped cables—carrying out their duties in the war zone made it doubly so.[8] During the landings at Leyte, for example, the 609th Port Company had a platoon aboard three different ships. Even as enemy fire rained down on them, the three platoons unloaded troops and their equipment and did so in record time. Two of the platoons followed the troops on shore, this when the infantry had advanced only two hundred yards. And the danger persisted long after the platoons returned to their ships. A Japanese bomber on fire dove and hit a ship on which the crews were working on deck, and on another ship under attack a hatch exploded, killing three sailors. Charles Hall, injured during a strafing incident over the landing beaches, died of his wounds on October 24, though at an unknown hour.[9]

For PFC Thomas Golden, the Leyte invasion was as close to routine as it could be. He complained only of the delays he encountered. Some were nothing more than a display of the privilege of senior officers. Golden had deployed with a QMC truck company on Hollandia, fifteen hundred miles southeast of the landing sites at Leyte. He was subject to being called whenever and wherever his duties were required. In a postwar interview, he recounted one memorable trip from Hollandia. While transporting ammunition inland to the front, he and the other drivers in his convoy were halted two miles from the battle lines. They were ordered to remain in place and allow the road dust to settle. Soon, a convoy transporting General MacArthur approached and passed the truckers, kicking up the dust again and cloaking Golden and the idling convoy in a murky haze. He said, with a touch of wry humor, "No dust for him. It's alright for us and the others, you know."[10]

As it was for Charles Hall, however, the operation was also a deadly one for another black soldier, CPL Howard C. Bridgett, also a member of the QMC's transportation unit and another "indispensable" soldier. He had registered for the military in his hometown of Lancaster, Pennsylvania. There, with only a grammar school education, Bridgett had to rely on the registrar to complete his draft registration and sign his name to the document. As was typically the case for African American inductees, he had no say in where or what he might be doing in the service. The Army assigned Bridgett to the 3521st Quartermaster Truck Company.[11]

On Tuesday, October 24, four days after the invasion, Howard Bridgett was busy shuttling supplies between the shore and the QMC depots. He might have hoped for nothing more than the inconvenience of being stopped to allow General MacArthur to pass. Instead, an enemy aircraft took that precise moment to strafe a US convoy, with Bridgett wounded in the attack. By the time he reached a military hospital, he was beyond saving and pronounced dead.[12]

A military postwar assessment of black soldiers and the performance of their segregated units noted that "quartermaster truck and service companies, the laundry and dump truck companies, the engineer separate and the port units performed their routine duties as assigned. . . . There were few heroics and few chances for them." Neither Howard Bridgett nor Charles Hall would likely have asked to be called a hero. They simply performed their duty as they saw it and paid the ultimate price for their country.[13]

Howard Bridgett was buried in the Manila American Cemetery. He was awarded a Bronze Star for his service.

Charles Hall was initially buried in the Philippines, but today rests in Arlington National Cemetery.

CHAPTER 23

A Shark with Torpedoes

Dive with our men beneath the sea;
Traverse the depths protectively.
O hear us when we pray, and keep
Them safe from peril in the deep.
—"Navy Hymn," by David B. Miller

5:00 p.m., Pacific Theater, Philippine Sea

The USS *Shark* (SS-314) was a *Balao*-class submarine and the sixth US Navy ship christened after the ocean's fiercest predator. Launched into the fray in 1943, it boasted the latest in maritime design and technology, including a hull fortified by a thicker, higher-strength steel, allowing it to dive to greater operating depths than its counterparts. The ship's specifications listed its test depth at four hundred feet, one hundred feet deeper than the earlier *Gato* class, and the potential to survive at a bone-crushing depth of eight hundred feet.[1] For some aboard, the enhancements offered a measure of comfort, but the more superstitious souls could not shake the history of the *Shark*'s predecessors. Three of the five had met with disaster. The first, a schooner, had run aground while exploring the Columbia River in 1846. Although the crew survived, the ship was a total loss. The third, a World War I–submarine (A-7 and SS-8), suffered serious damage after fuel ignited and caused an explosion in the engine room. Eight men perished while battling the flames

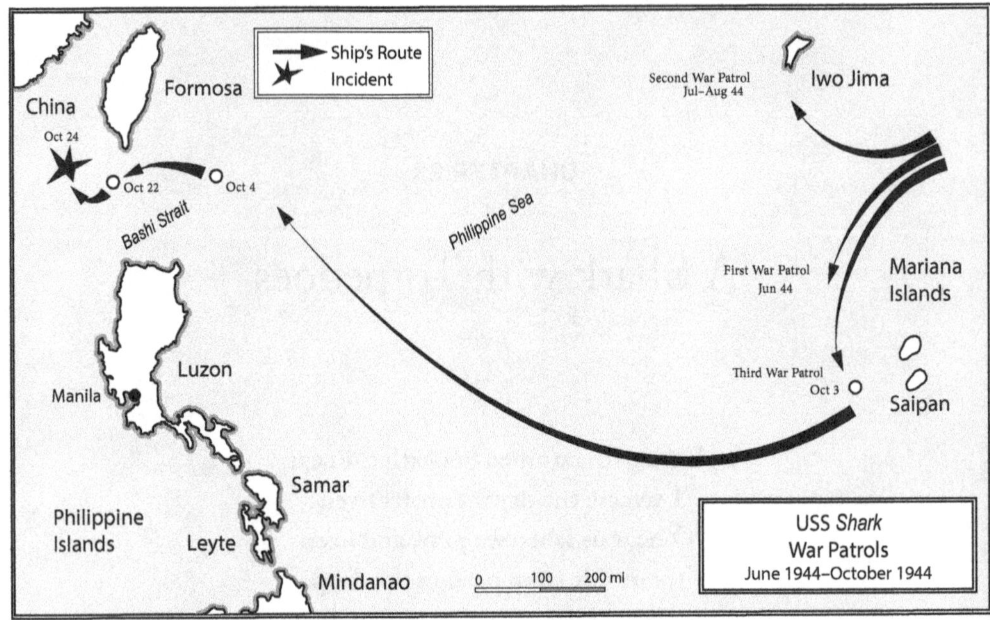

20. USS *Shark* War Patrols, June 1944–October 1944

or in the days after from injuries they had sustained. The fifth, USS *Shark* (SS-174), was at sea in the Philippines when the Japanese attacked Manila in December 1941. Later, while on patrol in the Makassar Strait, the waters between the islands of Borneo and Sulawesi in Indonesia, it vanished without a trace. In March 1942, the Navy declared it lost to unknown causes. Nevertheless, speculation as to the submarine's fate persisted. Postwar reports, although unconfirmed, claimed that while patrolling in Indonesian waters, the Japanese destroyer *Yamakaze* had sunk the fifth *Shark*.[2]

No matter their disposition, the SS-314 crew came together under the leadership of their commander, Edward Noe Blakely. The thirty-one-year-old was a proud alumnus of the US Naval Academy class of 1934. He had played for two of the school's athletic teams, football and track, and was active in the school's campus life. Both extracurricular activities helped him gain the leadership and team-building skills that would one day earn him command of a ship. Gentle barbs posted by his name in the academy's memorial hall are further testament to his acumen and congeniality. One post from a classmate read, "This man has a certain little way all of his own of getting along," by which the writer insinuated with *anyone* he encountered, including women of all description. Another added, "That cheery disposition, even in the teeth of a Monday Morning, is something to talk about."[3] It was no surprise that after graduating and receiving his commission, the born leader progressed from ensign to commander in ten years.

And, further to his credit, under his command, the sixth *Shark* had amassed a notable record. During its first patrol in June 1944, while operating with the *Pintado* (SS-387) and *Pilotfish* (SS-386) as part of a coordinated attack group, the *Shark* submerged ahead of an unsuspecting enemy convoy sailing west of the Marianas. It fired its torpedoes and sank the *Chiyo Maru*, a forty-seven-hundred-ton cargo ship. Then, over the course of the next two days, its torpedoes found their marks again, sinking the *Katsukawa Maru*, a cargo ship, and the *Tamahime Maru*, a freighter. Finally, on the following day, the *Shark* sank the *Takaoka Maru*, a passenger and cargo transport. The string of successes disrupted Japanese troop- and supply-transport activities and sent the enemy scrambling to recover. In the interim, the Allies made the most of the situation and captured the islands of Saipan and Guam.[4]

The ship's second patrol, in which it served on "lifeguard duty" for carrier air strikes off Iwo Jima in July and August, proved less remarkable. It sank no enemy ships but fulfilled its crucial role successfully, rescuing two Navy airmen from a downed torpedo plane.[5]

Before setting out on a third war patrol, the *Shark* returned to Pearl Harbor for routine maintenance. By the end of September, it was ready to resume operations and joined the *Seadragon* (SS-194) and *Blackfish* (SS-221) to form another three-ship coordinated attack group. With Commander Blakely in the lead, the fearsome trio, dubbed "Blakely's Behemoths," arrived in Saipan on the morning of October 3. The next day, they began patrolling the Luzon Strait.[6]

By this time, life in pursuit of the enemy had become routine for the *Shark*'s crew. Watches came and went, as predictable as the tides, until the moment the enemy came into view. In the blink of an eye, everything changed as the crew assumed their battle stations. Even the cooks halted the meal they were preparing and stowed their pots and pans to take their positions. Unless the commander had broadcast his intentions widely, however, men like George W. Pittman, a ship's cook at work in the galley, would know little about the hunt under way or their target. In his formal Navy portrait, Pittman bears a shy half-smile. He appears pleased with his position, coming as he did from a family of cotton and tobacco farmers in the township of Scotland Neck, North Carolina. He had learned to hold his own among his six siblings—five brothers and a sister—and prosper despite having only a seventh grade education. Pittman had much to live up to, carrying the full given name of George Washington Pittman and having the responsibility for a young wife, Mary Lee Bennett Pittman. The couple had only a short time to get to know each other. In 1942, he enlisted in the Navy, beginning a journey that would take him far beyond the crowded home and rural classroom of his youth. The Navy assigned Pittman to the USS *O-8* (SS-69), a World War I vintage submarine designed for coastal defenses. At the time he was a mess attendant second class, a traditional role for young black recruits. In September 1943, he transferred to the USS *Marlin* (SS-205), also assigned to patrol the East Coast of the United States. Aboard the *Marlin* he rose to steward's mate first class and then officer's cook third class before transferring to the *Shark* at its commissioning in 1944.[7]

"Tracking party, man your stations!" Commander Blakely's voice called out over the *Shark*'s intercom on October 22. The hunt was on. The *Shark* had spotted four large enemy ships in the Philippine Sea off the southern coast of Formosa. It reported the sightings to the commander of the Submarine Force of the Pacific Fleet and noted the *Shark* had its full complement of twenty-four torpedoes—evidence it had not engaged with the enemy since departing Saipan.

Unfortunately, as Blakely's Behemoths approached, the convoy dispersed. The *Shark* pressed on, Blakely now more anxious to find a target for the two dozen torpedoes resting in his fore and aft torpedo rooms.[8]

He did not have to wait long. Two days later, at 6:15 a.m., the *Shark* made radar contact with a lone Japanese freighter in the Bashi Straits. The ship's radio crackled to life as Commander Blakely sent word of contact with an enemy ship to his partner the *Seadragon*. In response, the *Seadragon* rose to periscope depth and spotted the *Shark*'s enemy ship in the distance. It had no markings, but the ship's profile was that of a Japanese merchant vessel designed to carry raw materials. Closer and more tempting to the *Seadragon* was an array of other targets. The *Seadragon* set a course to attack the closer ships, leaving the *Shark* to pursue the lone freighter on its own.[9]

After hours of stalking the freighter and maneuvering into position, late on the afternoon of October 24, the *Shark* fired its torpedoes and waited for the sound of explosions. The sub may have surfaced to assess the damage and search for survivors, as required under Navy protocol. This humanitarian policy had been in place since September 1944 when, after several enemy ship sinkings, Allied submarines had rescued Australian and British prisoners of war from ships transporting prisoners to the Japanese mainland. Had it done as required, the *Shark* would have witnessed a most grievous event, for the freighter was none other than the *Arisan Maru*, with eighteen hundred American prisoners in its hold who were now fighting for survival in the water. Before it could begin rescue operations, destroyers in the enemy convoy spotted the *Shark* and turned in its direction. The lone freighter was not alone, after all. The *Shark* rigged for depth charges and dove below the surface.

Japanese naval records note the destroyers *Harukaze* and *Take* were operating in the Bashi Straits on October 24. After the attack on the *Arisan Maru*, the records claim the destroyers spotted an Allied submarine and gave chase, circling over the submarine's presumed location. *Harukaze* made seventeen depth-charge attacks, each with from one to six depth charges. Soon the crew spotted "bubbles, and heavy oil, clothes, cork," and other debris in the water—believed to be signs of the destruction of the *Shark*.[10]

Two hours later, after its own hunt concluded, the *Seadragon*'s commander recorded in the ship's log: "1858 hours: Surfaced and set course for assigned patrol area. Attempted to contact SHARK to give her results of day's attacks, but was unable to raise her."

And at 4:30 in the morning the next day: "Established SJ radar communications with BLACKFISH and asked her if she had radar interference from SHARK. BLACKFISH answered negative."[11]

The *Seadragon* and *Blackfish* remained briefly in the area and made several more attempts to contact the *Shark*, but received no response. On November 27, just over a month after the ship's last communication, the US Navy declared the *Shark* presumed lost. The commander of the Naval Group China later confirmed the sinking of a Japanese freighter in a convoy of fifteen ships headed to the Japanese mainland on October 24. Of the three torpedoes fired at the freighter, the third struck it amidships on the starboard side at 5:10 p.m. As no other submarines had reported attacks in that location, the fleet credited the *Shark* with the sinking and concluded it, in turn, was likely sunk by a Japanese counterattack. The credit came at the high cost of the lives of the *Shark*'s entire crew of eighty-seven, including Commander Blakely and George Washington Pittman.[12]

Edward Blakely commanded the *Shark* from its commissioning in February 1944 to its loss eight months later on October 24. He left behind his wife and a son, Edward. Blakely was awarded a Navy Cross, Silver Star, and Purple Heart.[13]

When the Pittman family learned of George Pittman's death, they were already grieving the loss of one of George's younger brothers, Dennis Pittman. Dennis had served as a sergeant in the Army Air Forces and died in January 1944. Carlton Pittman, twelve years younger than George and the youngest of the Pittman children, may have been inspired by the wartime service of George and Dennis. He enlisted in the Army and served in and survived the Korean War.[14]

Two other US Naval Academy graduates, Lt. Cdr. John D. Harper Jr., assistant approach officer and recipient of two Silver Star Medals, and Lt. (j.g.) William H. Turner, awarded a Bronze Star, were lost aboard the *Shark*. Ironically, onboard the *Arisan Maru* were ten other academy graduates: Cdrs. Alfred E. Grove, Francis D. Jordan, Egbert A. Roth, Douglas E. Smith, and Morris H. Spriggs; a lieutenant commander, Daniel S. Gothie; Navy lieutenant Robert A. Gallaher; Marine Corps lieutenant colonel Charles W. Kail and major Robert F. Ruge; and Army lieutenant Harold F. Monson.[15]

William Emerson, the bomber pilot the *Shark* had plucked from the sea on its second war patrol, returned to the *Lexington* and flew from its deck during the Battle of Leyte Gulf. He remained in the Navy, serving in the Korean War and retiring as a lieutenant commander in 1969. Fifty years later, the Navy awarded Emerson its highest award, the Navy Cross—the delay attributed to the misplacement of paperwork submitted in 1944. In 1995, at the dedication of the Submarine Wall of Honor in Connecticut, Emerson was invited to represent the more than five hundred naval aviators rescued by submarines in World War II. As he rose to make his remarks, he no doubt thought of one lifeguard in particular, the *Shark*.[16]

The *Shark* received one battle star for its World War II service.

PART THREE
EVENING

5:00 p.m., Pacific Theater, the Arisan Maru, Bashi Channel in the South China Sea

Little changed aboard the *Arisan Maru* as it made its way northward toward Formosa. Although the sun had lowered in the sky, the oppressive heat in the hold remained oppressive, the empty bellies of the men empty, their parched throats parched. The shrieks of those who were going mad or had already done so continued, their agony weighing increasingly heavily on those who clung to the threads of their sanity. To wall themselves off from the most desperate, friends chatted in raised voices to be heard over the din. Their conversations ranged widely, from their family back home to their sweethearts, from their favorite foods to what they would do first when they returned, if they returned, and then back to their family and their sweethearts again. When they had exhausted the litany of familiar topics, they made solemn pledges to each other to contact their loved ones should one or the other friend survive.

Just before five o'clock, shouts and the slap of dozens of pairs of feet sounded above their heads. As Robert Overbeck, a civilian prisoner, remembered, "Distant explosions, and the sharp crack of our ship's guns, made us realize something was up. A tremendous crash, which filled the air in the hold with dust and rust, told us that we had been hit."[1] Sgt. Calvin R. Graef, one of a group of prisoners on deck preparing the evening meal, was an eyewitness to the commotion. Years later after the war ended, he remembered several of the Japanese crew ran toward the bow. While they were distracted, he risked a glance over the side of the ship where a series of ripples in the water outlined the path of a torpedo headed toward the stern. It missed, but seconds later another came through the water, aiming for the bow. "It missed by inches," he said.[2]

In the confusion, the Japanese herded the men on deck together and shoved them back into the hold. There they relayed the news of what was occurring topside. Excitement spread across the throng of desperate souls. All had prayed for their deliverance, be it by bomb or torpedo, even if by the hands of their own military, and now their prayers seemed to be answered.[3]

In minutes, a third torpedo struck the hull on the starboard side, ripping into the empty number-three hold. Pvt. Anton Cichy remembered hearing shouts of "Hit her again!" Some postwar accounts claim the blast killed no one or only a few men, although Calvin Graef recalled the situation differently, saying he saw hundreds of dead and dying after the strike. Regardless, seawater flooded in and spread in an instant to the holds containing the prisoners.[4]

Robert Overbeck had heard what had happened after another hellship was torpedoed off the Philippines. Survivors reported that "their ship had gone down like a stone and most of the prisoners had been trapped below decks." Overbeck deliberated and watched as the men crowded near the makeshift stairs in the number-two hold and at the center of the number-one hold, waiting for the hatches to open. Rather than join in the pushing and shoving, he went back and grabbed the life vest he had been issued earlier in the day—one the crew had thrown into the hold not for humanitarian reasons but to make room for loading more cargo in Formosa. Then he changed the overalls he was wearing for a pair of shorts. The fortuitous decision and the delay saved his life—at least for the moment.[5]

Shortly, the hatch cover to the number-one hold flew back. Daylight flooded the compartment, momentarily blinding the men directly below. A guard reached down, drew his knife, and cut the rope escape ladder, dropping the ends into the hold. The hatch slammed shut, and darkness returned.[6] Panic ensued, and a mass of arms and legs and torsos scrambled over each other to gain purchase. A few prisoners managed to shinny up a stanchion, exit the hold, and find two ropes on the ship's deck. They lowered one end of each of the ropes into the hold, allowing the prisoners below to reattach the escape ladder. Shortly, six hundred prisoners made their way out of the hold and onto the deck.[7]

To their surprise and relief, the expected beating or execution from the Japanese guards did not materialize. Most of the crew were nowhere to be seen. The few that remained, although armed, were too busy trying to lower themselves into lifeboats to be bothered with the escaping prisoners. Already, most had abandoned the ship and were rowing frantically toward an approaching Japanese vessel.

Soon, the pressure of the intruding seawater forced the hull to expand. With a crack of splitting timbers, the stern broke away, but both the stern and the ship's main section remained afloat. Still, sensing the end was near, a few dozen men chose to enter the water and then swam toward the nearest of the circling Japanese vessels. The men on deck watched as the Japanese sailors aboard the approaching ship fired shots toward the swimmers, pushed the men away with the butts of long poles, or beat the nearest with clubs. Despite the dire circumstances of their own ship sinking lower in the water with every passing moment and now the realization the circling Japanese vessels would not rescue them, a sense of freedom washed over the prisoners. In the galley, vats of food the crew had been preparing for their evening meal sat untouched, the aroma calling to the men's hunger and thirst. Having consumed only a few sips of water and a handful of rice each day in the hold, they stuffed their throats with whatever they could gather by bowl, cup, spoon, or bare hands. They drank as much as they could swallow in large gulps from the vats of soup and the water barrels, slaking weeks of agonizing thirst. Once their initial pangs of hunger subsided, those who could not swim and others who were fearful of entering the water simply wandered across the crowded deck and peered out at the ships on the sea and the distant and vacant horizon.[8]

The Japanese destroyers *Take* and *Harukaze* that had been sailing with the convoy came to avenge the *Arisan Maru*'s destruction. They found and attacked the Allied submarine they believed had released its torpedoes on the freighter. After firing a series of depth charges, an oil slick, pieces of clothing, and cork floated to the surface—signs the Japanese took to mean their attack had been successful. With the submarine dispatched, the destroyers went about rescuing the men in the water—that is, the *Japanese* men in the water.[9]

The two halves of the *Arisan Maru* remained afloat for more than two hours. "I could see people still on the ship when it went down," Cpl. Glenn S. Oliver recalled. "I could see people against the skyline, just standing there." Then the ship sank, forcing everyone into the sea. The men who had managed to grab one of the life vests glanced at the swales around them and back at the sinking ship and held the vests more tightly to their chests. It did not take a Navy sailor to realize, with the crew having taken the lifeboats, the life vests were now their only hope. What many might not have known was the life-preserving capability of the kapok life vests was estimated to be up to two hours. The less fortunate men, those with no life vests, floated and treaded water where they were and gathered near others and scouted for floating remnants of the ship on which they had been imprisoned.[10]

As darkness fell, men called out to each other or blew their GI whistles.[11] And, weakened by their long captivity, lack of food and water, and wounds, the men in the water began to die. Soon the calls turned to moans and then to silence save for the sound of the crashing of waves in what was reported as rough and cold seas.[12] Of all the Americans who had awoken that morning in the hold of the hellship, only nine survived.

Whether it was the *Snook* or the *Shark* that attacked the *Arisan Maru* is unknown. Samuel Eliot Morrison, an American serviceman, historian, and author of notable maritime histories, maintains that while the *Shark* had informed the *Seadragon* it was pursuing a lone freighter and was itself sunk by Japanese convoy escorts, the *Arisan Mau* was not hit during this attack.[13] And so the argument proceeded. Regardless, neither US submarine was blamed for the tragic loss of life. The hellship, like other hellships, had been sailing without white crosses or other markings to indicate it was carrying prisoners. The Allied submarines had no way of knowing there were friendlies aboard. In any case, as the *Shark* lay at the bottom of the Bashi Channel, the *Snook* continued its seventh war patrol. The ship would be lost on its ninth patrol while in the South China Sea in April 1945.[14]

CHAPTER 24

Lost in the Vosges

We kept telling the long tall Texan we had for a commander that our flanks weren't keeping up with us.

—Sgt. Bruce Estes

9:00 p.m., European Theater, Forêt de Champs, Vosges Mountains, France

On September 9, 1943, with Maj. Gen. Fred L. Walker in command, the Thirty-Sixth Infantry Division became the first US Army division to touch ground on European soil during World War II. They landed near the ancient Greek city of Paestum, southeast of Salerno, Italy, along the Tyrrhenian Sea. Italy had surrendered the day before, but Germany remained defiant and launched a fierce and swift offensive. The untested troops of the Thirty-Sixth, however, proved themselves worthy opponents.[1] Despite a barrage of fire over the beaches and heavy fighting as they moved inland, the troops broke through the German defenses and reached their initial targets. Both sides incurred significant losses of personnel, but after nine grueling days, the Germans withdrew. Men, matériel, and supplies flooded onto the open beaches for what lay ahead. The Allies turned their sights northward, with plans to advance along the coast to Naples and then inland to Cassino. As they clawed their way north, they met heavy resistance and engaged in ceaseless combat.[2]

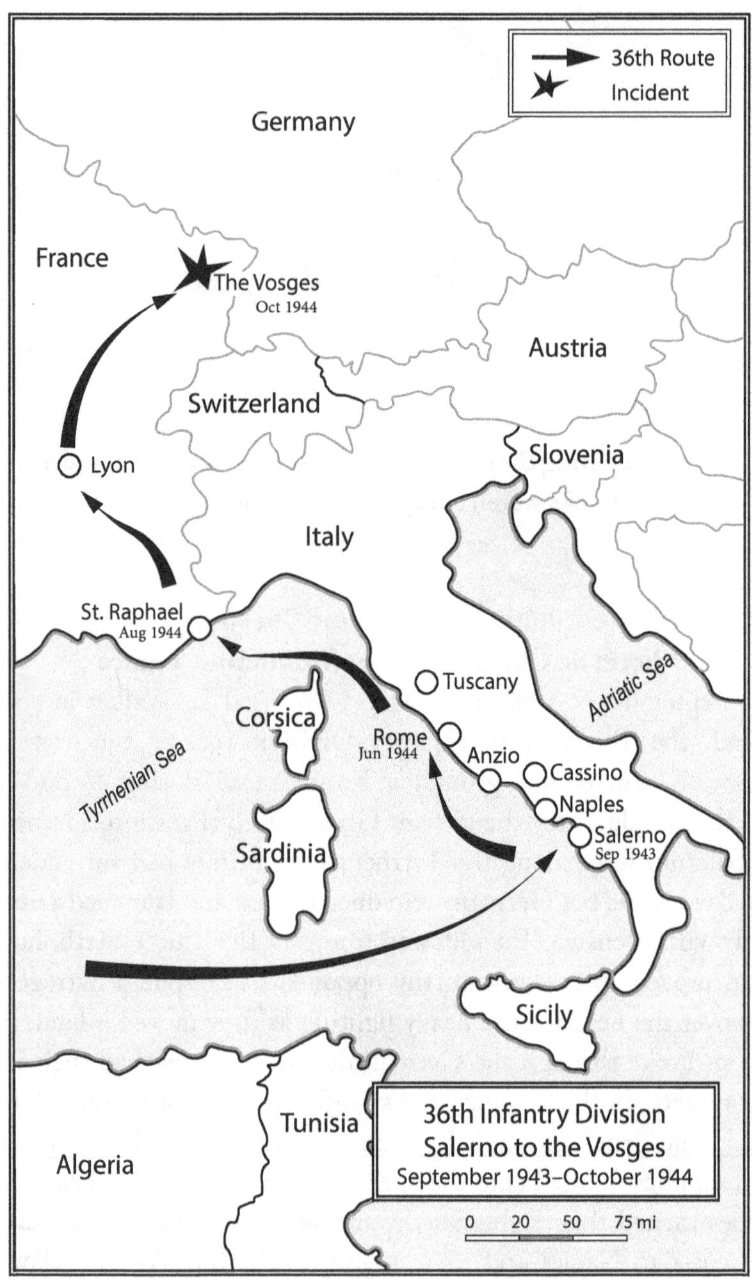

21. 36th Infantry Division, Salerno to the Vosges, September 1943–October 1944

In May 1944, with signs of success at Cassino, the Thirty-Sixth pivoted. They returned to Naples for amphibious training in preparation for a landing in southern France. But then, in response to seemingly ever-changing Army orders, they detoured to Anzio to support a full-scale Allied offensive aimed at capturing Rome. A month later, after achieving their objectives, the men of the Thirty-Sixth earned their bit of victory and celebrated, riding atop tanks or clinging to the sides of jeeps and half-tracks as they paraded through streets crowded with cheering citizens. The celebration was soon over, and the Thirty-Sixth moved up the coast. Bruised and beaten, the Wehrmacht failed to delay, much less stop, the Allied advance. In August, after another change in direction and a thirty-six-hour sea voyage from Naples, the division arrived off the coast of southern France, with its turquoise waters and golden-sand beaches. The anticipated amphibious landing was back in play near St. Raphael on beaches renamed Yellow, Green, and Blue.[3]

The action proved a tactical success, but this time there was no time to regroup, resupply, or celebrate. Instead, they surged forward at a breakneck pace, at times covering close to a hundred miles a day. As they advanced, they liberated a series of French villages and then the cities of Grenoble and Lyon before continuing their relentless march north and east toward the craggy peaks of the Alps and the German border beyond.[4]

In the late fall, the Thirty-Sixth arrived in the shadows of the Vosges Mountains, a range of low peaks and ridges running in a northeasterly line near France's border with Germany. Crossing the range through its mountain passes would put the Allies on the banks of the Rhine River and the edge of the German homeland. But first, the Thirty-Sixth would have to clear the area of stubborn German resistance, an effort that proved more protracted than anticipated. Seven weeks of constant skirmishes ensued as the troops clambered through the foothills. Then they began their ascent of the mountains, trudging along the rugged terrain and up densely forested slopes. As if the terrain was not challenge enough, the weather worsened, bringing cold and wet conditions to the battlefield.[5]

Mostly, the unit's armored tanks and heavy vehicles were ineffective. The rain made a quagmire of sodden back roads and trails and ensnared the vehicles in thick mud. The weather worsened, with "wet snow, fog, mist and low hanging clouds" settling in, impeding the Allies' ability to sight the enemy and target their artillery and hampering air support and resupply. The fight fell into the laps of the infantry. Where once they had advanced miles per day, they now proceeded at a crawl, fighting hard for every foot and yard in their slog forward and upward.[6]

Finally, reinforcements were brought in, including the 442nd Regimental Combat Team, known as a "Nisei" unit—*Nisei* being the term used to refer to second-generation Japanese Americans who were born in the United States and thus had always been US citizens. Their unit was a segregated unit of Japanese Americans with white officers in command positions. Most of the men in the 442nd had, by executive order of President Roosevelt, been placed in incarceration camps in the United States at the beginning of the war. Rather than languish in the camps, the young men chose to join the military to fight for their country of birth—despite how the country had just treated them and their families—and face what some figured was the lesser of two evils.

Until this point, the 442nd had been doing a good job of fighting its way across France. One of the Nisei was Staff Sgt. Robert Kuroda. On October 20, near Bruyères, he distinguished himself with extraordinary heroism as he advanced with his men to destroy snipers and machine-gun nests on the forested slopes. Firing repeatedly, he alone killed more than a half-dozen enemy and destroyed at least two of the enemy's gun emplacements. While Kuroda was embroiled in his efforts, an unseen sniper took aim and killed him. Kuroda was awarded a Medal of Honor posthumously. Now, the 442nd joined forces with the Thirty-Sixth for the assault in the Vosges.[7]

By this time, the Thirty-Sixth's 141st Regiment had been in constant fighting for weeks with only a brief reprieve. Realizing they needed to rest, the Army sent in the 142nd Regiment, allowing the 141st troops to shower, eat a hot meal, rest, and then reassemble for the ascent of a promontory a thousand feet above the valley floor. Four days later, on October 24, the 141st was back at the front line. At dawn the unit's First Battalion advanced through dense woods in an attempt to rout the Germans from their positions. "By mid-afternoon the soldiers had traveled nearly six miles into enemy territory, flanked by the Third Battalion on a ridge to the north. . . . Suddenly the enemy counter-attacked splitting the two Battalions." Although the Germans had withdrawn, they were not finished. They had dug in where they were and had kept a watchful eye on the Americans. When they found the situation advantageous, they pounced, encircling the 141st and severing 270 men of Companies A and B and parts of Companies C and D from the rest.[8]

Sergeant Bruce Estes was a member of the stranded Company C. He had entered the Army in early September 1943 and weeks later found himself in Italy. In an interview decades after the war, he shared his harrowing experience of that day in October 1944. He knew they were headed for trouble and recalled saying, "We kept telling the long tall Texan we had for a commander that our flanks weren't keeping up with us." Once they were cut off, they waited for a lull in the fighting to try to evacuate the wounded from the front line, sending back teams of men carrying their injured comrades on litters. Minutes later, the litter bearers came under enemy fire. They dropped the cumbersome litters, clutched the wounded, and scrambled back to the front lines. It was then that the stranded men realized they were surrounded. Ironically, they were in a region of the Forêt de Champs known as "le Trapin des Saules," or "the Trap of the Willows."[9]

Atop the mountain, the stranded troops set a perimeter in an elliptical ring with outposts scattered a stone's throw away to warn of impending attacks. Wired phones connected the outposts to the men inside the perimeter. Estes recalled they had taken only enough supplies for a single day. And as the day progressed, those rations, ammunition, and supplies dwindled along with their hopes.[10] Realizing how dire their predicament was, the men divided their supplies and sent a desperate, barely audible message to their headquarters, saying, "No rations, no water, no communications with headquarters." Then they dug in for the night, the Americans scratching vigorously to deepen their foxholes and slit trenches in the wet, muddy soil, some adding a cover of dirt, rocks, and tree limbs. Everyone knew the Germans would try to reclaim the lost ground. When the shelling began, the trees burst around them, sending shrapnel and razor-sharp splinters into their flimsy, make-shift shelters.[11]

Regimental headquarters had surmised enough from the desperate but garbled communications to send a rescue effort, the Second and Third Battalions taking on the challenge. They were soon halted, however, by the constant German artillery pounding the ridges and withdrew empty-handed.[12]

It would be a weeklong effort to rescue the "lost battalion." In the interim, Hitler had become aware of the situation and issued orders to his troops to prevent the Americans from escaping or being rescued.[13] And so the ferocious bombardment continued. Casualties in the early stage were surprisingly light. Among the fallen on October 24 was 1st Lt. Charles R. Mattis. The son of Lithuanian immigrants, he had grown up in humble Midwest surroundings. His father, a widower, worked as a mechanic and later a laborer with the railroad to put food on the table and keep the household. Charles attended Harrison Technical High School in Chicago, but when his father died in 1939, he took a job as a store clerk. Two years later, in 1941, he joined the local police force and married Clare Elizabeth Lasky. Still a newlywed, he enlisted in the Army when the war broke out. In no time, he found himself far from his bride and serving in Europe. Assigned to the 141st Infantry Regiment, he distinguished himself in the early days of the Italian

Campaign, receiving a Silver Star for his actions. Now, stranded with his fellow soldiers, Mattis distinguished himself again. He led a platoon to destroy an enemy strongpoint that threatened the battalion's supply and communications route. When they came under a heavy artillery and mortar barrage, Mattis rose to direct his men to better-covered positions. After regrouping, they resumed their charge, but the Germans responded again with heavy fire. Mattis knew his platoon needed to move to an even safer point, and, as the citation for his second Silver Star noted, he "selflessly braved the hostile fire to cover the withdrawal of his men. While protecting his platoon's movement, he was killed by direct small arms fire. His gallant action reflects great credit upon himself and the Armed Forces of the United States."[14]

Another casualty on that fateful day was another staff sergeant from Company H of the 442nd, Shiro Sugiyama Togo, one of the Nisei brought in initially as reinforcements. Now the regiment commanders called on them to join the rescue effort. The choice was not coincidental; the 442nd had a reputation for success in precisely the type of mission the US Army contemplated. Their motto, "Go for Broke," spoke volumes. Shiro Togo was born in Kahuku, Oahu, and graduated from Kahuku High and Elementary School before going to work as a carpenter at the Pacific Naval Base in the Hawaiian Islands. In 1940, he joined the US Army and was in training in the continental United States when the Japanese attacked Pearl Harbor. While logic might have argued for sending Shiro Togo to the Pacific, instead the Army sent him to North Africa. From there, with the 442nd, he took part in the Italian Campaign, which brought him to the Vosges and to his death on October 24.[15]

With each passing hour, the situation on the mountain deteriorated, and the number of fallen rose precipitously. The men sheltered in their foxholes and responded as best they could to the German attacks. As ammunition ran precariously low, they supplemented their supply by retrieving arms and ammunition from dead German soldiers on the perimeter of their holdout. Food supplies dwindled too, and stomachs grumbled louder and longer in protest. The Army attempted to parachute in rations, medical supplies, and ammunition, but the supplies were largely compromised by the enemy, who reached many of the dropped packets first and retrieved them for their own use. Nevertheless, the trapped men hung on, drinking from pools of water left in craters even after they exhausted their supply of water-purification tablets.[16]

During the six-day incident, fifty-nine of the three hundred men trapped on the mountain were killed, mostly while on failed patrols. One patrol occurred on October 25 when the regiment's headquarters sent a thirty-six-man squadron out to scout a for a possible breakout route. Only five of the thirty-six men returned that day, while a sixth stumbled into the headquarters camp days later.[17] The rescue of the lost battalion finally unfolded on October 30, largely thanks to the efforts of the 442nd, aided by the Second and Third Battalions of the 141st. In all, the 442nd sent in three thousand troops and suffered eight hundred wounded and two hundred killed in action.[18] The rescue only added to the unit's reputation, which, in part, prompted Gen. Mark Clark of the Fifth Army to call for the 442nd to lead an attack against the Gothic Line in April 1945. Once again, the Nisei unit proved their worth, breaking through the line and allowing the Allies to push the retreating Germans back, weeks before Germany surrendered.[19] The 442nd would go on to become one of the most decorated units of the war, with 5,200 Bronze Star medals, 588 Silver Stars, 52 Distinguished Service Crosses, 7 Distinguished Unit Citations, and 21 Congressional Medals of Honor.[20] Of the 442nd, Bruce Estes said, "The Japanese came in and relieved us. . . . I didn't see it, but I heard that the first ones to come through were hugged and kissed."[21]

Unfortunately, the rescue came six days too late for Charles Mattis and Shiro Togo.

Despite the 442nd's many awards, after the war questions arose about the choice of sending the Japanese American troops to rescue the lost battalion. No accusations were officially levied and no blame assigned. The insinuation was, however, that because of their heritage the US military willingly risked the lives of the 442nd's troops in what amounted to a suicide mission. Nearly twenty years later, Texas governor John Connally granted honorary Texan status to the men of the 442nd Regimental Combat Team of the US Army from World War II. The award went to thousands. Then, in 2000, President William Clinton upgraded several of the medals the men had received, including twenty of the twenty-one Medals of Honor mentioned above. One of the Medals of Honor awarded was made to then 2nd Lt. Daniel K. Inouye, who later served as a US senator from Hawaii.[22]

Charles Mattis, as noted above, received a second Silver Star Medal (Oak Leaf Cluster) for his actions during the entrapment of the 141st Infantry Regiment. Clare Lasky Mattis never remarried and lived in Chicago until her death in 2010.[23]

Shiro Togo received posthumously one of the fifty-two Distinguished Service Crosses awarded to the 442nd Regiment. He also earned a Bronze Star and other medals.[24]

Bruce Estes remained in combat through the end of the war and was discharged in December 1945. He became a carpenter and an electrician, married, and had two children, three grandchildren, and ten great-grandchildren. He died in 2016 at the age of ninety-one.[25]

CHAPTER 25

Under Cover of Darkness

The low slow target was "capable of absorbing a great deal of punishment."

—Lt. Cdr. Deane Freeman

11:35 p.m., Pacific Theater, Hollandia, Indonesia

The last hammer had struck, the last welder's torch spark doused, in April 1944 when LST-695 launched from Jeffersonville, Indiana. After winding its way down the Mississippi, the "landing ship, tank" arrived in the vibrant port of New Orleans, where it received its commission and Lt. Deane Freeman Jr. took command. He oversaw the shakedown and gunnery exercises in the waters off the Florida panhandle and then sailed to Cuba and on to the Canal Zone, reporting for duty with the Seventh Fleet. Traffic through the Panama Canal caused the LST to moor at the canal's entrance for two days, finally making the eight-hour passage through the iconic passageway on July 9. With the confines of the Mississippi River, the canal, and even the relatively small Gulf of Mexico behind it, the LST entered the vast expanse of the Pacific Ocean. Thousands of miles of open water lay ahead. Lieutenant Freeman set a course for Noumea, New Caledonia, to join the US Seventh Amphibious Force.[1]

Throughout August and September, LST-695 ferried men and materials into place from New Caledonia to the Admiralty

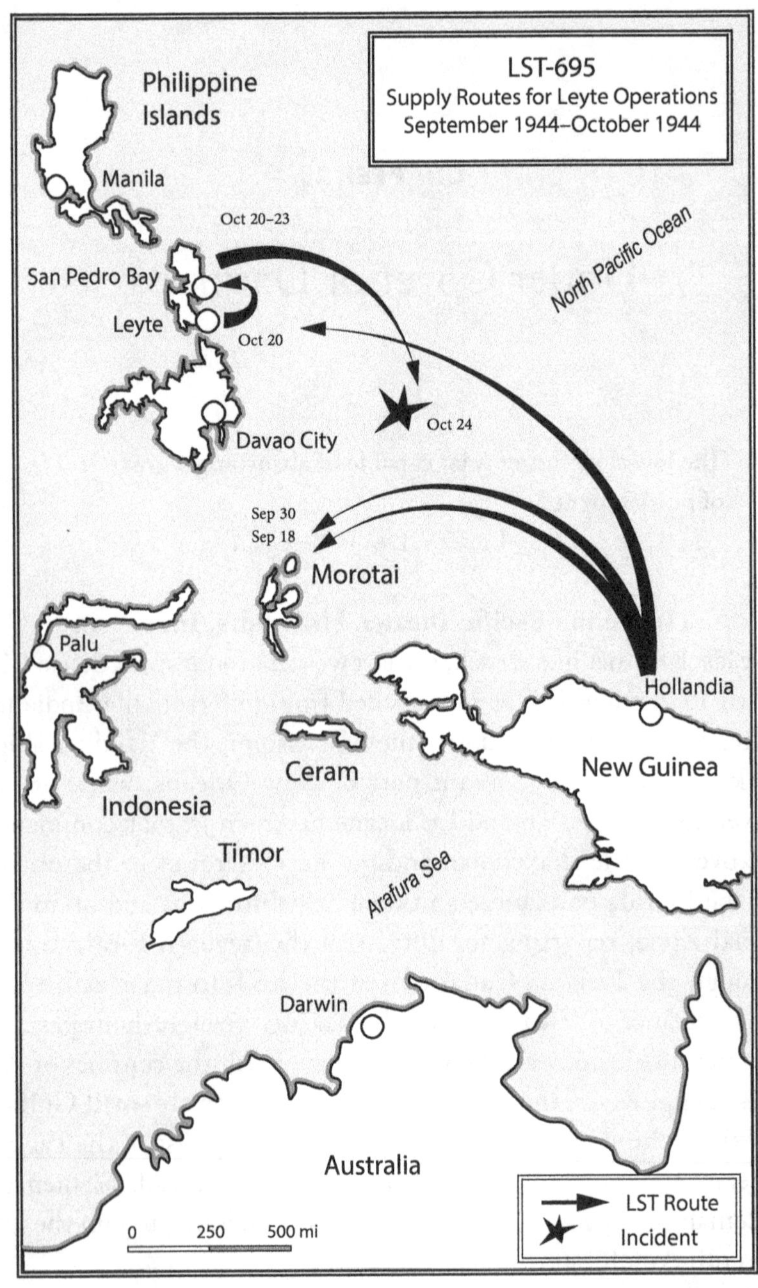

22. LST-695, Supply Routes for Leyte Operations, September 1944–October 1944

Islands and to New Guinea and wherever the Allied island-hopping campaign required. On September 18, as the landing ship, tank, approached the harbor at Morotai Island, Netherlands East Indies, Freeman and his crew saw their first signs of war, a Japanese bomber. The aircraft, at first only a distant speck, grew ominously closer, "flying very high, out of range, coming up over the ship's stern and heading north." When the plane came within range, antiaircraft fire erupted from ships in the harbor, their artillery dotting the sky with tiny black clouds. Electricity charged the air around the crew on the LST's deck, standing the hair on their arms upright.[2]

Unscathed by the barrage, the bomber released its payload, one bomb missing a landing ship, tank, on LST-695's port side and another a destroyer escort on its starboard. The attack was over in minutes, the bomber disappearing as quickly as it had come. LST-695 beached, unloaded its cargo, and then headed with the convoy back to the north coast of New Guinea.[3] The trip to Hollandia, the ship's home port, proceeded without further incident, but for the men onboard the craft, the world had changed. Suddenly, the mundane routine of boarding men and materials on the beach of one South Pacific island and transporting them nine hundred miles to another was neither mundane nor routine. This was war, and the reality of it grabbed everyone's attention.

For five-foot-ten-inch, 140-pound Petty Officer Vernie E. Musgrove, the encounter had set his heart racing. As a shipfitter, his job was to make vital repairs while at sea, a job that took him to every nook and cranny of the ship. Whether the young man was making repairs on deck or pulling some other duty topside, that particular day in September, he might have caught a glimpse of the bomber and noticed the bombs hitting to his right and left. After the bomber disappeared, Musgrove breathed a sigh of relief—LST-695 had escaped without damage, and his ship-fitting skills were not required. But the experience was not one he would forget. It would fill his next letter home to his family in Virginia.[4]

Musgrove had dropped out of school in 1942 and picked up the trade of welding, following in his father's footsteps. He took a job as a railway repairman before joining his father as an employee of the Norfolk Naval Shipyard. Once the war broke out, he changed direction, taking his skills to the military. He enlisted in the Navy as a shipfitter and had the good fortune to train close to home in Norfolk's Amphibious Warfare Training Center. In February 1944, the Navy assigned Musgrove to LST-695, where he became a "plank owner," an unofficial but cherished award designating him as a member of the ship's crew at commissioning. After five months at sea, his aptitude proven, he was promoted to shipfitter second class.[5]

As September waned, LST-695 made another run to Morotai, seeing enemy action for the second time as it pulled away from Pitoe Beach, an idyllic strip of white sand and turquoise waters on the island's southern coast. Two enemy planes were spotted approaching the beach, seemingly intent on attacking men the LST had disembarked moments earlier. On shore, guns unleashed heavy antiaircraft fire, and LST-695 joined the effort with its 40- and 20-millimeter batteries. Lieutenant Freeman reported later, "No bombs were dropped by the enemy on the convoy, though several were observed bursting on shore."[6]

A month later, on October 16, the landing ship set sail from Hollandia to the Philippines to assist with the October 20 Allied invasion. Its decks were laden with troops. Besides its crew, twenty-three officers and nearly five hundred enlisted men of the US Sixth Army were aboard. And below, in the holds, sat more than four hundred tons of mobile cargo and one hundred tons of bulk cargo. By the time the ship arrived, White Beach on Leyte was stacked high with cargo from earlier supply deliveries. Nevertheless, it disembarked the Sixth Army troops, along with their tanks and trucks, and added the remaining cargo to the rapidly growing mountain of crates, cartons, and boxes on shore. Then LST-695 pulled away and anchored in San Pedro Bay to wait for a convoy to assemble for the return voyage to Hollandia. At 3:23 p.m. on October 23, the convoy having formed, the landing ship was under way and homeward bound to New Guinea with other ships of Task Group 78.1.[7]

By nightfall, all was peaceful. The seas were relatively calm, the air clear, with the moon breaking the horizon. Belowdecks, another member of LST-695's crew, Seaman Wanza E. Matthews, who, at nineteen years old, was the youngest man aboard, was perhaps writing home to his parents in Arcadia, Florida. It was a letter his mother would read aloud to his eight younger siblings: five boys (Millard, Willard, Eugene, Willie Dean, and Wilburn) and three girls (Wilma, Mildred, and Christine). Matthews was a slight young man, weighing a mere one hundred pounds and standing five feet, three inches tall in his stocking feet. His diminutive stature was due, in part, to a traumatic incident at the age of thirteen in which he was shot in the abdomen. The incident was the classic case of two young boys playing with a loaded handgun, one aiming it at the other and, thinking the gun was unloaded, pulling the trigger. Wanza suffered multiple punctures to his intestines and spent a year recovering from his wounds. Later, he had the added misfortune of being in his bed when the family's house caught fire. Undaunted, and despite his still tender wound, in a demonstration of ingenuity and good sense, he pushed his mattress out the window and followed it outside. According to his sister Christine, Wanza never managed to put on weight after the shooting. Even the Navy recruiting office turned him away, telling him to eat bananas for two weeks and come back and try again. He did as the recruiter had suggested, gained the needed weight, returned, and signed on the dotted line.[8]

Apparently, Wanza Matthews had a cat's nine lives. Besides surviving the gunshot and the house fire, he survived drinking kerosene as a toddler. And once, during a family fishing trip, he wandered off into the woods and had to be rescued by a search team. Then later, on another sojourn into the woods, the boy was bitten by a water moccasin and forced to suck the venom from the bite to save himself. But he could not cheat death forever. And at sea on that seemingly peaceful night in 1944, Wanza's luck ran out.[9]

At 11:35 p.m. on October 24, LST-695 was two hours out of Leyte and making its way east at nine knots through low swells.[10] Lt. Hugo O. Stevens, the executive officer, was at the helm, anticipating the change of watch coming at midnight. Across the ship, men awakened and prepared to relieve their shipmates. Lieutenant Freeman was in his quarters sleeping restlessly, if at all. For the last week, he had been frustrated with the poor seamanship he witnessed in the convoy to Hollandia. He described the experience in his log as "poor station keeping by LST-744, necessitating LST-695 pulling out of column several times." The condition persisted, and a few days later he wrote that ships in the convoy were steaming "dangerously close during the [mid] watch."[11]

As Freeman tossed and turned, unbeknownst to him and to all the others aboard LST-695 or, for that matter, aboard any ship in the convoy, a powerful threat lurked beneath the waves. An Imperial Japanese Navy submarine had spotted the convoy and was stalking the ships under cover of darkness. In command of the Japanese submarine *I-56* was Lt. Cdr. Morinaga Masahiko. This was the ship's first war patrol, and he was determined to make it a successful one. It had departed Kure, Japan, on October 15 with orders to patrol the seas east of Mindanao in the Philippines—its arrival date estimated to be October 24. From the array of ships in the convoy, Morinaga selected LST-695 as his target and called for a torpedo strike. At 11:35 p.m., three magnetic exploder-equipped conventional torpedoes shot from their tubes and sped toward the homeward-bound craft. Seconds later, three explosions echoed back through the water. Morinaga was elated, believing he had struck three transports.[12]

The first torpedo struck LST-695, sending shock waves throughout the ship. Seconds later, another torpedo followed, tossing Seaman Maynard Swisher and Seaman Robert Lambert into the sea. They had been standing watch in the 40-millimeter gun tub at the ship's stern. Freeman scrambled from his bunk, dressed hastily, and took command from Hugo Stevens. General quarters sounded.[13]

The strike caused significant damage, mostly at the stern, where it had blown off the port-side rudder and jammed the starboard rudder into "a nearly horizontal position." An ensuing explosion forced the decks at the stern into each other, raising the fantail (the deck above the rudder) two feet and tearing a thirty-foot-by-fifteen-foot hole in the deck. The skin of the ship bent upward around the hole and buckled the hull forward while indenting the ship's side and bottom, caving in the surface and distorting the starboard side. One observer wrote later, "The port side of the stern, below the second deck is nonexistent." As a result, the mangled ship lost steering control and power in the port engine. Twenty minutes later, the starboard engine overheated as well.[14]

Hugo Stevens summoned officers and enlisted men to help recover the wounded and dead from across the ship and to search for men who had fallen into the water. Despite their own injuries and ignoring the possibility of further injury, volunteers ventured into the dark and heavily damaged crew quarters. Simultaneously, a four-man damage-control party slogged through water-filled compartments and ducked below and around twisted metal to assess the damage and determine if the ship could be made watertight. Within fifteen minutes, they reported to the commander that the LST was stable and no longer taking on water. Freeman's belief in the sturdiness of his vessel was validated. He had once said of the "low slow target" that it was "exceptionally good—capable of absorbing a great deal of punishment."[15] Much the same could be said for the crew. As Freeman later wrote of the exemplary action of his men, "In the immediate wake of the attack, when there was imminent danger of further enemy action (a possibility of foundering many miles offshore, and when many) [*sic*] shipmates were dead and dying her men had rendered assistance when it was badly needed and conducted themselves most creditably."[16]

By this time, other ships in the convoy had come to LST-695's aid. LST-170 sent boats into the water to help locate those blown overboard, finding and rescuing Seaman First Class Lambert. LST-170 also transferred medical staff and supplies to the damaged ship to help triage the wounded, identifying those most in need of medical attention and those they believed were past help. Morphine was in short supply, and so it fell to the commander and the medical officers to determine who could benefit most from a shot of the painkiller and who would receive a simple saline solution. The horrific task so disturbed Freeman that it haunted him for the rest of his life. The mere mention of morphine, regardless of context, caused him considerable stress.[17]

As soon as the chaos subsided, LST-986 took LST-695 under tow, and LST-170 followed closely behind. For defense, a submarine accompanied the three-ship convoy as they headed to the closest repair facility at Peleliu, some two hundred miles east. While under way, LST-695's crew prepared for burials at sea. On October 26, with Deane Freeman officiating the somber ceremony, the LST sent twenty-two of its crew into the water. Freeman then began the most heart-wrenching task reserved for him by virtue of his command—notifying the next of kin of those who had perished. His daughter recalled him stating that the day he wrote the letters was the worst day of his life.[18]

The US Navy awarded eight Bronze Stars and five Silver Star Medals to crew members who retrieved wounded and deceased men trapped in the crew quarters and those who helped establish the ship's seaworthiness in the aftermath of the attack.

Vernie Musgrove and Wanza Matthews were among those buried at sea. All five of Matthews's brothers served in the military. Millard served in the Army in Germany during World War II, Willie in the Air Force and Eugene in the Army during the Korean War, and Willard and Wilburn in the Air Force during the Vietnam War. All five returned home safely.[19]

Maynard Swisher's remains were not recovered, and he was declared Missing in Action. Seaman 2C Leonard D. Gooden had been unaccounted for since the attack, but on November 1 his body was discovered in the ship's mangled crew quarters. He, too, was committed to the deep with the commander and eleven of LST-695's surviving crew in attendance.[20]

On October 24, one of the convoy's escorts, the frigate USS *Carson City* (PF-50), made an unsuccessful attempt to sink the *I-56*. Six months later, however, LST-695 would have its revenge. Five destroyers and a TBD Avenger torpedo plane from the USS *Bataan* (CVL-29) sank the *I-56* while about 150 miles east of Okinawa.[21] By then, LST-695 was preparing to be towed, first to Pearl Harbor and then to the West Coast of the United States, for repairs. But when the war ended in the summer of 1945, work on LST-695 was halted, the Navy deeming the ship "surplus to Navy needs." Salvageable material was removed and what remained sold for scrap. Deane Freeman received the ship's bell, a lasting memento of his resilient "low slow target." Today, on special occasions, Freeman's family rings the bell in his memory.[22]

PART FOUR

DAY'S END

We just wanted to survive.
—Pvt. Anton E. Cichy

Midnight, Pacific Theater, the *Arisan Maru*, Bashi Channel in the South China Sea

Nightfall brought no relief to the men in the water. On the contrary, if anything, their situation had grown more dire. The cold wind blew stiffer, and the ocean swells continued to chop, buffeting the men, sapping their last ounce of strength, and dashing any hope of survival to which any of them still clung. Most who had gone into the water in the aftermath of the attack on the hellship had by now slipped below the surface. The calls and cries and whistles of distress that pierced the air in the first hours had grown more intermittent, more distant, their tone having gone from desperate to plaintive. Now they amounted to the whimpers of men resigned to facing death.[1]

Men lucky enough to have grabbed a life vest earlier wore them to keep afloat in the high wind-whipped sea. The rest relied on flotsam scattered across the water, wooden planks from the ship's deck and sections of storage compartments, hatch covers, bamboo poles, and crates.[2]

Robert S. Overbeck was a civilian working as a mine superintendent in the Philippines before the war and joined the Army immediately after the Japanese attack in 1941, becoming a lieutenant. An educated, decisive, and determined young man, he had not lingered aboard the *Arisan Maru* after the torpedo strike but instead was among the first to enter the water. There, as he treaded to keep afloat, he watched the enemy escorts turned rescue ships pull fleeing *Arisan Maru* crewmen aboard from their lifeboats. Inexplicably, but fortunately, once emptied of its passengers, rather than destroy the lifeboats, the sailors allowed the craft to drift away. Overbeck swam toward one boat, reaching it after dark and pulling himself aboard. To his great surprise, inside he found ten gallons of water. Later, he hoisted in a box that drifted by only to find within a sail designed for his lifeboat. For now, lacking oars, he rested, sprawled across the bottom, and let the current take his small craft where it would.[3]

Yards away, two other men, Sgt. Avery E. Wilber, from Appleton, Wisconsin, and Pvt. Anton Cichy, from Urbank, Minnesota, who had been in the water for four and a half hours, spotted a lifeboat and its passenger, Robert Overbeck, who helped them aboard. Relieved and spared the need to tread water or cling to improvised floats, they still could not escape the cold and wet, as water sloshed over the gunwales, covering the bottom of the boat. For now, however, they were alive—exhausted and choking on seawater, but alive.[4]

The next morning's first light revealed the gray outline of the lifeboat and its three passengers to Master Sgt. Calvin R. Graef from New York Mills, Minnesota, and Cpl. Donald E. Meyer from Whiting Lake, Indiana. Together, they released their hold on the bamboo poles that had kept them afloat through the night and, with all the strength they could muster, swam toward the boat and joined Robert, Avery, and Anton. As the five took stock of their situation and made rudimentary plans, they scanned the sea for other survivors. But the cries and whistles had ended. Only the haunting sound of the vastness of the ocean prevailed. No one could be seen in the water, if indeed anyone else had survived.[5]

Overbeck had studied astronomy while at Columbia University before the war, never imagining the knowledge could save his life. Based on his estimate of their position, the direction of the winds, and a basic knowledge of the outline of the coast of China, he charted a rudimentary course to reach the Chinese mainland, some three hundred miles distant. In what can only be described as an epic effort of survival, the men sailed west for two days. On the third day, while twenty-five miles off the coast, the crew of a Chinese junk spotted them and brought the weary men aboard.[6]

After an exchange with their rescuers, largely conducted in sign language, the Chinese understood the men were Americans and needed to reach land and friendly forces. Two and a half days later, they came ashore in China and were handed over to a Chinese guerrilla force who took them to a town in Lufeng, Shanwei Prefecture, Guangdong, and then up the coast to Hoifung. From there, with the aid of the Chinese, they made a cross-country journey of eight hundred miles on foot and by car, truck, bicycle, and plane. In fourteen days, they reached the US military post in Kunming, the eastern terminus of the Himalayan supply route, known as "the Hump." At the end of November, the United States flew the five *Arisan Maru* survivors from Kunming to India and then to North Africa and Bermuda. On December 2, they reached Washington, DC, where George C. Marshall pinned Purple Heart Medals on the four soldiers in the group. Finally, the men went home to be reunited with their families.[7]

While newspapers across the country regularly printed accounts of prisoners of war, the five survivors of the *Arisan Maru* sinking received little press. In fact, reports of the award ceremony in Marshall's DC office were ignored by the major papers, perhaps as the government was still investigating the account and had asked the young men to refrain from speaking of the incident until later. A photo of the men with Marshall appears not in the *Los Angeles Times* or *Chicago Tribune* but in Donald Meyer's hometown newspaper in Wilmington, California. The three-sentence article reads, in part, "Four American soldiers, escaped prisoners of war from the Japanese, were awarded the Purple Heart by General George C. Marshall." There was no mention of the *Arisan Maru* or the other eighteen hundred prisoners and their fate.[8]

The first reports of the sinking were printed in February 1945, but even they were often relegated to a brief mention on the front or a few paragraphs in later pages of America's newspapers. The headlines focused on the firebombing of Tokyo and the US Fleet's hunt for the Imperial Japanese Navy ships in the Pacific. At the bottom of page 1 of the *Pittsburgh Sun* on February 16, 1945, for example, was an easy-to-overlook title, "2nd Jap Prison Ship Sunk, 5 Yanks Say." The War Department was still investigating the reports and had not released the survivors' names or confirmed the number of prisoners lost. Congress, if it had known about the incident, remained silent as well. During the congressional session for February 15, while the House deliberated pending cabinet nominations, the national debt, and economic reform, the Senate paused to honor Susan B. Anthony on the 125th anniversary of her birth. The four-thousand-word tribute, no doubt one that had consumed days or weeks to write, was read into the record. Whether anyone in Congress knew the names of the five survivors, the names and faces of Cichy, Graef, Meyer, Overbeck, and Wilber soon became known, and more stories, even more page 1 stories, appeared.[9]

Families of the nearly eighteen hundred who perished did not receive official notice of their family members' demise for almost a year. The signature of Maj. Gen. Ulio, Army adjutant general, was on the letters sent to the next of kin. The letter to PFC Frederick J. Elkes's family, dated June 18, 1945, read, in part, "The International Red Cross has transmitted to this Government an official list obtained from the Japanese Government, after long delay, of American prisoners of war who were lost while being transported northward from the Philippine Islands on a Japanese ship which was sunk on 24 October 1944. It is with deep regret that I inform you that your son . . . was among those lost when that sinking occurred and, in the absence of any probability of survival, must be considered to have lost his life."[10]

Notice of the deaths of other prisoners on the *Arisan Maru* also found their way to the public that summer. On June 21, the *Fort Worth Star-Telegram* announced the death of 1st Lt. Edgar B. Burgess, a Fort Worth native, under the page 6 heading "Captive since Fall of Bataan: Family Learns Husband Was Killed When Jap Prison Ship Was Sunk."[11] Notice of the death of William Wight, one of the twins who served in the Philippines, as mentioned earlier, was announced in the *Cambridge (NE) Clarion* on June 28, 1945. William's parents had taken matters into their own hands. After first learning he had become a prisoner, they traveled around the country to meet and speak with men who had served in the South Pacific with the hope of learning more. Now they needed search no further. According to the newspaper, the International Red Cross found that William had died on October 24, 1944.[12] Hometown newspapers across the country did the same, highlighting their local heroes, one by one, city by city, a steady drip of lives.

As it so happens, there were other survivors of the tragedy. Cpl. Glenn S. Oliver created a makeshift raft from bits and pieces of the sunken hellship. He was soon joined by Sgt. Philip Brodsky, who had a broken hand. The two worked together to improve their raft, and, although Brodsky later said they did not get along, they survived, eating two tiny fish that washed onto their raft and drinking what rainwater they could capture. An Imperial Japanese Navy destroyer found the two men on the fourth day at sea and turned them over to the authorities in Manila where, in a bit of déjà vu, they were sent aboard the *Hakusen Maru* to Takao, Formosa. On board, they met PFC Charles W. Hughes, yet another *Arisan Maru* survivor. For a period, Oliver and Brodsky were interned at the Toroku POW Camp, one that had less severe work requirements, in consideration of the men's poor state of health.[13]

From Formosa, Glenn Oliver was sent to the Osaka POW Camp No. 10-B Maibara, Shiga Prefecture, in Japan, where he worked as a stevedore until the war ended. Oliver, who had served with the 192nd Tank Battalion, attributed his survival to his being "'a good Minnesota boy who went into the war fit from eating lots of farm vegetables and drinking his milk." He also credited the survival tips he learned as a Boy Scout; his desire to return to his wife, Esther; and plain old good luck.[14]

Philip Brodsky was transferred among a series of camps on the Japanese home island for the remainder of the war.[15]

Charles Hughes died a month after reaching the Shirakawa POW Camp.[16]

Besides the five men who reached China and freedom and the three who survived but were recaptured, a ninth man, BSN Martin Binder, survived the torpedoing of the notorious hellship. Binder, who had been aboard the USS *Pigeon* before surrendering to the Japanese on Luzon, had been floating on a makeshift raft on his own until picked up by a Japanese transport. He, too, was sent to Japan and spent the rest of the war interned in prisoner-of-war camps near Tokyo, including Toroku, where he may have found Glenn Oliver and Philip Brodsky, at Sendai Camp No. 3.[17]

After forty months in captivity, upon the surrender of Japan in 1945, Oliver, Brodsky, and Binder were repatriated to the United States.[18]

Although thirst, heat, and beatings accounted for many deaths of the Allied prisoners of the hellships, the vast majority of loss of life onboard was attributed to the sinking of the makeshift prisoner transports by Allied attacks. Indeed, the *Arisan Maru* was the fifteenth hellship to be sunk by Allied forces. The loss of the ship's eighteen hundred prisoners remains one of the largest maritime disasters and losses of American lives in history. But it would not be the last hellship to suffer "friendly fire" before the war ended. In December 1944, after departing Manila,

American bombers struck the *Oryoku Maru*, sinking the ship and resulting in the death of roughly six hundred Allied prisoners aboard. The surviving one thousand of the ship's original sixteen hundred prisoners, were placed on another hellship and less than two hundred survived the war. And, in January 1945, American planes targeted the *Enoura Maru*, damaging the ship and resulting in the death of approximately four hundred of the thirteen hundred prisoners (three hundred of which were Americans).[19] The Japanese were able to corral the surviving prisoners of both hellships and send them on to Japanese labor camps. These sinkings, too, escaped notice of the press until the war's end when the survivors were repatriated. By then, although there were occasional articles about the mistreatment the prisoners suffered as well as uplifting stories of returning soldiers, the country was looking forward and moving on.[20]

On a more positive note, the eight *Arisan Maru* survivors who were repatriated to the United States prospered at home, most living well into their later years.

Robert Overbeck was fortunate to have escaped work detail in a prisoner-of-war camp where his knowledge of mining would have been invaluable to the Japanese—should he have made his skill known. After the war ended, however, he did leverage his knowledge for a career at Alcoa, becoming the head of Alcoa of Costa Rica. He died at age fifty-five in 1972 while working in San José, Costa Rica.[21]

Anton Cichy died on October 27, 2009, at the age of ninety-five in his home state of Minnesota.[22]

Avery Wilber, a native of Wisconsin, died in Michigan in 1999. He was eighty-six years old.[23]

Calvin Graef, initially forbidden by the US government to speak of the fates of individuals aboard the *Arisan Maru*, later spoke to many families of the prisoners, sharing his experience and providing what comfort he could. Graef, who was from Minnesota, died in New Mexico in 1997 at the age of eighty-one.[24]

Donald Meyer, of Whiting Lake, Indiana, died in 1999 at age seventy-nine in California.[25]

Glenn Oliver died in Minnesota in November 2012 at ninety-three. During a reunion with his family, he and his wife, Esther, whom he had married just prior to deployment, cut a celebratory cake with a Japanese saber Oliver had brought home from Japan.[26]

Philip Brodsky of Atlantic City, New Jersey, was born in 1919. He recorded his memories of the war and as a survivor of Bataan and the *Arisan Maru* in an oral interview in 1981. He lived to the age of ninety, passing away in 2009.[27]

Martin Binder of New Castle, Pennsylvania, died in 1982 at the age of seventy-eight.[28]

Epilogue

Setting aside the familiar stories of the attack on Pearl Harbor and the invasion of Normandy, there are other days through which similar stories of American fallen could be told. August 9, 1942, for example, during the Battle of Savo Island when America lost four heavy cruisers and twelve hundred men. Or November 13 that year, with the loss of five Navy vessels, including the *Juneau* with five Sullivan brothers aboard, claiming a total of one thousand lives. Or December 18, 1944, when a typhoon sank ship after ship in the Pacific and killed close to twelve hundred. Or March 19, 1945, when twenty-five US bombers were shot down over Berlin and enemy aircraft strafed and bombed American ships in the Pacific for a loss of eleven hundred lives. But October 24, 1944, is notable for both the magnitude of the losses and the number of theaters of war in which those losses occurred. They include the casualties from the sinking of the *Arisan Maru*, but also from those aboard the USS *Birmingham* and USS *Princeton* and those lost during the landings on Leyte in the Philippines. They include the loss of life in locations scattered across the United States. And they include the fallen from skirmishes in the mountains of northern Italy and eastern France as the Allies pushed the German Wehrmacht back toward their homeland.

These pages have been filled with tales of death of, for the most part, "common" soldiers, sailors, airmen, and marines, the "small" men and "small" deaths referenced at the outset. They range from Paul Miller in the early-morning hours of Tuesday, October 24, 1944, to Wanza Matthews who perished in the waning minutes of that same day.

Some who perished that day were fortunate to have been beside a brother or a close friend who might have given them comfort in their last moments. Others died alone in a foxhole or as they scrambled through thickets toward a machine-gun nest or after having been swept into dark waters. For many of those who survived, the images of the carnage stayed with them. The survivors of the *Arisan Maru* tragedy spoke of the dwindling cries of the weak and wounded men clinging to whatever might have kept them afloat until they lost their purchase. The survivors of the explosion on the *Princeton* never lost the sight of the blood that drained in rivers from the decks of the *Birmingham*.

Grief at the loss of a son or husband washed over the families and friends of the fallen. Fathers and mothers wept for having willingly sent their sons to the fight, no matter how noble the cause. Countless wives clung to the memory of their dead husbands and never remarried. The fallen were heroes to their loved ones and to those who chose to honor them with a medal for their valor. Mostly, however, they were young men who did what they had signed up to do. And when called on, in some of the darkest moments, they stepped forward despite the danger and the cost.

One particularly poignant account comes from the chaplain aboard the *Birmingham* as the wardroom and corridors filled with the grievously wounded.

> Throughout this initial period, there was no sign of confusion, even though suffering shock and in many cases probably in great pain until the morphine began to take effect. They remained quiet and fully cooperative with those attempting to render first aid. Again and again, I was urged by those horribly wounded to help others before themselves. There were no

> out-crys and in cases of those with clean outs which were not hemorrhaging too fast, agreed cheerfully in every case saying, "O. I am all right, don't worry about me." . . . For sheer courage, bravery, and in many cases out right heroism, that first hour in the wardroom following the explosion surpasses anything I could ever have imagined or have believed possible.[1]

Today, long after the conflict ended, the twenty-six hundred fallen are remembered by faithful and dedicated sons and daughters, nieces and nephews, and grandchildren who heard firsthand from family members who knew the young men and women before they went off to do their duty. Increasingly, however, as in all wars past, there remains only a frayed letter or journal, a creased photograph or newspaper clipping, a medal attached to a faded ribbon, a name mentioned in a footnote of a book about the war, or nothing at all.

Those who fell are commemorated by tombstones or on the tablets of the missing in one of America's 16 cemeteries on foreign soil and in Hawaii, in one of the 155 national cemeteries from Maine to New Mexico across the United States, or in individual cemeteries and family plots across the country from Sgt. Charles Olsen's grave in Oak Hill Cemetery in Blackearth, Wisconsin, to 2nd Lt. Fred Swank's in Live Oak Cemetery in Manchaca, Texas. In their day, newspapers took pride in publishing news of their hometown heroes. They printed the names of local men who had joined the military, wrote of their send-offs, their furloughs home, their engagements and weddings, their brave actions in combat, their awards for valor, and their homecomings or obituaries.

Still, in a postwar interview of survivors of the *Arisan Maru* tragedy, Calvin Graef and Donald Meyer concurred: "Deep within at least two of the surviving soldiers is a sense that history has somehow failed them, that the magnitude of their experience and the lives of their comrades have not been properly acknowledged. Today, Graef and Meyer suggest, is the perfect time for Americans to pause and remember, just as they have done every day for the past 50 years."[2] Coming as it did six to nine months from the end of hostilities after many decisive battles had been fought, and when the end was in sight, the October 24 incident is an outlier. Had the sinking of the *Arisan Maru* not occurred, the loss of the remaining eight hundred souls would make that Tuesday just another terrible day in the war. But outlier or not, the stories here representing the fallen on that day provide a better sense of the size and scope of the war and encourage us to look more closely at the events and stories of other days in the war—even the most average of them.

May these twenty-six hundred service members and all those who fell whether in the major battles of the war or in the sinking of supply ships, in air-reconnaissance patrols, in truck convoys, in accidents, or from diseases or maltreatment, regardless of theater, whether on the first day of the war or the last, have a chance to have their story told and be remembered.

In their honor, the names of those who perished on October 24, 1944, are listed in the appendix.

APPENDIX

American Military Who Died on October 24, 1944

Rank and Rating Abbreviations

1, 2, . . . 5	Class or Grade	JG	Junior Grade
1LT	First Lieutenant	LCDR	Lieutenant Commander
1SGT	First Sergeant	LT	Lieutenant
2LT	Second Lieutenant	LTC	Lieutenant Colonel
AMM	Aviation Machinist's Mate	MAJ	Major
AOM	Aviation Ordnanceman	MM	Machinist's Mate
ARM	Aviation Radioman	MOMM	Motor Machinist's Mate
ART	Aviation Radio Technician	MSGT	Master Seargeant
BG	Brigadier General	PFC	Private First Class
BkR	Baker	PhM	Pharmacist's Mate
BM	Boatswain's Mate	PLGT	Platoon Sergeant
C	Chief	PO	Petty Officer
CDR	Commander	PTR	Painter
CK	Cook	PVT	Private
CO	Commanding Officer	QM	Quartermaster
COL	Colonel	RdM	Radarman
COX	Coxswain	RM	Radioman
CPL	Corporal	RT	Radio Technician
CPT	Captain	S	Seaman
CS	Commissary Steward	SC	Ship's Cook
EM	Electrician's Mate	SF	Shipfitter
ENS	Ensign	SGT	Sergeant
F	Fireman	SK	Storekeeper
FCO	Fire Controlman	SM	Signalman
GNR	Gunner	SP(X)	Specialist
GSGT	Gunnery Sergeant	SSGT	Staff Sergeant
HA	Hospital Assistant	SSM	Ship's Serviceman

ST	Sonar Technician	WO	Warrant Officer
TEC3, 4, 5	Technician X Grade	WT	Water Tender
TSGT	Tech Sergeant	XO	Executive Officer
TM	Torpedoman's Mate	Y	Yeoman

List of American Military Who Died by Time of Day

3:00 a.m., Pacific Theater, Hanawa, Japan (20th Infantry Regiment, 30th Infantry Division)

Miller, Paul Henry / PFC

3:45 a.m., Zone of the Interior, Baltimore, Maryland

Neubauer, Margaret Nancy / SP(X)

4:00 a.m., Zone of the Interior, Barksdale Field, Bossier City, Louisiana (484th Bomb Squadron, 505th Bomb Group)

Dowling, Paul T. / CPT
Fueyo, Louis M. / 2LT
Lentz, Kent A. / PFC
Martin, Cyril T. / SGT
Newfield, Harold / PFC
Nowak, John I. / PFC
Olsen, Charles F. / TSGT
Plunkett, Melvin R. / 2LT
Powers, Robert E. / 2LT
Ramos, Joaquin J. / PFC
Schmidt, Werner F. / CPL

6:30 a.m., Zone of the Interior, March Field, Riverside, California (420th Base Unit)

Bentley, Harold D. / SSGT
Bertrand, James E. / CPL
Bowman, Joseph E. / 1LT
Cole, Roy Sawyers / 2LT
Deverell, William A. / 2LT
Galioto, Anthony Vito / 1LT

—— a.m., Zone of the Interior, Walker Airfield, Russell, Kansas (248th Base Unit)

Bartimo, Marco / SGT
Gibson, Charles E., Jr. / CPT
Keadin, Herbert James "Bud" / MAJ
Oleksyk, John Turlesky / LT
Palmer, Donald A. / CPL
Rector, James N., Jr. / 2LT
Sheats, Lloyd / CPL
Simmons, Armand P. / TSGT
Smith, Jack Willard / CPL
Smith, Peter J. / CPL
Snyder, Andrew L. / CPL
Swank, Fred B. / LT

8:40 a.m., Pacific Theater, San Juanico Strait, Philippine Islands (LCI(G)-65, LST 452, LST-746, and LSM-19)

Aiston, Lester E. / SC3c
Bunce, William Arthur / SK2c
Dunn, James A. / LT
Ryan, Earl / MoMM2c
Theiler, Frank Mathew / MoMM3c
Weingartz, Lawrence William / S1c

—— a.m., Pacific Theater, Palo, Leyte Island, Philippine Islands (24th Infantry Division)

Baran, Walter J. / PVT
Bracknell, Artee / PVT
Coger, Ollie Alva, Jr. / PFC
Glum, Garret John / TEC5
LeBron, Raul / PVT
McClung, Virgil W. / PFC
O'Hara, Francis W. / PVT
Petrowski, Walter John / PVT
Plante, Joseph Z. / PFC
Sclafani, Frank J. / PVT
Willden, Myron R., Jr. / PFC

—— a.m., Pacific Theater, Dagami, Leyte Island, Philippine Islands (383rd Infantry Regiment, 96th Infantry Division)

Baty, Donald E. / PFC
Bennett, Norris / SSGT
Kjorvistad, Beryle H. / PVT

—— a.m., Pacific Theater, Dagami, Leyte Island, Philippine Islands (7th Infantry Division)

Alvarado, Julian Rios / SSGT
Brunson, Charles Edward / PFC
Carter, Norval V. / PVT
Clement Bruce Edward / SGT
Copeland, William Edward / 1LT
Coppola, Frank M. / PFC
Gardner, David Franklin / PVT
Greer, Kenneth T. / TEC4
Griffin, Grover L. / PFC
Hoffer, Norman Martin / PFC
Hudnutt, George Demming / 1LT
King, James T. / TEC5
Kite, Samuel Balous / PFC
Loveland, John V. / PFC
Medina, Vincent / PFC
Shanks, Willis / PFC
Sorenson, Eldridge V. / PFC
Williams, Gordon E. / PFC

—— a.m., Pacific Theater, Caibaan, Leyte Island, Philippine Islands (1st Cavalry)

Fontenot, Jessie J. / PFC
Hudgens, Denver Thomas / PFC

8:45 a.m., Pacific Theater, San Pedro Bay and Dio Island, Philippine Islands (LCI-1065 and the USS *Sonoma*)

Becker, Roy Ervin, Jr. / SC2c
Bjertness, Sigurd John / ENS
Disciano, Frank J. / MM1c
Griffin, Thomas Stansell / PhM1c
Judson, Gordon A. / RM3c
McMillan, Roy Lewis / MM2c
Mellott, Thomas Boyd / S2c
Meyer, Melvin Frederick / S2c
Shaw, Robert Mark / CM2c
Thornton, Tullie Clarence / S1c

9:00 a.m., Pacific Theater, Ceram Island, Netherlands East Indies (26th Photo Reconnaissance Squadron, 6th Photo Reconnaissance Group)

Bardsley, Clair James / 1LT

—— a.m., Pacific Theater, Adak Naval Operations Base 230, The Aleutian Islands

McElroy, George Henry / S1c

—— a.m., European Theater, Dunkirk, France (313th Air Transport Squadron, 31st Air Transport Group)

Adolfae, Herman Joseph / 1LT
Goodwin, Glen Earle / 1LT
Holliday, Leroy W., Jr. / SGT
Myers, Floyd Raymond / SGT

9:39 a.m., Pacific Theater, Gulf of Leyte, Philippine Islands (USS *Birmingham*)

The list below contains 233 named individuals, which includes 4 members of the ship's Marine detachment. The ship reported 229 killed, 4 missing, and 420 wounded of which 8 died within hours, but at an unspecified time.

Agnew, Charles Vincent / RDM3c
Austin, Carl S. / S2c
Babbs, Marshall L. / S2c
Barger, Thomas Earl / EM2c
Barron, Samuel J. / S1c
Bassett, Albert J., Jr. / S2c
Bates, Robert H. / QM1c
Benzie, Paul / GM3c
Bishop, Joseph E. / CEM
Blanco, Anthony P. / S1c
Blankenship, Cleo / S2c
Bodnar, John Paul / SC1c
Bowers Harry L. / CRT
Buckingham, Ernest Archie. / MM2c
Burckhard, Mike T. / S1c
Burnham, Robert Lee / S1c
Burns, Rodger M. / COX
Butkiewicz, Daniel / S1c
Butler, Collie H. / S2c
Caputo, Vincenzo J. / RDM3c
Carl, Robert Paul / S1c
Carmody, Kenneth J. / GM3c
Carr, James R. / SF3c
Carroll, John Francis / S1c
Cooper, Roland / LT
Corbin, Charles Oswald / S2c
Corini, Carlo Louis / S1c
Costigan, Joseph Frank / S2c
Cottrill, Harold Richard / S2c
Cramer, Winfred Lee / S1c
Creaven, John Anthony / COX
Crockett Thaddeus Hamp / SC3c
Culotta, Dominic Peter / S1c
Deakin, Billy Wayne / MM2c
Dean, Norwin Goodwin / CWT
Decenzo, Frank Joseph / F2c
Dickerson, Alfonzo J., Jr. / S1c
Dietrich, Howard R. / GM1c
Dobbins, Robert Henry / S2c
Doughman, Clarence L. / S2c
Droste, Albert Henry / SSML3c
Duke, Robert Clayton / S2c
Dymond, Charles David / S1c
Ekstrom, Stanley Edson / LT
Elkins, Samuel Eli / S2c
Ellison, Harold Pond, Jr. / S1c
Elsinger, Francis Joseph / S2c
Elson, William Junior / F1c
Englert, Harry Joseph / S1c
Ericksen, Ralph John / WT1c
Estes, George / S2c
Evankoe, Steve / F1c
Farish, James William / MM1c
Filip, James William / CSP
Flynn, Gerard Edward. / GM3c
Folkman, Leon Junior / SK3c

Ford, Simon Patrick / COX
Fowler, Arthur Jesse / GM3c
Frazier, Paul Dewitt / S1c
Fulton, Richard E. / MM3c
Gerson, Paul William / WT3c
Gifford, Winferd Bundy / COX
Gilbert, Charles Hugo, Jr. / EM1c
Gluscic, Joseph John / S1c
Godin, Vincent Richard / Y2c
Golitko, Edward Paul / S2c
Graham, James Paul / S1c
Graves, Joe Earl / S1c
Griger, Arthur / Y3c
Gwinn, Charles Parker / S1c
Haas, Edward Joseph / S1c
Hahn, John Edward / GM3c
Hartle, Raymond Lewis / S2c
Hedges, Wilbert / GM3c
Hoagwood, George H. / WO
Hoegerl, Anthony Joseph / MM2c
Hoff, Ralph William / SSML3c
Holley, Hubert Henry / S2c
Howard, Henry Franklin / S2c
Howze, James Edward / QM3c
Hoyt, Dale Hoel / SGT
Huey, Hubbard Pool / S1c
Huls, Joseph Francis / S2c
Hunter, Norman Elwood / S2c
Jackson, David Elwood / S1c
James, Raymond / S1c
Jaramillo, William / S2c
Johnson, John Thomas, Jr. / S3c
Johnston, Richard H. / GM3c
Jones, George Franklin / FCO3c
Kenley, Lee Charles / F1c
Kerr, Robert C. / ENS
Kuminga, Chester Stanley / MM3c
Kwikowski, Peter Paul / BM1c
Kwolek, John Joseph / MM3c
Landin, Johan Ambrose / F1c
Large, George Hathaway / SC3c
Latorre, Joseph / F1c
Lavalle, John A. / S2c
Lawson, William Dallas / M3c
LeClaire, Ovila Joseph / S2c
Leonard, Daniel, Jr. / SC3c
Leta, Domenico Michael / S2c
Libengood, James Ralph / GM3c
Liebman, Marion Albert / S1c
Loeber, Edward Conrad / RT3c
Longkabel, Gordon, Jr. / S2c
Low, Frederick John / S1c
Lowe, Burnis W. / F1c
Marker, Franklin Leroy / GM3c
Marriott, Oscar Ferdinand / CEM
Marsland, Alvah Irwin / MM3c
Martin. Wendell Linzy / S1c
Maunter, Paul Thomas / F1c
Maxwell, Harry Guy, Jr. / PFC
McCormick, Donald / LT
McGee, Donald Eugene / S1c
McGinnis, Arthur James / S1c
McLain, Charles Edward / F1c
Medellin, Pedro Martinez / S1c
Medina, Norberto / RT3c
Menius, Billy Odell / MM3c
Mensenkamp, Walworth T. / S1c
Metallo, Nunzio Daniel / BM2c
Michalik, George Edward / S1c
Mierzejewski, Paul Raymond / WT2c
Miller, Joseph James / COX
Miller, Robert Williams / FC3c
Minahan, John Patrick / S1c
Minks, Everett Russell / S2c
Mitchell, Wallace Harry / S2c
Molzahn, Albert Lewter / S2c
Moore, Carroll Edward / MM2c
Moss, Robert Francis / WT2c
Mount, James Watson / S2c
Mugridge, Paul Clayton / COX
Neal, Earl A. / AMM3c
Nelson, Laverne Nets / S2c
Nelson, Lowell Rainard / GM3c
Nettles, Edward Marvin / S1c
Nielson, Kenneth Reber / WT3c
Oleson, Harald Reio Arild / CTC
Owens, Luther Birchel / S1c
Payton, Larus Elmer / SF2c
Peregud, Harry / S2c
Perkins, Van Ostrand / CDR
Peterson, Robert H. / EM2c
Piggott, Tom Edward / BkR3c
Pires, John Paul / F1c
Popa, Emil / S1c

Postle, Lewis Wiley, Jr. / RM3c
Pote, Robert Lee / S2c
Purvis, John Mitchell / GM3c
Quinn, Edward Joseph, Jr. / S1c
Ramsey, Charles Homer / COX
Reed, Alan / LT
Reed, Donald Otis / S1c
Reed, Harold Onell / S1c
Richard, Omar Adrian / S2c
Richie, Eugene Anthony / S1c
Ritchey, Edward Gilbert / MM2c
Roberts, Robert Ewing / CCS
Rogers, Harold Floyd / S1c
Rogers, Louis Richard / S2c
Roleder, Howard Stanley / MM2c
Romo, Jesuse Antenna / S2c
Russo, Anthony Thomas / MM2c
Sabino, Peter Anthony / S1c
Samuelsen, Laurence Albert / S1c
Sanders, Charles Ernest / S1c
Savage, Jack Milton / CPhM
Savey, John Henry / S1c
Schaefer, William Arthur / MM3c
Schieble, Robert Francis / S1c
Schmidt, John Mathew / S1c
Schoen, Roy Adam / BM2c
Schultz, Alvin Leo / COX
Sears, Billy D. / S2c
Shaver, Frank, Jr. / BkR1c
Sheil, Joseph Patrick / S1c
Sidor, John / S1c
Simkins, Clarence Marcellus / GM2c
Smith, Harold Truman / F1c
Smith, Mirel Ralph / WO
Solano, Isidro / CST
Spillane, Charles William / COX
Staymates, Albert Harrison / S2c
Stepp, Billie / S2c
Studden, Arthur / MM3c
Taylor, Clair Elwood / BM2c
Taylor, Lloyd / S2c
Teague, Jesse Zachaus / S2c
Thompson, John Robert / RT1c
Thurman, Joseph Allen / S2c
Tice, William Lester / SC1c
Tipps, Everett Shirman / S2c
Tomlinson, Frank Ellis / S1c
Tonka, George Joseph / S2c
Trevethan, Vernon Ervin / MM3c
Truett, James Melvin / S2c
Trujillo, Daniel Carmen, Jr. / S1c
Turcott, Charles Augustus / PFC
Turner, Daniel Junior / S2c
Ulery, Roy Levon / MM1c
Vaughn, Clyde Everett / MM2c
Vicknair, Warren Joseph, Jr. / EM2c
Voelker, Delmar O. / S2c
Voigt, Ferdinand Max / F1c
Volk, Wendelin J. / COX
Wade, Jack Wayne / S2c
Walden, Charles Orville / S2c
Walker, Paul Allen / S2c
Walls, William Howard / S2c
Walters, James Truman / S2c
Waterman, Lee / F1c
Waynick, Delbert Lee / S2c
Weaver, Bruce Edward / S1c
Weaver, Marlin Andrew / S2c
Webb, Edward Perry, Jr. / SC1c
Wedeking, James L. / FC3c
Weigand, Ralph John / S1c
Wells, Paul Raymond / SK3c
West, Clayton Clifford / F1c
Westfall, Howard Venton / S2c
White, Fred Hoyt / S2c
Wilczynski, Tadeusz Bernard / S2c
Wilson, Max Earl / FCO3c
Wolff, Warren William / S2c
Wollerman, Fritz August / GM3c
Wong, Harry / BkR3c
Wood, Russell Devere / F1c
Wytrykowski, Henry Thomas. / F1c
Zespy, Jerome Anthony / GM3c

9:39 a.m., Pacific Theater, USS *Princeton*

The list below contains 106 named individuals of the 108 the ship claimed were lost on October 24, 1944.

Adolph, Adrian L. / F1c
Arsics, Michael G. / EM1c
Bentley, John Steele / MM1c
Bloecher, Fred W. / BkR1c

Bradley, Robert Graham. / LT
Brunelle, Joseph A. / S1c
Brustoski, Joseph John / PFC
Bryant, Theodore W. / SF1c
Burns, James P. / CM
Cardoza, David F. / MM3c
Cerny, Joseph I. / WT3c
Chagnon, Oscar O. / AM2c
Christie, Alexander A. / ENS
Corum, Paul I. / S1c
Daly, Walter L. / EM3c
Doherty, James B. / SF3c
Fiorita, Frank E. / SF3c
Flynn, John Francis / EM2c
Fredette, John A. / F1c
Garrison, Dorris Gwin / RM3c
Gentry, James Everett / SGT
Glen, Richard H. / F2c
Gormley, John F. / AOM2c
Gravell, William McCormick / AMM1c
Harrell, Robert Reed / WT3c
Harwood, Bruce Lawrence / CDR
Hauser, Gary / PTR3c
Heisler, Donald R. / S1c
Hill, Donald N. / AM3c
Hirleman, Richard D. / WT3c
Hoecker, Esper H. / CPC
Holden, Paul L. / EM3c
Jarrell, James C. / S1c
Jones, John Norbert / WT3c
Kaser, John M. / LTjg
Kotlas, Johnny / EM3c
Krall, Henry / SGT
Laird, Richard F. / GM2c
Lamb, Lonnie L. / EM3c
Lawrence, Austin L., Jr. / BkR3c
Letton, James W. / SC3c
Lewis, John S. / S1c
Lind, Herbert J. / SM2c
Mason, Booker T. / STM2c
Mason, Farrell D. / SC2c
Maxon, Henry D. / MM2c
McLendon, Wallace Howard / WT2c
Meza, Vicente Onesimo / SK3c
Milano, Ralph F. / S1c
Mirando, Mario G. / AMM3c
Moon, Bernard P. / S1c
Morrison, Lewis Henry / AMM3c
Morrissey, Fred J. / AMM3c
Newton, Lester F. / F1c
Nolan, Ernest Laverne / PFC
Nulph, Harold Walker / PFC
O'Leary, James J. / AMM3c
Padula, Joseph M. / S1c
Page, Nelson K. / F2c
Patton, Jimmy Don / S2c
Pelletier, Lucien E. / AMM2c
Pino, Manuel Lupe / ST3c
Probst, Herbert L. / PhM2c
Rattler, Mark J. / PFC
Reed, Wayne M. / S1c
Reimers, Fred Lee / Y2c
Reynolds, Earl R. / PTR3c
Ricketts, Henry Thomas / S1c
Rigdon, David M., Jr. / S1c
Ringwelski, Frank / S2c
Robbe, Robert R. / S2c
Rogers, Everett K. / F1c
Ross, Bernard M. / F1c
Sargent, William Thomas / S2c
Sassenberger, James A. / S2c
Saxton, William A., Jr. / AM3c
Scott, Oliver L. / ENS
Seabrooks, Charlie / Ck3c
Shannon, William J. / AMM3c
Smith, George T. / S1c
Smith, Milford Hoyt / BkR3c
Spencer, William J. / WT2c
Steele, James Clinton / CE
Stevens, Russell / S1c
Strauch, Adam / CEM
Strickland, Young Edward / CWT
Suarez, Jesse Lee / MM1c
Tanner, William J. / S1c
Thurman, Ralph E. / LTjg
Tilley, Owen Edgar / AOM3c
Toporski, Edward / S1c
Vallante, Pasquale / F1c
Vandenberg, Edward J. / LT
Van Dusen, Robert Jay / WT3c
Van Winkle, James Alexander / S2c
Vendrely, Donald L. / F1c
Vickers, Lawrence V. / BM2c
Vincent. Ivan R. / S1c
Vydfol, Fred A. / MM1c
Wachunas, Charles S. / EM3c
Walker, Ernest Eugene / S1c
Walsh, David Samuel / MS1c

Westfall, Robert W. / MM1c
White, Ralph Alexander / SFC
Zalcek, Ralph S. / WT2c
Zlatnik, Henry Frederick / MM3c

10:00 a.m., European Theater, Honington Airfield, England (1st Scouting Force)

Hess, Charles Frank / CPT

10:22 a.m., Pacific Theater, Gulf of Leyte, Philippine Islands (*Cabot*, *Essex*, *Franklin*, *Intrepid*, *Kalinin Bay*, *Lexington*, *Santee*, *Savo Island*)

Anderson, Norman Earnest / ARM1c
Barnett, Marshall David / LTjg
Barrett, Guy Jennings, Jr. / LTjg
Black, Eugene Edmond / ARM2c
Blalock, Dennis Pershing / AMM2c
Bogert, Robert W. / AMM3c
Boyle, John Joseph / ENS
Christman, George E., Jr. / AMM2c
Clive, Richard Howard / LTjg
Crellin, Conrad Wesley / LTjg
English, Clarence Frederick / ARM2c
Ewart, William Cameron / ARM3c
Fletcher, Willard Merle / ENS
Galbraith, Byron Blair / ARM2c
Granger, Albert Alexander / AMM1c
Hubbuch, Francis P. / ENS
Kohut, Edward J. / ARM2c
Lampson, Donald / ENS
Mayhew, Ralph Albert / ENS
McGowan, Richard / CDR
McNeill, Wilson Carroll / LT
Odom, William H. / ARM3c
Pickens, Leonard / ARM3c
Shetler, Carl Edward / ARM3c
Simpson, William E. / LT
Skelly, Raymond J. / LTjg
Southard, Paul Edward / LTjg
Teilliard, William Joseph / AOM2c
Westmoreland, Robert G. / ARM3c

10:30 a.m., Pacific Theater, Yap Island, Micronesia (2nd Marine Air Wing and 81st Infantry Division)

Grinlinton, Clarence A. / 2LT
Haltom, Girvis, Jr. / 1LT
Randolph, Thomas Edison / PFC

11:00 a.m., European Theater, Dodewaard, the Netherlands (327th Glider Infantry Regiment, 377th Field Artillery Battalion, 502nd and 506th Parachute Infantry Regiments, 101st Airborne)

Marnye, John Charles / PFC
Murphy, John Thomas / TEC5
Thompson, Sylvester J. / PVT
Trishaw, Floyd J. / PVT
Weber, George L. / PFC

Noon, European Theater, Emberménil, France (313th and 315th Infantry Regiments, 79th Infantry Division)

Arredondo, Francisco C. / PVT
Bauknecht, Russell Harry / PVT
Beason, Glen / PFC
Cooper, John George / PVT
Dempster, Elwood / PFC
Edwards, John Clark / CPL
Fousek, Lewis John / SGT
Gaar, Shirley M. / PFC
Groiser, Joseph / PFC
Johnson, Earl L. / SGT
Lake, Forest A. / PFC
Lynch, Archie D. / PVT
Magre, Peter Francis / CPL
Mandermach, Nicolas / PFV

McCallum, John / PFC
Murray, M. C. / PVT
Opdahl, Glenn C. / PVT
Osborn, James O. / PVT
Parish, Thomas L. / PVT
Pitts, John A., Jr. / PVT
Roberts, Harley John / SSGT
Rossman, Freeman Ordell / PVT
Shinault, William Robert / PFC
Spinn, Michael F. / TSGT
Thompson, James Patterson / SGT
Walker, Earl A. / SGT
Wisvari, Theodore / PVT
Wygant, Paul F. / PVT

—— European Theater, Moncourt Woods, France (101st and 104th Infantry Regiments, 26th Infantry Division)

Baum, Mortimer J. / TEC
Blake, Kenneth / PFC
Conroy, Robert M. / PFC
Giglio, Joseph R. / PFC
Kuhl, Robert Bruce / PFC
Nadybal, Theodore S. / PFC
Venditti, Frank P. / PFC
Wroten, Wallace S., Jr. / SGT

—— Europe Middle East Africa Theater, the Vosges Mountains, France (7th, 15th, and 30th Infantry Regiments, 3rd Infantry Division)

Burkes, James Monroe / SGT
Champagne, Leon F. / PVT
Gerrol, Marvin M. / PFC
Harris, Walter J. / TSGT
Kinsella, Robert A. / PFC
Papak, Stanley A. / PFC
Pian, Seymour A. / 1LT
Rewers, Joseph F. / PFC
Samuels, Patrick G. / SGT
Teachout, James Edward / PVT

12:16 p.m., Pacific Theater, Pitu Airfield, Morotai, Indonesia (72nd Bomb Squadron, 5th Bomb Group)

Albert, William A., Jr. / 2LT
Bailes, Keith C. / SSGT
Faust, George Henry / PVT
Holland, Calvin Silas / SSGT
Ivey, Josie Wells / SGT
Lape, Dwane E. / 2LT
McLaughlin, Warren F. / SGT
Palmer, Donald N. / TSGT
Runde, Kenneth P. / 2LT
Schow, Mason R. / 2LT
Worley, Charles Donald / SSGT

1:42 p.m., China Burma India Theater, Maymyo, Burma (490th Bomb Squadron, 341st Bomb Group)

Dixon, George W. / CPL
Finney, Frank M. / 2LT
Loew, Franklin E. A. / CPL
Martin, James Stafford / CPL
Mueller, Eugene C. / 2LT
Wonnell, Robert E. / 2LT

2:00 p.m., Pacific and European Theaters

Adamson, George Anthony / S1c
Anderson, Bror Henry / CPT
Hart, Edwin Clyde / CPL
Humes, William Patrick / SSGT
McGirk, Clarence E. / PVT
Miller, Germain F. / PFC
Padgett, Donald M. / PFC
Poovey, Lloyd William Lee / ART2c
Sheehan, Daniel P. / PVT
Solesbee, Milo / S2c

2:00 p.m., European Theater, Vedriano, North Apennines, Italy (133rd, 135th, and 186th Infantry Regiments, 34th Infantry Division)

Baker, Robert J. / PFC
Black, Lowell A. / PFC
Bradshaw, Gordon Ransom / PVT
Crum, Hubert K. / SGT
Davis, Frank L. / PFC
Gunn, Francis R. / PFC
Haim, Morton E. / 1LT
Hurley, John Joseph / PFC
Logan, William M. / PFC
Nystul, Joseph Allen / TEC4
Pendergast, John V. / 1LT
Qualls, Joseph Stewart / TEC4
Stecewicz, Walter A. / TSGT

—— p.m. (337th and 338th Infantry Regiments, 85th Infantry Division)

Bruns, Alfred P. / PVT
Craft, J. T. / PFC
Frisbey, James LeRoy / PVT
Harutunian, Harry / PVT
Kreitner, Jack / PFC
LaPointe, Louis J. / PFC
Morgan, Roland E. / CPL

—— p.m. (349th, 350th, and 351st Infantry Regiments, 88th Infantry Division)

Berard, Leo J. / PVT
Berns, William H., Jr. / PVT
Bolin, Ed / SGT
Cama, Paul J. / PCT
Cox, Robert / PVT
Ellis, Harry Francis, Jr. / PVT
Kohut, John / PFC
Marquez, Francisco A. / SGT
McDonough, Thomas P., Jr. / CPL
McMahon Jack J. / PVT
Miller, Francis J. / PFC
Murphy, John J. / PVT
Parrish, Harless / PFC
Pazuchowski, Henry V. / PVT
Perfetti, Louis P. / PVT
Petrie, Willard Franklin, Jr. / PVT
Phillips, Charles O. / PFC
Podulka, Edward G. / PVT
Putnam, John Grant / PVT
Rudd, Louis Lee / PFC
Sanders, Charlie W / PVT
Spradling, Donald L. / PVT
Stevens, James Garland / PVT
Vasholz, Alfred Herbert / 2LT
Voss, Raymond G. / PVT
Wesson. Alfred E. / PVT
Yanez, Joe Paredez / PVT

—— p.m. (361st Infantry Regiment, 91st Infantry Division, and 35th Signal Company)

Hull, James C. / PVT
McDonald, Thomas Graham / SM
McGrath, James A. / PVT
Melvin, Percy Linstrome / PVT
Miller, Lawrence Otis / PFC
Verke, Clayton E. / PFC

4:15 p.m., European Theater, the Netherlands (61st and 62nd Fighter Squadrons, 56th Fighter Group)

Choate, George R. / 2LT
Osborne, William J., Jr. / 2LT

5:00 p.m., Pacific Theater, Leyte Island, Philippine Islands (Quartermaster Corps and Transportation Corps)

Baker, Arvell R. / PVT
Bell, Augustus Lichenstein / CK
Bridgett, Howard Curtis / TEC5
Hall, Charles B. / TEC4
Johnson, Robert R. / PVT
Murphy, Peter / PVT
Planty, George Vincent / SGT

—— p.m., Pacific Theater, Philippine Sea (USS *Shark* [SS-314])

Adams, Steven Douglas / ENS
Adamson, James Marshall / F1c
Babig, Joseph William / TM1c
Bailey, Donald Eugene / EM2
Baker, Charles Marvin / S1c
Barrett, James Joseph / SC1cc
Barton, Claude Anthony, Jr. / EM2c
Black, Henry Roy, Jr. / SM1c
Blakely, Edward Noe / CDR-CO
Borusiewicz, Walter Eugene / GM3c
Brown, Charles Richard / TM3c
Brown, Leon Maurice / CPhM
Buckey, William Emmett, Jr. / S1c
Burns, John Edward / MoMM2c
Burns, Rolland T. / MoMM1c
Cerruti, Ralph Michael / RT1c
Chilcote, Orville Gross / MoMM1c
Click, Robert Ford / MoMM2c
Constantinos, William Anthony / RM3c
Cupper, Herbert Andrew / MoMM2c
Davis, Jesse Andrew, Jr. / LT
Davis, John Scott / MoMM2c
Delehanty, Mark Arthur / F1c
Dobson, Leslie Garbutt / SC3c
Doyen, Louis Jackson / TM2cc
Drury, Franklin Charles / MoMM1c
Dryer, Perry Leo / MoMM1c
Dupuy, Hal Hunter / TM3
Elko, Andrews / TM3
Ferguson, Lawrence Howard / RM3c
Giles, Arthur Lewis / MoMM1c
Harper, John Dott / LCDR-XO
Hawthorn, Willie Edwin / CMoMM
Hoffman, Ross Charles, Jr. / F2
Hooker, Richard Edward / StM1
Houston, Sam Kenneth / SM2c
Hudgins, Bunyan Cleveland, Jr. / TM1c
Huffman, James Royal / S1c
Hunting, Eugene Nathan, Jr. / LT
Josephs, Arthur Thomas / EM2c
Jurovaty, Steven / MoMM2c
Kibbons, Clarence Vernon / CTM
Kirstein, Alvin Ewald / LT
Kneib, Thomas Francis / MoMM2c
Krecker, Sterling Schlichter / MoMM2c
Lawson, Kenneth Eugene / S1c
Leecy, Raymond Arthur / CTM
Leonard, Charles Upham / S1c
Lewis, William Theodore / ENS
Luedemann, Frederick / F1c
Lyon, Daniel Benjamin / RM2c
MacIntyre, James Clyde / F1c
Masincupp, Byron Tucker / RM3c
McDonald, Robert Scrysmer / LT
Muntz, Robert William / Y3c
Olson, Walter Everett / S1c
Ongerth, William Ralph / GM2c
Oothoudt, Marvin Dwaine / RM1c
Paulsen, William Oneil / CEM
Perkins, Royalston Elijah / RM1cc
Perrin, Irby Carl / CRM
Perry, John Michael / F2c
Pittman, George Washington / Ck2c
Polikowski, Michael / RM3c
Porter, Willis Woodrow / CMoMM
Reed, Floyd Earnest / CEM
Reich, Kenneth Anthony / FC3c
Reilly, Francis Steven / CSM
Reinthaler, Rudolph Henry / FC2c
Ridgeway, Arlin Lee / EM1c
Satterfield, Herbert Austin / EM3c
Schuermann, Lloyd Bernhard / CMoMM

Scutiero, Anthony Edward / EM3c
Selig, Jesse Lee / QM2c
Shaffer, Donald Eugene / Y1c
Shaw, Bernon Foche / SC2c
Shefcheck, Henry, Jr. / ENS
Simko, William Anthony / EM3c
Thommen, Harvey Hubbell / TM3c
Tien, Kenneth Raymond / TM3c
Tiller, Forrest Sterling / EM1c
Turner, William Harlan / LTjg
Wall, William Riefler / TM3c
Wansky, Richard Warren / BM1c
Wells, Richard Warren / TM3c
Williams, Martin Luther / SC3c
Zidziunas, John Joseph / MOMM3c

—— p.m., Pacific Theater, Philippine Sea (*Arisan Maru*)

Army Headquarters Units

Includes Headquarters Company, Adjutant General Corps, and Finance Department, US Army

Ballew, Herbert Keene / PFC
Brassington, Theodore J. / TSGT
Bridgman, Ernest H. / SGT
Britt, George Thomas / MAJ
Cathey, Henry Norris / SSGT
Cohen, Robert Lee / TEC4
Cooper, Oscar Lehman / SGT
Davis, William R. / MAJ
Deter, Dwight Meyer / LTC
Gregory, Roy Dunscomb / LTC
Hampton, Velton C. / PFC
Haralson, Henry Benjamin / SGT
Henderson, Charles W. / TSGT
Hettinger, Gund / MSGT
Hilliard, Richard / PVT
Hough, Meridith L. / SSGT
Irby, Richard / CWO
Maness, Choice Roland / PFC
McPherson, John D., Jr. / MAJ
McShane, John R. / 1LT
Moyer, Paul Frederick / SSGT
Newton, William B. / SSGT
Reed, Fitz L. / MAJ
Renshaw, Kieth Junior / PFC
Richard, Gerard A. / PVT
Trentham, Allen J. / SGT
Watson, Festus George / CPT
Williams, Edward A. / MSGT
Williams, Robert W. / SGT
Williams, Harold Morton / SSGT

Army Headquarters Military Police

Includes 12th Military Police Company, Philippine Division and 808th Military Police Company, US Army

Carpenter, Manuel R. / CPL
Hasson, Ernest / SGT
Houston, Leonard / SGT
Lindsay, Dean W. / PVT
Manuel, Lawrence / PVT
McKnight, Vernon F. / PFC
Mueller, Charles F. / CPT
Pagan, Kenneth Gibson / PFC
Parsons, Murl B. / PFC
Smith, Oscar L. / CPL
Tracy, Clifford Lee / PFC
Whitaker, Wilfred Gene / SSGT

Army Infantry Regiments, Field Artillery, and Cavalry

Includes 31st Infantry Regiment and 301st Field Artillery, Philippine Division and 23rd Field Artillery, 26th Cavalry, 45th and 57th Infantry Regiments, and 86th Field Artillery, Philippine Scouts, and other Philippine units

Adkins, Joseph Herschel / PFC
Amend, Donald Alvin / CPT
Anderson, Roy C. / PVT
Anthony, Newton Darman / 1LT

Armantrout, George Oliver / 1LT
Armstrong, Doyle Ray / 1LT
Arriola, Frank B., Jr. / PVT
Ashby, Henry Bourbon / SGT
Baca, Bernard O. / PVT
Ball, Russell W. / PFC
Ballantyne, Kyle Thomas / CPT
Ballard, George Wilton / TEC4
Baruch, Benjamin / CPL
Bennett, Earl / PVT
Berkelhamer, Ralph C. / CPT
Bigelow, James E. / 2LT
Bigger, Arthur H. / PVT
Bograd, Heimie / SGT
Bostick, Paul Roy / PVT
Braddy, George Curtis, Jr. / PVT
Bradford, Harry A. / CPL
Brickman, Albert Harvey / PFC
Brittan, Robert Neil / LTC
Brown, Charles Dyer / WO
Brown, Frank O. / CPT
Burgess, Harland Fremont / LTC
Burns, Albert R. / PVT
Buyatt, Clinton H. / PVT
Campbell, Oren A. / 1LT
Carleton, Robert K. / 2LT
Casey, Orman W. / 1LT
Catterlin, Dail / PVT
Childers, Donald Thomas / CPT
Chisenhall, Theopalus Stevens / CPL
Cloutier, George Wohn / SSGT
Collins, Lewis Fontain, Jr. / PVT
Coppock, Robert Bell, Jr. / PFC
Couch, Thomas A. / PVT
Craig, Jewel D. / PFC
Crane, Theodore Poole "Feny" / MAJ
Creader, John Bennie / PFC
Croom, Clifton Arthur / CPT
Cruikshank, Edward Harold / WO
DuBose, Ethan A. / PVT
Duquette, Anthony M., Jr. / PVT
Durachko, Victor W. / CPL
Durham, William D. / 2LT
Ellett, Charles A. / 2LT
Emerson, Robert G. / 1LT
Evans, Frank T. / 2LT
Exceen, Leonard R. / SSGT
Fleeger, Harry James / MAJ
Fletcher, Ray / PFC
Foreman, Charles C. / PFC
Forte, William / PVT
Fortune, Thomas Willis / SSGT
Frandsen, Earl C. / MAJ
Garrett, Charles Irvan / CPT
George, Keith E. / 1LT
Goodwin, Gene L. "Bud" / CPL
Gray, Roy B. / CPT
Haberman, Edward A. / SGT
Hall, Ralph C. / PFC
Hall, Walter H. / 1SGT
Harrington, Thomas Charles / PVT
Harris, Henry / CPT
Harvey, Clarence J. / PVT
Head, Joseph Thomas / PVT
Henderson, Charles Austel, Jr. / PVT
Hendricks, Jay L. / PFC
Hendry, Roderick. K. / CPT
Herbert, Harry Taylor / 1LT
Hicks, Leroy / PFC
Higgins, Arlie W. / MAJ
Holladay, Otha L. / SSGT
Holland, Frank Lane / LTC
Hooper, Ronald Gerald / PVT
Houston, Van Frederick / MAJ
Hunter, Richard Grant / LTC
Ingraham, Clarence Woodrow / TEC5
Isbell, Gerald Warren / PVT
Jackson, Albert Joel / PFC
James, Jack L. / PFC
Jarycranzki, Edward M. / SGT
Johnson, Donald Widmer / PFC
Johnston, Lee W. / 1LT
Jolley, Curtis / 2LT
Jones, Paul M. / MAJ
Kelley, James W. / TEC5
Kincaid, Dewey / PFC
Kopelke, Bernard Charles / 2LT
Korn, Emanuel / PVT
Kramer, Milton / MAJ
Krummel, Edward Lee / 1LT
Labasewski, John / PFC
Laro, Jack M. / 1LT
Lawhon, William Allen, Jr. / CPT
Leisenring, William Pearson / 1LT

Lonergan, James J. / CPL
Long, Owen Gardner / SGT
Loyal, Joe Washington / PVT
MacPhail, Archie John / 2LT
Martin, Charles O. / PFC
Martinez, Lazaro / PFC
Martinez, Manuel Davio / PFC
Matney, Robert Earl / PVT
May, Eugene L. / PVT
Mazzucca, Fiorino Francis / PVT
McCollum, Offa Shivers / LTC
McDonald, James S. / CPT
McKee, Montgomery / LTC
McSorley, Raymond Audrey / 2LT
Meier, Hix W. / CPT
Meredith, John Carroll / PFC
Metcalf, William S. / SSGT
Meyers Olin Eugene / PFC
Miles, Francis D. / CPL
Mock, William E. / CPL
Monson, Harold Frederick / 1LT
Moore, Samuel B. "Jack" / PVT
Morales, Joseph M., Jr. / PVT
Morgan, James A / PVT
Morrison, Edgar Murrel / PVT
Mott, Charles Frederick, Jr. / PFC
Moyers, Glenn William / PFC
Muir, Robert W. / 1LT
Muldoon, Charles Elroy / PVT
Myers, Hershell L. / CPL
Myers, Lloyd Erwin / 2LT
Mygrant, Clifford Harry / PVT
Nance, Truman / PVT
Oates, Earnest Clifford / 2LT
O'Connor, James O. / PVT
Oliver, William P., Jr. / 1LT
Olson, Harry W. / 1SGT
Oster, Roy Joseph / CPT
Palmer, Johnnie William / PVT
Patterson, Russell D. / CPT
Pedigo, John Lee "Johnnie" / PVT
Perryman, Conrad Clellan / PVT
Pieczonka, Edward F. / 2LT
Pierpont, Robert Patterson / 1LT
Pock, Edward J. / MAJ
Porter, George E., Jr. / CPT
Prater, Chester J. / PFC
Reinhardt, Norman F. / PVT
Rice, Emery Leslie / CPT
Roberts, William R. / PVT
Roesner, Lawrence Edward / PVT
Rowley, Charles W. / 2LT
Sayer, Clarence Emmett / SGT
Sayre, Vinal F. / CPT
Scecina, Fr. Thomas John / CPT
Schildroth, Robert C. / PFC
Seay, James A. / CPT
Sechrist, Bert / PFC
Seldomridge, Charles McKinley / 2LT
Sharp, Abiel Thomas / 1LT
Sherbuck, Joe S. / PFC
Slack, Leland D. / PFC
Slawek, Walter S. / PVT
Smith, Clarence Harwood. / LTC
Smith, Cleatus O. / PVT
Smith, Harold L. / CPL
Smyers, Webster Cullen / CPT
Spanelle, Theodore / CPL
Stewart, Julius William / PFC
Stout, Jesse Earl / PFC
Stroud, Ray B. / CPT
Strout, Durwood / SGT
Stukenburg, John Darrell / 1LT
Sullivan, Logan Jackson, Jr. / PVT
Sumrell, Bertie W. / PVT
Swanson, Ray G. / PVT
Talvy, Samuel / 1SGT
Terry, Joseph E. / CPT
Thompson, John Ward / CPT
Toney, Emmett B. / PFC
Trevillian, Jesse O. / SGT
Trotter, Conrad E. / PVT
Troutman, William / 2LT
Van Sant, Benjamin Franklin / 1LT
Van Sickle, J. C. / PFC
Vargas, Charles Garcia / PVT
Veatch, Doyle W. / CPL
Walker, Friedman H. / SGT
Weigel, Robert P. / PFC
Weiland, George F. / CPT
Whalen, Edward L. / CPL
Whitehurst, Collin Batson, Jr. / MAJ
Widerynski, Steffan / MSGT
Williams, Ottis C. / PFC

Wingfield, Henry J. / PVT
Wisniewski, Stanley L. / CPL
Wohler, Glenn W. / CPT
Wright, Elliott David / 2LT
Wroten, Fred Millard / PFC
Zenchenko, Charles C. / PVT
Zinn, Jack P. / PVT

Army Tank Groups

Includes 192nd and 194th Tank Battalions and 17th Ordnance Company, Provisional Tank Group, USAFFE

Ainsworth, Robert Sterling / PFC
Altman, Jack Cary / CPT
Anderson, Leroy Clark / SGT
Andrews, John Robert / 1SGT
Angelone, Joseph Nicholas / PVT
Atha, Leon Foster / PFC
Babb, John Barnett / PVT
Baldon, Fay Walter / PVT
Bandych, Joseph S. / TEC4
Barden, Donald M. / SSGT
Baugh, David Joseph / PVT
Bennett, Charles E. / 2LT
Boni, Daniel Joseph / PVT
Boyce, George H. / PVT
Boyd, William Giles / MSGT
Boysen, Adam Thayer / TEC5
Brewer, Hubert O. / PFC
Brown, Charles Race / PFC
Brown, Vincent Russell / SGT
Buggs, Melvin Emil / PVT
Burke, John Francis / PVT
Bussell, Vernon H. / SGT
Cahill, Martin Anthony / PFC
Cale, Lester C. / PVT
Callison, Wilbur C. / PVT
Campbell, Hays C. / CPL
Canby, Charles S. / MAJ
Carter, James Melvin / PFC
Cloyd, Robert Vernon / PFC
Crick, Ancel Edgar / PFC
Cummins, John L. / PFC
Danforth, Claude C. / PVT
DiBenedetti, Edmund Nicholas / PVT
Dobson, Maxwell Stephen / PVT
Dutt, Homer Rae / PFC
Edwards, Albert Thomas / SSGT
Ehrhardt, Clyde David / PFC
Ellis, Ralph Arnold / PVT
Elwell, Olen C. / SSGT
Fanson, Wayne Ross / 1LT
Flippen, Roy J. / PVT
Fontes, Edwin M. / PVT
Franklin, Carl H. / PVT
Giachino, Martin / PVT
Gorr, Alexander G. / PFC
Hall, Norman W. / PVT
Hampton, Jay Alexander / PVT
Heard, Willie Stokes, Jr. / 1LT
Heilig, Roger James / 1SGT
Hickman, Harry Samuel / CPT
Hildebrand, Warren A. / SSGT
Holland, Arthur A. / 2LT
Hurtt, Thomas Edward / PVT
James, Edward A., Jr. / PVT
Jardot, William H. / PVT
Joyce, Thomas Stephen / PFC
Kissinger, Hugh Patrick / SGT
Knipshield, Donald Eugene / PFC
Kopek, Alexander Raymond / PVT
Krause, Leslie Herman / SGT
Lemke, Steve / TEC4
Long, Hubert H. / SGT
Lustig, Maurice E. / PFC
Luther, Henry M. / SSGT
Luther, John P. / SSGT
MacDonald, Robert / PVT
Mahone, Arthur Glen / PFC
Martini, Clement Frank / PVT
McCage, Neil B. / TEC5
Mitchell, Robert E. / PVT
Montero, Salvador J. / PVT
Moser, Paul E., III / TEC5
Nakavich, Peter / PVT
Napier, Andrew Jackson / TEC4
Nordstrom, Roy M. / PFC
Ortez, Manuel F. / PFC

Paden, Paul Alexander / PFC
Peterson, Marvel V. / CPL
Pierotti, Bruno Jacob / CPL
Rickman, Howard Edward / PVT
Robertson, James Henry / PFC
Russell, Willard / SGT
Russell, Wilbur Forrest, Jr. / PFC
Sallee, James William / PVT
Schilling, William / PFC
Schoeberle, Kenneth Edward / PFC
Simms, Clarence E. / PVT
Smith, Armand P. / PVT
Smith, William J. / PVT
South, Frank E. / CPL
Spornitz, John C. / SGT
Stickel, Howard Frank / CPL
Talley, Herman / PFC
Wierzchon, Joseph J., Jr. / SSGT
Wodrich, Howard Milton / CPL
Zimmerman, George / PFC

Army Harbor Defenses

Includes 59th, 60th, 91st, 92nd, 200th, and 515th Coast Artillery units and the USAMP *Harrison*

Aftuck, Anthony A. / PVT
Akin, Earl K. / PVT
Allen, Barney Marvin / CPL
Almeraz, Manuel G. / PVT
Analla, Santiago Saavedra / PVT
Andreoli, Guido / CPL
Andrews, Herbert K. / MSGT
April, Armand Joseph / SGT
Arnold, Thomas Ching / PFC
Ashby, Jack G. / CPT
Aubol, Phillip Elmer / PFC
Baca, Juan E. / PVT
Bain, Harley / PVT
Baranek, Joseph C. / SGT
Barela, Herman P. / CPL
Barnes, Bulen June / PFC
Barnett, John B. / SSGT
Barton, Neville Lewis, Jr. / PVT
Bayne, Alvin Leroy / CPT
Bedwell, Alan Warren / PVT
Beem, Fred Eldon / PFC
Begley, Samuel Clarence / PFC
Bell, Chunkie Francis / CPL
Bendas, Steven / PFC
Bennett, John William / GUN
Bever, Spencer / PFC
Beyer, Glenn Howard / CPL
Biri, Henry Francis / PFC
Blanford, Leslie Munford / SGT
Blanscett, Roy J. / PVT
Boly, Harold Samuel / PFC
Bores, Sixto / PFC
Bostock, William LaVon / PFC
Bouton, Herman Richard "Buck" / SSGT
Bowers, Robert S. / PFC
Bowman, Thomas Charles / SGT
Boyd, Donald Lawrence / CPL
Braswell, Joe Lee / PVT
Briggs, Harold L. / PVT
Bright, William Lincoln / PFC
Brinkerhoff, Walter Whiting / PFC
Broderhausen, John W. / PVT
Brodsky, Bernard / CPL
Brown, Jack R. / PVT
Bruce, Reid H. / PFC
Brumitt, Ernest Loren / PFC
Bryant, Otis Connor / CPT
Burrell, Donald William / SGT
Burruss, Eugene / PVT
Calafato, Charles C. / SGT
Carmichael, Earl W. / PVT
Carter, Casey / PVT
Carter, Edgar H. / PVT
Cash, Douglas C. / PVT
Cashman, Russell Gill / PVT
Cates, Earl Eugene / SGT
Chambers, Robert L. / PVT
Chavez, Horacio S. / CPL
Chavez, Ralph P. / PFC
Clark, Everett Oscar / PVT
Clark, Manson Owen / PFC
Clothier, Maurice Elden / PVT
Coaker, William Arthur / PVT

Cochrane, Henry L. / PVT
Coffey, Kenneth / PFC
Collier, William J., Jr. / PVT
Connelly, Jack W. / TSGT
Cook, Steen Charles / CPL
Copeland, Kirby O. / PVT
Cordova, Hilario Ortiz, Jr. / PVT
Cordova, Jose / PVT
Cornelius, Edmund Oliver / PVT
Cox, Alfred R. / PFC
Cretsinger, Frank D. / PVT
Cummings, Warner Waldo / PVT
Curtis, William Mark / CPT
Daniels, Richard Holbrook / CPL
Davenport, Herschel Robert / PFC
Davenport, Rubin H. Delmo / PVT
Davis, Alfred T. / PVT
Davis, Dwayne Ardell / 2LT
Davis, Eugene Ray / SGT
Deel, John H. / CPL
Deets, Albert Donaldson / PFC
Deffenbaugh, Joseph Eugene / PVT
Dewey, Fred S., Jr. / 1LT
Didich, Nicholas, Jr. / SGT
Dorrance, Arthur Albert / PVT
Dreadin, Raymond / PVT
Duke, Lewis Edward / SGT
Duncan, Charles L. / PFC
Dunwoody, Raymond S. / CPL
Ellis, Emmett Edward / PVT
Emitz, Alex / PVT
Erich, George Henry / PVT
Estu, Andrew / SGT
Everett, Riley A. / SSGT
Fackler, Roy / 1SGT
Falk, Victor Arnold / SGT
Fallon, Richard Mick / CPL
Farley, Philip H. / 1LT
Fedinets, John, Jr. / CPL
Ferguson, Edward H. / SGT
Fessler, Clay George / PFC
Field, Albert Kilman, Jr. / CPT
Fillyaw, Luther Edward / CPL
Findley, Lewis F. / CPL
Finney, William H. / PFC
Fisher, Frank Vernon / PVT
Fleck, Anton T. / PVT
Fullmer, Don Bernard / 1LT
Galayda, Andrew / PFC
Gallagher, Robert Anthony / LT
Garcia, Benny Charles / PFC
Garcia, Leonides Lujan / PVT
Garcia, Manuel / PFC
Garcia, Raymond Joe / CPL
Garcia, Valentin M. / PVT
Garde, Pascual / PVT
Garris, Banks Edgar / SGT
George, John Kingston / SGT
Gerlich, Frederick John, Jr. / CPT
Gibson, Harold H. / PVT
Gittins, Venord J. / PVT
Goldman, Juluis / PVT
Gomez, Fernando, Jr. / PVT
Gonzales, Carlos G., Jr. / PFC
Gonzales, John Joseph / PFC
Gonzalez, Anatolio / PFC
Gosnell, Grady / SGT
Graves, Reed / LTC
Gray, Harry McReynolds / MAJ
Grinden, Donald Henry / PFC
Grogan, Howard V. / PFC
Gruska, Casimir A. / PFC
Gulden, Royal Scott, Jr. / 1LT
Gyles, Ernest W. / PFC
Haggerty, James A. / PVT
Hall, Elton Elvis / PVT
Hamm, William Estes / 1SGT
Handshy, Eugene F. / PVT
Hardin, David E. / SSGT
Hardy, Willmer Lee / PVT
Harrison, Benjamin F. / 1SGT
Harvey, Pershing Hobby / PVT
Hauck, Herman Huebner / CPT
Hawkins, B. M. / PVT
Head, Herbert Heron, Jr. / PFC
Hearn, William Cloyd / PVT
Hebert, James G. / PFC
Hein, Edward Herman / SGT
Henry, Boyd Nolan / PFC
Hiatt, Joseph Colonel / PFC
Hill, Samuel Jefferson / PVT
Hinson, Odis James / PVT
Hite, James McDonald / SGT
Hixon, Oda R. / CPL

Hoelting, Robert / PVT
Hoffman, Theodore C., Jr. / PFC
Hogan, Rhondel L. / PVT
Holmes, Charley A., Jr. / PVT
Holmes, James Russell / CPT
Hopkins, Bernard O. / SSGT
Horner, Warren P. / PFC
House, Jess Clifton / PVT
Howell, Burl Clifton / SGT
Howell, John F. / SGT
Hubbard, Charles Henry, II / SSGT
Hubbard, Charles M. / PVT
Huck, William B. / PFC
Huerta, Paul / CPL
Hughes, William E. / PFC
Humphrey, Bernice Francis / 1LT
Hunt, Perry A. / SSGT
Hunt, Richard Baker / PFC
Hunter, James Phillip / SGT
Hupp, Charles E. / SGT
Irish, Clayton Earl / 1LT
James, Vernie Lee / PFC
Jeffus, Hubert Preston / CPT
Jennings, Aubrey Bob / CPL
Jewell, Fred T. / SSGT
Jezek, Joseph Edward, Jr. / PFC
Joas, Herbert William / CPL
Johnson, Blair Reed / PFC
Johnson, Einar S. / SGT
Johnson, Howard W. / CPL
Jones, George Malcolm "Mack" / TSGT
Jones, James Jackson, Jr. / SSGT
Jones, Robert D. / PVT
Julian, Harry Appleton / MAJ
Kanally, Billy Bert / PFC
Kappes, George / CPT
Karell, Carl, Jr. / CPL
Kasero, Antonio / PVT
Kelly, Harry / CPL
Kelsey, Gustav / SGT
Kendall, Arthur G. / 1SGT
Kenna, Robert Nash / CPL
Kenny, Richard J. / SGT
Kent, Robert Kenneth / PVT
Kerr, John Wesley / PFC
Kimble, Dwight Ferguson / TEC5
Kime, Boyde A. / PFC
Kindle, Edward G. / SSGT
King, Warner Archibald / PFC
Kohler, Martin John / PFC
Kratz, John Henry, Jr. / PFC
Kryscinski, Edward / PFC
Kuhn, Lawrence M. / PFC
Kuznia, Ferdinand Vincent / CPL
Langeles, Albert Bernard / 2LT
Lavix, Leo A. / CPL
Lawson, Bishop. / SGT
Lawson, Dave B. / PVT
Leaird, Harley H. / PFC
Lee, Roy / CPL
Leech, Everett Clarence / PVT
Lemke, John Anton / PFC
Lente, Seferino / PVT
Leyba, Ramon B. / PVT
Lindsey, William Otto / PVT
Lines, Robert E. / CPL
Livingston, Raymond P. / PVT
Loftus, Francis E. / PVT
Loggins, Larry Allen / CPL
Long, Julian Oliver / CPT
Looney, Eldon Ray / PFC
Lowe, Harold Seldon / PVT
Lucero, Lupe / PFC
Lueras, Ernest George / CPL
Luna, Candido / PVT
Luth, John Rolland / SGT
Maillette, William H. / PVT
Mann, Chester Norton / PFC
Marquez, Manuel Ortega / PFC
Martin, Andrew J. / PFC
Martin, Clyde Levon / CPL
Martin, Harry / PVT
Martinez, Edward A. / PVT
Martinez, Joe C. / PVT
Mash, Jessie Frederick / SGT
Massie, Roy W. / CPT
Mathews, Burton Joseph / CPL
Mayes, James Alva / CPL
Maynard, Ennis Murray / PVT
McAlexander, Ernest Leighton / 1SGT
McBride, Blaine Rex / PVT
McClintock, Edward R. / PFC
McClintock, William Henry, Jr. / 1SGT
McClung, Dennie C. / PFC

McClure, Chester R. / PFC
McCluskey, John Brown, Jr. / 1LT
McCoy, Kenneth / PVT
McCray, Archie Evert / PFC
McCreary, Paul Easton / PFC
McMillan, George Perry, Jr. / CPL
McNeil, Joseph A. / PFC
Midkiff, James H. / PFC
Miera, Moises / PFC
Millard, Melvin Ray / 1LT
Miller, Albert Delmar / LTC
Miller, Frederick Adam / CPT
Miller, William J. / PVT
Mize, Edwin D. / PVT
Moore, John Isaac, III / 2LT
Moore, William Judson, Jr. / PFC
Mora, Trine / PFC
Morris, Jack C. / MSGT
Morrison, Charles D. / PFC
Morton, Roy Monasco / SGT
Moscato, Michael Richard / SGT
Murphy, Timothy F. / SGT
Nail, Robert Aaron / SGT
Neubauer, David / PVT
Nevedale, Mike / SGT
Nicely, Strother / SSGT
Nispel, Milton G. / CPL
Norman, William Perry / PVT
Northrup, Roy Richard / CPL
Nunez, Inocencio V. / PVT
Odneal, La Vaughn / CPL
Oglesby, James W. / PFC
O'Neal, John Franklin / CPL
Orosco, Arnold A. / SSGT
Osborne, Owen A. / CPL
O'Toole, Edward J. / CPL
Owen, William Henry, III / MAJ
Owens, Charles Leroy / PVT
Ozinkiemwicz, Stanley F. / PVT
Pace, Charles Andrew / 2LT
Paitsel, Ernest O. / TEC4
Palanuk, Emil W. / PVT
Palkovic, Lawrence C. / PVT
Palmer, Jesse A. / PFC
Palmer, Paul E. / PVT
Papadeas, Constantine L. / SGT
Paquin, Stephen L. / PFC
Parker, John W. / PVT
Parrish, Jack Albert / PVT
Patoile, Robert Thorald, PVT
Patton, John Pershing / CPL
Paul, Philip Charles / PFC
Paulk, Arthur C. / PVT
Pearcy, George Washington / 1LT
Pento, Nicholas D. / PVT
Peoples, Donald L. / PFC
Peters, Samuel L. / PFC
Peterson, Clifford G. / PFC
Petty, Ernest W. / PVT
Phillips, Connie Doyle / SGT
Pintarelli, Robert Pete / PFC
Piskorowski, Edward F. / SSGT
Platt, Robert T. / PFC
Plomteaux, Francis Albert / CPL
Pollock, Stephen E. / CPL
Powell, Horace Roy / CPL
Powers, Rufus / PVT
Queen, William D. / PVT
Quintero, James P. / PFC
Race, Arthur J. / SSGT
Rada, Emanuel / CPL
Rauhauser, Glenn Marvin / CPL
Ray, Reuben Earl, Jr. / CPL
Reed, Thomas C. / PVT
Reini, Terho Evert / PFC
Reynolds, John Edward / SGT
Riley, Edwin Anthony / CPL
Roberts, Andrew Joseph / PVT
Robinson, Franklin M. / PFC
Rocco, John B. / PFC
Rohrback, Gilbert / PVT
Romero, Richard George / PFC
Rosenberry, Kenneth R. / PFC
Rowell, Ralph W. / PFC
Ruiz, Joel Ruiz / PVT
Russell, Francis / PVT
Safin, Benny J. / PVT
Salas, Martin D. / PFC
Salaz, Luciano G. / PVT
Salazar, Samuel D. / PFC
Sandidge, Waymon W. / PVT
Sandoval, Ambrocio Juan, Jr. / PVT
Santistevan, Thomas / SGT
Saputo, Vincent / PVT

Sarracino, Frank B. / TSGT
Sarty, William W. / PFC
Satherfield, Howard W. / PFC
Savage, George, Jr. / PVT
Schutte, Henry J., Jr. / CPT
Self, James Peale / CPL
Sena, Jose Albino / PVT
Seward, Charles Marse / CPL
Sharp, Harry G. / PVT
Shimp, Neil Bertrand / CPT
Shirley, Hallford M. / PVT
Shoup, William H. / 2LT
Simons, Edward F. / SGT
Skoskie, George A., Jr. / SGT
Slade, James Richard / PVT
Slaughter, Lonnie Thomas / PVT
Slavik, Jerome / PVT
Slonecker, Gerald C. / PFC
Smalley, Richard Samuel / CPL
Smith, Albert Daniel / PFC
Smith, Averill Howard / PVT
Smith, Bernard H. / PFC
Smith, Connie Lewis / PVT
Smith, Earl H. / PFC
Smith, Francis M. / PVT
Smith, Frank B. / PVT
Smith, Gordon C. / SGT
Smith, Onie R. / SGT
Smith, Wilbur Clarence / PVT
Smolen, George / RM3c
Soichtic Rudolph M. / SSGT
Sprague, Arthur Lamar / CPL
Sprunk, Jack Daniel / TSGT
Stevens, Major / PFC
Straschitz, Mike M. / PVT
Straus, James E. / PVT
Streitenberger, Elmer E. / PVT
Strus, Walter P. / PVT
Susanka, Clarence R. / PVT
Suttles, Ernest Oscar / PFC
Taylor, Albert M. / PFC
Taylor, Paul G. / PVT
Test, Charles Daniel / PVT
Thomas, Charles Byron / PFC
Thomas, James M. / PVT
Thomason, Kenneth G. / PVT
Thompson, William M. / MSGT
Ticer, Neal Curtis / CPL
Trujillo, Charles Alfredo / PFC
Trujillo, Dionicio R. / PVT
Trujillo, Reynaldo / PFC
Trumble, George R. / SGT
Tubbleville, H. M. / SGT
Tubbleville, Oscar Wilburn, Jr. / SGT
Tucker, Raymond Thomas / CPL
Turnipseed, John Lincoln, Jr. / PVT
Ulibarri, Manuel / PFC
Utley, James L. / PFC
Vaale, Truman Edwin / PVT
Van, Charles E. / PFC
Vandagriff, Thurman Lester / CPL
Van Slyke, Loren E. / PVT
Vaughn, Miller / 1SGT
Verdi, Paul P. / SGT
Vetesnik, Irwin A. / 1LT
Vick, Roy McMahan, Jr. / CPT
Vincent, Harold / SGT
Von Schriltz, Max Leo / PVT
Ward, Floyd Eugene / 1SGT
Ward, Marvin D., Jr. / PFC
Wardlaw, Guy / 1SGT
Warner, Glenn O. / SSGT
Watters, Walter J. / SSGT
Weaver, Charles J. / PFC
Webb, Nathan Elder / PVT
Weigel, Daniel R. / TEC4
Westbrook, Joe W. / PFC
Wexler, Robert James / PVT
Wheet, Joe H. / PVT
White, Clifford Ross / SGT
White, Elmer Dee / SGT
Whitfield, Henry Draffin / 1SGT
Whittaker, Carl Coulter / CPL
Wiest, John H. / PFC
Wight, William M. / PFC
Wilburn, James C. / PVT
Wilkerson, John T. / CPL
Willbanks, Elkanah H. / PFC
Williams, Arthur R. / PVT
Williams, Joe Mack / PVT
Williams, Mervin Jeff / CPL
Williamson, R. D. / PVT
Williamson, Vernon J. / PFC
Wilson, Jack / SGT

Wilson, William, Jr. / PFC
Winther, Chris H. / PFC
Wirship, William / WOJG
Wold, Lynn Eugene / PFC
Wood, John D. / CPT
Woodson, James / PFC
Workman, Claud Leonard, Jr. / PVT
Wright, Ralph C. / PVT
Wurzel, Victor / PVT
Wyper, Menzies, Jr. / 1SGT
York, John F. / PVT
Young, Robert Edwin / PFC
Zdunek, Stanley Thomas / PVT
Zumwalt, Frederic Willam / PFC
Zwolle, Charles Wesley / PVT

Army Service Units—Other

Includes Ordnance and Signal Companies of the Philippine Division and Ordnance Department, Signal Corps, and Corps of Engineers of the US Army

Beyer, Frederick H. / PFC
Blaskewicz, John A. / PFC
Block, Gerald Francis / PVT
Bowen, William E. / CPT
Brodginski, Henry M. / PVT
Cauvel, Chester Monroe / SSGT
Connolly, Clarence L. / MSGT
Coughlin, John J. / CPT
Dugan, James Carr / PFC
Farmer, Harry L. / PFC
Francisco, Peter Joseph / PVT
Gallup, Brewster Garroway / CPT
Gartner, Morris A. / PFC
Gilbert, Leslie Bergen / CPT
Goss, Frank Milne / 2LT
Griset, John Daniel / CPL
Heady, Roy D. / CPL
Herring, Ralph Curtis / 1LT
Hucke, Lewis R. / PVT
Hutchens, Henry Harvey / PVT
Lothrop, Robert Blake / MAJ
Meek, Ernest W. / 1LT
Mowder, Harold Lawrence / 2LT
Myers, Bertram F. / 1LT
Polk, Reginald M. / 1LT
Proctor, Robert Delos / 1LT
Rosensweig, Robert M. / PFC
Ruan, James Stanley / CPL
Saulnier, Roland G. "Frenchy" / 2LT
Schmidt, Marvin F. / CPT
Smith, James E. / PVT
Wallick, Roy E. / CPL
Ward, Richard B. / SGT
Wilson, Einar / TSGT

Quartermaster Corps

Abell, Gilbert Roy / 2LT
Allen, Morris / SSGT
Bauer, Louis Edward / SGT
Bernard, Samuel / WOJG
Bovey, Franklyn W. / 1LT
Bryant, Charles William / CPL
Burrell, Walter William / 1LT
Campbell, Lorne M. / 2LT
Carnett, Franklin / PVT
Castillo, Ignacio Chavez / PVT
Clausen, Jessie Maynard / 2LT
Cox, Hershel B. / PFC
Cradit, Ralph H. / PFC
Cramer, Roger L. / PFC
Earl, Mervin Claude / PFC
Estus, Merritt B. / PFC
Fisher, Frederick T. / SGT
Garcia, Pete / PVT
Grossman, Bernard / PVT
Hoyt, Neil Freeland McGinnis / 1LT
Hudnall, Weldon Smith / SGT
Hull, Harry D. / MAJ
Hyson, Earl E. / SGT
Jacobson, Samuel / TEC5
Jones, Jesse Herbert / PVT
Kazart, Woodrow Wilson / PVT
Kolinski, Stanley J. / 2LT
Lambert, Arthur Frederick / PVT

Lay, Marlin M. / PVT
Lewis, Frank P. / PVT
McFarlin, Otha D. / SGT
McGrath, Robert Arthur / PVT
Minotte, Mike J. / PVT
Morrison, Harry E. / MSGT
Neer, Walter / SGT
Ocedek, John T. / TSGT
Palmer, Harold I. / SGT
Pentecost, Leo B. / PVT
Price, John Arthur / WO
Ramos, Frederick / PVT
Riley, Walter Lee / PFC
Roach, Glenn C. / PFC
Robertson, Howard E. / PVT
Schrami, Henry J. / PVT
Shy, James R. / CPL
Smith, Albert Elias / PVT
Smith, Willie M. / PVT
Thornton, George B. / PVT
Turnbull, Jerome J. / SGT
Wieczorek, Anthony P. / TEC4
Wilds, Kedron Sharum / PVT

Army—Other

Evers, Robert Martin / PVT
Lackey, John Woodrow / 1LT
Lasa, Tomas / PVT
Mays, Unknown / SGT
O'Brien, Fr. James Walter / 1LT
Wallbaum, Robert F. / SSGT

Army Air Force Headquarters Units

Bass, Harold F. / TSGT
Blackadar, Thomas R. / SGT
De Paoli, Frank V. / 1SGT
Gelb, Daniel / 2LT
Guearin, Victor E. / SSGT
Hawks, Albert Edmond / SSGT
James, Andrew Marmaduke, Jr. / 2LT
Kayser, Otto Bismarck / CPT
Lash, Russell Leroy / CPL
Martin, David G. / SSGT
Napier, Johnnie / SGT
Nelson, Donald A. / TEC4
Oetmann, Emil / CPT
Robinson, Vincent S. / TEC4
Sanders, Arthur Monroe / CPL
Schneider, Louis W. / MAJ
Serna, Philip Joseph / PVT
Spence, Fremen J. R. / SGT
Svihra, Albert / LTC.
Tidwell, Crawford M. / SSGT
Vetters, Clifford M. / WOJG

Army Air Force Base Units

Includes 5th and 20th Air Base Groups

Anderson, Alton Lyndell / PFC
Angus, Sidney / 2LT
Armond, Cleveland / PVT
Austin, Chalmer Wayne / PVT
Bates, Arthur E. / PVT
Blackanic, Frank / PFC
Blume, Basil Lawrence / PFC
Booth, Edwin T. / PFC
Brown, Herbert R. / PVT
Brumwell, William Scott / PVT
Cahayla, John / PFC
Causey, Charles Ben / MSGT
Colpitts, Walter William, II / 1LT
Cook, Lawrence E. / SGT
Danforth, Vernon Richard / PVT
Delamater, John Wesley / PFC
De Laurentis, Dante Antonio / PVT
Delo, Ethmer Ellsworth, Jr. / TSGT
Dickie, John, Jr. / PVT
Donley, Alvie R. / PVT

Dorsett, William / TSGT
Dove, Paul Whitney / CPT
Durnan, Thomas R. / SSGT
Eberle, Frank Aaron / PFC
Estes, Clarence Albert / SSGT
Ewens, Loyal Earl / PFC
Fay, Donald D. / SSGT
Fernandez, Salvador M. / CPL
Flowers, Walter T. / PFC
Fontaine, William F. / SGT
Foster, Frank L. / PVT
Gaines, Gaylord Virgil / SGT
Gaston, Lawrence W. / WOJG
Gottlieb, Murray / PVT
Green, Edgar P. / CPL
Guccione, Charles Jerry / PVT
Hales, Blaine Arthur / PVT
Hanson, Kenneth Henry / CPL
Harrell, Carl Raymond / PFC
Hayes, John H. / PFC
Hejkal, Milton Miro / PVT
Hendricks, Carl F. / SGT
Jenkins, William J. / PVT
Joers, Frederick / SSGT
Jurczak, Stephen / PFC
Kerner, Benjamin / SSGT
Kinard, Dorris Lavelle / PVT
Klein, Nicholas M. / TSGT
Kraig, Joseph R. / PVT
Kruchowsky, Steve Joseph, Jr. / SSGT
Lakey, Webster C. / PFC
Leonard, John T. / PVT
Loika, Pete / PVT
Ludwick, Gale A. / PVT
Mariello, James / PFC
Martin, Hollis A. / CPL
Mason, Nat J. / WOJG
May, Raymond Wingfield / PVT
McIntosh, Alexander R. / PFC
Merrick, Herman D. / TEC4
Miller, Joseph L. / SSGT
Moore, Joseph E. / PFC
Moore, Rodney H. / CPL
Morrison, Harold L. E. / PVT
Mossel, Benjamin / 1LT
Page, Wilfred Tennis / TEC4
Palumbo, Angelo Joseph / CPL
Pedota, Bennie, Jr. / PVT
Perron, Albert J. / PVT
Pippin, Millard Irvin / PFC
Potter, Richard A. / PFC
Rabinovitz, Harold J. / SSGT
Ratcliff, Fred Eugene / PVT
Reynolds, Peter W. / CPT
Richardson, Oran Homer / PVT
Ritchie, Kenneth O. / PVT
Robertson, Norris J. / TEC4
Rouse, Kenneth / SGT
Russell, Dalton Dwight / 1SGT
Sachleben, Frank K. / PVT
Sadesky, Edward James / PVT
Sakowski, Frank / PFC
Salata, Joseph J. / CPL
Sample, Carl A., Jr. / PFC
Scott, Roderick S. / WOJG
Seymour, Theodore W. / PVT
Sinclair, J. W. / PVT
Snodgrass, Thomas A. / PVT
Spurlock, Charles Leon / PFC
Stevenson, John / PVT
Struble, Edwin Chester. / PFC
Szymanik, Stanley / PVT
Tisdale, Howard C. / SSGT
Tolson, Charles E., Jr. / PVT
Tripp, Zebulon, Jr. / PVT
Van Steenberg, Clayton E. / PFC
Vargo, Joseph, Jr. / PVT
Vladich, Peter / PVT
Walker, Max W. / TSGT
Watkins, Reynolds H. / SSGT
White, William J. / PFC
Wigington, James Thomas / PVT
Wisz, Edward J. / CPL
Wuest, Charles M. / CPL
Wydel, Joseph A. / PVT
Young, Jack C. / SSGT
Young, Henry Levi / PVT
Young, Roy Edgar / PFC
Ziefle, William J. / PVT
Zitone, Joseph George / PFC

Army Air Force Pursuit Groups

Includes Headquarters, 3rd, 17th, 20th, 21st, and 34th Pursuit Squadrons, 24th Pursuit Group

Barter, Adelbert Ellery / SGT
Bryant, Camden R. / PVT
Canady, Bruce Truman / SSGT
Carevich, Stephan W. / CPL
Carroll, Thomas P. / 1SGT
Causey, Whitley F. / PFC
Chenoweth, Rolland Elmer / PVT
Chism, Frank Joe / SSGT
Dabney, Edmund Reed, Jr. / SSGT
Davis, Robert R. / PFC
Day, Jack E. / WOJG
Domenick, Joseph / PFC
Dort, Herbert F. / TSGT
Doyle, James Albert / CPL
Elkes, Frederick William / PFC
Engstrom, Walter F. / 2LT
Fields, J. Harold / SGT
Garrett, Cleitus Roy / 2LT
Garrett, James E. / CPT
Garrison, John Robert / SGT
Gaskell, Charles Earl "Jack" / 1LT
Godby, David Cleveland, Jr. / SGT
Grigg, Ralph J. / PFC
Halversen, Max B. / 1LT
Hankins, Curtis L. / PFC
Hegdal, Martin Judson / PFC
Henry, James M. / 1LT
Houseman, Edward Eugene / 2LT
Hughes, Harrison Sterling / 2LT
Iversen, Guy Wittrup / 2LT
Kenel, William Arthur / SGT
Kirsch, Charles / SSGT
Kitzmiller, Harold W. / SGT
Krueger, William Edward / PVT
Krysak, John / SGT
Libby, Hiram D., Jr. / CPL
Maimonis, James P. / PVT
Malone, Harlan Edward / SGT
Marvin, William Henry / PVT
Massey, John Earl "Jack," Jr. / TEC4
Matisovsky, Stephen / SSGT
McBeath, John / WOJG
McFarland, James B. / SSGT
Nowak, Taddeusz / PVT
Peterson, Phillip C. / SGT
Price, Hugh L. / SGT
Racicot, Paul / 1LT
Raker, John Newlin / CPT
Ramsey, Percy Elzie / 2LT
Risen, Coleman L. / SSGT
Roberts, Robert Frank / 1LT
Rooney, Thomas / PFC
Ross, De Wolfe / PVT
Salter, Robert M. / PVT
Schattel, Albert / SSGT
Schenning, Kenneth L. / SSGT
Schmidt, Duane J. / SGT
Schuh, Harry A. / TSGT
Shapiro, Daniel A. / CPT
Shea, Paul Dennis / SGT
Shelton, Kenneth B. / 1LT
Terrell, Harry W. / SGT
Tosh, Nathaniel Jackson, Jr. / SGT
Wenzel, Frederick W. / PVT
Winn, Will Roy / CPL

Army Air Force Bomber Groups

Includes Headquarters, 14th, 28th, 30th, and 93rd Bomb Squadrons, and 440th Ordnance Company, 19th Bomb Group; Headquarters, 14th, 16th, 17th, and 91st Bomb Squadrons, 14th Materials Squadron, 2nd Observation Squadron, and 454th Ordnance Company, 27th Bomb Group

Akers, Earl N. / PFC
Amox, Bryant Cornelius / TSGT
Ball, Freddie Louis / CPL
Barnie, Joseph W. / PVT
Baze, Buster K. / CPL
Bennett, Willard Earl / PVT

Bockman, Judge Samuel / PVT
Bonds, Dorsey Monroe / PFC
Brevdy, Oscar L. / SGT
Brewton, Marvin Virgil / PFC
Browne, Pope Lott / 1LT
Bullard, Willie B. / WOJG
Burgess, Edgar Beaumont / 1LT
Chaney, Edward A. / SSGT
Choban, Stephen P. / PVT
Collette, Francis Arthur / PVT
Craft, Paul / PFC
Crull, Scott W. / PVT
Cummings, William / TEC4
Dale, Eldon Milton / PFC
Damon, Robert Eggert / CPL
Dawson, Charles Patterson / PVT
Deak, Joseph Dumond, Jr. / PVT
Delude, Leon Wifred / PFC
Derringer, Francis E. / PFC
Dey, James John / 1LT
Donnelly, William Joseph / CPL
Duren, Robert N. / PVT
Edwards, Lewis Arthur / 1LT
Engel, Emanuel "Boots," Jr. / 1LT
English, Jack C. / CPL
Falk, Gottfred N. / CPL
Foster, Benjamin F. / PVT
Gates, Fentress D. / PFC
Gatti, Patsy Vincent / PVT
Gerson, William Earl / PFC
Graham, Owen Russell / 1LT
Halat, Joseph / SGT
Halterman, Austin L. / PFC
Hana, Leonard E. / PVT
Harrell, Jack Lott / TEC5
Hart, John Curtis / SSGT
Herndon, Elihu Z. / PVT
Hill, Charles Roger / PVT
Howard, Elmer Theron / TSGT
Hughes, Samuel Johnston / PVT
Hurst, James Clanton / SGT
Jackson, Mantie Lee, Jr. / PFC
Jordan, Nylon Floyd / PFC
King, Donald Woodrow / PVT
Lang, William Joseph, Jr. / 2LT
La Roe, James E. / PVT
Larson, Lewis R. / PVT
Lee, Robert E. "R. E.," Jr. / PFC
Lisk, James A. / PVT
Livergood, Wayne / 1LT
London, Harold June / SSGT
Lossett, Eugene E. / TSGT
MacMath, Donald / PVT
Mangrum, Max Ray / SGT
Martel, Lionel J. / TSGT
McClure, Robert Fisher / 1LT
McCormick, Robert F. / PFC
Medlin, Charles Raymond / PVT
Miller, William Tollie / PVT
Mitchler, Paul Eugene / 1LT
Molnar, Gaza J. / PVT
Moore, J. W. / PFC
Neil, Eugene A. "Mickey" / SGT
Noble, John Arthur / SGT
Oden, Tommy G. / CPL
Orta, John Lara / CPL
Owens, Westley Homer / MSGT
Poole, Samuel E. / SGT
Pryor, John S. / 2Lt
Putnam, John Joseph, Jr. / PFC
Ramsey, Jack Dayton / TEC4
Reynolds, Charles W. / PFC
Rice, Walter E. / PFC
Ringer, Graham L. / PVT
Ripley, Robert R. / SGT
Robins, Donald D. / 2LT
Rose, Norman / SSGT
Roth, Harry Robert / 2LT
Salter, Robert R. / CPL
Savage, Ottis L. / PFC
Scarboro, Pearly Hortance, Jr. / 1LT
Schroedl, George Stanley / CPL
Sears, Tommy S. / PFC
Sikes, Joe H. / SGT
Springer, Duey Everett / PVT
Stewart, Lamar Nelson / TSGT
Tanner, William R. / SSGT
Tefft, Erving Wooley, Jr. / PVT
Thomas, Lester / TSGT
Tompkins, James D. T. / PVT
Vos, Eugene L. / SSGT
Ward, Rankin Hershel / SSGT
Watkins, Ross E. / TSGT
Watson, Kearby L. / PVT

Weaver, William M. / CPL
Whally, Alvin E. / 2LT
Wiest, Arnold F. / PVT
Williams, Leon Franklin, Jr. / 1LT
Wolfe, James Franklin / PVT
Woodson, Everett Eugene / PVT
Wyatt, Rufus H. / PVT
Yankevich, John J. / CPL

Army Air Force Service Units—Other

Includes Signal Corps, Ordnance Department, Corps of Engineers, and Chemical Warfare Service

Alford, George / PFC
Allen, Daniel Dale / PVT
Baer, William Joseph / PFC
Bailey, Ernest / PFC
Barlow, Emil M. / CPL
Bernd, Peter Paul / CPT
Blair, Amon Max / PVT
Bradley, James C. / PVT
Brown, Peter J. / SGT
Butler, James Dwight / PVT
Carmichael, Cephus Lee / PVT
Case, Louis D. / TSGT
Clark, Richard Joseph / PFC
Combs, Johnie M. / PVT
Cox, Chick / 1SGT
Daniel, Blueford Fowler / CPT
Dawson, Joseph Albert / PVT
Elechko, John A. / PVT
Fadorchak, Michael / PVT
Farmer, Dellyn Ardine / PVT
Gastelum, Alfred J. / PVT
Gonzales, Richard Christopher. / PVT
Goodrich, Eugene R. / PFC
Hamilton, Oliver / TSGT
Hollingsworth, James L. / PVT
Illiscavitch, Joseph A. / SGT
Lawson, Andrew Harris / PFC
MacNeven, Robert Lee / PVT
Malcher, Rudolph / MSGT
McBride, Isaac Madison / PVT
McKinley, Leonard Wood / PFC
McLaughlin, Patrick Thomas / PVT
Miner, James J. / PFC
Moore, Junius Dodge / PVT
Norton, Louis D. / PVT
Pall, Wilbur D. / PVT
Pearson, Robert V. / PVT
Perrow, LaFayette A. / PVT
Roberts, Isaac "Ikey" / PVT
Rood, William Robert / PVT
Salzmann, Wesley John / CPL
Walker, George E. / PFC
Wasser, John V. / PVT
Zubik, Vincent / SGT

Army Air Force—Other

Grossman, James Swiler / TSGT
Haskins, Clifford A. / PFC
Karns, Charles F. / SGT
McFarland, Cecil Scott / MAJ
Munton, Harold Victor / CPT
Ranson, Joseph C. / TEC4
Spengler, Charles / CPL

Navy ships Canopus, Finch, Houston, Napa, Pigeon, *and* Tanager

Adams, Harry Edward / S1c
Ambro, Eugene Allen / PhM2c
Arnaud, John Bertram / BM2c
Autrey, Benjamin Franklin / CTM
Baer, Robert William / HA1c
Bishop, Charles Acle / SC3c
Burns, William L. / CBM
Butler, George Dwight / SF3c
Calhoun, Waid Bertram / COX
Carpenter, William Theodore / BM1c
Casey, John Franklin / MM1c
Ciulla, Michael Angelo / SC2c
Clack, Roy Lee / EM3c
Collins, Nathan Mayo / MM1c

Combs, Claude DeWitt / CBM
Coon, Benjamin Franklin / CM2c
Cox, Joseph Theodore / S1c
Craig, Willard Homer / BM1c
Deck, Vernon Melvin / MM2c
Engebretsen, Wilbert Ferdinand / CM1c
Foss, Clarence Stewart / F2c
France, Kenneth Carl / MM1c
Gammon, Eugene Arthur / WO
Girkin, Farrell Cyrus / EM2c
Goslin, Edgar Henry / MM2c
Graham, Turner / GNR
Grayson, Elton / WO
Grove, Alfred Edgar / CDR
Gutierrez, Anthony Aralio / CEM
Hampton, Rupert Lee / MM2c
Hershey, William Louis / S1c
Hippler, Ross Eldon / PM2c
Hirst, Allen Albert / EM3c
Hughes, Lawrence Thomas / MM2c
Kalamaja, Leo Benedict / QM2c
Kanae, John Edward / COX
Karwoski, Harry Edwin / S1c
Klupp, Adam Jack / EM2c
Latham, David Lexton / S2c
Lee, George Waldon / S1c
Lovering, Lauren Lionel / CEM
Lowrey, John Jackson / S1c
Lyon, Otto James / S1c
Matchett, Kenneth James / BM2c
McCranie, William Thomas / S1c
McCuen, Walter Rea / MM2c
Miller, Charles Ervin / HA1c
Nash, Jack Kenneth / CTM
Nollette, David Daniel / GM1c
Osborne, Raymond Daniel Alfred / RM1c
Patrick, William Harrison / BM1c
Patterson, Woodrow David / EM1c
Penter, Loren Boyd / S1c
Phifer, Jim Bob / ENS
Pinkham, Paul Webster / MM3c
Pliler, Luther Melvin / CPhM
Potter, Frank Jay / EM2c
Powell, John Michael / BM1c
Rauch, Benjamin Nathan, Jr. / BM3c
Roth, Egbert Adolph / CDR
Shumway, Kenneth Woodrow / PhM2c
Smith, Howard Bruce / CFC
Smith, Ralph Lowell / MM1c
Sturgell, Stephen Raymond / WO
Swinconos, Peter Paul / PTR1c
Sylvester, Valleon / CQM
Taylor, Forest Lee / PhM2c
Taylor, James Leon / S1c
Tinker, Charles Richard / S1c
Tyree, Lawrence Franklin / PhM2c
Watts, Edwin Allan / CQM
Webber, Edward Clarence / CEM
Wojtkielewicz, William / EM3c
Wresinski, Thaddeus / BR1c

Navy—Other

Abruzzino, Thomas Joseph / AM1c
Athey, John Francis / WOJG
Bean, Russel Chase / ENS
Bell, Richard Eugene / COX
Biron, Arthur Stanley / SC1c
Bouck, Ralph Richtmyer / BM2c
Brodsky, Charles / CBM
Burridge, George T. / CRM
Carl, Jeff Charles / GM2c
Cary, Oran Francis / RM1c
Casimiri, Nunzio Nichola / S1c
Chaison, Marshall Frederick / RM1c
Cox, James Leslie / RM1c
Dahlgren, John Adolf / RE
Daugherty, Elwood Alonzo / BM2c
Deeds, Buferd Alvin / BM2c
Deisinger, George M. / S1c
Demanio, Joseph Jack / RM3c
Duquette, William George / S1c
Ehrhardt, Melvin Edward / EM2c
Ewell, Parker Thomas Nelson / RM1c
Fager, Burl Dwain / SM3c
Fisher, James R. / S1c
Garrett, Walter Kenneth / LTCDR
Glass, William Henry / WO
Golden, Marion Eugene / S2c
Gooding, George Brewer / WO
Gothie, Daniel Shinton / LTCDR

Gregory, Robert Amis / RM3c
Gribbons, George Thomas / CCM
Grosse, William Frederick / CMM
Harrison, Vernon Frank / Y1c
Hausam, Alfred William "Bud" / TM1c
Henke, William Leonard / S1c
Herren, Albert Felix, Jr. / AMM1c
Hillman, Robert Stephen / WT2c
Hogue, William Austin / EM1c
Hughes, Lyall Arthur / EM1c
Hutchison, William Adolphus / WO
Jenkins, Alvin / RE
Keaton, Thomas James Salter / CMM
Killian, Charles Henry / BM2c
Lamb, James Shelton "Mike," Jr. / Y3c
Lowman, Ralph Seaton / S3c
Lyle, Wagner Dewitt / AMM1c
Maass, Adolph Rudolph / PhM2c
Morrissey, Thomas Leroy / EM2c
Murphy, John W., Jr. / MM3c
Musick, Arthur Benton / MM2c
Norgren, Oscar William / CTM
Olen, Leo James / RM1c
Oster, James Charles / CBM
Paine, Robert, Jr. / CGM
Payne, Harold Keysar / AGM3c
Probasco, Ellsworth Lincoln / WT2c
Regan, Richard Arthur / CMM
Ridgway, William Harold / TM1c
Ristau, Herbert Paul / ACOM
Saalfield, Herbert Albert / S2c
Senter, Claude David / S1c
Short, William Lawrence / GNR
Sigman, Carter Enloe / CCS
Spencer, George Raymond / MM1c
Stambaugh, William Allen / CY
Stemen, John Isaac / S1c
Steve, John / CBM
Stickman, William Frederick / MMC
Thompson, John Robert / RT1c
Tysinger, Raymond Luther / ACMM
Watson, Earl Earnest / S1c
Winig, Charles Anthony / FC1c
Winsor, Willard Ira / CY
Wright, William Jesse / BM1c
Zelazny, Leo Frank / RM3c

Marines

Amos, Robert Allen / SGT
Anderson, Albert Arthur / PFC
Anderson, Robert Louis / PFC
Anderson, Roy Arnold / Field Cook
Augustyn, Anthony Andrew / CPL
Austin, John Herbert / PFC
Baldwin, George William / PFC
Barker, Russell Pershing / PFC
Barnes, Roy Franklin, Jr. / PFC
Biggers, Huey Astas / PFC
Billingsley, Jack Maurice / PFC
Bingham, John Coleman, Jr. / SGT
Blancett, Jesse Ralph / PhM3c
Blaydes, Wilbur Kassel, Jr. / PhM3c
Boots, Morris Arthur / PFC
Brainard, John Thompson / 2LT
Breese, Paul Raymond / PFC
Brent, Claude Lester / SGT
Brohman, Henry George / PhM1c
Broski, Xavier Ulysses / SGT
Brown, Joseph Clifton / CPL
Brown, Lyle Junior / PFC
Browne, Edward Raymond / 1SGT
Burden, Joseph Dennis / PFC
Bynum, Cecil Woodrow / PFC
Byrne, Michael / CCK
Carrier, Wilton Maurice / PFC
Clark, Duane Jack / PFC
Clark, Max / LTC
Clubine, Robert Melton / CPL
Conder, Archer Wesley / PFC
Corbin, Leonard Roy / SGT
Craig, Kermit Elmer / SGT
Crain, Kenneth Eugene / PFC
Davies, James Edward / PFC
Davis, Rex Vern / CCK
De Mouth, Lester Jacob / PFC
Dubois, William Lubie / 2LT
Duncan, Richard "Bozo" / 1SGT
Fawcett, Albert William / PFC
Fitzgerald, John Patrick / SGT
Fowler, Harry Park / CPL

Fulton, James Wesley / SSGT
Garrett, Donald J. / PFC
Garrison, Alfie Theodore / CPL
Girardot, Carl Francis / FM1c
Gordon, Harvey / PhM1c
Grenz, Jesse Earl / PFC
Hale, Robert Lee / PFC
Hall, Jack Quentin / SSGT
Harris, Adrian Forrest / SGT
Harter, Harlan Dayton / CPL
Hartzog, Shelton / PFC
Havlena, James Joseph / PFC
Helmick, Raymond Arnett / SGT
Henderson, Ralph Lee, Jr. / PFC
Hicks, Thomas Randolph / SSGT
Hobbs, Earl Russell / SGT
Hobbs, Richard A. / PFC
Hodge, Roy Ray / PFC
Hoff, Ruben Samuel / FM1c
Hoover, John Horsford / PhM2c
Hubbard, A. G. / PFC
Huckabay, Uri Lloyd, Jr. / SGT
Humphreys, Howard Winston / CPL
Ianuzzo, George Robert / PFC
James, Howard Edwin / PFC
Jenkins, Louis / PFC
Jennings, Hugh Dale / PFC
Johanson, Willie D. / PFC
Jonaitis, Charles Frank / PFC
Jones, Paul Robert / PFC
Kail, Charles William / LTC
Kapplinger, Jarvis Max / CPL
Katauskas, Frank John / CPL
Kelner, John Raymond / PFC
Kenney, Donald Wilbur / SSGT
Keough, Stanley James / PFC
Koehler, Linroy / CPL
Kovalcik, John Paul, Jr. / PFC
Krigas, George Michael / 2LT
Kubeth, Joseph / PFC
La Pointe, Henry Dennis, Jr. / PFC
Larson, Leonard Edward / SGT
Leaders, John Griffith / CPL
Leininger, Paul William / PLSGT
Lewis, Robert Stuart / CPL
Linville, Bert Sackett / PLSGT
Luther, William Glyn / PFC
Lutz, Frederick Clair / PVT
Maddox, Morrison Buel / PFC
Mancuso, Ernest Joseph / PFC
Manning, Alan Shearer / CPT
Marquez, Trancito Garcia / CPL
Marshall, William Elmer / GSGT
Mathias, Robert Abel / PFC
McCoy, Marvin Marshall / PFC
Mikula, Joseph Edward / SGT
Miles, Walter Jefferson / PFC
Miley, Clifton Spencer / PVT
Miller, Roy Waltman / PFC
Moore, Clarence R., Jr. / PFC
Murray, Grady / CPL
Murray, Sylvester Elmo / CPL
Nolan, Emmett Franklin / SSGT
Nowlin, James Alex / CPL
Olson John Carney "Olie" / 2LT
Osborne, Howard Robinson / SGT
Parks, Edgar George / PFC
Pickering, Ray Wood / 2LT
Pickup, Lewis Herman / MAJ
Porche, William Robert / PFC
Prange, Edward Herman / PhM3c
Price, Theodore John, Jr. / PFC
Reifschneider, Wilmer James / SGT
Rice, Granville Jackson / SGT
Robison, Francis Edward / PFC
Rossell, Frank George, Jr. / PLSGT
Ruge, Robert Franklin / MAJ
Ruzicka, Albert / CPL
Sanford, Egbert Everett / CPL
Schlegel, Stanley Riechers / SGT
Selby, Harold Vernon / CPL
Sirota, John Francis / PFC
Smith, Hobert Lee, Jr. / PO1c
Smith, Jay Durfey / PFC
Smith, John Wescot / SGT
Smith, William Albert / SGT
Stahlecker, Harold Rienhart / CPL
Standefer, John Young / PhM3c
Stapp, Kenneth Wayne / PFC
Stokes, John Blanchard / PFC
Studnicki, Edward Joseph / PFC
Taylor, James Cullen / PFC
Taylor, James Edward / PLSGT
Thomas, Frederick "Fritz" / PFC

Toohig, Thomas Davis, Jr. / SGT
Trupiano, Peter Joseph / CPL
Van Hoenacker, Jerome Arthur / PFC
Vicentini, Tullio Vincent / CPL
Wallace, Ray Walker / PFC
Wells, Noble William / 1SGT
White, Wilbur Wasson / PFC
Wood, Jack Walter / CPL
Yakovich, Anthony / PFC
Yakowchyk, William / CPL
Yamolovich, Albert J. / CPL
Zink, Joseph Jacob / PL/SGT

Medical Personnel

Includes 1st General, 2nd General, Canacao, and Station Hospitals, Cavite Dispensary, and Medical Department

Allee, William Sylvanus / 1LT
Anderson, Irwin Henry / PhM2c
Arnold, George Marvin / PhM3c
Avery, Roy Elvin / HA1c
Bartz, Walter Frederick / CPT
Benison, Arthur Louis / 1LT
Bennett, Wilmurt Addison, Jr. / ENS
Bloomingdale, Leslie Frank / PhM3c
Bress, Philip / MAJ
Brokenshire, Herbert Cecil / LTCDR
Brower, Charles W. / PVT
Buckhold, Wilbert William / 1LT
Burr, Neil Maynard / CPT
Byrd, Hershel Wayne / PhM3c
Carawan, Benago Green, Jr. / PhM2c
Carey, Jerry Dalton / PhM2c
Castle, Elbert Eugene / PVT
Christensen, Ernest Lawrence / PhM2c
Collins, Fred Ernest / CPhM
Czarnek, Edmond R. / PVT
Davis, David Waverly / PhM2c
Davis, Leo Norman / PFC
De Backer, William / 1LT
Demuth, Paul Vincent / PhM2c
Diaz, Arthur Irving / CPhM
Dick, Robert James / PhM2c
Dobbs, Louis James / PhM2c
Donehue, William Eugene / PhM3c
Durham, Irwin Washington / HA1c
Eldredge, William Earl, Jr. / PFC
Fenton, Benjamin Arthur / SGT
Ferguson, George Theodore / LT
Fitzgerald, Albert B. / PFC
Fleming, Kenneth Earl / PhM1c
Francis, Lloyd J. / PhM3c
Frasier, Clarence Alvin / CPhM
Fuller, Eddy Warren / PhM3c
Fulton, Judson Paul / PhM2c
Galbraith, Robert Edward / PVT
Gallaher, Robert Neal / PhM1c
Gardella, Francis Adellio / PhM3c
Gaspa, Leonard Joseph / PhM2c
Glick, David A. Myers / PhM3c
Glover, Herbert Preston / PhM2c
Godwin, Luther Hartzel / PhM3c
Guthrie, George Truitt / PhM3c
Haines, John Wister / CPT
Hall, Joseph Leslie / 1LT
Halversen, Lloyd Henry, Jr. / PhM3c
Halweg, Stanley Martin / PhM2c
Harrington, Edward Douglas / PhM2c
Hartz, William Albert / PhM3c
Hayden, Elliot Alexander / CPT
Helms, William Arnold / PhM2c
Hempelman, Wayne Vincent / PhM1c
Hetzler, Marvin Leroy / PhM2c
Hogshire, George Riley, Jr. / CDR
Hoyle, Jack Mills / PhM3c
Humphreys, Bernard Francis / PFC
Hunt, Jack Earnest / PhM2c
Janney, General Arnold, Jr. / PhM3c
Jay, John Patrick / PhM3c
Jenkins, Jack Wilber / PhM2c
Johnson, John David / BM2c
Jones, Ernest W. / CPT
Jordan, Francis Dixon "Dick" / CDR
Junker, Dana Saladin / PhM2c
Kelly, Shirley Henry / PhM1c
Keltz, Charles / CPT
King, Orville William / PhM3c
Kirby, Henry Luther / PhM2c
Klumker, George Gerald / PhM2c

Koehler, Ralph Carl / PhM1c
Krumholz, William A. / PhM2c
Laudicina, August / 1LT
Lenhart, Albert L. / PVT
Linville, Jesse William, Jr. / PhM2c
Lipscy, James W. / PFC
Lisman, Edward Sherman / PFC
Mariette, Maxwell Albert / PhM3c
Marshall, William Lloyd / PhM2c
Matheson, Roy Lambert / PhM3c
McClatchey, Virgil Ford / PhM3c
McKinnon, Richard Lewis / HA1c
McLendon, Darwin Albert / PhM3c
Mohn, George / PFC
Morris, George H. / PVT
Nelson, Joseph Doyle / PFC
Noyes, Elton Leland / PhM1c
Osborne, Charles Eugene / CPT
Owenby, Clifford W. / PVT
Peachey, Gerald Ross / PhM2c
Peck, Gordon H. / CPT
Perciful, Victor F. / PhM1c
Philson, Clark Allen / PhM3c
Polk, Almus / CPL
Powell, Odeen Delano / PhM3c
Proffit, Leonard Melvin / PhM3c
Rader, George Andrew / CPT
Rice, Jack / PhM2c
Rihn, James Joseph / PhM1c
Riker, Dorman Neal / PhM2c
Ritter, Edward Francis, Jr. / LT
Sanford, Tebe Dewitt, Jr. / PhM3c
Sauers, Loran / PFC
Scheurer, Phillip L. / PFC
Shillington, Thomas Willdey / PhM2c
Shipman, Wesley Everett / PhM3c
Smith, Douglas Elwin / CDR
Sparkman, Eldon Ellis / CPhM
Spiess, Norman Joseph / PhM3c
Spriggs, Morris Homer / CDR
Stevens, James Jackson / CPhM
Stewart, Russell Clifton / PhM3c
Stueve, Emmett Gregory / PhM3c
Templeton, Elbert Lee / PVT
Terrell, Bishop Wade / CPL
Tiffany, Frank Leslie / CPT
Tousignant, Dr. Albert Noel / MAJ
Turner, Kenneth Earl / PhM2c
Vincent, Oland Melvin / PhM2c
Vise, William George / PhM3c
Walker, Myron D. / CPL
Warshell, Arnold H. / 1LT
Washburn, Lowell Lorenzo / PVT
Wawrzonek, Louis Joseph / PhM3c
Wells, Arthur, Jr. / PhM1c
Wendroff, Robert / PhM3c
Weselman, Julius / PVT
Wildermuth, Loren Burnham / PFC
Woodmansee, Cecil Stephen / PFC
Writebol, Charles / PFC

Merchant Marine

Berkowitz, Morris
Harrington, James C.
Hatton, Ivan Henry
Owens, Arthur G.

Civilians

Includes eight foreign-born individuals working for US entities

Abbott, John H.
Anderson, Ray W.
Arnold, Horatio S.
Asheim, Bjahne
Bailey, Richard Gunnison
Baker, Louis Linton
Barr, Donald P.
Bennett, John M.
Berger, Maurice L.
Black, Frederick James
Blackman, Dwight W.
Blackman, Harvey P.
Bloom, Frank Olaf
Booker, Harold H.
Browne, Verl R.
Browning, Horace B.
Buttner, Richard Lorin
Caldwell, Tracy J.

Casad, Thomas Harold
Chambers, Donald D.
Clamp, Jim
Coble, Urban L.
Coleman, William L.
Corkle, Richard C.
Cottrell, Floyd Furno
Davis, Chester J.
Downey, Merton B.
Dunlop, Kenneth A.
Durbin, Frank
Elliott, Charles A.
Fields, Robert J.
Flowers, Richard Felix
Fournier, George H.
Funston, Mathew W.
Ganfield, Cary G.
Gomm, Albert Benjamin
Grant, William
Haines, Wilbert Orin "Nukie"
Hart, Louis Boyd
Hart, Willard L.
Hedges, William F.
Hessenberger, Ben Bernhard
Heyda, Charles W.
Hogen, Olaf Olsen
Hotsenpiller, Winston R.
Jasten, Walter
Johnson, Carl Chick
Judge, John "Paddy"
Juel, Audnu
Kelly, Raymond
Kinder, Burl B.
Krom, Max M.
La Compte, Arthur G.
Lashley, James V.
Martin, Albert Roland
McKay, George N.
McLean, Hector D.
Merrill, Frank Smith
Michaelson, Oliver M.
Mitchell, Thomas Loy
Monroe, Lynn
Mundell, Rameous L.
O'Brien, Ray E.
Olferieff, Sergei
Padgett, Marvin H.
Peoples, Thayer World
Piland, James Edward
Porter, Otis Ollie
Riggs, John H.
Rose, Frank, Jr.
Rowland, Jess C., Jr.
Sandin, Billy Gosney
Sargeant, Warren D.
Schwab, Lester L
Selk, Ernest F.
Smith, Alfred T.
Snyder, Gordon
Snyder, Samuel L.
Stefansie, Martin, Jr.
Stenger, Arno J.
Stout, Vincent
Taylor, Orvillel Lee
Thompson, Francis Sigle
Trapp, Edward R.
Vallero, Lawrence J.
Varelas, Anastsios G.
Vicha, William Francis
Vincent, Charles M.
Vining, Carl J.
Weidlich, Charles Richard
Weisman, Joseph
Woodham, Howard A.
Wylie, James Edward
Zeitlin, William

9:00 p.m., European Theater, Forêt de Champs, Vosges Mountains, France (141st Infantry Regiment, 36th Infantry Division, and 442nd Infantry Regiment)

Dowden, Frank Nathaniel / PVT
Eastman, Alan R. / SGT
Hall, Albert E. / PVT
Hooter, Willard Joseph / PVT
Howard, John A. C. / PVT
Kilburg, Stanley Everett / PFC
Lengacher, John W. / PFC
Levy, Milton B. / PVT
Mattis, Charles Richard / 1LT
McClanahan, Ray H. / PVT
Togo, Shiro Sugiyama / SSGT

11:35 p.m., Pacific Theater, Hollandia, Indonesia (LST-695)

Clotfelter, Clifton Bunion / S1c
Coca, Johnny Joe / COX
Gebauer, Chester William / S1c
Gooden, Leonard Douglas / S2c
Holt, John Godkin / QM2c
Horan, Edward Thomas / S2c
Ilges, Harry John, Jr. / S2c
Kessler, Walter Wesley / PhM1c
Lemacks, Francis Glover / S2c
Lockwood, Charles William / COX
Matthews Wanza Ealam, Jr. / S2c
McEnaney, Thomas Francis / GM3c
McGinnis, Orville Lee / S1c
McIlrath, J. B. / SC3c
Moore, Donald Earl / COX
Musgrove, Vernie Elegia / SF2c
Pinkham, Eben Lewis / GM2c
Stefan, Robert Wayne / S1c
Strong, Charles H. / S2c
Swisher, Maynard / S1c
Van Houten, Arthur Frederick / S1c
Williams, John Russell, Jr. / S2c
Wojniak, Edward H. / TM3
Wolf, Charles Frederick / GM3c
Wozniak, Harry / UNK

All Other—Air Force

Anderton, Joseph G. / PVT
Archie, Aron / SGT
Brooks, George M. / 1LT
Burdick, Charles Edward / LT
DeLisle, Donald / 1LT
Diard, Gordon Roger / LT
Foster, James R. / LT
Hedler, Robert Walter / 1LT
Landrum, Jack C. / 2LT
Norrie, Richard R. / 1LT
Pilgrim, Edgar R, Jr. / TEC4
Radowicz, Zenna A. / PVT
Rand, Malcom / CPT
Reese, Charles Athol / TSGT
Smith, William Arless / CPL
Twilley, John F. / PFC
Winrick, Ralph Edward / PVT
Wright, Max, J. / CPT

All Other—Army

Alexander, Herschel F. "Buddy" / SSGT
Anders, Herman Albert / SSGT
Anglada, Salvador J. / PVT
Benton, Cecil / PFC
Bretschneider, George / CPL
Bryson, Donald G. / PVT
Burgess, William Freddie / PVT
Calvi, John Francis / PFC
Carbone, Frank Joseph / TSGT
Carnell, James E. / PVT
Church, Edward John / CPT
Clause, Junior Neal / SGT
Cole, Eugene E. / TEC
Collins, Trela Dempsey, Jr. / 1LT
Cote, Clarence J. / PFC
Crisp, Dennis Sherrill / PVT
Cruz, Tomas / SSGT
Daniel, Edwin Leroy / PVT
Felteau, Lionel W. / PVT
Forcum, Ted Francis / LT
Fortney, David Ashford / PVT
Freund, Robert W. / PFC
Fromm, Norman C. / PVT
Fulton, John R., Jr. / PFC
Gaston, J. C. / SGT
Green, William H. / PVT
Hall, Austin Elliott / PFC
Hamann, Alfred F. / PVT
Hammond, Sylvan Cicero / SGT
Harple, Chester F. / PVT
Harsh, Earl Edward / PVT
Hayes, John M. / TEC3
Heller, Ralph H. / PFC
Hering, Edgar Theodore / PVT
Herndon, Arch D., Jr. / SSGT
Hyams, Jack / PFC
Isaacs, Walter B. / LT
Jones, Lee Leonard / PVT

Jossund, Jens A. / PFC
Keran, Gerald L. / TEC5
Kisor, Glen Raymond / PFC
Linville, William F. / PVT
Manliclic, Federico L. / PVT
Marks, Thomas Virgil / UNK
Martin, William J. / PFC
McInnis, Frederick C. / PVT
McKeon, Thomas J. / PVT
Mynatt, James William / PFC
Nebe, Rudolph H. / PVT
Newberry, James G., Jr. / PVT
Newborn, Eddie R. / SSGT
Nichols, Jesse M. / PVT
Pehle, Richard C. / 1LT`
Perez, Jose / PVT
Picha, James F. / PFC
Poindexter, Robert Dale / SGT
Prather, James / PFC
Roager, Wesley John / PVT
Roberts, Walter J. / PVT
Rogers, Royal Rufus / PFC
Roubedeaux, Robert R. / PVT
Sasina, Raymond C. / SGT
Seamon, Ernest H. / PFC
Silva, William Charles / PVT
Smutko, George / PVT
Spiedell, Willie J. / UNK
Strohl, John L. / PO
Thomas, William Max / PFC
Tichawa, Robert A. / 2LT
Tubridy, Joseph F. / PFC
Unger, Frank S. / PVT
Vafeas, Paul P. / PVT
Vanover, Thomas / PVT
Voss, Burvel Allen / SGT
Whitfield, Steven Ralph / PFC
Wilson, James C. / PVT
Wright, Cecil Byron / PVT
Wydra, Stanley S. / PFC
Wylie, Thomas / TEC3
Wytrwal, Frydryk / UNK
Zaikowsky, George Joseph / PVT

All Other—Marines

Hall, Donald Raymond / PVT
McGuire, Raleigh M. / PFC
Quinn, James / PFC
Walston, Billie Ray / PVT

All Other—Navy

Davis, Warren / ENS
Eberhardt, Fred Lorrence / F1c
Flanery, Fred Virgil / S1c
Greenhagen, David Frank / ENS
Gunter, Berchard Kenneth / RM2c
Howard, Ralph Conrad / ENS
Lewis, George Titus, III / EM1c
Jeffress, Willard T. / F1c
McLeskey, Charlie Cleo / S2c
Pollard, Allen Albert / ENS
Rusch, Harry O. / 1LT
Smith, James Newton / S2c

The author is indebted to Bill Bowen, son of Capt. William E. Bowen who perished aboard the *Arisan Maru*, for creating a list of the prisoners aboard the hellship from the original Japanese handwritten records. Bowen's database is viewable online on the West-Point.Org website (www.west-point.org/family/japanese-pow/Bowen_AM.htm). Since the list's first publication, it has been amended as new information became available. Notable updates are included in a list maintained by the American Defenders of Bataan & Corregidor (ADBC) Descendants Group. A number of the prisoners aboard the *Arisan Maru* perished before the hellship sank. However, as reliable records of these deaths do not exist, the list above includes all those known to have boarded the *Arisan Maru* in Manila on October 12, 1944.

Other sources consulted to compile the list include the virtual cemetery of *Arisan Maru* prisoners viewable at the FindAGrave.com website (www.findagrave.com/virtual-cemetery/676430?), individual and military unit records on HonorStates.org (www.honorstates.org/), Ancestry.com (https://www.ancestry.com), and Fold3.com (www.fold3.com/).

NOTES

Preface

1. "Research Starters: Worldwide Deaths in World War II," National World War II Museum, accessed March 11, 2024, https://www.nationalww2museum.org/students-teachers/student-resources/research-starters/research-starters-worldwide-deaths-world-war; "The Battle of Stalingrad," World Atlas, accessed March 11, 2024, https://www.worldatlas.com/ancient-world/the-battle-of-stalingrad.html. Military personnel losses for other major powers are estimated at five million for Germany (7 percent of its population), three to four million for China (0.65 percent), and two million for Japan (3 percent).

2. "D-Day Editions," *Tacoma News Tribune*, June 7, 1944, https://www.newspapers.com/image/733641709/; "Heavy Fighting Rages on Normandy Beachhead," *Brooklyn Daily Eagle*, June 7, 1944, https://www.newspapers.com/image/52681741/.

Part One. Morning

1. Louis Morton. "The Decision to Withdraw to Bataan," 151–72.

2. Louis Morton, *The Fall of the Philippines*, 14–24.

3. Morton, *Fall of the Philippines*, 77–113.

4. "Historical Report: U.S. Casualties and Burials at Cabanatuan POW Camp #1," Defense POW/MIA Accounting Agency (DPAA), 4–6, accessed April 20, 2023, https://www.dpaa.mil/Portals/85/.

5. "Historical Report," DPAA, 4–6.

6. "Historical Report," DPAA, 4–6.

7. "Historical Report," DPAA, 6; Raymond LaMont-Brown, *Ships from Hell: Japanese War Crimes on the High Seas*, 117–18; Van Waterford, *Prisoners of the Japanese in World War II: Statistical History, Personal Narratives, and Memorials Concerning POWs in Camps and on Hellships, Civilian Internees, Asian Slave Laborers, and Others Captured in the Pacific Theater*, 150. A Naval History and Heritage Command article lists the number of hellships as 134, the number of voyages as 150, and the number of Allied prisoners transported as 126,000. Sources include

Gregory F. Michno's work *Death on the Hellships: Prisoners at Sea in the Pacific War*. The site notes, "There is considerable disagreement among historians on the number of hell ships and the number of sinkings." In *Silent Victory: The US Submarine War against Japan*, Clay Blair Jr. presents an exhaustive account of the various war patrols in the Pacific and notes the attempts during and after the war by multiple parties, including most notably the Joint Army Navy Assessment Committee, to determine which ships were sunk by which submarine or other ship or land- or ship-based aircraft or artillery. For the most part those records have stood the test of time, but are arguably prone to error.

8. "*Arisan Maru*," POW Research Network Japan, accessed April 21, 2023, http://powresearch.jp/en/archive/ship/arisan.html. The number of prisoners on board the *Arisan Maru* varies by source, ranging generally between 1,780 and 1,800. Bill Bowen (son of Capt. William E. Bowen, a prisoner aboard the *Arisan Maru*) created a list of the prisoners from original Japanese handwritten records. The database is viewable online at www.west-point.org/family/japanese-pow/Bowen_AM.htm.

9. Jonathan Mayhew Wainwright, *General Wainwright's Story*, 174–87.

10. Wainwright, *General Wainwright's Story*, 174.

11. "*Arisan Maru*," POW Research Network Japan.

12. John Glusman, *Conduct under Fire: Four American Doctors and Their Fight for Life as Prisoners of the Japanese, 1941–1945*, 356; R. Stevens, "Voyage to China," Overbeck.org, accessed May 25, 2023, https://overbeck.org/rso.

13. Glusman, *Conduct under Fire*, 356; "Cichy, Pvt. Anton E.," BataanProject.com, accessed May 25, 2023, https://bataanproject.com/provisional-tank-group/cichy-pvt-anton-e/. Anton Cichy was a Japanese prisoner of war; he survived the Bataan Death March and was transported to Japan aboard the *Arisan Maru* hellship. Cichy's comment that serves as an epigraph for this chapter appeared in Milton Kaplan, "Minnesotan Tells Horrors," *Minneapolis Star Tribune*, February 25, 1945, https://www.newspapers.com/image/182562657/.

14. "James Murphy Archive Record," American Defenders of Bataan and Corregidor Museum, accessed May 20, 2023, http://philippinedefenders.pastperfectonline.com/Archive/B5AD4C8C-A9C9-47A4-9B37-328643324531.

15. James T. Murphy, "Hanawa Camp History," 1, Mansell.com, accessed May 20, 2023, http://mansell.com/pow_resources/camplists/sendai/hanawa/murph_1.html.

16. "Cichy, Pvt. Anton E.," BataanProject.com.

17. "Cichy, Pvt. Anton E.," BataanProject.com. Accounts differ between survivors' memories, from stating the men were loaded in two holds at the outset by Charles Overbeck's posting of his father Robert Overbeck's account, "Voyage to China," to saying eight hundred were moved to a second hold (hold number one) partially filled with coal in Lee Gladwin's article for the National Archives' *Prologue Magazine*, "American POWs on Japanese Ships Take a Voyage into Hell," *Prologue Magazine* 35, no. 4 (2003), https://www.archives.gov/publications/prologue/2003/winter/hell-ships-1.html.

18. Waterford, *Prisoners of the Japanese in World War II*, 150.

19. "Hard-Pounded Corregidor Is Proud of Its Torrid 'Pick Up' Jazz Band," *Stockton (CA) Daily Evening Record*, April 27, 1942, https://www.newspapers.com/image/843878050/; Eugene C. Jacobs (Col.), *Blood Brothers: A Medic's Sketch Book*, 70–72.

20. "Phoenician Aids Fort Musically," *Arizona Republic* (Phoenix), April 28, 1942, https://www.newspapers.com/image/116885140/; Jacobs, *Blood Brothers*, 70–72.

21. Cichy, Pvt. Anton E.," BataanProject.com.

22. The ships in the convoy were three destroyer escorts (the *Harukaze*, *Kurekaze*, and *Take*); a subchaser, the *Kimikawa Maru*; a seaplane tender; and the cargo and passenger ships *Eiko Maru*, *Fuyukawa*, *Kikusui*, *Kokuryu Maru*, *Ryofu Maru*, *Shikisan Maru*, *Shinsei Maru*, *Taiten Maru*, *Tenshin Maru*, and *Arisan Maru*.

23. "Arisan Maru," WreckSite.eu, December 20, 2018, https://www.wrecksite.eu/wreck.aspx?57991.

24. "*Sawfish* (SS-276)," Naval History and Heritage Command, April 25, 2016, https://www.history.Navy.mil/research/histories/ship-histories/danfs/s/sawfish.html; US Submarine War Patrol Reports, 1941–1945: USS *Sawfish* (Eighth), September–November 1944, 29–37, USS *Snook* (Seventh), September–November 1944, 5–9, National Archives, Fold3.com, accessed May 20, 2023, https://www.fold3.com/publication/494/wwii-submarine-patrol-reports/; JANAC (Joint Army Navy Assessment Committee), "*Arisan Maru*." The USS *Seadragon* (SS-194) received credit for sinking three ships, the *Eiko Maru*, *Taiten Maru*, and *Kokuryu Maru*. The *Snook* scored a second hit at 2:00 a.m., sinking the *Kikusui Maru*. The USS *Drum* (SS-228) and the USS *Icefish* (SS-367) each sank a ship, the *Shikisan Maru* and the *Tenshin Maru*, respectively.

Chapter 1. A Pencil for a Pick

1. "Paul Henry Miller," Find a Grave, accessed August 29, 2023, https://www.findagrave.com/memorial/71213056/paul-henry-miller; Linda Bolen and Robert Miller, interviews by the author.

2. "American Historical Collection," BobBlume.com, accessed August 29, 2023, 48–60, https://bobblume.com/wp-content/uploads/2016/07/The-Story-of-US-Army-Officer-George-Moore.pdf; "Paul Henry Miller," Find a Grave.

3. "Paul Henry Miller," Find a Grave; Morton, *Fall of the Philippines*, 71, 237–38.

4. Morton, *Fall of the Philippines*, 565.

5. "Family Rejoices: Hears Son Is Safe," *Staunton (VA) Evening-Leader*, February 6, 1943, https://www.newspapers.com/image/315466620/.

6. "*Ija Noto Maru*: Tabular Record of Movement," Rikugun Yusosen, accessed July 22, 2023, www.combinedfleet.com/Noto_t.htm.

7. Waterford, *Prisoners of the Japanese in World War II*, 187. The number of camps varies based on the source and date. Often camps were renamed and sometimes relocated to other jurisdictions. The POW Research Japan website lists 126 camps in the Japanese home islands, 33 in Tokyo, 26 in Osaka, 23 in

Fukuoka, 12 in Sendai, 12 in Nagoya, 12 in Hiroshima, and 8 in Hakodate. Tokyo No. 8 was transferred to the jurisdiction of Sendai and took on the name Sendai No. 6-B in April 1945. "POW Camps in Japan Proper," POW Research Network Japan, accessed May 12, 2013, http://www.powresearch.jp/en/archive/camplist/index.html.

8. James T. Murphy, "Hanawa Camp History," 1–2, Mansell.com, accessed May 20, 2023, http://mansell.com/pow_resources/camplists/sendai/hanawa/murph_1.html.

9. Murphy, "Hanawa Camp History," 1.

10. Murphy, "Hanawa Camp History," 2–3.

11. Alan E. Mesches, *Major General James A. Ulio: How the Adjutant General of the U.S. Army Enabled Allied Victory* (Philadelphia: Casemate, 2020), 22–25; Lee A. Gladwin, "Reference Copy of Technical Documentation for Accessioned Electronic Records," National Archives and Records Administration, December 16, 2005, https://aad.archives.gov/aad/content/aad_docs/rg389_wwii_pow_nara_doc.pdf.

12. "Sendai #6 Hanawa POW Camp: Deceased Roster," Mansell.com, accessed May 20, 2023, http://www.mansell.com/pow_resources/camplists/sendai/hanawa/deceased.html.

13. Bolen and Miller, interviews by the author.

14. Kirk Spitzer, "Apology, Memorial in Japan Mark Reconciliation for American POWs," *USA Today*, December 1, 2016, https://www.usatoday.com/story/news/world/2016/12/01/apology-memorial-japan-mark-reconciliation-american-pows/94729644/.

15. "Japan Offers 'Heartfelt Apology' to US POWs," *NBC News*, September 13, 2010, https://www.nbcnews.com/id/wbna39145098.

16. Sam Sanders, "Morning Edition," NPR, accessed August 28, 2023, https://www.npr.org/2015/07/20/424571375/mitsubishi-apologizes-to-u-s-world-war-ii-veterans-for-forced-labor; Spitzer, "Apology, Memorial in Japan Mark Reconciliation."

17. "Japan's Apologies for World War II," *New York Times,* August 14, 2015, https://www.nytimes.com/interactive/2015/08/13/world/asia/japan-ww2-shinzo-abe.html?

Chapter 2. A Petty Officer of Pigeons

1. SP(X)3c Margaret N. Neubauer, Fold3.com, accessed June 1, 2024, https://www.fold3.com/memorial/657805491/spx3c-margaret-n-neubauer/stories.

2. Melissa A. McEuen, "Women, Gender, and World War II," American History, in Oxford Research Encyclopedia, June 9, 2016, https://oxfordre.com/americanhistory/display/10.1093/acrefore/9780199329175.001.0001/acrefore-9780199329175-e-55.

3. Neubauer, Fold3.com; "A Half Century of Learning: Historical Census Statistics on Educational Attainment in the United States: 1940 to 2000," US Census Bureau, April 2006; "Bring Him Home Sooner," Naval History and Heritage Command, accessed June 2, 2024, https://www.census.gov/library/publi

cations/2010/demo/educational-attainment-1940-2000.html; https://www.history.navy.mil/our-collections/art/exhibits/conflicts-and-operations/wwii/recruiting-posters-for-women/bring-him-home-sooner.html.

4. "Research Starters: US Military by the Numbers," National World War II Museum, accessed July 21, 2023, https://www.nationalww2museum.org/students-teachers/student-resources/research-starters/research-starters-us-military-numbers.

5. Eleanor Millican Frye, interview by the author.

6. Susan H. Goodson, Serving Proudly: A History of Women in the U.S. Navy (Annapolis, MD: Naval Institute Press, 2001), 125–27.

7. Jordan Grimes, "Pigeons: The Navy's First Aviators," Chips, January 5, 2024, https://www.doncio.navy.mil/CHIPS/ArticleDetails.aspx?ID=16584; "G. Paul Garson, Warfare's Unsung Pigeon," Warfare History Network, Fall 2017, https://warfarehistorynetwork.com/article/warfares-unsung-pigeon/; Donna Williamson, "Wacoan Recalls WWII Work as Pigeoneer," Winston-Salem (NC) Journal, November 11, 2018, https://journalnow.com/news/trending/texas-woman-now-became-a-pigeoneer-and-pioneer-in-her/article_ffd083d3-73d5-59a2-ade7-f7df37266b4e.html.

8. "A Brief List of Old, Obscure, and Obsolete U.S. Navy Jobs," USNI.org, December 3, 2014, https://news.usni.org/2014/12/03/brief-list-old-obscure-obsolete-u-s-navy-jobs.

9. Kaitlyn Kanzler via the Associated Press, "A Missing Pilot, a Mustang, and an Enduring Mystery: What Happened to This WASP Aviator? Gertrude Vreeland Tompkins," Army Times, October 5, 2019, https://www.armytimes.com/news/your-army/2019/10/05/a-missing-pilot-a-mustang-and-an-enduring-mystery-what-happened-to-this-wasp-aviator/.

Chapter 3. A Dress Rehearsal

1. "Here's Why Hap Arnold, a Practical Visionary, Became the 'Father of the Air Force,'" *Air Force Times*, November 18, 2018, originally published in *World War II Magazine*, October 13, 2016, https://www.airforcetimes.com/news/your-air-force/2018/11/18/heres-why-hap-arnold-a-practical-visionary-became-the-father-of-the-air-force/; Wesley Frank Craven and James Lea Cates, eds., *The Pacific: Matterhorn to Nagasaki, June 1944 to August 1945*, 6–8, 12–24; "Boeing History: B-29 Boeing Superfortress," Boeing.com, accessed August 29, 2023, https://www.boeing.com/resources/boeingdotcom/history/pdf/Boeing_Products.pdf; Victor Margolin, "The United States in World War II: Scientists, Engineers, Designers," *MIT Press* 29, no. 1 (2013): 14–29, https://www.jstor.org/stable/24267099.

2. Phil Dougherty, "Prototype Boeing B-29 Superfortress Bomber Crashes into Seattle's Frye Packing Company on February 18, 1943," HistoryLink.org, December 28, 2021, https://www.historylink.org/File/2874.

3. Rosemary Giles, "Men Were Too Scared to Fly B-29 Superfortress—until Two Women Did," War History Online, accessed July 15, 2022, https://www.warhistoryonline.com/world-war-ii/women-b29-superfortress.html.

4.ASN Wikibase Occurrence #98459, Aviation Safety Network, accessed October 4, 2022, https://aviation-safety.net/wikibase/98459; John Andrew Prime, "Our History: October Crashes at BAFB," *USA Today*, accessed October 4, 2022, https://www.usatoday.com/story/news/2015/10/05/our-history-october-crashes-bafb/73028366/.

5. "Barksdale AFB, LA Weather History," Wunderground, accessed October 4, 2022, https://www.wunderground.com/history/daily/us/la/barksdale-afb.

6. Aviation Safety Network, ASN Aviation Safety Database, accessed October 4, 2022, https://aviation-safety.net/wikibase/type/B29.

7. "Local Girl to Be Married to Capt. Dowling," *Albuquerque Tribune*, March 24, 1944, https://www.newspapers.com/image/782763685/.

8. "Bomber Hits Tree, Eleven Men Killed," *Shreveport (LA) Times*, October 25, 1944, https://www.newspapers.com/image/210681124/.

9. "6 Barksdale Airmen Dead in Arkansas," *Shreveport (LA) Times*, October 24, 1944, https://www.newspapers.com/image/210680128/.

10. ASN Wikibase Occurrence #98126, Aviation Safety Network, accessed October 4, 2022, https://aviation-safety.net/wikibase/98126, narrative taken from "B-17 Low over Worthington," *Worthington (MN) Daily Globe*, October 24, 1944.

11. "Bomber Crash Kills Six near March Field," *Los Angeles Times*, October 26, 1944, https://www.newspapers.com/image/380790229/; "Cpl. James E. Bertrand Dies in Plane Accident," *Sleepy Eye (MN) Herald Dispatch*, October 26, 1944, Find a Grave, accessed October 6, 2022, https://www.findagrave.com/memorial/137747533/james-e-bertrand.

12. "El Toro Marines Will Play Fliers," *Fresno Bee*, October 18, 1944, https://www.newspapers.com/image/701612977/; "March Field Whips Marines in Hard Game," *San Bernardino Sun*, October 23, 1944, https://www.newspapers.com/image/49423652/; "Far from Outside," *Fresno Bee*, October 25, 1944, https://www.newspapers.com/image/701613305/.

13. "Plane Lands Then Explodes," *Hutchinson (KS) News*, October 28, 1944, https://www.newspapers.com/image/1034208/; "Capt. H. J. Keadin Dies in Plane Crash," *Troy (NY) Record*, October 31, 1944, https://www.newspapers.com/image/61029917/.

14. "ASN Wikibase Occurrence #98458," Aviation Safety Network, accessed October 4, 2022, https://aviation-safety.net/wikibase/98458; Michael D. Roberts, *Dictionary of American Naval Aviation Squadrons* (Washington, DC: Naval History and Heritage Command, Department of the Navy, n.d.), 2:367, accessed October 6, 2023, https://www.history.navy.mil/content/dam/nhhc/research/histories/naval-aviation/dictionary-of-american-naval-aviation-squadrons-volume-2/pdfs/chap3-12.pdf; "Women Marines, 11 Downed on Desert Island," *San Bernardino Daily Sun*, October 31, 1944, https://www.newspapers.com/image/49424056/.

15. "Women Marines, 11 Downed on Desert Island"; "Girl Marines Marooned 4 Days on Desert Isle with 11 Men," *Oroville (CA) Mercury Register*, October 31,

1944, https://www.newspapers.com/image/679273576/; United Press, "Girls Decide It's Hardly Paradise, Even with Lots of Men Around," *Mansfield (OH) News-Journal*, October 31, 1944, https://www.newspapers.com/image/292383562/.

16. "ASN Wikibase Occurrence #98458," Aviation Safety Network.

17. Robert Blanchard, "Sobering Stats: 15,000 U.S. Airmen Killed in Training in WW II," Real Clear History, February 12, 2019, accessed October 21, 2022, https://www.realclearhistory.com/articles/2019/02/12/staggering_statistics_15000_us_airmen_killed_in_training_in_ww_ii_412.html. The 14,903 aircrew lost to accidents in the United States were considerably more than the 10,921 lost to accidents abroad, and the total (25,844) amounted to half that of the 52,173 aircrew lost to combat. The 21,583 planes lost to accidents in the United States compared with almost an equal number (20,633) lost to accidents overseas and to the number lost to combat (22,948) and was just under a third of the 66,073 total lost. The total includes 909 lost during delivery of aircraft from the United States to their duty stations. *Army Air Forces Statistical Digest World War II* (Office of Statistical Control, December 1945), https://apps.dtic.mil/dtic/tr/fulltext/u2/a542518.pdf. Glider pilots from both Britain and the United States also called their aircraft—designed for one-way flights behind enemy lines—flying coffins.

Chapter 4. The First "Kamikaze"

1. General Orders, No. 13, Headquarters Department of the Army, Washington, DC, April 6, 1964, https://web.archive.org/web/20131103165818/; http://armypubs.army.mil/epubs/pdf/go6413.pdf.

2. M. Hamlin Cannon, ed., *Leyte: The Return to the Philippines*, 22–24.

3. Joseph Connor, "Shore Party: The Truth behind the Famous MacArthur Photo," HistoryNet.com, December 12, 2016, https://www.historynet.com/shore-party-macarthur-photo/; Douglas A. MacArthur, *A Soldier Speaks: Public Papers and Speeches of General of the Army, Douglas MacArthur*, 132–33.

4. Cannon, *Leyte*, 21–23.

5. Charles Robert Anderson, *Leyte: The US Army Campaigns of World War II*, 10–15.

6. *Encyclopedia Britannica*, s.v. "Battle of Leyte Gulf," July 7, 2023, https://www.britannica.com/event/Battle-of-Leyte-Gulf.

7. Douglas A. MacArthur, *Reports of General MacArthur: The Campaigns of MacArthur in the Pacific*, 203–7.

8. Cannon, *Leyte*, 21–23.

9. Cannon, *Leyte*, 60.

10. Cannon, *Leyte*, 61–73.

11. Cannon, *Leyte*, 68.

12. MacArthur, *Reports of General MacArthur*, 226–28.

13. Cannon, *Leyte*, 80.

14. John Keegan, *The Second World War*, 554–60.

15. "LCI Facts," USS Landing Craft Infantry National Association, accessed August 23, 2023, http://usslci.org/facts/; C. J. Macaluso, "LCI(G)-65 Action

Report: Initial Landing Leyte Island, November 13, 1944," Navsource.org, accessed August 24, 2023, 1–5, http://www.navsource.org/archives/10/15/pdf/150065a.pdf.

16. Trent Hone, "Countering the Kamikaze," *Naval History Magazine* 34, no. 5 (2020), https://www.usni.org/magazines/naval-history-magazine/2020/october/countering-kamikaze. Further support for not characterizing the attacks on October 24, as organized suicide bombers: "Japanese records (e.g., Tokkōtai Senbotsusha 1990, 130–312) do not include any Navy or Army special attack pilots who died on October 24, 1944." These sources also do not list the *Franklin* or *Belleau Wood* attacks. See Bill Gordon, "47 Ships Sunk by Kamikaze Aircraft," Kamikaze Images, accessed August 24, 2023, https://www.kamikazeimages.net/background/ships-sunk/index.htm.

17. Macaluso, "LCI(G)-65 Action Report."

18. "Lester Eugene Aiston," Ancestry.com, accessed July 19, 2022, https://www.ancestryinstitution.com/search/?name=lester_aiston; Macaluso, "LCI(G)-65 Action Report," 5.

19. Tank Landing Ship (LST) and USS LST-452, Navsource.org, accessed August 24, 2023, https://www.navsource.org/archives/10/16/16idx.htm-.

20. Ernie Pyle, "LSTs Are Tough to Sail, but Crews Swear by Them," *Buffalo News*, March 24, 1944, https://www.newspapers.com/image/842384042/.

21. Lt. (j.g.) Phineas Stevens, comp., "History of LST Flotilla Seven," NavSource.org, accessed August 24, 2023, 7–9, http://www.navsource.org/archives/10/16/pdf/160018a.pdf.

22. "LST-171 War Diary, 12/1–31/43," US World War II War Diaries, 1941–45, National Archives, Fold3.com, accessed August 28, 2023, 4, https://www.fold3.com/image/302085746/war-history-page-4-us-world-war-ii-war-diaries-1941-1945.

23. "James Andrew Dunn," Find a Grave, accessed August 21, 2023, https://www.findagrave.com/memorial/158153338/james-andrew-dunn.

24. G. W. Morris, Commanding, "LST-452 Action Report: Leyte Operation, Oct. 27, 1944," National Archives, Fold3.com, accessed October 1, 2023, https://www.fold3.com/image/292498349/rep-of-amphibious-ops-in-the-invasion-of-leyte-is-philippines-1020-2144-page-1-us-world-war-ii-war-d.

25. "James Andrew Dunn," article in *Waseca (MN) Journal*, November 22, 1944, Find a Grave, accessed August 21, 2023, https://www.findagrave.com/memorial/158153338/james-andrew-dunn.

26. Stevens, "History of LST Flotilla Seven," 20–21.

27. Cannon, *Leyte*, 82–84.

28. "Garret Glum," Find a Grave, accessed August 21, 2023, https://www.findagrave.com/memorial/56788347/garret-j-glum; "Praise Soldier Who Gave Life at Leyte," *Bismarck (ND) Tribune*, February 29, 1945, https://www.newspapers.com/image/55141501/.

29. "Praise Soldier Who Gave Life at Leyte."

30. MacArthur, *Reports of General MacArthur*, 367–68; Anderson, *Leyte*, 30.

31. MacArthur, *Reports of General MacArthur*, 203.

32. "Yanks Win Philippine Foothold," *St. Louis Post-Dispatch*, October 20, 1944, https://www.newspapers.com/image/139859549/.

33. MacArthur, *Reports of General MacArthur*, 236.

34. "Aubrey S. Newman; 'Follow Me!' Army General," *Los Angeles Times*, January 23, 1994, https://www.latimes.com/archives/la-xpm-1994-01-23-mn-14612-story.html.

35. "James Andrew Dunn," Find a Grave; "Commanding Officer Visits Home of Winonan Who Died," *Winona (MN) Daily News*, January 12, 1945, https://www.newspapers.com/image/546499412/.

Chapter 5. And Then Another

1. Edwin H. Lundquist, Commander, Navy Office of Information, "Fleet Tugs in World War II," http://ships.bouwman.com/Navy/Tugs/ATR-7/WWII.html, reprinted from http://www.chinfo.navy.mil/navpalib/wwii/facts/fleettug.txt; "ATO-12," DANFS Online Auxiliaries, accessed August 20, 2023, https://www.hazegray.org/danfs/auxil/at12.txt.

2. Michael Sharpe, Jerry Scutts, and Dan March, *Aircraft of World War II: A Visual Encyclopedia* (London: PRC, 1999), 340–50.

3. W. R. Wurzler to Commander-in-Chief, United States Fleet, USS *Sonoma* (ATO-12), "Action Report: Report of Operations in the Invasion of Leyte Islands, Philippines, 10/20–24/44, Including Sinking of after Being Crash-Dived by Jap Betty on 10/24/44," 7.

4. Wurzler, USS *Sonoma* (ATO-12), "Action Report," 2; Bud Shortridge, "SS *Augustus Thomas*: Liberty Freighter," ShipsNostalgia.com, comments, accessed August 23, 2023, https://www.shipsnostalgia.com/threads/ss-augustus-thomas-liberty-freighter.46349/.

5. Wurzler, USS *Sonoma* (ATO-12), "Action Report," 2.

6. Wurzler, USS *Sonoma* (ATO-12), "Action Report," 3.

7. " Roy Lewis McMillan," Find a Grave, accessed August 8, 2023, https://www.findagrave.com/memorial/18311750/roy-lewis-mcmillan.

8. Wurzler, USS *Sonoma* (ATO-12), "Action Report," 6; "Donnas Hank Boyd," Find a Grave, accessed August 8 2023, https://www.findagrave.com/memorial/56781320/donnas-hank-boyd.

9. Lundquist, "Fleet Tugs in World War II."

10. Wurzler, USS *Sonoma* (ATO-12), "Action Report," 6.

11. S. A. Thompson, Medical Officer, to the Commanding Officer, USS *Fremont* (APA-44), "Action Report: Medical Department," 19; Paul Tackett, Commanding, LCI(L)-978, "Action Report: Leyte Island Operation, Oct. 24, 1944," 6–7.

12. "Pastor Will Conduct Services for Two Sons," *Minneapolis Star*, May 30, 1945, https://www.newspapers.com/image/187523820/; "RM3c Gordon A. Judson," Find a Grave, accessed August 10, 2023, https://www.findagrave.com/memorial/56752343/gordon-a-judson; "Radioman Reported Lost in the Pacific," *Rochester (NY) Democrat and Chronicle*, December 8, 1944, https://www.newspapers.com/image/136348595/.

13. Reports by Denis and Peggy Warner claim a Sally-type bomber, not a Nell, crashed into LCI-1065. Denis Warner and Peggy Warner, with Cmdr. Sadao Seno, *The Sacred Warriors: Japan's Suicide Legions* (New York: Van Nostrand Reinhold, 1982), https://www.kamikazeimages.net/background/ships-sunk/index.htm.

14. "Donnas Hank Boyd," Navy Cross Citation by Commanding Officer, USS *Sonoma*, File Pers 8249-MS, 19, 1944, MilitaryTimes.com, https://valor.militarytimes.com/hero/19820.

15. "Pastor Will Conduct Services for Two Sons"; "Bedford Sailor Listed as Dead," *Bedford (PA) Gazette*, December 21, 1945, https://www.newspapers.com/image/15492565/.

16. "Walter R. Wurzler, USNR," uboat.net, accessed September 19, 2023, https://www.uboat.net/allies/commanders/6311.html.

Chapter 6. The "Photo Joes"

1. Missing Aircraft Report #42-68274, Report No. 9803, Missing Crew Reports of the US Army Air Forces, 1942–47, National Archives, Fold3.com, accessed August 18, 2022, https://www.fold3.com/image/139122540; John Stanaway and Bob Rocker, *The Eightballers: Eyes of the Fifth Air Force, the 8th Photo Reconnaissance Squadron in WWII*, 44–45.

2. Stanaway and Rocker, *Eightballers*, 51.

3. "Lockheed P-38 Lightning," Aviation History Online Museum, accessed August 17, 2022, http://www.aviation-history.com/lockheed/p38.html; Stanaway and Rocker, *Eightballers*, 47; "P-38 Variation: Photo Recon," P38assn.org, accessed August 17, 2022, https://p38assn.org/variations/.

4. Stanaway and Rocker, *Eightballers*, 60.

5. Walter J. Boyne, "Reconnaissance on the Wing," *Air & Space Forces Magazine*, October 1, 1999, https://www.airandspaceforces.com/article/1099recon/.

6. "US Distinguished Flying Cross Awarded Capt. Alexander Guerry," *Chattanooga Times*, August 28, 1943, 3.

7. Stanaway and Rocker, *Eightballers*, 35.

8. "John W. Gunnison," adapted from Eric Paddock, "Looking across the Divide: The Visual Legacy of Captain John W. Gunnison," *Colorado Heritage Magazine* 26, no. 2 (n.d.), ColoradoEncyclopedia.org, accessed August 20, 2023, https://coloradoencyclopedia.org/article/john-w-gunnison.

9. "Clair Bardsley Missing," *Gunnison Valley (UT) News*, November 16, 1944, https://www.newspapers.com/image/612756137/.

10. "Boys in Service," *Gunnison Valley (UT) News*, June 8, 1944, https://www.newspapers.com/image/612754987/.

11. "6th Reconnaissance Group," USAFUnitHistory.com, accessed August 18, 2022, http://ww45.usafunithistory.com/PDF/.

12. Missing Aircraft Report #42-68274.

13. "26th Photo Reconnaissance Squadron Book," 6thPRG.yolasite.com, accessed August 18, 2022, http://6thprg.yolasite.com/26th-prs.php.

14. Missing Aircraft Report #42-68274.
15. Missing Aircraft Report #42-68274.
16. "6th Reconnaissance Group," USAFUnitHistory.com.
17. "Clair Bardsley Missing."
18. Stanaway and Rocker, *Eightballers*, 90.
19. "Guerry, Alex," Tennessee Sports Hall of Fame, accessed August 20, 2023, https://tshf.net/halloffame/guerry-alex/.

Chapter 7. The Second Time Around

1. "George McElroy Succumbs to Heart Attack at Alaska Base," *Mason City (IA) Globe Gazette,* October 28, 1944, https://www.newspapers.com/image/391308058/.
2. "USS *Rowe* (DD-564)," Naval History and Heritage Command, accessed August 11, 2023, https://www.history.navy.mil/content/history/nhhc/research/histories/ship-histories/danfs/r/rowe.html.
3. "USS *Rowe* (DD-564)," Naval History and Heritage Command.
4. Department of the Navy, Bureau of Yards and Docks, *Building the Navy's Bases in World War II: History of the Bureau of Yards and Docks and the Civil Engineer Corps, 1940–1946*, 178–84.
5. Department of the Navy, Bureau of Yards and Docks, *Building the Navy's Bases in World War II*, 178–84.
6. Earl William Long Collection (AFC/2001/001/2316), Personal Narrative, Veterans History Project, American Folklife Center, Library of Congress, 1943, accessed August 11, 2023, https://www.loc.gov/item/afc2001001.02316/.
7. George L. MacGariggle, *Aleutian Islands: The US Army Campaigns of World War II* (Washington, DC: Center of Military History), 1–12.
8. MacGariggle, *Aleutian Islands*, 1–12.
9. Department of the Navy, Bureau of Yards and Docks, *Building the Navy's Bases in World War II*, 178–84.
10. "Franklin D. Roosevelt Day by Day," Day by Day, accessed August 18, 2023, http://www.fdrlibrary.marist.edu/daybyday/daylog/august-3rd-1944/. President Roosevelt arrived in Adak aboard the USS *Baltimore* on a "bluebird" day for the area, with a low of forty-two degrees. After his lunch the weather worsened, but after dinner aboard the *Baltimore*, he had time to fish. With his hook dangling over the side, the president caught several small Dolly Varden trout and a few other fish.
11. "History of the USS *Rowe* (DD-564)," letter from A. L. Young Jr., Commanding Officer, to the Secretary of the Navy, October 27, 1945, 3–4, Fold3.com, accessed August 11, 2023, https://www.fold3.com/image/301979906.
12. Richard Layman, *Shadow Man: The Life of Dashiell Hammett* (New York: Harcourt, Brace, and Jovanovich, 1981), 186–99; Peter Porco, "Deadline Adak: Dashing Dashiell Hammett's Adak Newspaper for the Troops," *Anchorage Daily News*, January 18, 2015, https://www.adn.com/we-alaskans/article/deadline-adak-dashing-dashiell-hammett-adak-newspaper-troops/2015/01/18/.

13. "Features Salesman Now on Shore Duty at Alaskan Base," *Mason City (IA) Globe Gazette*, October 19, 1944, https://www.newspapers.com/image/391305401/.

14. Department of the Navy, Bureau of Yards and Docks, *Building the Navy's Bases in World War II*, 178–84.

Chapter 8. A Most Unlikely Place to Land

1. Defense POW/MIA Accounting Agency (DPAA) records provided by the Adolfae family; Michael H. Adolfae, interview by the author.

2. "Americans in the RCAF," Bomber Command Museum, accessed August 2, 2023, https://www.bombercommandmuseum.ca/bomber-command/americans-in-the-rcaf/.

3. Spencer Dunmore, *Wings for Victory: The Remarkable Story of the British Commonwealth Air Training Plan in Canada*, 242.

4. DPAA records provided by the Adolfae family; Adolfae, interview by the author.

5. "Americans in the RCAF," Bomber Command Museum.

6. Wesley Frank Craven and James Lee Cate, *Europe: Argument to V-E Day, January 1944–May 1945*, 558–60.

7. Craven and Cate, *Europe*.

8. "302nd Transport Wing," American Air Museum in Britain, accessed August 11, 2023, https://www.americanairmuseum.com/archive/unit/302nd-transport-wing.

9. Missing Aircraft Report #41-18627, Report No. 10712, Missing Crew Reports of the US Army Air Forces, 1942–47, National Archives, Fold3.com, accessed May 21, 2023, https://www.fold3.com/image/28713229.

10. DPAA Investigation report, April 2013.

11. Missing Aircraft Report #41-18627.

12. DPAA Investigation report, April 2013.

13. DPAA Investigation report, April 2013: Memorandum, March 17, 1949, Officer in Charge, Casualty Section: Report of Death by Maj. T. J. Collum, records provided by the Adolfae family.

14. DPAA Investigation report, April 2013: Narrative of Investigation, US Army Graves Registration Detachment, October 17, 1950 by Capt. Edward Towsey, QMC, records provided by the Adolfae family.

15. DPAA Investigation report, April 2013.

16. DPAA records provided by the Adolfae family; Adolfae, interview by the author.

Chapter 9. To the Rescue

1. "Cdr. Bruce Lawrence Harwood," Find a Grave, accessed July 24, 2022, https://www.findagrave.com/memorial/56755792/bruce-lawrence-harwood; "Claremont," *Pomona (CA) Progress Bulletin*, September 12, 1931, https://www.newspapers.com/image/623411046/.

2. Bernard C. Nalty, *Winged Shield, Winged Sword: A History of the United States Air Force* (Washington, DC: Air Force History and Museum Programs, 1997), 155–68.

3. "Cdr. Bruce Lawrence Harwood," Find a Grave.

4. "The U.S. Goes on the Offensive," *Santa Barbara News-Press*, July 2, 1943, https://www.newspapers.com/image/997296793/; "Clark Lee, Bombed on Bataan, Helps Dish It Out in Solomon Islands," *Fresno Bee*, September 6, 1942, https://www.newspapers.com/image/701702864/.

5. "U.S. Torpedo Planes Plant Fish in Jap Carrier's Hull," *Pomona (CA) Progress Bulletin*, September 15, 1942 (delayed), https://www.newspapers.com/image/623410129/.

6. "Claremont Officer Decorated by Nimitz," *Los Angeles Evening Citizen News*, December 2, 1942, https://www.newspapers.com/image/683770655/.

7. Lt. H. H. Larsen, Commanding, Torpedo Squadron 8, Letter of Commendation to Commanding Officer, USS *Saratoga*, August 31, 1942, 294, Fold3.com, accessed July 23, 2022, https://www.fold3.com/image/268394585/war-diary-52242-to-111742; "Bruce Lawrence Harwood," Hall of Valor Project, MilitaryTimes.com, accessed August 20, 2023, https://valor.militarytimes.com/hero/20502.

8. "Bruce Lawrence Harwood," Hall of Valor Project.

9. "Bruce Lawrence Harwood," Hall of Valor Project.

10. Mark L. Evans, "*Princeton* IV (CVL-23), 1943–1944."

11. Evans, "*Princeton* IV (CVL-23), 1943–1944."

12. Evans, "*Princeton* IV (CVL-23), 1943–1944."

13. Evans, "*Princeton* IV (CVL-23), 1943–1944."

14. "Our Peg-Leg Admiral," *Life*, August 14, 1950, 72–77.

15. "Battle of Leyte Gulf, October 1944: Loss of USS *Princeton* (CVL-23), 24 Oct. 1944"; Evans, "*Princeton* IV (CVL-23), 1943–1944."

16. "Harry Junior Popham," Ancestry.com, accessed July 19, 2022, https://www.ancestryinstitution.com/search/?name=harry_popham&birth=1922; Vernon Ervin Trevethan, Ancestry.com, accessed July 19, 2022, https://www.ancestryinstitution.com/search/?name=vernon_trevethan.

17. "*Birmingham* II (CL-62)."

18. "*Birmingham* II (CL-62)."

19. "*Birmingham* II (CL-62)."

20. "*Birmingham* II (CL-62)."

21. "*Birmingham* II (CL-62)."

22. E. W. Litch, Commanding Officer, USS *Lexington*, War Diary, 1–31 October 1944, Serial No. 040, 11, National Archives, Fold3.com, accessed July 22, 2022, https://www.fold3.com/image/293488468/war-diary-10144-to-113044-page-11-us-world-war-ii-war-diaries-1941-1945; Evans, "*Princeton* IV (CVL-23), 1943–1944."

23. "*Birmingham* II (CL-62)."

24. Harry Popham, "Eyewitness to Tragedy: Death of USS *Princeton*," August 19, 1997, HistoryNet.com, https://www.historynet.com/eyewitness-to-tragedy-death-of-uss-Princeton-may-97-world-war-ii-feature/.

25. Litch, Commanding Officer, USS *Lexington*, War Diary, 1–31 October 1944.

26. W. H. Buracker, Commanding, USS *Princeton* (CVL-23), "Action Report: Battle of the Philippines, November 24, 1944," Serial No. 0020, 1–3, National Archives, Fold3.com, accessed July 25, 2022, https://www.fold3.com/image/292506071/rep-of-ops-loss-of-the-uss-princeton-on-102444-east-of-luzon-is-philippines-page-2-us-world-war-ii-w.

27. Thomas B. Inglis, Commanding Officer, USS *Birmingham* (CL-62), "Action Report of Operations in the Philippines Area, November 14, 1944," Serial No. 0048, 1, National Archives, Fold3.com, accessed July 18, 2022, https://www.fold3.com/image/292492506/rep-of-ops-in-the-philippines-area-1018-2444-including-aa-act-ops-in-connection-with-loss-of-uss-pri; Marc D. Bernstein, "'Hell Broke Loose' at Leyte Gulf," *Naval History Magazine* 23, no. 5 (2009), https://www.usni.org/magazines/naval-history-magazine/2009/october/hell-broke-loose-leyte-gulf; Ellen Knight, "75 Years Ago Men Survived Dangers and Disasters in the Pacific," *Winchester (MA) Daily Times Chronicle*, June 26, 2020, http://homenewshere.com/daily_times_chronicle/news/winchester/article.

28. "Battle of Leyte Gulf, October 1944."

29. Evans, "*Princeton* IV (CVL-23), 1943–1944."

30. Evans, "*Princeton* IV (CVL-23), 1943–1944."

31. "Valiant, Futile Fight to Save the Princeton," *San Bernardino County Sun*, November 28, 1944, https://www.newspapers.com/image/50322879/.

32. "Manuel Lupe Pino," Ancestry.com, accessed July 19, 2022, https://www.ancestryinstitution.com/search/?name=manuel+lupe_pino.

33. Evans, "*Princeton* IV (CVL-23), 1943–1944."

34. Bernstein, "'Hell Broke Loose' at Leyte Gulf."

35. *The Saga of the U.S.S.* Birmingham*: A Compilation of Her Officers & Men*, World War Regimental Histories (Washington, DC: United States Navy, 1945), 163, Bangor Public Library, http://digicom.bpl.lib.me.us/ww_reg_his/163.

36. Evans, "*Princeton* IV (CVL-23), 1943–1944"; Samuel Eliot Morison, *History of the United States Naval Operations in World War II*, vol. 12, *Leyte: June 1944–January 1945*, 177–83.

37. "USS *Princeton* (CVL-23) Loss in Action, Battle for Leyte Gulf, October 24, 1944," War Damage Report No. 62, October 30, 1947, 1–6, https://www.history.Navy.mil/research/library/online-reading-room/title-list-alphabetically/w/war-damage-reports/uss-Princeton-cvl23-war-damage-report-no-62.html; Evans, "*Princeton* IV (CVL-23), 1943–1944"; "Cdr. Bruce Lawrence Harwood," Find a Grave.

38. "Our Peg-Leg Admiral," 72–77.

39. "Cmdr. Bruce Harwood Was Lost on Princeton," *Pomona (CA) Progress Bulletin*, November 28, 1944, https://www.newspapers.com/image/623409589/.

40. Popham, "Eyewitness to Tragedy"; Bernstein, "'Hell Broke Loose' at Leyte Gulf."

41. Popham, "Eyewitness to Tragedy."

42. Winston Folk, Commanding Officer, War Diary, 10/1–31/1944, Serial No. 95531, 23–25, National Archives, Fold3.com, accessed September 21, 2023, https://www.fold3.com/image/292508585/war-diary-101-3144-page-1-us-world-war-ii-war-diaries-1941-1945.

43. Bernstein, "'Hell Broke Loose' at Leyte Gulf."

44. Popham, "Eyewitness to Tragedy"; Evans, "*Princeton* IV (CVL-23), 1943–1944."

45. Morison, *History of United States Naval Operations*, 12:177–83.

46. "Battle of Leyte Gulf, October 1944."

47. Neil Whalen Wirick, "1944 Princeton Story," interview by unnamed interviewer, accessed August 6, 2022, https://www.youtube.com/watch?v=2u6LR1eQh6M.

48. Inglis, USS *Birmingham* (CL-62), "Action Report," 51.

49. Admiral Bardshar and Captain Mooney, interview by Carol Deck and Marsha Clark, June 1980, Transcript of Interviews, Seely G. Mudd Manuscript Library, Princeton University, Princeton, NJ, accessed August 29, 2022, https://blogs.princeton.edu/mudd/wp-content/uploads/sites/41/2013/10/AC008_B1_F1-9.pdf.

50. Bernstein, "'Hell Broke Loose' at Leyte Gulf"; *Saga of the U.S.S.* Birmingham; Evans, "*Princeton* IV (CVL-23), 1943–1944." The exact numbers of those killed, wounded, and missing vary slightly between sources.

51. Evans, "*Princeton* IV (CVL-23), 1943–1944."

52. Knight, "75 Years Ago Men Survived Dangers and Disasters in the Pacific."

53. "Vice Adm. John Hoskins Dead; Saw Action in Pacific and Korea; Navy Leader, Called 'Pegleg,' Lost Foot in Combat—Decorated Many Times," *New York Times*, March 31, 1964, 35, nytimes.com https://www.nytimes.com/1964/03/31/archives/vice-adm-john-hoskins-dead-saw-action-in-pacific-and-korea-navy.html; "Our Peg-Leg Admiral," 72–77.

54. "Cdr. Bruce Lawrence Harwood," Find a Grave.

55. Bernstein, "'Hell Broke Loose' at Leyte Gulf"; "Thomas Browning Inglis Sr.," Find a Grave, accessed July 19, 2022, https://www.findagrave.com/memorial/29688449/thomas-browning-inglis.

56. Popham, "Eyewitness to Tragedy"; "Harry Junior Popham," Ancestry.com.

57. "Vernon Ervin Trevethan," Ancestry.com.

58. "Manuel Lupe Pino," Ancestry.com.

59. "Neil Wahlen Wirick," Find a Grave, accessed July 19, 2022, https://www.findagrave.com/memorial/127635985/neil-wahlen-wirick.

Chapter 10. Qualifying for the Scouts

1. "Hess Charles F.," 401st Bomb Group Association, accessed June 29, 2023, http://401bg.org/Main/History/Members/Details.aspx?ID=123; "Combat Crew Rotation, World War II and Korean War," Historical Studies Branch, USAF Historical Division, Aerospace Studies Institute, Air University, Maxwell Air Force Base, Alabama, January 1968, 7–8, accessed January 15, 2023, https://web

.archive.org/web/20141212095416/http://www.afhra.af.mil/shared/media/document/AFD-080424-048.pdf. Air Force tours of duty varied considerably by theater of war, numbered air force, and type of aircraft.

2. "Hess, Charles F.," Chester County Hall of Heroes, research by Matt Mericle and Alex Ullifer, Avon Grove High School, West Grove, Chester County, PA, accessed January 17, 2023, http://www.chescoheroes.org/468/Hess-Charles-F.

3. Wesley Frank Craven and James Lea Cate, *Men and Planes*, 488–94.

4. "613th Bombardment Squadron (H) Squadron History," 401st Bomb Group Association, 5–6, accessed June 30, 2023, http://401bg.org/Main/People/Maslen/613th.pdf.

5. Jim O'Connell, "The Second Schweinfurt Mission: Bomber Command's Darkest Day," Fairchild Air Force Base, accessed October 14, 2014, https://www.fairchild.af.mil/News/Article-Display/Article/762942/the-second-schweinfurt-missionbomber-commands-darkest-day/.

6. Bill Marshall, "The Scouting Force at Steeple Morden (F-122)," WWII Aircraft Performance, April 23, 2007, http://www.wwiiaircraftperformance.org/mustang/scouting-force.html; E. Richard Atkins, *Fighting Scouts of the 8th Air Force* (Dallas: Taylor, 1996), 5.

7. "North American P-51D Mustang," National Museum of the United States Air Force, accessed August 16, 2023, https://www.nationalmuseum.af.mil/Visit/Museum-Exhibits/Fact-Sheets/Display/Article/196263/north-american-p-51d-mustang/.

8. Marshall, "Scouting Force at Steeple Morden"; "Richard T. Bennett," American Air Museum, accessed February 26, 2024, https://www.americanairmuseum.com/archive/person/richard-t-bennett; "Richard Thomas Bennett," Honor States, accessed February 26, 2024, https://www.honorstates.org/profiles/91924/; Atkins, *Fighting Scouts*, 15.

9. Jon Guttman, "The P-51 Pioneers: Breaking in the Mustang," History Net, November 14, 2022, https://www.historynet.com/breaking-in-the-p51-mustang/; Marshall, "Scouting Force at Steeple Morden."

10. "Scouting Force (Experimental) SFX," American Air Museum, accessed March 3, 2023, https://www.americanairmuseum.com/archive/unit/scouting-force-experimental-sfx; Atkins, *Fighting Scouts*, 40.

11. "Charles Frank Hess," American Air Museum, accessed March 3, 2023, https://www.americanairmuseum.com/archive/person/charles-frank-hess.

12. "Charles Frank Hess," Find a Grave, accessed August 17, 2023, https://www.findagrave.com/memorial/56290660/charles-frank-hess.

13. Marshall, "Scouting Force at Steeple Morden"; "357th Fighter Squadron," AFHRA.af.mil, accessed August 17, 2023, https://www.afhra.af.mil/About-Us/Fact-Sheets/Display/Article/431972/357-fighter-squadron-acc/.

14. Bill Marshall, *Angels, Bulldogs & Dragons: The 355th Fighter Group in World War II*.

15. "Charles Frank Hess," Find a Grave.

16. "613th Bombardment Squadron (H) Squadron History," 401st Bomb Group Association, 14.

17. "Gen. Allison Cochran Brooks," Find a Grave, accessed August 17, 2023, https://www.findagrave.com/memorial/149904479/allison-cochran-brooks; Atkins, *Fighting Scouts*, 25.

Chapter 11. Even the Best of the Best

1. Sebastien Roblin, "What Made the *Essex*-Class Carriers So Powerful," *National Interest*, January 22, 2021, https://nationalinterest.org/blog/reboot/what-made-essex-class-aircraft-carriers-so-powerful-176913.

2. "USS *Intrepid* (CV-11)," Naval History and Heritage Command, December 19, 2017, https://www.history.navy.mil/research/histories/ship-histories/danfs/i/intrepid-iv.html/.

3. "USS *Intrepid* (CV-11)."

4. J. F. Bolger, Commanding, USS *Intrepid* (CV-11), "War Diary, Month of October 1944," 1–6.

5. Bolger, "War Diary," 7–9; "USS *Intrepid* (CV-11)."

6. Bolger, "War Diary," 10–14, 18.

7. Bolger, "War Diary," 28.

8. Samuel J. Cox, "H-038-2: The Battle of Leyte Gulf in Detail."

9. Cox, "H-038-2: The Battle of Leyte Gulf in Detail."

10. Samuel J. Cox, "H-044-3: Operation Heaven Number One (*Ten-ichi-go*)—the Death of *Yamato, April 7, 1945*."

11. Bolger, "War Diary," 35.

12. J. M. Shoemaker, Captain, Commanding, USS *Franklin* (CV-13), "Action Report: Operations against the Enemy in the Philippine Islands and the Philippine Sea from 22 October 1944 to 31 October 1944," 2.

13. Bolger, "War Diary," 36.

14. "Lt. Wilson C. McNeil," Find a Grave, accessed August 20, 2023, https://www.findagrave.com/memorial/56779791/wilson-c-mcneill.

15. J. F. Bolger, Commanding, USS *Intrepid* (CV-11), "Action Report: Operations against the Ryukyu Islands, Formosa, & Philippines, October 10–31, 1944," 67.

16. S. J. Michael, Commanding, "War Diary: October 2, 1944–November 9, 1944," 8; "Ens. Donald Lampson, Jr.," Find a Grave, accessed August 20, 2023, https://www.findagrave.com/memorial/56773281/donald-lampson; "Albert Alexander Granger," Find a Grave, https://www.findagrave.com/memorial/56788395/albert-alexander-granger; "William Hoyle Odom," Find a Grave, https://www.findagrave.com/memorial/56784566/william-hoyle-odom.

17. Richard Howard Clive, Commander, VB-13: Serial O25, November 2, 1944, Navy Cross Citation, MilitaryTimes.com, accessed August 21, 2023, https://valor.militarytimes.com/hero/19018.

18. Shoemaker, "Action Report," 4. Freligh and Plonsky crash-landed and with the help of Filipino guerrillas evaded capture by Japanese patrols for seven weeks. "Aviation Radio Man Weds," *Boston Globe*, May 25, 1945, https://www.newspapers.com/image/433980253/.

19. Richard McGowan, CDR, USN, US Naval Academy Virtual Memorial Wall, accessed August 23, 2023, https://usnamemorialhall.org/index.php/RICHARD_MCGOWAN,_CDR,_USN.

20. Martin R. Waldman, *Calmness, Courage, and Efficiency: Remembering the Battle of Leyte Gulf*, 31.

21. Edwin P. Hoyt, *McCampbell's Heroes: The Story of the U.S. Navy's Celebrated Carrier Fighters of the Pacific War*, prelude, 15.

22. "David McCampbell," Congressional Medal of Honor Society, accessed August 23, 2023, https://www.cmohs.org/recipients/david-mccampbell; Cox, "H-038-2: The Battle of Leyte Gulf in Detail."

23. C. W. Wieber, Commanding, USS *Essex* (CV-9), "Action Report: Battle of the Philippines, 24–25 October 1944," 52, National Archives, Fold3.com, accessed August 23, 2023, https://www.fold3.com/image/292515806; Hoyt, *McCampbell's Heroes*, 214. While Crellin and Shetler were shot down and crashed into the sea, their attack contributed to the sinking of the *Musashi* later that day.

24. Wieber, "Action Report," 52.

25. "USS *Intrepid* (CV-11)."

26. Bolger, "War Diary," 37.

27. Michael, "War Diary," 8.

28. S. E. Smith, ed., *The United States Navy in World War II* (New York: William Morrow, 1966), 875–79; *Britannica*, s.v. "Battle of Leyte Gulf," accessed August 29, 2023, https://www.britannica.com/event/Battle-of-Leyte-Gulf.

29. "Lt. Wilson C. McNeil," Find a Grave; "Wilson C. McNeil," Honor States, accessed August 21, 2023, https://www.honorstates.org/profiles/87141/; "Clarence F. English," Honor States, https://www.honorstates.org/profiles/99034/.

30. "Ens. Donald Lampson, Jr.," Find a Grave; "Albert Alexander Granger," Find a Grave; "William Hoyle Odom," Find a Grave.

31. "Marshall David Barnett, Jr.," Find a Grave, accessed August 21, 2023, https://www.findagrave.com/memorial/53882516/marshall-david-barnett; "LtJG Richard Howard Clive," Find a Grave, https://www.findagrave.com/memorial/56754890/richard-howard-clive; "Leonard Pickens," Honor States, https://www.honorstates.org/profiles/353058/; "Eugene E. Black," Honor States, https://www.honorstates.org/profiles/353058/; "Robert W. Bogert," Honor States, https://www.honorstates.org/profiles/87141/.

32. "Richard McGowan, CDR, USN."

33. "David McCampbell," Congressional Medal of Honor Society; "David McCampbell," Naval Aviation Hall of Fame, accessed August 29, 2023, https://nationalaviation.org/enshrinee/david-mccampbell/.

34. "Conrad Wesley Crellin, Lieutenant, (j.g.)," VB-15: Bulletin No. 342, September 1945, Navy Cross Citation, MilitaryTimes.com, accessed August 21, 2023, https://valor.militarytimes.com/hero/19919; "Carl Edward Shetler," Aviation Radioman Third Class, Bulletin no. 345, December 1945, Distinguished Flying Cross Citation, MilitaryTimes.com, accessed August 21, 2023, https://valor.militarytimes.com/hero/310618.

35. "Ralph A. Mayhew," Ensign, Bulletin no. 340, July 1945, Distinguished Flying Cross Citation, MilitaryTimes.com, accessed August 21, 2023, https://valor.militarytimes.com/hero/310439.

Chapter 12. A Distant and Unnecessary Death

1. "Magnolia A&M Goes to War," University Archives, Southern Arkansas University, accessed August 6, 2023, https://web.saumag.edu/archives/archives/history/illustrated/magnolia-am-1941-1951/magnolia-am-goes-to-war/; "Girvis Haltom," Find a Grave, accessed August 6, 2023, https://www.findagrave.com/memorial/171228052/girvis-haltom; "Girvis W. Haltom," Ancestry.com, accessed August 6, 2023, https://www.ancestryinstitution.com/discoveryui-content/view/1362085090.

2. Allan Reed Millett, *Semper Fidelis: The History of the United States Marines*, 419–24, https://archive.org/details/semperfidelis00mill_eud/page/430/mode/2up?q=yap.

3. Stanley Falk, *Bloodiest Victory: Palaus*, 143.

4. "Vought F4U-1D Corsair," National Air and Space Museum, Smithsonian Institution, https://airandspace.si.edu/collection-objects/vought-f4u-1d-corsair/nasm_A19610124000.

5. Falk, *Bloodiest Victory: Palaus,* 138.

6. "Letters from Girvis Haltom to Harold G. Alford," Missing Air Crew: The Search for the Coleman B-24 Crew, MissingAirCrew.com, accessed August 6, 2023, http://www.missingaircrew.com/yap/mac/24oct1944.asp.

7. Rolfe L. Hillman III, "Grim Peleliu: The Aircraft," *Naval History Magazine* 3, no. 2 (1989), citing from Capt. Donald A. Stauffer, "Marine Aviation at Peleliu," *Marine Corps Gazette*, February 1945, https://www.usni.org/magazines/naval-history-magazine/1989/april/grim-peleliu-aircraft.

8. Falk, *Bloodiest Victory: Palaus,* 143–44. At the end of the battle for Peleliu, Colonel Nakagawa and his adviser, Maj. Gen. K. Murai, committed seppuku, ceremonial suicide, in their last command post situated inside a cave in the Umurbrogol Mountains. Japanese resistance officially ended there on November 25, 1944. Corydon Wagner Jr., "The Bones of Nakagawa," *Naval History Magazine* 17, no. 1 (2003), https://www.usni.org/magazines/naval-history-magazine/2003/february/bones-nakagawa.

9. "Newspaper Articles about Girvis," Missing Air Crew: The Search for the Coleman B-24 Crew, MissingAirCrew.com, http://www.missingaircrew.com/yap/mac/24oct1944.asp.

10. Robert Lee Sherrod, *History of Marine Corps Aviation in World War II*, 258.

11. CINCPAC Communiqués No. 137–No. 170, Navy Department Communiqués and Pertinent Press releases, December 10, 1941, to May 24, 1945, Month of October, 251–59, accessed December 17, 2022, https://www.ibiblio.org/pha/comms/1944-10.html.

12. "Missing Air Crew Report," Missing Air Crew: The Search for the Coleman B-24 Crew, MissingAirCrew.com, accessed August 10, 2023, http://missingaircrew.com/pdf/24oct44.pdf.

13. "Letter Tells of Flier's Death," Missing Air Crew: The Search for the Coleman B-24 Crew, MissingAirCrew.com, accessed August 10, 2023, http://www.missingaircrew.com/yap/mac/24oct1944.asp.

14. "Unknown Flier Buried on Yap Island," *Corvallis (OR) Gazette-Times*, April 2, 1947, https://www.newspapers.com/image/383154081/. The story of another instance of local inhabitants burying and caring for fallen American pilots is the account of Lt. George R. Choate in the Netherlands in chapter 21.

15. Edwin H. Simmons, *The United States Marines: A History*, 132–34, 163–67.

16. Thomas D. Sheppard, "Peleliu: Heroism and Grit," Naval History and Heritage Command, August 2019, https://www.history.navy.mil/browse-by-topic/wars-conflicts-and-operations/world-war-ii/1944/peleliu/peleliu-essay.html.

17. Millett, *Semper Fidelis*, 419–24.

18. "Third Haltom Killed in War," *Fort Worth Star-Telegram*, September 2, 1943, https://www.newspapers.com/image/637529665/.

19. "1Lt Gambrell W. Haltom," Find a Grave, accessed August 10, 2023, https://www.findagrave.com/memorial/35663900/gambrell-w-haltom.

20. Missing Air Crew: The Search for the Coleman B-24 Crew, MissingAirCrew.com.

21. "Girvis Haltom," Find a Grave.

Chapter 13. Boots on the Ground and in the Air

1. "About Us," Onondaga Nation, accessed September 2, 2023, https://www.onondaganation.org/aboutus/.

2. Thomas D. Morgan, "Native Americans in World War II," *Excerpted from Army History: The Professional Bulletin of Army History*, no. 35 (Fall 1995), 22–27, https://web.archive.org/web/20170327110226/http://www.shsu.edu/~his_ncp/NAWWII.html. American Indians had different citizenship statuses. Those who had accepted the terms of the Dawes Act of 1887 regarding their land allotments, approximately one-third of the population, became citizens.

3. Morgan, "Native Americans in World War II," 93–106.

4. "Thompson, Sylvester J.," Fields of Honor, accessed August 19, 2023, https://www.fieldsofhonor-database.com/index.php/en/american-war-cemetery-margraten-t/57597-thompson-sylvester-j.

5. Laurel Schlegel, "A Native American Member of the Band of Brothers," More than a Headstone, accessed August 19, 2023, https://www.morethanaheadstone.org/all-stories/a-native-american-member-of-the-band-of-brothers?rq=mcclung.

6. Matt Fratus, "How Paratroopers Honored Their Native American Heritage on D-Day," November 2, 2021, Coffee or Die, https://coffeeordie.com/the-filthy-13.

7. Kevin M. Hymel, "The World War II Paratrooper: First Hand Accounts of the D-Day Invasion," Warfare History Network, Winter 2015, https://warfarehistorynetwork.com/article/ww2-paratrooper-first-hand-accounts-of-the-d-day-invasion/; "The 101st Airborne during World War II," 101st Airborne, accessed September 2, 2023, http://www.ww2-airborne.us/18corps/101abn/101_overview.html.

8. "The 101st Airborne during World War II"; Alex Kershaw, "First in France: The World War II Pathfinder Who Led the Way on D-Day," June 6, 2019, History Net, https://www.historynet.com/first-in-france-the-world-war-ii-pathfinder-who-led-the-way-on-d-day/.

9. Antony Beevor, *The Battle of Arnhem: The Deadliest Airborne Operation of World War II*, 36, 317.

10. Ted Ballard, *Rhineland: 15 September 1944–21 March 1945*, 10–14, https://history.army.mil/brochures/rhineland/rhineland.htm.

11. Charles B. MacDonald, *The Siegfried Line Campaign*, 142–46; Ballard, *Rhineland*, 13–16.

12. Beevor, *Battle of Arnhem*, 109–25.

13. MacDonald, *The Siegfried Line Campaign*, 142–43.

14. Leonard Rappaport and Arthur Norwood Jr., *Rendezvous with Destiny: A History of the 101st Airborne*, 378–80.

15. "Thompson, Sylvester J.," Fields of Honor.

16. "The 502nd Parachute Infantry Regiment, Unit History," Airborne, accessed August 15, 2023, http://www.ww2-airborne.us/units/502/502.html; MacDonald, *The Siegfried Line Campaign*, 150–53; Rappaport and Northwood, *Rendezvous with Destiny*, 326.

17. "Thompson, Sylvester J.," Fields of Honor; MacDonald, *The Siegfried Line Campaign*, 229; "502nd PIR," Airborne, accessed August 16, 2023, https://www.usairborne.be/101/101_502_us_txt.htm#3.Hollande; Rappaport and Northwood, *Rendezvous with Destiny*, 378–79.

18. Schlegel, "Native American Member of the Band of Brothers."

19. Ballard, *Rhineland*, 12–14.

20. Rappaport and Northwood, *Rendezvous with Destiny*, 826; Airborne in Normandy, accessed August 15, 2023, https://www.airborneinnormandy.com/company_rosters_normandy.htm.

21. "Thompson, Sylvester J.," Fields of Honor; Office of Indian Affairs, *Indians in the War* (Chicago: Department of the Interior, 1945), 20, https://archive.org/details/IndiansInTheWar/page/n27/mode/2up.

22. Fratus, "How Paratroopers Honored Their Native American Heritage on D-Day"; "James Elbert 'Jake' McNiece," Find a Grave, accessed August 15, 2023, https://www.findagrave.com/memorial/103882659/james-elbert-mcniece; "Jake McNiece, WWII Hero and Self-Described 'Troublemaker,'" NPR, May 27, 2013, https://www.npr.org/2013/05/27/186273553/jake-mcniece-wwii-hero-and-self-described-troublemaker.

23. Schlegel, "Native American Member of the Band of Brothers."

24. Morgan, "Native Americans in World War II," 22–27; Congressional Medal of Honor Society, accessed August 16, 2023, https://www.cmohs.org/recipients/lists/native-american-indian-recipients/.

Part Two: Noon

1. "Temperature on Tuesday October 24, 1944, at Tacloban Airport, WeatherSpark.com, accessed July 30, 2023, https://weatherspark.com/h/d/149298/1944

/10/24/Historical-Weather-on-Tuesday-October-24-1944-at-Tacloban-Airport-Philippines#Figures-Temperature.

2. "Bill Bowen's *Arisan Maru* Roster," accessed February 21, 2023, https://www.west-point.org/family/japanese-pow/Bowen_AM.htm.

3. "The Sullivan Brothers," Naval History and Heritage Command, April 26, 2022, https://www.history.Navy.mil/browse-by-topic/disasters-and-phenomena/the-sullivan-brothers-and-the-assignment-of-family-members0.html.

4. "Oscar Wilburn Tubbleville," Find a Grave, accessed July 31, 2023, https://www.findagrave.com/memorial/56750618/oscar-wilburn-tubbleville; "H.M. Tubbleville," Find a Grave, https://www.findagrave.com/memorial/56750617/h-m-tubbleville; "Alba, Texas," TexasEscapes.com, accessed July 31, 2023, http://texasescapes.com/EastTexasTowns/Alba-Texas.htm.

5. "Henry M. Luther," Find a Grave, accessed May 26, 2023, https://www.findagrave.com/memorial/56783918/henry-m-luther; "Henry Luther," Ancestry.com, accessed May 26, 2023, https://www.ancestryinstitution.com/mediaui-viewer/collection/1030/tree/185874/person/-2113296920/media/. In some cases, the Japanese dragged disabled American tanks from the jungles outside Manila and forced the prisoners to repair the tanks for service.

6. "Luther, S/Sgt. Henry M.," Bataan Project, accessed May 25, 2023, https://bataanproject.com/provisional-tank-group/luther-s-sgt-henry-m/; "Luther, Sgt. John P.," Bataan Project, accessed May 25, 2023, https://bataanproject.com/provisional-tank-group/luther-sgt-john-p/.

7. "Baldon, Pvt. Fay W," Bataan Project, accessed May 25, 2023, https://bataanproject.com/provisional-tank-group/192nd-tank-battalion/baldon-pvt-fay-w/; "Baldon, Cpl. Ray," Bataan Project, accessed May 25, 2023, https://bataanproject.com/provisional-tank-group/baldon-cpl-ray/; "Fay Walter Baldon," Find a Grave, accessed May 25, 2023, https://www.findagrave.com/memorial/56780996/fay-walter-baldon.

8. "Corporal Pascual Garde," Fold3.com, accessed May 25, 2023, https://www.fold3.com/memorial/90171725/pascual-garde/stories.

9. "Pvt. John W Parker," Find a Grave, accessed May 25, 2023, https://www.findagrave.com/memorial/56784678/john-w-parker; "Don Franklin Parker," Ancestry.com, accessed May 25, 2023, https://www.ancestryinstitution.com/; "Don F. Parker," National Archives, Washington, DC, Record Group title *Records of the Office of the Provost Marshal General, 1920–1975*; Record Group number 389, Ancestry.com, accessed June 11, 2023, https://www.ancestryinstitution.com/.

10. "Sgt. Joe Stanley Smith Tells Experience in Japanese Camp," *Carlsbad (NM) Daily Current-Argus*, March 28, 1945, https://www.newspapers.com/image/503157409/; "Both Davis Boys Given Up for Lost in Sinking of Japanese Prison Ship," *Carlsbad (NM) Daily Current-Argus*, June 14, 1945, https://www.newspapers.com/image/503161415/.

11. "Donald C. Wight," Ancestry.com, accessed June 11, 2023, https://www.ancestryinstitution.com/; Pacific POW Roster, Mansell.com, accessed June 11, 2023, http://www.mansell.com/pow_resources/pacific_pow_roster.html.

12. "Frederick Thomas," Find a Grave, accessed July 31, 2023, https://www.findagrave.com/memorial/56771755/frederick-thomas#view-photo=264473880; "2 from Bensenville Lost in Action," *Roselle (IL) Register*, July 30, 1943, https://www.newspapers.com/image/44496631/.

13. Roosevelt, Eleanor, "My Day," *Evansville (IN) Press*, October 26, 1944, https://www.newspapers.com/image/763608772/.

Chapter 14. Rumors of a Rest

1. "PFC Elwood Dempster," Find a Grave, accessed June 24, 2023, https://www.findagrave.com/memorial/56371982/elwood-dempster.

2. "Elwood Dempster," Find a Grave; "The Cross of Lorraine Division: The Story of the 79th Division," LoneSentry.com, accessed June 23, 2023, http://www.lonesentry.com/gi_stories_booklets/79thinfantry/index.html (the source of the epigraph regarding Tennessee maneuvers); Army, 79th Division, *The Cross of Lorraine: A Combat History of the 79th Division, June 1942–December 1945*, 1986, 18–27, accessed June 4, 2023, 8–9, https://archive.org/details/TheCrossOfLorraine/page/n21/mode/2up.

3. US Army, 79th Division, *Cross of Lorraine*, 18–27, 68–72.

4. "Elwood Dempster," Find a Grave.

5. US Army, 79th Division, *Cross of Lorraine*, 7; "Elwood Dempster," Find a Grave.

6. Actions of the 26th Infantry Division are discussed in chapter 15 and those of the Third Division in chapter 16.

7. US Army, 79th Division, *Cross of Lorraine*, 68–72; "79th Infantry," Researching World War II, accessed June 15, 2023, http://worldwar2files.com/79thinfantrydivision/index.html; Jeffrey J. Clarke and Robert Ross Smith, *Riviera to the Rhine*, 263–64.

8. US Army, 79th Division, *Cross of Lorraine*, 68–72; Combat Studies Institute, *CSI Battlebook 11-C: Forêt de Parroy* (Fort Leavenworth, KS: Combat Studies Institute, 1984), 52–59, accessed June 15, 2023, https://apps.dtic.mil/sti/pdfs/ADA151630.pdf; Clarke and Smith, *Riviera to the Rhine*, 266.

9. Combat Studies Institute, *CSI Battlebook 11-C*, 41, 64–65. Hitler would frequently request that lines be held. See chapter 15 when he insisted they hold Moncourt Woods where he had fought in World War I and chapter 16 when the führer ordered troops to prevent the escape of the Lost Battalion in the Vosges Mountains.

10. US Army, 79th Division, *Cross of Lorraine*, 72.

11. Sterling A. Wood, *History of the 313th Infantry Regiment in World War II* (Washington, DC: Infantry Journal Press, 1947), accessed June 24, 2023, https://archive.org/details/HistoryOfThe313thInfantryInWorldWarII/; US Army, 79th Division, *Cross of Lorraine*, 75.

12. Combat Studies Institute, *CSI Battlebook 11-C*; US Army, 79th Division, *Cross of Lorraine*, 73–74.

13. "The WW2 Letters of Private Melvin W. Johnson," accessed June 12, 2023, https://web.archive.org/web/20180128190401/http://privateletters.net/10.26.44.html.

14. "79th Infantry," Researching World War II; "Elwood Dempster," Fold3.com, accessed June 12, 2023, https://www.fold3.com/record/704939090/dempster-elwood-us-wwii-hospital-admission-card-files-1942-1954; Roy Morris Jr., "The Race to the Rhine: How the US 79th Division Took Down the Nazis," History Net, June 15, 2021, https://www.historynet.com/the-race-to-the-rhine/.

15. Clarke and Smith, *Riviera to the Rhine,* 270.

16. US Army, 79th Division, *Cross of Lorraine*, 74.

Chapter 15. Yankees in France

1. Maj. Gen. Ralph A. Paladino, ed., *History of a Combat Regiment, 1639–1945* (Baton Rouge, LA: Army and Navy, 1960), 26–35; Frank Burns, "Second Army (Tennessee) Maneuvers," in *The Tennessee Encyclopedia*, Tennessee Historical Society, October 2017, https://tennesseeencyclopedia.net/entries/second-Army-tennessee-maneuvers/. According to an article by Bill Carey in the *Tennessee Magazine* on May 1, 2022, the conditions were in fact so realistic, some 250 men (of the 850,000 trainees) died during the exercises.

2. Paladino, *History of a Combat Regiment*, 39.

3. Paladino, *History of a Combat Regiment*, 39; "PFC Robert Bruce Kuhl," Find a Grave, accessed July 11, 2023, https://www.findagrave.com/memorial/56657323/robert-bruce-kuhl.

4. Paladino, *History of a Combat Regiment*, 39.

5. Paladino, *History of a Combat Regiment*, 40.

6. Paladino, *History of a Combat Regiment*, 40–42.

7. "The History of the 26th Yankee Division: 1917–1919, 1941–1945," Yankee Division Veterans Association, Deschamps Brothers, Salem, MA, 32, accessed July 12, 2023, https://www.fold3.com/image/676405992.

8. Paladino, *History of a Combat Regiment*, 43; "History of the 26th Yankee Division," 34.

9. Paladino, *History of a Combat Regiment*, 43; Hugh M. Cole, *The Lorraine Campaign* (Washington, DC: Center of Military History, US Army, 1993), 256–59, 289–90.

10. Paladino, *History of a Combat Regiment*, 46; "History of the 26th Yankee Division," 36.

11. Paladino, *History of a Combat Regiment*, 50–54.

12. Paladino, *History of a Combat Regiment*, 54; "History of the 26th Yankee Division," 36–37.

13. "History of the 26th Yankee Division," 37.

14. "History of the 26th Yankee Division," 40.

15. Paladino, *History of a Combat Regiment*, 50–52.

16. "PFC Robert Bruce Kuhl," Find a Grave.

17. "PFC Robert Bruce Kuhl," Find a Grave.

18. Paladino, *History of a Combat Regiment*, 48; "Dwight Townsend Colley," Find a Grave, accessed July 11, 2023, https://www.findagrave.com/memorial/133357344/dwight-townsend-colley.

Chapter 16. Clinging to the Scrabble

1. "Technical Sergeant Walter Jackson Harris," World War Two Veterans, accessed July 7, 2023, https://worldwartwoveterans.org/harris-walter-jackson-39676072-kia-eto/; Philip A. St. John, *History of the Third Infantry Division*, 12.

2. Donald G. Taggart, ed., *History of the Third Infantry Division in WWII* (Washington, DC: Infantry Journal Press, 1947), 5–11; Charles R. Anderson, *Algeria-French Morocco*, U.S. Army Campaigns of World War II Commemorative Series (Washington, DC: Center of Military History, n.d.), 12–14.

3. Taylor Downing, "War on Film—*Casablanca*," The Past, accessed January 10, 2023, https://the-past.com/review/tv-film/war-on-film-casablanca/; "Remembering Operation Torch: Allied Forces Land in North Africa during Operation Torch," American Battle Monuments Commission, accessed November 8, 2017, https://www.abmc.gov/news-events/.

4. Taggart, *History of the Third Infantry Division*, 37–39; St. John, *History of the Third Infantry Division*, 13; George F. Howe, *Northwest Africa: Seizing the Initiative in the West*, 663–71.

5. Taggart, *History of the Third Infantry Division*, 51–76; St. John, *History of the Third Infantry Division*, 13–14.

6. Taggart, *History of the Third Infantry Division*, 79–80; "3rd Infantry Division—Rock of the Marne," US Army Divisions, accessed June 15, 2023, https://www.Armydivs.com/3rd-infantry-division.

7. Taggart, *History of the Third Infantry Division*, 90–102, 150, 188; *From the Volturno to the Winter Line (6 October–15 November 1943)* (Washington, DC: Center of Military History, 1944, 1990), 8–9.

8. Taggart, *History of the Third Infantry Division*, 105.

9. Taggart, *History of the Third Infantry Division*, 237.

10. Taggart, *History of the Third Infantry Division*, 202, 237–41; Clarke and Smith, *Riviera to the Rhine*, 231–45, 561–69.

11. Ben Phlegar, "World Series Notes," *Moberly (MO) Monitor Index*, October 7, 1944, https://www.newspapers.com/image/19591863/; "World Series Is Broadcast to GI-Joe in Italy," *St. Louis Star and Times*, October 5, 1944, https://www.newspapers.com/image/204718629/.

12. Taggart, *History of the Third Infantry Division*, 245–50; Clarke and Smith, *Riviera to the Rhine*, 285–96.

13. "Huntsville Youth with Yanks Rout the Germans in Surprise 9 Hour Attack," *Moberly (MO) Monitor-Index*, November 1, 1944, https://www.newspapers.com/image/19596960/.

14. Clarke and Smith, *Riviera to the Rhine*, 285–96.

15. Taggart, *History of the Third Infantry Division*, 248–56; Clarke and Smith, *Riviera to the Rhine*, 319–25.

16. "Walter J. Harris Wounded Seriously," *Moberly (MO) Monitor-Index*, November 11, 1944, https://www.newspapers.com/image/19597868/; "Walter Harris of Huntsville Killed October 24," *Moberly (MO) Monitor-Index*, November 14, 1944, https://www.newspapers.com/image/19598134/.

17. "Walter J. Harris," Wall of Valor Project, accessed July 3, 2023, https://valor.militarytimes.com/hero/95297.

18. "Audie Leon Murphy," Wall of Valor Project, accessed October 10, 2023, https://valor.militarytimes.com/hero/209.

Chapter 17. Into Thin Air

1. Craven and Cate, *Men and Planes*, 206–9; Sam McGowan, "The Boeing B-17 Flying Fortress or the Consolidated B-24 Liberator?," Warfare History Network, accessed July 15, 2023, https://warfarehistorynetwork.com/boeing-b-17-flying-fortress-vs-the-consolidated-b-24-liberator/; Bruce Bromelow, "Here Are the Bombers the US Has Used to Dominate Skies All Over the World for over 80 Years," *Business Insider*, September 10, 2020, https://www.businessinsider.com/air-force-bombers-b17-b24-b29-b52-b1-b2-b21-2020-9?op=1; Consolidated B-24 Liberator, National World War II Museum, accessed July 21, 2023, https://www.nationalww2museum.org/visit/museum-campus/us-freedom-pavilion/warbirds/consolidated-b-24-liberator.

2. "William Albert," Ancestry.com, accessed July 29, 2023, https://www.ancestryinstitution.com/search/?name=william_albert&event=_manitoba-canada_5003&birth=1923; MACR 10018, Fold3.com, accessed July 29, 2023, https://www.fold3.com/image/139274292; "1LT William A. Albert, Jr.," Find a Grave, accessed July 29, 2023, https://www.findagrave.com/memorial/56780832/william-a-albert.

3. "William Albert," Ancestry.com.

4. *The Story of the 5th Bombardment Group (Heavy), US Army Air Forces, 5th Bomb Group* (Raleigh, NC: Hillsborough House, 1946), accessed July 17, 2023, 42–43, https://archive.org/details/TheStoryOfTheFifthBombardmentGroupHeavy-nsia/page/n41/mode/2up?q=72nd.

5. Robert Ross Smith, *The Approach to the Philippines*, 491–93; *Story of the 5th Bombardment Group*, 74.

6. MACR 10018, Fold3.com.

7. MACR 10018, Fold3.com.

8. "B-24J-185-CO Liberator Serial Number 44-40947," Pacific Wrecks, January 12, 2023, https://pacificwrecks.com/aircraft/b-24/44-40947.html.

9. Shuichi Yutaka, "Group Compiling Encyclopedia on POW Camps, Captives in Japan," Asahi Shimbum, October 17, 2020, https://www.asahi.com/ajw/articles/13796164. The camp reference in the article is "Kempi-Tai" camp in Makassar. Lists of prisoner-of-war camps include the likely Kampili Camp near Makassar on South Celebese Island (Sulawesi today). The Japanese Kempai-Tai or Kempeitai were the Imperial Japanese Navy's military police who oversaw interrogation and punishment protocols at several internment camps.

10. "B-24J-185-CO Liberator Serial Number 44-40947," Pacific Wrecks. The military provided the report to Josie Ivey's widow, Ardelle Stanley Ivey.

11. MACR 10018, Fold3.com.

12. Jared Morgan, "This Non-profit Organization Works to Recover WWII MIAs Still Missing," *Military Times*, September 18, 2020, https://www.militarytimes.com/news/your-military/2020/09/18/nonprofit-works-to-recover-wwii-mias-still-missing/.

Chapter 18. Burma Bridge Busters

1. Charles F. Romanus and Riley Sunderland, *Stillwell's Mission to China*, United States Army in World War II: China-Burma-India Theater (Washington DC: Center of Military History, 1987), 3–48, 191–220, https://history.army.mil/html/books/009/9-1/CMH_Pub_9-1.pdf; David W. Hogan, *India-Burma, 2 April 1942–28 January 1945*, The US Army Campaigns of World War II (Washington, DC: Center for Military History, United States Army, 1992), 7–30, accessed April 15, 2023, https://history.Army.mil/brochures/indiaburma/indiaburma.htm.

2. Edward M. Young, *B-25 Mitchell Units of the CBI* (Oxford: Osprey, 2018), 9; Hogan, *India-Burma*, 7–30.

3. Clayton R. Newell, *Burma, 1942*, 12–14, 16–23.

4. E. Kathleen Williams, "Army Air Forces in the War against Japan, 1941–1942, Army Air Forces Study No. 34, 1945," 96–99, 169–70, Army Air Forces, accessed April 20, 2023, https://www.afhra.af.mil/Portals/16/documents/Studies/1-50/AFD-090602-078.pdf; Romanus and Sunderland, *Stillwell's Mission to China*, 92, 199.

5. Hogan, *India-Burma*, 7–9; Williams, "Army Air Forces in the War against Japan," 95–97; Romanus and Sunderland, *Stillwell's Mission to China*, 82.

6. Young, *B-25 Mitchell Units*, 11–12, 24–26; Williams, "Army Air Forces in the War against Japan," 170, 181; Tony Strotman, "341st Bomb Group, History 1943," Army Air Forces in China Burma India, accessed April 30, 2023, http://aafincbi.com/341st_web/bg341_history_43.html.

7. "More Midsouth Men Are Reported Missing," *Memphis Commercial Appeal*, November 30, 1944, https://www.newspapers.com/image/769640781/.

8. Strotman, "341st Bomb Group, History 1943."

9. Young, *B-25 Mitchell Units*, 13.

10. Strotman, "341st Bomb Group, History 1943."

11. Sgt. Dave Richardson, "The Burma Bridge Busters: They Invented New Bombing Technique," Ex-CBI Roundup, November 1971, CBE Order of Battle: Lineages and History, accessed April 15, 2023, http://www.cbi-history.com/part_vi_490th_bomb_sq3.html.

12. Richardson, *Burma Bridge Busters*.

13. Wesley Frank Craven and James Lea Cate, *The Pacific: Guadalcanal to Saipan, August 1942–July 1945*, 490–93.

14. CBI Order of Battle: Lineages and History, 490th Bombardment Squadron, accessed April 5, 2023, http://www.cbi-history.com/part_vi_490th_bomb_sq.html; "CBI Roundup," *Delhi* 3, no. 7 (1944), https://www.cbi-theater.com/roundup/roundup102644.html.

15. Missing Air Crew Report #9452, Fold3.com, accessed April 6, 2023, https://www.fold3.com/image/28710530?terms=macr,9452.

16. Missing Air Crew Report #9452.

17. Strotman, "341st Bomb Group, History 1943."

18. "Robert A. Erdin Wins Colonelcy," *Columbia (SC) State*, December 29, 1944, https://www.newspapers.com/image/748910686/.

19. "2LT Frank M. Finney," Find a Grave, accessed April 6, 2023, https://www.findagrave.com/memorial/3298956/frank-m-finney#view-photo=72183984; "Finney, Frank M.," Fold3.com, accessed April 6, 2023, https://www.fold3.com/record/706932989/finney-frank-m-us-veterans-gravesites-ca1775-2019.

Chapter 19. A Day at the Beach

1. "Lloyd William Lee Poovey, Jr.," Find a Grave, accessed August 10, 2022, https://www.findagrave.com/memorial/47425259/lloyd-william_lee-poovey; "War Diary, 5/1–31/44 Mission Reports," National Archives, Fold3.com, accessed August 10, 2022, https://www.fold3.com/image/279776042/war-diary-51-3144-mission-reports-p-10-page-9-wwii-war-diaries?terms=lloyd,poovey.

2. "Lloyd W. Poovey Aviation Technician Reported by Navy Drowned in Service," *Charlotte (NC) Observer*, October 29, 1944, https://www.newspapers.com/image/618071075/.

3. US Pacific Fleet Air Force, Torpedo Squadron 99, "War Diary, Oct. 1–31, 1944," National Archives, Fold3.com, accessed August 10, 2022, https://www.fold3.com/image/292496661.

4. "Warren County Ohio World War II Veterans," Military Heritage, accessed August 10, 2022, https://warren.ohgenweb.org/military/ww2p.html; Muster Roll of Officers and Enlisted Men of the U.S. Marine Corps, San Diego, Fold3.com, accessed August 10, 2022, https://www.fold3.com/image/714483307?rec=646606486.

5. "Catholicity of Pfc. Miller Is Praised by Commander," *Lake Shore Visitor* (Erie, PA), December 8, 1944, https://www.newspapers.com/image/951932802/.

6. "Army Battle Casualties and Nonbattle Deaths in World War II: Final Report," Department of the Army, Office of the Comptroller of the Army, 99, https://apps.dtic.mil/sti/pdfs/ADA438106.pdf.

7. Nese F. DeBruyne, "American War and Military Operations Casualties: Lists and Statistics," Congressional Research Services, RL32492, 2–4, https://www.census.gov/history/pdf/wwi-casualties112018.pdf.

8. "Capt. Bror Henry Anderson," Find a Grave, accessed August 12, 2022, https://www.findagrave.com/memorial/65430970/bror-henry-anderson; "4 Area Servicemen Give Lives," *Rochester (NY) Democrat and Chronicle*, November 9, 1944, https://www.newspapers.com/image/136826972/.

9. "Clarence E. McGirk," Find a Grave, accessed August 15, 2022, https://www.findagrave.com/memorial/21384983/clarence-e-mcgirk; "Private Clarence E. McGirk," *Philadelphia Inquirer*, November 10, 1944, https://www.newspapers.com/image/172138460/.

10. "Lloyd William Lee Poovey, Jr.," Find a Grave; "War Diary, Oct. 1–31, 1944," Fold3.com, accessed August 12, 2022, https://www.fold3.com/image/292496681/war-diary-101-3144-page-3-wwii-war-diaries?terms=torpedo,ninety,squadron,nine.

11. "Donald M. Padgett," Find a Grave, accessed August 12, 2022, https://www.findagrave.com/memorial/177059135/donald-m-padgett.

12. "Germain Miller," Find a Grave, accessed August 12, 2022, https://www.findagrave.com/memorial/56365428/germain-f-miller.

13. "Capt. Bror Henry Anderson," Find a Grave.

14. "Clarence E. McGirk," Find a Grave.

Chapter 20. A Not So Quiet War

1. Jami Bryan, "The 88th Infantry Division in Italy," Army Historical Foundation, accessed August 3, 2023, https://Armyhistory.org/the-88th-infantry-division-in-italy/; *We Were There, from Gruber to Brenner Pass with the 88th Division in Italy*, Information and Education Section MTOUSA, 6–8, https://www.mtmestas.com/88th-infantrydivision/wewerethere/88th-infantrydivision-wewerethere-88.htm; John Sloan Brown, *Draftee Division* (Lexington: University Press of Kentucky, 1986), 11, 37, 103.

2. Bryan, "88th Infantry Division in Italy."

3. Bryan, " 88th Infantry Division in Italy"; Norman Black, *Combat Veterans' Stories of World War II*, vol. 1, *North Africa and Europe, November 1942–May 1945*, 84–86.

4. *We Were There*, 13–14.

5. Colin Fraser, "The Battle of Monte Cassino and the Breaking of the Gustav Line," War History Online, February 21, 2018, https://www.warhistoryonline.com/world-war-ii/battle-monte-cassino-gustav-line.html?safari=1; Brown, *Draftee Division*, 1–2.

6. Clayton D. Laurie, *The Campaigns of World War II: Rome-Arno*, 7, 20–23; Brown, *Draftee Division*, 143.

7. Ernest F. Fisher Jr., *The Mediterranean Theater of Operation: Cassino to the Alps*, 285–88.

8. *We Were There*, 74; *The Final Campaign across Northwest Italy, 14 April–2 May 1945* (Washington, DC: Headquarters IV Corps, US Army, 1945), 2, https://88thinfantrydivisionarchive.com/italy/finalcampaign-acrossnorthwestitaly-145pgs.pdf.

9. Fisher, *Mediterranean Theater of Operation*, 315–16.

10. Fisher, *Mediterranean Theater of Operation*, 323–29.

11. Michael E. Haskew, "The Gothic Line: How the Allies Breached Germany's Defenses in Italy," War History Network, accessed August 12, 2022, https://

warfarehistorynetwork.com/article/the-gothic-line-how-the-allies-breached-germanys-defenses-in-italy/; Fisher, *Mediterranean Theater of Operation*, 339, 350–54.

12. *We Were There*, 77–78; Haskew, "Gothic Line"; Fisher, *Mediterranean Theater of Operation*, 378–91.

13. Lt. John P. Campbell, ed., *351st Infantry Regiment, World War II, July 1942–July 1945*, 45–57, accessed July 30, 2023, https://www.88thinfantrydivisionarchive.com/351st-infantryregiment/1942-1945-88th-id-351st-ir-history-82pgs.pdf.

14. Haskew, "Gothic Line"; Campbell, *351st Infantry Regiment*, 45–47; Fisher, *Mediterranean Theater of Operation*, 386–92.

15. Arthurs Champeny, "History of the 351st Infantry Regiment for the Month of October 1944," November 8, 1944, 351info.com, https://www.351inf.com/opsreports/October-1944.

16. *We Were There*, 19.

17. Black, *Combat Veterans' Stories*, 94.

18. "Alfred Vasholz," Ancestry.com, accessed July 30, 2023, https://www.ancestryinstitution.com/mediaui-viewer/collection/1030/tree/113550114/person/180116383854/. The untitled poem written by Mrs. O. Huebscher opens with a dedication to her nephew: "In memory of Second Lieutenant Alfred Vasholz who died on the battlefield in Italy October 24, 1944." "2LT Alfred Herbert Vasholz," Find a Grave, accessed July 30, 2023, https://www.findagrave.com/memorial/56367156/alfred-herbert-vasholz.

19. 88th Infantry Division Archive, accessed July 30, 2023, https://www.88thinfantrydivisionarchive.com/88th-infantrydivision/88th-id-history-7pgs.pdf.

20. "Delphia E. Garris," Find a Grave, accessed July 21, 2023, https://www.findagrave.com/memorial/89954268/delphia-e-garris.

21. "William Maxmillian Savich," Find a Grave, accessed July 21, 2023, https://www.findagrave.com/memorial/177321141/william-maxmillian-savich.

Chapter 21. Of Wolfpacks and Windmills

1. "A Brief History of the 56th Fighter Group," 56th Fighter Group in World War II, accessed July 6, 2023, http://www.56thfightergroup.co.uk/history.htm.

2. "Brief History of the 56th Fighter Group."

3. "Brief History of the 56th Fighter Group." The Army Air Force became increasingly dependent on the P-47. In the summer of 1944, more than thirty fighter groups flew the P-47. Production of the fighters rose from 532 planes in 1942 to 4,428 in 1943 and to more than 7,000 in 1944. Craven and Cate, *Men and Planes*, 215.

4. Craven and Cate, *Men and Planes*, 216–17.

5. "56th Fighter Group," Boxted Airfield, accessed July 6, 2023, https://www.boxted-airfield.com/groups/56th-fighter-group.

6. "Brief History of the 56th Fighter Group"; Don Hollway, "Wolfpack at War," DonHollway.com, accessed July 2, 2023, https://donhollway.com/wolfpack/.HistoryNetStaff; "56th Fighter Group in World War II," June 12, 2006, from an article

by Don Hollway, originally published in *Aviation History Magazine*, September 1999, accessed July 2, 2023, https://www.historynet.com/56th-fighter-group-in-world-war-ii/; "56th Fighter Group," Boxted Airfield; "Colonel Hubert Zemke Prisoner in Germany," *Daily Missoulian*, November 25, 1944, https://www.newspapers.com/image/349318834/.

7. "Brief History of the 56th Fighter Group."

8. Roger A. Freeman, *Zemke's Wolf Pack: The True Story of Hub Zemke and the 56th Fighter Group as Told to Roger A. Freeman* (New York: Pocket Books, 1988), 215.

9. "Brief History of the 56th Fighter Group."

10. Captain Eugene E. Barnum, 61st Fighter Squadron, Missing Air Crew Report #10115, Osborne Aircraft #42-26646, October 24, 1944, Fold3.com, accessed July 6, 2023, https://www.fold3.com/image/28716549; "George Rudolph Choate," Fold3.com, accessed July 6, 2023, https://www.fold3.com/record/84845383/george-r-choate-jr-wwii-army-enlistment-records.

11. "George R Choate, Jr.," Fold3.com, accessed July 6, 2023, https://www.fold3.com/memorial/529874727/george-r-choate-jr; "More about Squads Rights," *Watonga (OK) Republican*, October 12, 1944, https://www.newspapers.com/image/904617657/.

12. Captain Barnum, Missing Air Crew Report #10115.

13. Captain Barnum, Missing Air Crew Report #10115.

14. First Lieutenant Francis A. Nolan and Second Lieutenant Don Henley, Missing Air Crew Report #10117, October 24, 1944, Choate Aircraft #44-19929, Fold3.com, accessed, July 2, 2023, https://www.fold3.com/image/28717001/28716825.

15. Captain Barnum, Missing Air Crew Report #10115; First Lieutenant Nolan, Missing Air Crew Report #10117.

16. First Lieutenant Nolan, Missing Air Crew Report #10117.

17. "Dutch Family Cares for American Soldier's Grave for over 60 Years," *CT Insider*, accessed July 2, 2023, https://www.ctinsider.com/news/article/Dutch-family-cares-for-American-soldier-s-grave-16853374.php. See chapter 12 for another incident of local residents burying and caring for the graves of American fallen, in this instance 1st Lt. Girvis Haltom in the western Caroline Islands in the South Pacific.

18. John L. Frisbee, "Valor: Col. Hubert 'Hub' Zemke," *Air & Space Forces Magazine*, April 1, 1995, https://www.airandspaceforces.com/article/valor-col-hubert-hub-zemke/; "Col. Hubert A. 'Hub' Zemke," Find a Grave, accessed October 3, 2023, https://www.findagrave.com/memorial/123396067/hubert-a-zemke.

Chapter 22. Rough Roads and Seas

1. Erna Risch, *The Quartermaster Corps: Organization, Supply, and Services* (Washington, DC: Center of Military History, United States Army, 1995), 1:xi, xii, https://history.army.mil/html/books/010/10-12/CMH_Pub_10-12-1.pdf; "Quartermaster History," US Army Quartermaster Corps, accessed July 27, 2023, https://quartermaster.Army.mil/history/.

2. Matthew Delmont, "The Black WWII Soldiers Who Spirited Supplies to the Allied Front Line," *Smithsonian Magazine*, April 8, 2022, https://www.smithsonianmag.com/history/the-black-wwii-soldiers-who-spirited-supplies-to-the-allied-front-line-180979886/.

3. "Quartermasters of World War II," US Army Quartermaster Corps, accessed July 27, 2023, https://www.quartermasterfoundation.org/quartermasters-of-world-war-ii/; Alvin P. Stauffer, *The Quartermaster Corps: Operations in the War against Japan*, 259–69.

4. Stauffer, *Quartermaster Corps*, 259–69.

5. Stauffer, *Quartermaster Corps*, 289.

6. Douglas Bristol Jr., "What Can We Learn about World War II from Black Quartermasters?," August 27, 2021, National World War II Museum, accessed July 28, 2023, https://www.nationalww2museum.org/war/articles/world-war-ii-black-quartermasters (the latter is also the source for the chapter epigraph). In Europe, for example, 75 percent of the Red Ball Express drivers were black soldiers. Delmont, "Black WWII Soldiers Who Spirited Supplies to the Allied Front Line."

7. "Charles B. Hall," Find a Grave, accessed July 28, 2023, https://www.findagrave.com/memorial/49195848/charles-b-hall; Ancestry.com, https://www.ancestryinstitution.com/discoveryui-content/view/5894622:8783; Alan M. Morrison, "Port Men Truly Sweat Out Invasion," *Stars and Stripes*, May 20, 1944, Fold3.com, accessed July 31, 2023, https://www.fold3.com/image/713465582/.

8. John S. Kinloch, "Kinloch's Corner," *California Eagle* (Los Angeles), November 9, 1944, https://www.newspapers.com/image/692882844/; "Record of Tan Yanks in Pacific Saga of Courage, Devotion," *Pittsburgh Courier*, September 8, 1945, https://www.newspapers.com/image/40123893/; "Negro Troops at Fox Hills Cantonment to Be Reviewed by Maj. Gen. Groninger at Armory," *New York Age*, December 23, 1944, https://www.newspapers.com/image/40830517/.

9. Ulysses Lee, *The Employment of Negro Troops*, 637–43; "Charles B. Hall," Find a Grave.

10. Thomas Golden and David Byrd, "Thomas Golden Collection," personal narrative, Veterans History Project, American Folklife Center, Library of Congress, https://www.loc.gov/item/afc2001001.119449/.

11. Howard C. Bridgett, Memorial, Fold3.com, accessed July 25, 2023, https://www.fold3.com/record/86779334/howard-c-bridgett-us-wwii-army-enlistment-records-1938-1946.

12. Howard C. Bridgett, US WWII Hospital Admission Card Files, 1942–54, Fold3.com, accessed July 25, 2023, https://www.fold3.com/record/704984227/bridgett-howard-c-us-wwii-hospital-admission-card-files-1942-1954.

13. Lee, *Employment of Negro Troops*, 642–43.

Chapter 23. A Shark with Torpedoes

1. Blair, *Silent Victory*, 479. Test depth is the depth at which a submarine is permitted to operate in peacetime, established during sea trials and set at two-thirds the design depth.

2. "USS *Shark I** (SS 174)"; Randy Tucker, "The Incredible Stories of Nine Wyoming POWs," *Gunpowder Magazine*, November 20, 2019, https://gunpowdermagazine.com/the-incredible-stories-of-nine-wyoming-pows/.

3. "Edward N. Blakely, CDR, USN," US Naval Academy Virtual Memorial Wall, accessed June 21, 2023, https://usnamemorialhall.org/index.php/EDWARD_N._BLAKELY,_CDR,_USN.

4. John D. Alden and Craig R. McDonald, *United States and Allied Submarine Successes in the Pacific and Far East during World War II*, 163–64; Blair, *Silent Victory*, 617–19.

5. Submarines were assigned to lifeguard stations during carrier attacks and bomber raids. Their task was to retrieve airmen who ditched in the ocean.

6. "SS-314 *Shark* Submarine War Patrol Report," Commander Submarine Force US Pacific Fleet to the Commander in Chief US Fleet, accessed June 21, 2023, 187, https://issuu.com/hnsa/docs/ss-314_shark.

7. "George Pittman," Find a Grave, accessed July 25, 2023, https://www.findagrave.com/memorial/56777199/george-washington-pittman; "George Pittman," Ancestry.com, https://www.ancestryinstitution.com/; "Carlton Pittman," Find a Grave, accessed July 25, 2023, https://www.findagrave.com/memorial/189706659/carlton-pittman; US Navy Muster Rolls, National Archives and Records Administration, Ancestry.com, accessed July 24, 2023, https://www.ancestryinstitution.com/.

8. "SS-314 *Shark* Submarine War Patrol Report," 193–95.

9. USS *Seadragon* (SS 194), "Report of Eleventh War Patrol," US WWII Submarine War Patrol Reports, Fold3.com, 7, https://www.fold3.com/image/292505043/report-of-eleventh-war-patrol-page-7-us-world-war-ii-war-diaries-1941-1945; "*Seadragon*," Naval History and Heritage Command, September 8, 2015, https://www.history.navy.mil/research/histories/ship-histories/danfs/s/snook-i.html.

10. Alden and McDonald, *United States and Allied Submarine Successes*, 222–23; Blair, *Silent Victory*, 744–45; "Shark 2 (SS 314)," Naval History and Heritage Command, February 2, 2017, https://www.history.navy.mil/research/library/online-reading-room/title-list-alphabetically/u/united-states-submarine-losses/shark-2-ss-314.html.

11. USS *Seadragon* (SS 194), "Report of Eleventh War Patrol."

12. "Shark 2 (SS 314)," Naval History and Heritage Command.

13. "Edward N. Blakely, CDR, USN," US Naval Academy Virtual Memorial Wall.

14. George Pittman, Find a Grave; Carlton Pittman, Find a Grave.

15. "Harper, John Dott, Jr.," Traces of War, https://www.tracesofwar.com/persons/72363/Harper-Jr-John-Dott.htm; "William Harlan Turner, LTJG, USN," https://usnamemorialhall.org/index.php/WILLIAM_H._TURNER,_LTJG,_USN; "*Arisan Maru*," https://usnamemorialhall.org/index.php/Category:Arsan_Maru; "Former Valley Resident, Prisoner of Japs, Lost When Nip Ship Is Sunk," *Allentown (PA) Morning Call*, June 23, 1945, https://www.newspapers.com/clip/17562346/casualty-of-sinking-of-arisan-maru/.

16. "LCDR William Siggins 'Bill' Emerson," Find a Grave, accessed July 25, 2023, https://www.findagrave.com/memorial/194413307/william-siggins-emerson.

Part Three. Evening

1. R. Stevens, "Voyage to China," Overbeck.org, accessed May 25, 2023, https://overbeck.org/rso/VoyageToChina.md.

2. Glusman, *Conduct under Fire*, 358–61; R. Stevens, "Voyage to China."

3. Glusman, *Conduct under Fire*, 358–61.

4. "Cichy, Pvt. Anton E.," BataanProject.com, accessed May 25, 2023, https://bataanproject.com/provisional-tank-group/cichy-pvt-anton-e/; Sgt. Calvin Graef, interview, Bataan Corregidor Memorial Foundation of New Mexico, accessed May 31, 2023, https://www.angelfire.com/nm/bcmfofnm/themen/calvingraef.html.

5. R. Stevens, "Voyage to China."

6. Calvin Robert Graef with Harry T. Brundidge, "We Prayed to Die," *Cosmopolitan*, April 1945, 51–55, 177–79.

7. "*Arisan Maru*," POW Research Network Japan, accessed May 12, 2023, http://powresearch.jp/en/archive/ship/arisan.html.

8. Sally Macdonald, "He Survived—1,800 Fellow Prisoners aboard Japanese 'Hell Ship' Died 50 Years Ago Today," *Seattle Times*, October 24, 1994, https://archive.seattletimes.com/archive/?date=19941024&slug=1937653.

9. Glusman, *Conduct under Fire*, 358–61.

10. Graef with Brundidge, "We Prayed to Die."

11. Macdonald, "He Survived."

12. Macdonald, "He Survived."

13. Morison, *History of the United States Naval Operations*, 12:403–5.

14. "*Snook*," Naval History and Heritage Command, September 10, 2015, https://www.history.navy.mil/research/histories/ship-histories/danfs/s/snook-i.html.

Chapter 24. Lost in the Vosges

1. "36th Division in World War II," 36th Division Association, Texas Military Forces Museum, accessed October 22, 2022, https://texasmilitaryforcesmuseum.org/36division/archives/salerno/salerno.htm.

2. "36th Division in World War II."

3. "36th Division in World War II."

4. "36th Division in World War II."

5. "36th Division in World War II."

6. Clarke and Smith, *Riviera to the Rhine*, 280–85, 314–22, 329–32.

7. "36th Division in World War II"; "Robert Toshi Kuroda," Congressional Medal of Honor Society, accessed October 7, 2023, https://www.cmohs.org/recipients/robert-t-kuroda.

8. "36th Division in World War II"; Black, *Combat Veterans' Stories of World War II*, 1:106–11; C. Douglas Sterner, *Go for Broke: The Nisei Warriors of World War II Who Conquered Germany, Japan and American Bigotry*, 70–72.

9. "Estes, Bruce: The Lost Battalion," Oral History Recording, National World War II Museum, accessed June 22, 2023, https://www.ww2online.org/view/bruce-estes#the-lost-battalion; J. Herzig, "Stand Where They Fought," https://standwheretheyfought.jimdofree.com/the-vosges-2009-battle-of-bruyères-and-the-relief-of-the-lost-battalion-by-the-442nd-rct-then-and-now/.

10. Andrew Lam, "Dramatic Rescue 75 Years Ago," MassLive, October 28, 2019, https://www.masslive.com/living/2019/10/asian-american-soldiers-earned-reputation-for-valor.html.

11. Black, *Combat Veterans' Stories of World War II*, 1:108–9; W. F. Strong, "How the Japanese Americans Who Saved 'the Lost Battalion' of World War II Became Honorary Texans," *Texas Standard*, May 29, 2019, https://www.texasstandard.org/stories/how-the-japanese-americans-who-saved-the-lost-battalion-of-world-war-ii-became-honorary-texans/; Sterner, *Go for Broke*, 70–72.

12. "36th Division in World War II."

13. Strong, "Japanese Americans Who Saved 'the Lost Battalion.'"

14. "Charles R. Mattis," Find a Grave, accessed July 22, 2023, https://www.findagrave.com/memorial/56374030/charles-r-mattis.

15. "S/Sgt Shiro Togo," 100th Infantry Battalion Veterans, accessed July 22, 2023, https://www.100thbattalion.org/wp-content/uploads/Togo-Shiro.pdf.

16. "36th Division in World War II."

17. Black, *Combat Veterans' Stories of World War II*, 1:108–9; Clarke and Smith, *Riviera to the Rhine*, 329–32.

18. Strong, "Japanese Americans Who Saved 'the Lost Battalion.'"

19. *Densho Encyclopedia*, s.v. "442nd Regimental Combat Team," accessed September 8, 2023, https://encyclopedia.densho.org/442nd_Regimental_Combat_Team/; Sterner, *Go for Broke*, 104–15.

20. Strong, "Japanese Americans Who Saved 'the Lost Battalion.'"

21. Black, *Combat Veterans' Stories of World War II*, 1:110.

22. Strong, "Japanese Americans Who Saved 'the Lost Battalion.'"

23. General Orders, No. 56, Headquarters 36th Infantry Division, March 1, 1945, 36thDivisionArchive.com, https://www.36thdivisionarchive.com/_files/ugd/c1ecfd_79277f26591c40f58ab30271ff704d74.pdf; "Charles R. Mattis," Find a Grave.

24. "Togo," 100th Infantry Battalion Veterans.

25. "Bruce E. Estes," Hall of Valor Project, accessed June 30, 2023, https://valor.militarytimes.com/hero/67165.

Chapter 25: Under Cover of Darkness

1. Robert J. Cressman, "LST-695: 1944–1945."

2. Cressman, "LST-695: 1944–1945."

3. Cressman, "LST-695: 1944–1945."

4. "Musgrove, Vernie Elegia, SF2c," Fold3.com, accessed June 18, 2023, https://www.fold3.com/memorial/657808274/musgrove-vernie-eligia-sf2c/stories; Ross Patterson II, "Lost at Sea: The Last Cruise of a Portsmouth Sailor," Portsmouth Naval Shipyard Museum, https://portsmouthnavalshipyardmuseum.com/online-learning-archive/lost-at-sea-the-last-cruise-of-a-portsmouth-sailor/.

5. "Musgrove, Vernie, Elegia, SF2c"; Patterson "Lost at Sea."

6. Cressman, "LST-695: 1944–1945."

7. Cressman, "LST-695: 1944–1945."

8. Wanza Ealam Matthews, Fold3.com, accessed May 25, 2023, https://www.fold3.com/memorial/657803422/matthews-wanza-ealam/stories; Renne Corbin, interview by the author; "Wanza Ealam Matthews," Find a Grave, accessed May 25, 2023, https://www.findagrave.com/memorial/56776655/wanza-ealam-matthews; "13-Year -Old Arcadia Boy Is Accidently Shot," *Tampa Tribune*, July 20, 1938, https://www.newspapers.com/image/327471607/.

9. Corbin, interview by the author.

10. Cressman, "LST-695: 1944–1945."

11. Cressman, "LST-695: 1944–1945."

12. Bob Hackett and Sander Kingsepp, "Sensuikan! IJN Submarine I-56: Tabular Record of Movement," CombinedFleet.com, accessed May 30, 2023, http://www.combinedfleet.com/I-56.htm?fbclid=IwAR1U61Dr02DxdhvPYIPlpr7N6-u16fLfAIh8TJmzKiR08xBZzZVWvewmt_w.

13. Cressman, "LST-695: 1944–1945."

14. Cressman, "LST-695: 1944–1945."

15. Cressman, "LST-695: 1944–1945." The volunteers receiving Bronze Star Medals for their actions were Lt. Joseph F. White Jr., D-V(S); Ens. Harry D. Hendren, D-V(S); Petty Officers Edgar R. Snider, Leland G. Morlan (who had suffered back injuries), Samuel L. Mowder, Leonard C. Herm (who had suffered contusions to his nose and back and multiple lacerations to his feet), and John L. Hensley; and Seaman John S. Strzelczyk (who had suffered a fractured right arm). Five others who received commendations were Ens. James E. Walch, D-V(S), and Seamen Wellington C. Grant, Carl W. Puckett, Thorn P. Starkey, and William E. Tinsmith. The men on the damage-control party received Silver Star Medals. They were Lt. (j.g.) Matthew C. Cavoretto, E-V(S) (who had suffered a fractured right wrist); Ens. George E. Zillgitt, D-V(G); and Petty Officer Walter J. Bodeman (who had suffered perforated eardrums), aided by CPO David H. Stephens (who suffered facial contusions and a fractured nose).

16. Cressman, "LST-695: 1944–1945."

17. Laura F. Mills, interview by the author.

18. Cressman, "LST-695: 1944–1945"; Mills, interview by the author.

19. "Wanza Ealam Matthews," Find a Grave.

20. LST-695 Muster Rolls, October 31, 1944, Fold3.com, accessed May 3, 2023. https://www.fold3.com/image/305639502/305639488; Cressman, "LST-695: 1944–1945."

21. Wayne Scarpaci, "US Carson City: Ship of Three Flags," *Naval History Magazine*, December 2022, https://www.usni.org/magazines/naval-history-magazine/2022/december/uss-carson-city-ship-three-flags; "USS *Bataan*," Hullnumber.com, accessed June 20, 2023, https://www.hullnumber.com/CVL-29; "USS *Bataan* (CVL29)," Navysite.de, accessed June 20, 2023, https://www.Navysite.de/cvl/cvl29.htm. In their article "Sensuikan! IJN Submarine I-56," Hackett and

Kingsepp note that Japanese sources give credit to the USS *Hudson* (DD-475) for the *I-56* sinking.

22. Cressman, "LST-695: 1944–1945"; Mills, interview by the author.

Part Four. Day's End

1. "Cichy, Pvt. Anton E.," BataanProject.com, accessed May 25, 2023, https://bataanproject.com/provisional-tank-group/cichy-pvt-anton-e/; "Luther, S/Sgt HenryM.," Bataan Project.com, accessed May 25, 2023, https://bataanproject.co/provisional-tank-group/luther-s-sgt-henry-m/.

2. "Cichy, Pvt. Anton E." and "Luther, S/Sgt. Henry M.," BataanProject.com.

3. "75th Anniversary of the *Arisan Maru* Tragedy," American POWs of Japan, October 26, 2019, https://pows.jiaponline.org/2019/10/75th-anniversary-of-arisan-maru-tragedy.html.

4. Tom Hintgen, "WWII Vet Survived POW Camp," April 14, 2007, *Daily Journal Media* https://www.fergusfallsjournal.com/news/wwii-vet-survived-pow-camp/ (epigraph quote by Cichy); "Cichy, Pvt. Anton E.," BataanProject.com.

5. "75th Anniversary of the *Arisan Maru* Tragedy."

6. "Cichy, Pvt. Anton E.," BataanProject.com.

7. "75th Anniversary of the *Arisan Maru* Tragedy."

8. "Corp. Don F. Meyer Awarded Purple Heart by General George C. Marshall," *Wilmington (CA) Daily Press Journal*, December 21, 1944, https://www.newspapers.com/image/359018496/.

9. "2nd Jap Prison Ship Sunk, 5 Yanks Say," *Pittsburgh Sun-Telegraph*, February 16, 1945, https://www.newspapers.com/image/524094883/; 79th Congress, Records of the United States Senate, 1117–19; "Bataan 'a Picnic' to Jap 'Hell-Hold,'" *Dayton (OH) Journal*, February 17, 1945, https://www.newspapers.com/image/391703969/.

10. Letter, Major General J. A. Ulio, Office of the Adjutant General, War Department, to Michael J. Elkes, June 18, 1945, https://www.archivingwheeling.org/blog/frederick_elkes.

11. "Captive since Fall of Bataan: Family Learns Husband Was Killed When Jap Prison Ship Was Sunk," *Fort Worth Star-Telegram*, June 21, 1945, https://www.newspapers.com/image/636025590/.

12. "Service News," *Cambridge (NE) Clarion*, https://www.newspapers.com/image/674533435/, June 28, 1945.

13. "75th Anniversary of the *Arisan Maru* Tragedy"; Glusman, *Conduct under Fire*, 365–67; "Allied POWs under the Japanese," Center for Research, Mansell.com, accessed June 10, 2023, http://www.mansell.com/pow_resources/camplists/china_hk/toroku_roster.html.

14. Sally Macdonald, "He Survived—1,800 Fellow Prisoners aboard Japanese 'Hell Ship' Died 50 Years Ago Today," *Seattle Times*, October 24, 1994, https://archive.seattletimes.com/archive/?date=19941024&slug=1937653.

15. "75th Anniversary of the *Arisan Maru* Tragedy."

16. "75th Anniversary of the *Arisan Maru* Tragedy."

17. "75th Anniversary of the *Arisan Maru* Tragedy"; "Ex-Captive Bares Jap Brutalities," *Philadelphia Inquirer*, October 14, 1945, https://www.newspapers.com/image/171481694/.

18. Calvin Robert Graef with Harry T. Brundidge, "We Prayed to Die," *Cosmopolitan*, April 1945, 51–55, 177–79.

19. Adam Bisno, "The Japanese Hellships of WWII," November 2019, Naval History and Heritage Command, https://www.history.Navy.mil/content/history/nhhc/browse-by-topic/wars-conflicts-and-operations/world-war-ii/1944/oryoku-maru.html; Lee A. Gladwin, "American POWs on Japanese Ships Take a Voyage into Hell," *Prologue Magazine* 35, no. 4 (2003), National Archives, https://www.archives.gov/publications/prologue/2003/winter/hell-ships-1.html.

20. "Jap 'Oryoku' Atrocity Killed 1,269," *Atlanta Constitution*, September 9, 1945, https://www.newspapers.com/image/397781622/; Michael Hurst, "The Story of the *Enoura Maru*," accessed March 13, 2024, http://www.powtaiwan.org/archives_detail.php?The-Story-of-the-Bombing-of-the-Enoura-Maru-17.

21. "Robert S. Overbeck Dies at 55, Ex-Head of Alcoa of Costa Rica," *New York Times*, March 6, 1972, https://www.nytimes.com/1972/03/06/archives/robert-s-overbecl-dies-at-55-exhead-of-alcoa-of-costa-rica.html.

22. "Anton Ervin Cichy," Find a Grave, accessed June 30, 2023, https://www.findagrave.com/memorial/48572758/anton-ervin-cichy.

23. "Sgt Avery Edward Wilber," Find a Grave, accessed June 29, 2023, https://www.findagrave.com/memorial/66303496/avery-edward-wilber.

24. Associated Press, "Book Tells Bataan Shipwreck Survivor's Struggles," *Santa Fe New Mexican*, February 19, 2000, https://www.newspapers.com/image/584475493/.

25. "Donald Ernest Meyer," Find a Grave, accessed June 30, 2023, https://www.findagrave.com/memorial/71418410/donald-ernest-meyer.

26. "Glenn S. Oliver," Find a Grave, accessed June 29, 2023, https://www.findagrave.com/memorial/148638858/glenn-s-oliver.

27. "Philip Brodsky," Find a Grave, accessed June 29, 2023, https://www.findagrave.com/memorial/238744433/philip-brodsky.

28. "Martin William Binder," Find a Grave, accessed June 29, 2023, https://www.findagrave.com/memorial/207920368/martin-william-binder.

Epilogue

1. USS *Birmingham*, "War Diary, 10/24/44," US World War II War Diaries, 1941–45, 22–25, National Archives, Fold3.com, accessed August 28, 2023, https://www.fold3.com/image/292508915/war-diary-101-3144-page-24-us-world-war-ii-war-diaries-1941-1945.

2. Zack Van Eyck, "New Mexican Recalls the Ordeal of 50 Years Ago," *Santa Fe New Mexican*, October 24, 1994, https://www.newspapers.com/image/583638282/; Associated Press, "Book Tells Bataan Shipwreck Survivor's Struggles," *Santa Fe New Mexican*, February 19, 2000, https://www.newspapers.com/image/584475493/.

SELECTED BIBLIOGRAPHY

Books, Brochures, and Pamphlets

Alden, John D., and Craig R. McDonald. *United States and Allied Submarine Successes in the Pacific and Far East during World War II*. 4th ed. Jefferson, NC: McFarland, 2009.

Anderson, Charles Robert. *Leyte: The US Army Campaigns of World War II*. Washington, DC: Center of Military History, United States Army, 1943.

Ballard, Ted. *Rhineland: 15 September 1944–21 March 1945*. Washington, DC: Center of Military History, United States Army, 1995.

Beevor, Antony. *The Battle of Arnhem: The Deadliest Airborne Operation of World War II*. New York: Viking, 2018.

Black, Norman. *Combat Veterans' Stories of World War II*. Vol. 1, *North Africa and Europe, November 1942–May 1945*. N.p.: CreateSpace, 2015.

Blair, Clay, Jr. *Silent Victory: The US Submarine War against Japan*. Philadelphia: Lippincott, 1975.

Cannon, M. Hamlin, ed. *Leyte: The Return to the Philippines*. United States Army in World War II: War in the Pacific. Washington, DC: Center of Military History, United States Army, 1954.

Clarke, Jeffrey J., and Robert Ross Smith. *Riviera to the Rhine*. Washington, DC: Center of Military History, United States Army, 1993.

Craven, Wesley Frank, and James Lea Cate, eds. *Europe: Argument to V-E Day, January 1944–May 1945*. Vol. 3 of *The Army Air Forces in World War II*. Washington, DC: Office of Air Force History, 1951.

———. *Men and Planes*. Vol. 6 of *The Army Air Forces in World War II*. Washington, DC: Office of Air Force History, 1983.

———. *The Pacific: Guadalcanal to Saipan, August 1942–July 1945*. Vol. 4 of *The Army Air Forces in World War II*. Washington, DC: Office of Air Force History, 1983.

———. *The Pacific: Matterhorn to Nagasaki, June 1944 to August 1945*. Vol. 5 of *The Army Air Forces in World War II*. Washington, DC: Office of Air Force History, 1983.

Dunmore, Spencer. *Wings for Victory: The Remarkable Story of the British Commonwealth Air Training Plan in Canada*. Toronto: McClellan & Stuart, 1994.

Evans, Sterling, ed. *American Indians in American History, 1870–2001: A Companion Reader*. Westport, CT: Praeger, 2002.

Falk, Stanley. *Bloodiest Victory: Palaus*. New York: Ballantine Books, 1974.

Fisher, Ernest F., Jr. *The Mediterranean Theater of Operation: Cassino to the Alps*. Washington, DC: Center of Military History, United States Army, 2002.

From the Volturno to the Winter Line (6 October–15 November 1943). Washington DC: Center of Military History, United States Army, 1945.

Glusman, John. *Conduct under Fire: Four American Doctors and Their Fight for Life as Prisoners of the Japanese, 1941–1945*. New York: Viking, 2005.

Hogan, David W. *The US Army Campaigns of World War II: India-Burma, 2 April 1942–28 January 1945*. Washington, DC: Center of Military History, United States Army, 1992.

Howe, George F. *Northwest Africa: Seizing the Initiative in the West*. Washington, DC: Center of Military History, United States Army, 1957.

Hoyt, Edwin P. *McCampbell's Heroes: The Story of the U.S. Navy's Celebrated Carrier Fighters of the Pacific War*. New York: Avon, 1984.

Jacobs, Eugene C., (Col.). *Blood Brothers: A Medic's Sketch Book*. Edited by Sam Rohlfing. New York: Carlton Press, 1985.

Keegan, John. *The Second World War*. New York: Viking, 1989.

LaMont-Brown, Raymond. *Ships from Hell: Japanese War Crimes on the High Seas*. Stroud: Sutton, 2002.

Laurie, Clayton D. *The Campaigns of World War II: Rome-Arno*. Washington, DC: Center of Military History, United States Army, 1994.

Lee, Ulysses. *The Employment of Negro Troops*. Edited by Stetson Conn. United States Army in World War II: Special Studies. Washington, DC: Center of Military History, United States Army, 1966.

MacArthur, Douglas A. *Reports of General MacArthur: The Campaigns of MacArthur in the Pacific*. Vol. 1. Washington, DC: Center of Military History, United States Army, 1994.

MacDonald, Charles B. *The Siegfried Line Campaign*. Washington, DC: Center of Military History, United States Army, 1993.

Marshall, Bill. *Angels, Bulldogs & Dragons: The 355th Fighter Group in World War II*. Mesa, AZ: Champlain Fighter Museum, 1986.

Michno, Gregory F. *Death on the Hellships: Prisoners at Sea in the Pacific War*. Annapolis, MD: Naval Institute Press, 2001.

Millett, Allan Reed. *Semper Fidelis: The History of the United States Marines.* New York: Free Press, 1991.

Morison, Samuel Eliot. *The History of United States Naval Operations in World War II.* Vol. 12, *Leyte: June 1944–January 1945.* Boston: Little, Brown, 1958.

———. *The Two Ocean War: A Short History of the US Navy in the Second World War.* Boston: Little, Brown, 1963.

Morton, Louis. "The Decision to Withdraw to Bataan." In *Command Decisions.* Washington, DC: Center of Military History, United States Army, 2000.

———. *The Fall of the Philippines.* United States Army in World War II: War in the Pacific. Washington, DC: Center of Military History, United States Army, 1953.

Newell, Clayton R. *Burma, 1942.* Washington, DC: Center of Military History, United States Army, 1995.

Rappaport, Leonard, and Arthur Norwood Jr. *Rendezvous with Destiny: A History of the 101st Airborne.* Old Saybrook, CT: Konecky and Konecky, 2001.

Risch, Erna. *The Quartermaster Corps: Organization, Supply, and Services.* Washington, DC: Center of Military History, United States Army, 1995.

Russell, David Lee. *David McCampbell, Top Ace of US Naval Aviation in World War II.* Jefferson, NC: McFarland, 2019.

Sherrod, Robert Lee. *History of Marine Corps Aviation in World War II.* Washington, DC: Combat Forces Press, 1952.

Simmons, Edwin H. *The United States Marines: A History.* Annapolis, MD: Naval Institute Press, 1998.

Smith, Robert Ross. *The Approach to the Philippines.* Washington, DC: Center of Military History, United States Army, 1996.

St. John, Philip A. *History of the Third Infantry Division.* Paducah, KY: Turner, 1994.

Stanaway, John, and Bob Rocker. *The Eightballers: Eyes of the Fifth Air Force, the 8th Photo Reconnaissance Squadron in WWII.* Atglen, PA: Schiffer Military History, 1999.

Stauffer, Alvin P. *The Quartermaster Corps: Operations in the War against Japan.* Washington, DC: Center of Military History, United States Army, 1990.

Sterner, C. Douglas. *Go for Broke: The Nisei Warriors of World War II Who Conquered Germany, Japan and American Bigotry.* Clearfield, UT: American Legacy Historical Press, 2015.

Wainwright, Jonathan Mayhew. *General Wainwright's Story.* Westport, CT: Greenwood Press, 1946.

Waterford, Van. *Prisoners of the Japanese in World War II: Statistical History, Personal Narratives, and Memorials Concerning POWs in Camps and on Hellships, Civilian Internees, Asian Slave Laborers, and Others Captured in the Pacific Theater.* Jefferson, NC: McFarland, 1994.

Document, Public Papers, and Speeches

MacArthur, Douglas. *A Soldier Speaks: Public Papers and Speeches of General of the Army, Douglas MacArthur.* Edited by Vorin E. Whan. New York: Frederick A. Praeger, 1965.

Websites

"Battle of Leyte Gulf, October 1944: Loss of USS *Princeton* (CVL-23), 24 October 1944." Department of the Navy, Naval Historical Center. Accessed July 24, 2022. www.ibiblio.org/hyperwar/OnlineLibrary/photos/events/wwii-pac/leyteglf/cvl23-1.htm.

"*Birmingham* II (CL-62)." Naval History and Heritage Command, June 25, 2015. www.history.Navy.mil/research/histories/ship-histories/danfs/b/birmingham-ii.html.

Bisno, Adam. "The Japanese Hellships of WWII." Naval History and Heritage Command, November 2019. www.history.navy.mil/content/history/nhhc/browse-by-topic/wars-conflicts-and-operations/world-war-ii/1944/oryoku-maru.html.

Cox, Samuel J. "H-038-2: The Battle of Leyte Gulf in Detail." Naval History and Heritage Command, November 25, 2019. www.history.navy.mil/content/history/nhhc/about-us/leadership/director/directors-corner/h-grams/h-gram-038/h-038-2.html.

———. "H-044-3: Operation Heaven Number One (*Ten-ichi-go*)—the Death of *Yamato*, April 7, 1945." Naval History and Heritage Command, April 2020. www.history.navy.mil/about-us/leadership/director/directors-corner/h-grams/h-gram-044/h-044-3.html.

Cressman, Robert J. "LST-695: 1944–1945." Naval History and Heritage Command, November 29, 2016. www.history.navy.mil/research/histories/ship-histories/danfs/l/lst-695.html.

Department of the Navy, Bureau of Yards and Docks. *Building the Navy's Bases in World War II: History of the Bureau of Yards and Docks and the Civil Engineer Corps, 1940–1946*. Vol. 2. Washington, DC: US Government Printing Office, 1947. www.ibiblio.org/hyperwar/USN/Building_Bases/bases-23.html.

Evans, Mark L. "*Princeton* IV (CVL-23), 1943–1944." Naval History and Heritage Command, June 28, 2019. www.history.navy.mil/research/histories/ship-histories/danfs/p/Princeton-iv.html.

JANAC (Joint Army Navy Assessment Committee). "*Arisan Maru*." In *Japanese Naval and Merchant Shipping Losses during World War II by All Causes*. February 1947. http://powresearch.jp/en/archive/ship/arisan.html.

"*Rowe* (DD-564)." Naval History and Heritage Command, April 4, 2016. www.history.navy.mil/research/histories/ship-histories/danfs/r/rowe.html.

"*Sawfish* (SS-276)." Naval History and Heritage Command, April 25, 2016. www.history.navy.mil/research/histories/ship-histories/danfs/s/sawfish.html.

"*Snook*." Naval History and Heritage Command, September 10, 2015. www.history.navy.mil/research/histories/ship-histories/danfs/s/snook-i.html.

"The Sullivan Brothers." Naval History and Heritage Command, April 26, 2022.www.history.navy.mil/browse-by-topic/disasters-and-phenomena/the-sullivan-brothers-and-the-assignment-of-family-members0.html.

"USS *Intrepid* (CV-11)." Naval History and Heritage Command, January 11, 2023. www.history.navy.mil/browse-by-topic/ships/aircraft-carriers/uss-intrepid.html.

"USS *Shark* I* (SS 174)." Naval History and Heritage Command, January 31, 2017. www.history.navy.mil/research/library/online-reading-room/title-list-alphabetically/u/united-states-submarine-losses/shark-i-ss-174.html.

Waldman, Martin R. *Calmness, Courage, and Efficiency: Remembering the Battle of Leyte Gulf.* Washington, DC: Naval History and Heritage Command, Department of the Navy, 2022. www.history.navy.mil/content/dam/nhhc/research/publications/publication-508-pdf/battle_leyte_gulf_508.pdf.

Action Reports, War Diaries, and War Patrol Reports

Bolger, J. F., Commanding, USS *Intrepid* (CV-11). "Action Report: Operations against the Ryukyu Islands, Formosa, & Philippines, October 10–31, 1944." Serial No. 0166, n.d. National Archives, Fold3.com. Accessed August 20, 2023. www.fold3.com/image/292234058.

———. "War Diary, Month of October 1944." Serial No. 0195, November 9, 1944. National Archives, Fold3.com. Accessed August 21, 2023. https://www.fold3.com/image/292504278.

Buracker, W. H., Commanding, USS *Princeton (CVL-23)*, to the Secretary of the Navy. "Action Report: The Battle of the Philippines and Loss of USS *Princeton*, 24 October 1944." Serial No. 020, November 24, 1944.

Commander Task Unit 78.2. "Action Report, Leyte Island Operation of LCI(L)-978, Forwarding of, November 29, 1944."

Freeman, Deane M, Jr., Commanding, LST-695. "War Diary, 6/1/44–8/31/44." US World War II War Diaries, 1941–45, National Archives Catalog ID 4697018, 1–4.

"LST-171," War Diary: Ship's History," National Archives Catalog ID 4697018, 4.

Macaluso, C. J., Commanding. "Action Report: Initial Landing Leyte Island, November 13, 1944."

Michael, S. J., Commanding, USS *Cabot* (CVL-28). "War Diary: October 10, 1944–November 9, 1944." N.d. National Archives, Fold3.com. Accessed August 20, 2023, www.fold3.com/image/313864930.

Shoemaker, J. M., Commanding, USS *Franklin* (CV-13). "Action Report: Operations against the Enemy in the Philippine Islands and the Philippine Sea from 22 October 1944 to 31 October 1944." Serial No. 0041, November 4, 1944.

Tackett, Paul, Commanding, LCI(L)-978. "Action Report: Leyte Island Operation, October 24, 1944." Serial No. 084, November 29, 1944. National Archives, Fold3.com. Accessed August 8, 2023. https://www.fold3.com/image/295269294/fwding-of-lcil-978-act-reps-on-the-leyte-is-philippine-op-page-6-us-world-war-ii-war-diaries-1941-19.

Thompson, S. A., Medical Officer, to the Commanding Officer, USS *Fremont* (APA-44). "Action Report: Medical Department." Serial No. 00555, November 20, 1944. National Archives, Fold3.com. Accessed August 8, 2023. https://www.fold3.com/image/292495578/rep-of-ops-in-the-invasion-of-leyte-is-philippine-is-101244-11844-page-19-us-world-war-ii-war-diarie19-23.

USS *Birmingham* (CL-62). "Report of Operations in the Philippines Area, October 18–24, 1944, Including Anti-aircraft Action & Operations in Connection with Loss of USS *Princeton*, October 24, 1944." Serial No. 0048, November 14, 1944.

"USS *Sawfish*, War Patrol No. Eighth, September–November 1944." US Submarine War Patrol Reports, 1941–45, National Archives Microfiche Publication M1752.

USS *Seadragon*. "War Patrol No. Eleventh/Twelfth, September–November 1944." US Submarine War Patrol Reports, 1941–45, National Archives Microfiche Publication M1752.

USS *Snook*. "War Patrol No. Eighth, September–November 1944." US Submarine War Patrol Reports, 1941–45, National Archives Microfiche Publication M1752.

Wieber, C. W., Commanding, USS *Essex* (CV-9). "Action Report: Battle of the Philippines, October 24–25, 1944." Part VI, Serial No. 0195, November 21, 1944. National Archives, Fold3.com. Accessed August 23, 2023. https://www.fold3.com/image/292515806.

Wurzler, W. R., to Commander-in-Chief, United States Fleet, USS *Sonoma* (ATO-12). "Action Report: Report of Operations in the Invasion of Leyte Island, Philippines, 10/20–24/44, Including Sinking of after Being Crash-Dived by Jap Betty, on 10/24/44." Serial No, 113, November 3, 1944. National Archives, Fold3.com. Accessed August 19, 2023. https://www.fold3.com/image/292504477.

Interviews by the Author

Adolfae, Michael H. Son of Herman Joseph Adolfae. January 2023.
Bolen, Linda. Daughter of Paul Miller. April 17, 2023.
Corbin, Renne. Niece of Wanza Matthews. May 31, 2023.
Frye, Eleanor McMillan. April 6, 2017.
Miller, Robert. Son of Paul Miller. April 21, 2023.
Mills, Laura. Daughter of Deane Freeman. December 2022 and March 2023.

INDEX

Page numbers in italics refer to illustrations